AF262970

The Club

ArtCurious: Stories of the Unexpected, Slightly Odd, and Strangely Wonderful in Art History

The Club

*Where American Women Artists Found
Refuge in Belle Époque Paris*

Jennifer Dasal

BLOOMSBURY PUBLISHING

NEW YORK · LONDON · OXFORD · NEW DELHI · SYDNEY

BLOOMSBURY PUBLISHING
Bloomsbury Publishing Inc.
1359 Broadway, New York, NY 10018, USA
50 Bedford Square, London, WC1B 3DP, UK
Bloomsbury Publishing Ireland Limited,
29 Earlsfort Terrace, Dublin 2, D02 AY28, Ireland

BLOOMSBURY, BLOOMSBURY PUBLISHING, and the Diana logo
are trademarks of Bloomsbury Publishing Plc

First published in the United States 2025

Bloomsbury Publishing Plc does not have any control over, or responsibility for, any third-party websites referred to or in this book. All internet addresses given in this book were correct at the time of going to press. The author and publisher regret any inconvenience caused if addresses have changed or sites have ceased to exist, but can accept no responsibility for any such changes.

ISBN: HB: 978-1-63973-130-5; EBOOK: 978-1-63973-131-2

LIBRARY OF CONGRESS CATALOGING-IN-PUBLICATION DATA IS AVAILABLE.

Library of Congress Control Number: 2024943561

2 4 6 8 10 9 7 5 3 1

Typeset by Westchester Publishing Services
Printed in the United States at Lakeside Book Company

To find out more about our authors and books visit www.bloomsbury.com and sign up for our newsletters.

Bloomsbury books may be purchased for business or promotional use. For information on bulk purchases please contact Macmillan Corporate and Premium Sales Department at specialmarkets@macmillan.com.

For product safety–related questions contact productsafety@bloomsbury.com.

*To Josh, Felix, and my parents
and to American girls everywhere*

*The study of art in Paris is a chimera which is coming more and more
to haunt the brain of the American girl . . . it is a joy, it is a snare;
it is a life of privation, it is a bed of ease; it is costly, it is cheap;
it is satisfying, it is a fraud . . .*

—KATHARINE DE FOREST, "ART STUDENT LIFE IN PARIS,"
HARPER'S BAZAAR 33, NO. 27 (JULY 7, 1900)

*And so we come back to Paris, which we find just the same gay,
beautiful, encouraging, disheartening, flattering, indifferent, busy, idle,
heart-breaking, joyous Paris. Paris, with its thousands of rich, thousands of
poor, thousands of comfortable and thousands of destitute—and thousands
of students that sing in its streets, and slave in its studios, that ramble in its
gardens, and eat at cafes and dance at its balls, and find themselves happy
today and downcast tomorrow—and yet, we are [never] ready to leave,
no matter what treatment we receive at its hands.*

—ALICE RUMPH, "MISS ALICE RUMPH TELLS OF HER WORK AND TRAVELS
WHILE TWO YEARS ABROAD," *BIRMINGHAM NEWS*, AUGUST 2, 1902

CONTENTS

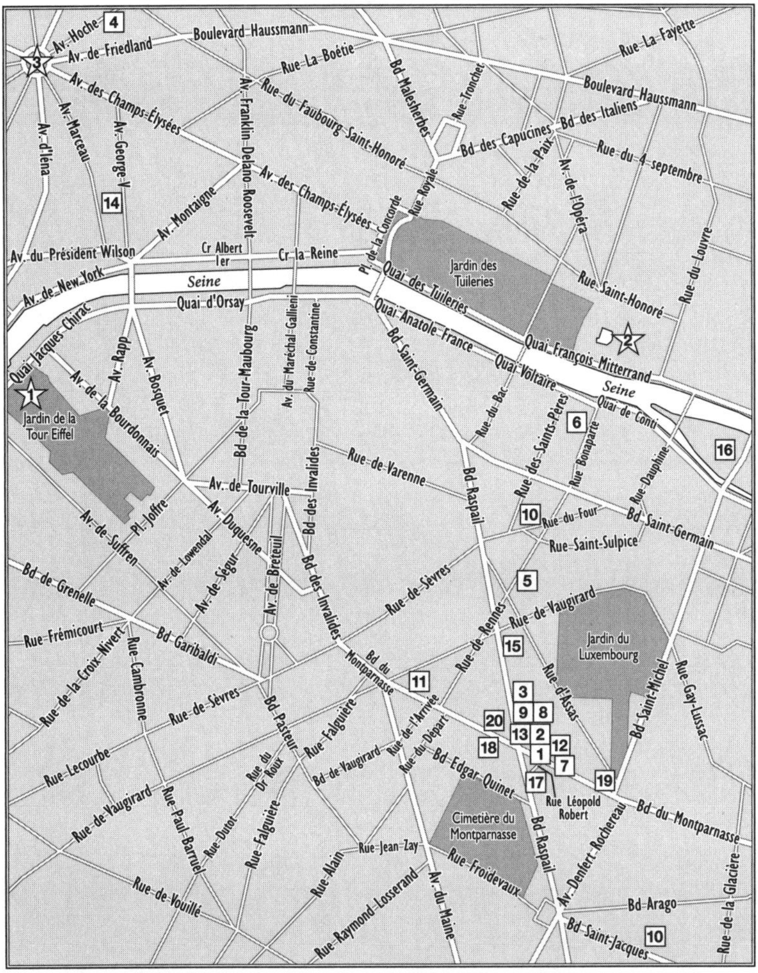

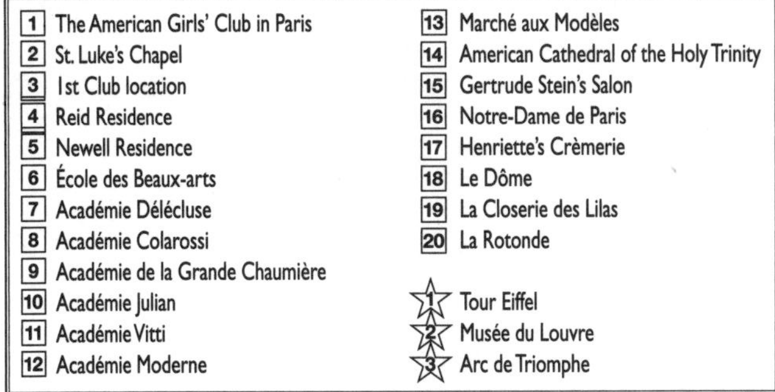

Av.-Hoche 4
Boulevard-Haussmann
Rue-La-Fayette
Av.-de-Friedland
Rue-La-Boétie
Boulevard-Haussmann
Av.-des-Champs-Élysées
Bd-Malesherbes
Rue-Tronchet
Bd-des-Italiens
Rue-du-Faubourg-Saint-Honoré
Bd-des-Capucines
Rue-du-4-septembre
Av.-Marceau
Av.-George-V
Av.-Montaigne
Av.-Franklin-Delano-Roosevelt
Av.-des-Champs-Élysées
Rue-Royale
Rue-de-la-Paix
Av.-de-l'Opéra
14
Av.-d'Iéna
Av.-du-Président-Wilson
Cr Albert 1er
Cr-la-Reine
Pl.-de-la-Concorde
Jardin des Tuileries
Rue-Saint-Honoré
Rue-du-Louvre
Av.-de-New-York
Seine
Quai-des-Tuileries
Quai-François-Mitterrand
2
Quai-d'Orsay
Quai-Anatole-France
Quai-Voltaire
Seine
Quai-Jacques-Chirac
Av.-Rapp
Av.-Bosquet
Av.-du-Maréchal-Gallieni
Rue-de-Constantine
Bd-Saint-Germain
Rue-du-Bac
Rue-des-Saints-Pères
Quai-de-Conti
Jardin de la Tour Eiffel
Av.-de-la-Bourdonnais
Bd-de-la-Tour-Maubourg
6
Rue-Bonaparte
Rue-Dauphine
16
Av.-de-Tourville
Rue-des-Invalides
Rue-de-Varenne
Bd-Raspail
10
Rue-du-Four
Bd-Saint-Germain
Pl.-Joffre
Av.-de-Suffren
Av.-Duquesne
Rue-Saint-Sulpice
Av.-de-Lowendal
Av.-de-Ségur
Av.-de-Breteuil
Bd-des-Invalides
Rue-de-Sèvres
5
Rue-de-Vaugirard
Bd-de-Grenelle
Jardin du Luxembourg
Rue-Frémicourt
Bd-Garibaldi
Rue-de-Rennes
15
Rue-d'Assas
Bd-Saint-Michel
Rue-Gay-Lussac
Rue-de-la-Croix-Nivert
Rue-Cambronne
Rue-de-Sèvres
Bd-du-Montparnasse
11
3
Rue-Lecourbe
Bd-Pasteur
Rue-Falguière
Av.-de-l'Arrivée
20
9
8
Rue-du-Dr-Roux
Rue-du-Départ
13
2
18
1
Rue-de-Vaugirard
Bd-de-Vaugirard
Bd-Edgar-Quinet
12
7
17
19
Rue-Paul-Barruel
Rue-Dutot
Rue-Falguière
Rue-Léopold Robert
Bd-du-Montparnasse
Rue-de-Vaugirard
Cimetière du Montparnasse
Bd-Raspail
Rue-de-Vouillé
Rue-Jean-Zay
Rue-Alain
Rue-Froidevaux
Av.-Denfert-Rochereau
Bd-Arago
Rue-de-la-Glacière
Rue-Raymond-Losserand
Av.-du-Maine
Bd-Saint-Jacques
10

1 The American Girls' Club in Paris
2 St. Luke's Chapel
3 1st Club location
4 Reid Residence
5 Newell Residence
6 École des Beaux-arts
7 Académie Délécluse
8 Académie Colarossi
9 Académie de la Grande Chaumière
10 Académie Julian
11 Académie Vitti
12 Académie Moderne
13 Marché aux Modèles
14 American Cathedral of the Holy Trinity
15 Gertrude Stein's Salon
16 Notre-Dame de Paris
17 Henriette's Crèmerie
18 Le Dôme
19 La Closerie des Lilas
20 La Rotonde
1 Tour Eiffel
2 Musée du Louvre
3 Arc de Triomphe

PROLOGUE

In the last half of 2021, I learned a secret.

Well, maybe it was not a secret to *everyone*, but it was one that I, as a longtime art historian, had never discovered in all my study of the history of art. This secret was about a place: a blink-and-you-miss-it, turn-of-the-century structure in Paris that, for two decades, successfully sheltered, supported, and spawned a generation of American women artists in a way that nothing else could—or, if truth be told, that perhaps no one else would. A place that gave them the opportunity to pursue paths that they had determined for themselves, without unwarranted judgment or obstacles. In news reports, published across the globe during its heyday from the final decade of the nineteenth century until the beginning of World War One, it was called by a number of similar names—"the American Art Students' Club," "the American Girls' Club for Artists," "the American Girls' Art Club," "the Ladies' Club," "The American Girls' Club in Paris" (abbreviated here as AGCP), or just "the Girls' Club."

But for a considerable number of its residents, this structure—tucked into a quiet building at 4 rue de Chevreuse in the French capital's sixth *arrondissement*—would simply, and forever, be known to them by the one word common to these variations: the Club.[1]

For the hundreds, perhaps thousands (there is no confirmed number), of intrepid women who crossed its threshold during the fabled Belle Époque—the "beautiful age" of Paris denoted as the years between 1870 and 1914—the Club provided a wealth of welcome services: a warm cup

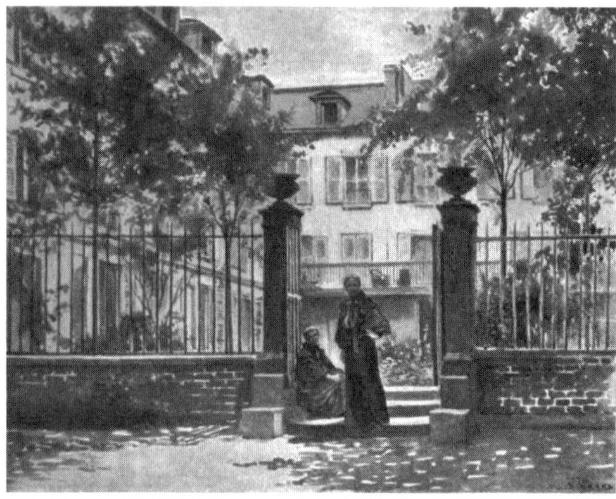

Figure P.1. *"Garden of the Art Club."* Scribner's Magazine, *November 1894.*

of tea, an American newspaper, an inexpensive meal, a room to rent, an exhibition space, a familiar face, a common language.

Such amenities were vital to these artists—painters, sculptors, miniaturists, the occasional pianist or two—who hailed from all over the United States, including cities like Albany, Baltimore, Birmingham, Indianapolis, New York, Sacramento, St. Louis, and beyond. These were women who were searching for an artistic education akin to those offered to their male colleagues, but which was often limited, if not denied, to them on the basis of their gender. An unlikely hero came to the rescue, a woman of means and influence who built the Club as a comfortable and safe place for female artists (much to the relief of their worried parents). The Club also provided a designated space, acceptable to both the Parisian and American public, to corral these paintbrush-toting "girls" rather than allowing them to cavort carelessly throughout the City of Light. For artists, their families, and society at large, it was the right solution at the right time.

The Club's lovely but unassuming building was adjacent to the city's Latin Quarter, the Left Bank enclave encapsulated by the fifth and sixth *arrondissements.* Home to the famed Sorbonne University as well as the epicenter of numerous independent art schools and ateliers, the Quarter has a long history of educational greatness, but like most student-heavy environments, it suffered from the vagaries of overuse and underappreciation during this era (think: odiferous street corners, cheap drink, and even cheaper food in less-than-appealing cafés). The Club at 4 rue de Chevreuse was the antidote to this environment, becoming a word-of-mouth sensation and the focal point for the lives of so many women, aged eighteen to forty-five, seeking comprehensive artistic training in hopes of becoming professional working artists.

The variety of American women who convened at the Club is fascinating. The most privileged arrived with bulging steamer trunks and pocketbooks, holding personal letters of introduction to the world's most prominent modernist sculptor or an acclaimed expatriate painter. Yet more than a few arrived with little else than a suitcase and the clothes on their backs. Several women gained the artistic fame that they sought, but many did not, falling into obscurity or never being recognized at all. Their lives often mirrored the trajectory of the Girls' Club itself: rising to prominence, only to disappear from the history books. But for all their differences, when these artists set foot inside the Club, they were *home*.

To claim I was intrigued by the tale would be to undersell my enthusiasm. Initially, I immersed myself in hundreds of books, newspaper articles, academic journals, and dusty archives, pursuing what details could be gleaned about this short-lived but influential artistic outpost. I read hundreds of letters—many of which you'll find included here, with their original language intact and with no corrections for misspellings or [*sic*]s included. Ultimately, though, nothing could be more meaningful to a historian than traveling to the source itself. So, in September 2022, I too set out for Paris. Upon landing, I headed directly to the rue de Chevreuse, echoing the movements of many of the American girls who came before me. What I discovered there began my journey in full to understand this place, its benefactor, its residents, and their art, and it resulted in what you are reading now.

Though the Club closed its doors for good at the onset of the First World War, its dignified location remains, still off the busy boulevard du Montparnasse. The four-story, white-walled *bâtiment* is nondescript amid its more conspicuous neighbors. This plainness is, perhaps, one more reason why the building, bedecked by only a simple "4" to denote its address, is likely ignored by most passersby today and by history at large.

But it is time to bring this special place back into the spotlight. Together, in the pages that follow, we will attempt to correct this historical and artistic forgetting. We will finally swing open the sky-blue French doors of this once proud but little appreciated artistic sanctuary, this embassy of American women's creativity on foreign soil, and trace the origins of the institution, the women who made it what it became, and the legacy it left behind in the history of art.

Welcome, one and all, to the Club.

CHAPTER I

The Splendor of Paris

*What is the secret of this enigmatic charm of Paris which, sooner or
later, takes possession of everyone? What is it about Paris which seizes people,
envelops them, holds them, and often keeps them forever, even those who
profess to have the greatest lack of sympathy for the French?*

—KATHARINE DE FOREST, *PARIS AS IT IS* (1894)[1]

There's only so much teaching that an artist can do, even if they enjoy it, thought Anna McNulty Lester (1862–1900), as she gazed out upon the vast lawns of the Augusta Female Seminary in the springtime of 1897. Lester, at thirty-four years old, had made her mark as an accomplished instructor and administrator at the Staunton, Virginia, academy. Even though she gamely headed the school's art department, she had reached a point of disillusionment in her life. She was tired and unfulfilled. And more than anything, she craved a new adventure. She needed to be *taught* again, for a change of pace.

Anna Lester had made unexpected pivots in her life before: after her own undergraduate days at the Augusta Female Seminary, the Georgia native opted out of pursuing a business career with her newly acquired bookkeeping degree and moved instead to New York City to pursue art classes at the famed Art Students League. This decision was

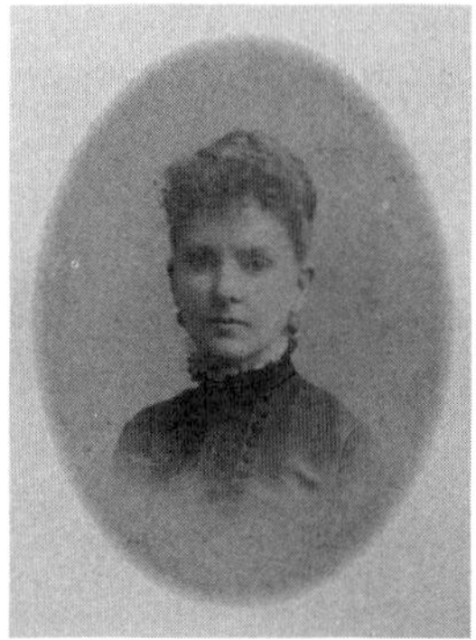

Figure 1.1. *Portrait of Anna Lester, undated. From* Tea with Sister Anna, *2005.*

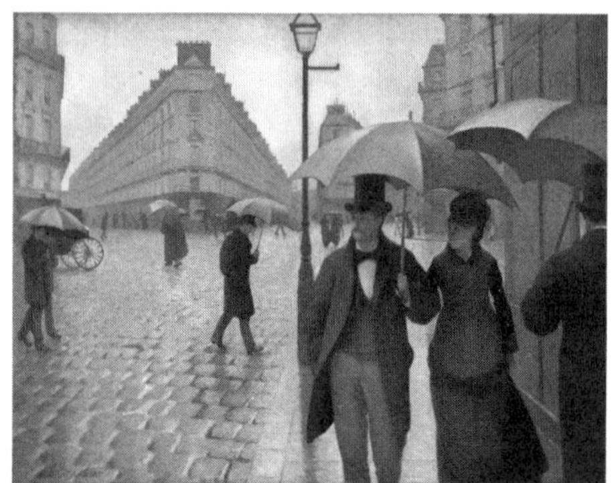

Figure 1.2. *Gustave Caillebotte,* Paris Street; Rainy Day, *1877. Art Institute of Chicago.*

not made lightly. In the final decade of the nineteenth century, for a woman to pursue a career as an artist was a risky maneuver, particularly when, in Lester's case, she was already adequately trained to seek stable and financially secure accounting positions. But Lester had shown great promise as a student of drawing and painting, even winning a gold medal for her creations at Augusta.[2] Art was a passion, a deep-set love; to chase such a dream seemed like a folly to many Americans, but for women like Lester, it was a calling.

After many years of teaching art, she was finally ready to answer that call: she moved to Paris, France, to finish her own art education in the most artistic and inspiring city in the world. The enthusiasm pouring from her letters to her family confirm that she had made the right choice: gushing to her sister Edith after her arrival in the French capital in 1897, she wrote, "I am so glad that I am learning to draw from Life full length. I always have wanted to and I like the work immensely! When you get here [for Christmas] you will wish you had come to stay [indefinitely]. One cannot help being in love with Paris!"[3]

Why Paris, though? When other European capitals, like London, Rome, and Berlin, boasted similar cultural enclaves and amenities, why did so many American women choose Paris as their destination?

Simple: because it was *Paris.*

ADMITTEDLY, PARIS HAD not always been so beloved, and by the dawn of the nineteenth century it was in dire need of an overhaul. Though certain elements of the capital had long exhibited signs of royal or imperial splendor, such as the Musée du Louvre (itself a palace until the late eighteenth century) and the monumental Arc de Triomphe, much of the city was mired in muck and overwhelmed by disease, devastated especially by cholera in major outbreaks of 1832 and 1849.[4] As Baron Georges-Eugène Haussmann, the great administrator of the city's renovations, wrote of central Paris, it was "a place choked by a mass of shacks inhabited by bad characters and crisscrossed by damp, twisted and filthy streets."[5] This reality had not been ignored or dismissed by previous generations of visitors. In 1784, future first lady of the United States Abigail Adams complained to her niece Lucy Cranch:

> You inquire of me how I like Paris? Why they tell me I am no judge, for that I have not seen it yet. One thing I know, and that is, that I have smelt it. If I was agreeably dissapointed in London, I am as much dissapointed in Paris. It is the very dirtyest place I ever saw. There are some Buildings and some Squares which are tolerable, but in general the streets are narrow, the shops, the houses inelegant, and dirty, the Streets full of Lumber and Stone with which they Build.[6]

The ascendancy of the French president Louis Napoléon, later known as Napoleon III when he became emperor of France in 1852—thus following in the authoritarian footsteps of his famous uncle for whom he was named, Napoléon Bonaparte—brought about one of the greatest undertakings of urban planning in modern history. As journalist Rupert Christiansen has deftly noted, Louis Napoléon's reign could be defined by *newness*: new buildings, new streets, new parks, new sewers, new monuments, new libraries, new bridges, anchored by an all-new opera house, and all at the behest of Louis's right-hand man, Baron Haussmann.[7] Though Haussmann's demolition crew largely sidestepped the city's medieval heart—several sections of the Île de la Cité, in the middle of the Seine, were maintained as historically important—they otherwise bulldozed entire neighborhoods to improve public works, safety, and salubrity.

But the aesthetics of this huge project were just as critical as its practicalities. The "Haussmannization" of Paris, which continued well into the first decades of the twentieth century, transformed the city into one of the most breathtaking in the world, with a visual uniformity that was firmly maintained via Haussmann's strictures on the height and design of the state-of-the-art buildings. New constructions, particularly luxurious apartments formed from white limestone replete with wrought iron balconies, were wreathed by public gardens and neatly landscaped parks, such as the Bois de Boulogne and the Parc Monceau. Planting crews cultivated more than 50,000 trees, and public green space skyrocketed from twenty hectares at the beginning of Haussmann's project to more than 1,600 hectares by 1870.[8] Grand edifices crowned those freshly widened boulevards, the most spectacular being Charles Garnier's glorious, green-domed opera house. Much of the Paris that visually delights tourists was born during this period. "Ah, Paris!" exclaimed Alice Rumph (1877–1957), a future Club resident, upon her first visit to the city. "A different atmosphere surrounds us as soon as we come within its walls and it strikes me immediately as being the gay, beautiful city it is always described to be. In the first drive from the station, its beauty is ravishing, and you wonder if it will not grow more commonplace on closer acquaintance. It never does."[9]

To the early witnesses of the transformed and beautified city, Paris was truly a remarkable sight—and for many American travelers, unused to the charm of the

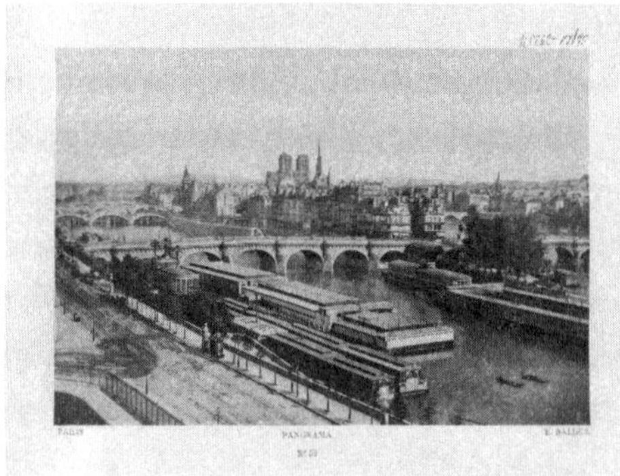

Figure 1.3. *Edouard Baldus,* Paris. Panorama, *between 1851 and 1870. Library of Congress.*

Old World, the spectacle was newsworthy. In 1858, writer Nathaniel Hawthorne recorded his thoughts in his notebook, writing:

> The splendor of Paris, so far as I have seen, takes me altogether by surprise; such stately edifices, prolonging themselves in unwearying magnificence and beauty, and, ever and anon, a long vista of a street, with a column rising at the end of it, or a triumphal arch, wrought in memory of some grand event . . . I never knew what a palace was, til I had a glimpse of the Louvre and the Tuilleries; never had any idea of a city gratified, till I trod these stately streets.[10]

But beauty was not the only component that enthralled the city's residents and visitors; its amenities did, too. The momentous changes accomplished by Haussmannization were equaled, especially in the latter years of the century, by a dedication to the pleasures of bourgeois life in Paris. As industrialization had inspired vast populations to relocate to the capital, a booming service industry followed to cater to their needs and wants. This was the era of the *Grands Magasins*, the large department stores, led by Le Bon Marché at the corner of the rue de Sèvres and rue de Bac on the Left Bank, where anyone could ogle the latest designer gowns and specialty home goods. After the delight of a shopping spree, one could be seated at any number of cafés or upscale restaurants for a leisurely meal, a *café crème*, or the popular *fine à l'eau,* a brandy or cognac diluted with a bit of tap water.[11] The Parisian dining scene had nearly doubled between 1870 and the mid-1880s, approaching a total of almost 45,000 eateries.[12]

Simply strolling down newly iconic wide boulevards like the Champs-Élysées was enchanting. By 1877, Paris was lit by the novel electric light, a feature befitting its nickname, "the City of Light." It is this vision of Paris that often springs to mind even from the vantage point of the twenty-first century: a city bursting with color in Toulouse-Lautrec's garish, beguiling images of the famed Moulin Rouge and other *café-concerts*; boulevards of nattily dressed flâneurs—the prototypical urban stroller—parading and living the good life. Paris was now elevated beyond simply a historically important city to an *experience* that could not be missed.

As Paris morphed into a city "where luxury is raised to a science," according to an 1889 Baedeker's guidebook,[13] its reputation as a must-see destination catapulted it into a star of global tourism, aided by a revolution in transportation. This included the expansion of rail systems across Europe, the development of undergrounds and subways throughout the world, including Paris's own Métropolitain in 1900, and, most importantly, an improved transatlantic steamship crossing that reduced the once-arduous voyage to a relatively speedy one: "New York's only a week away," liners reassured those traveling eastward.[14] This new transport meant visitors flooded the French capital in record numbers. To take one singular season as an example: social historian Harvey Levenstein has noted that "[b]etween April and October 1867, Paris hosted over eleven million visitors, ranging from the Czar of Russia and the Sultan of the Ottoman Empire to many thousands of less exalted excursionists from England and America."[15]

And oh, those excursionists from America: they positively *inundated* the city in the second half of the century, becoming one of the most prominent groups of foreign visitors. The period after the American Civil War coincided with a boom in the country's wealth, and that wealth spread rapidly into newly prestigious leisure activities, like international tourism. Though upper-class Americans—typically men— had long engaged in that British-inspired tradition of the "Grand Tour" of Europe to fulfill expectations of a cultured existence, travel in the post–Civil War era soared as one of the predominant ways for the rich to showcase their literal good fortunes.[16]

Once in Paris, tourists flooded recently inaugurated luxury hotels, with Americans in particular frequenting two monoliths: the Grand Hôtel du Louvre (place André Malraux, off the rue de Rivoli) and the Grand Hôtel de la Paix (2 rue Scribe, around the corner from the rue de l'Opéra, and today rebranded as the InterContinental Paris le Grand), where evenings could be whiled away playing billiards or sampling desserts in gilded dining halls. Just as Haussmann's alterations drove up housing prices, so, too, did the massive influx of tourists. By 1867,

Americans had "monopolized" both Grand Hôtels to such a large degree that the British travel entrepreneur Thomas Cook blamed Americans for a 50 percent spike in lodging prices.[17]

But it was not just the wealthiest of Americans who flooded into Paris. That same post–Civil War *richesse* grew a middle class yet unseen in the relatively new nation. For them, too, travel became a newly accessible luxury. Take, as an example, the competitive fares for transatlantic voyages beginning in the 1870s. While the most popular sailing routes from New York City ran to either Liverpool or Cherbourg for around $250 or $300 for a first-class round-trip fare (approximately $8,600 to $10,300 in today's dollars—certainly steep), budget-savvy Americans could save almost half the cost by seeking out slower boats departing from other cities like Baltimore, Philadelphia, or Boston. And it kept improving, too—by the 1890s, as Levenstein confirms, bargain-basement fares from New York to Glasgow bottomed out at $55 round-trip, or approximately $1,800 in today's currency.[18] It is no wonder that in the final two decades of the nineteenth century, the number of moneyed Americans visiting the French capital nearly tripled from 50,000 a year to 125,000.[19] For the first time, they could actually afford the journey.

Even more critically for our story of the Club: beginning in the 1870s and '80s, American *women*, for the first time in history, led the charge to travel to France. Less than a century prior, men had visited Paris for their edification and (perceived, perhaps) social refinement.[20] By the final decades of the nineteenth century, women were crossing the Atlantic in droves, often in small groups or alongside female family members to soak in its extravagances together. They enjoyed a freedom previously unimagined or historically only procured when in the company of male family members to chaperone them. These women would soon transform the city.

So delectable were their experiences that, not insignificantly, thousands of Americans opted to make their Parisian sojourns an extended one—perhaps even a permanent one. In 1874, Charles Carroll Fulton, editor of the *Baltimore American*, averred, "It is easy to get to Paris, but very hard to get away again, as most of the Americans now congregating here find . . . its attractions being so novel and varied."[21] Fulton focused his explanation of Paris's allure to women as being due almost entirely to its department stores. Of course, shopping, fine dining, and high fashion were only part of the city's charm. History, architecture, monuments, elegance, culture, sophistication—Paris had it all. But it lay an even greater claim in another vaunted area, one that was central to the lives of the French and foreigners alike: the fine arts.

It is almost laughable to list the hundreds of cultural institutions available to visit in Paris today—who has the time to document such abundance?—but it was similarly lush in the nineteenth century. Under Louis Napoléon's benefaction, major expansions of two significant arts institutions were begun, highlighting their prominence as important cultural bastions of French society and the world at large: the Musée du Louvre and the École des beaux-arts, the most prestigious school of fine arts in France (if not the entire world). Smaller art schools of various types flourished, too, and there a student could learn the latest techniques and trends at the feet of the great masters, who would groom them to enter the competitive spheres of annual exhibitions, like the highly coveted Parisian Salon, the top exhibition in all of Europe. Such an inclusion could, in theory, vault a student into the stratosphere of artistic glory.

So seductive were these visions of cultural excellence that, to an aesthete, Paris was unbeatable—and it quickly became the world's top art destination, particularly for painters and draftsmen of any gender.[22] In his partially autobiographical novel *The "Genius"* (1915), Theodore Dreiser's main character, an artist named Eugene, is so overcome not only by the city's beauty but by its wealth of cultural treasures at the Louvre and the Musée du Luxembourg that he proclaims, "When I die, I hope I come to Paris. It is all the heaven I want."[23]

CHAPTER 2

Trailing Painfully Behind

*I want no more of America, where there is no chance to do good work and
where people would prefer that you should paint badly rather than
try to do as well as circumstances will permit.*

—KENYON COX, AMERICAN ARTIST (1877)[1]

In 1893, Philadelphia-born and Paris-trained artist Katherine M.
Cohen (1859–1914) mounted a small stage in the Woman's Building
at the World's Columbian Exposition in Chicago, Illinois. The Exposition's Board of Lady Managers, tasked with arranging various lectures
and programs at the Woman's Building during the fair's six-month run,
requested that Cohen, then a renowned sculptor, participate. *Would she
consider lecturing about her experiences?* the managers asked. Indeed, Cohen
would, and she was prepared to share even the smallest details of a Parisian art student's day: toiling for hours on a wooden stool in a cramped
studio, producing charcoal studies of a live model; scrimping on heating
and food to save well-earned francs and sous for oil paints instead; the
blissful achievement of seeing one's masterpiece hanging in the desirable yearly Salon exhibition. To attendees and to the Board of Lady
Managers, such stories seemed exotic, a fascinating look at the life of a
very strange creature: *the artist.*

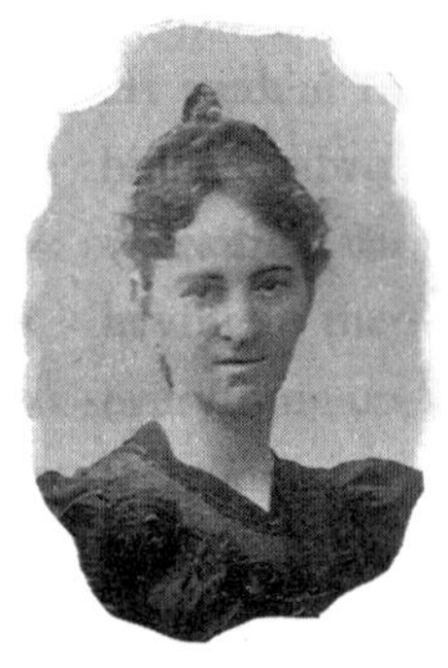

Figure 2.1. *Katherine M. Cohen, 1894. From* The Congress of Women: Held in the Woman's Building, World's Columbian Exposition, Chicago, USA, 1893, *1894.*

But the Managers got more than they asked for. Toward the end of Cohen's address, she transitioned into a fervent, if gentle, appeal for the support of artists in the United States. And a huge part of that support, she argued, was enabling them to leave their home country.

"When we arrive at the point that American art is better than anything we can get in Europe, then we shall stay at home to study," Cohen declared. "We can all of us help the quick realization of this, if we encourage our boys and girls to cultivate their artistic tastes instead of scoffing at them as impractical."[2]

In other words, to mold students into great creators of art, they had to leave the United States. They, like Cohen, had to go to Paris.

THE LURE OF Paris for American artists in the late nineteenth century was just as practical as it was passionate, because it helped solve one particular problem: training in American art schools was seen as subpar in comparison to the quality education offered by European masters. To be fair, U.S. art academies had some catching up to do, primarily because support and visibility for the visual arts had been limited, if not completely absent, for most of the country's first century.

An easy excuse for the nation's disinterest in art was America's newness. It was too busy, perhaps, establishing a government rather than focusing on what it considered frivolities—even then, art was typically viewed as a lesser endeavor (how little things change!). But this early indifference toward the visual arts was more than the result of the complicated business of managing a new nation. Americans purposefully disconnected from many European habits and ideals, deeming them antiquated and outdated at best, and fascistic and prejudiced at worst. Art was caught in the middle here, as it so often reflected the lives of the powerful and the wealthy. A single portrait could thus symbolize all the negativity that authoritarian European regimes like-wise represented: decadence, superficiality, inequality, neglect. In a new country built upon the ideals (if not the realities) of equality and freedom, art belonged to the unenlightened rather than the wise.

Given these unfavorable associations, it is no wonder that art educa-tion and appreciation in America were practically nonexistent for decades—and so, too, was "taste," something that one of the coun-try's first great painters, John Singleton Copley, knew all too well. In the 1760s, he complained about American colonists as "people entirely destitute of all just Ideas of the Arts."[3] No wonder he expa-triated, moving to England in 1774 and remaining there for the dura-tion of his life.

Yet as more foreign travelers descended upon this scrappy upstart country in the first decades of America's nationhood, the lack of interest in and encouragement of the visual arts gained more attention, and *not* the good kind. "The scarcity of taste and of skill in the fine arts of painting, sculpture, and architecture, in the United States, is a subject of great wonder to travellers," read one embarrassed op-ed published in March 1805. "It is a paradox of difficult, but surely not of impossible, solution, that a civilized, peaceful, free, industrious, and opulent nation . . . should have so few monuments of these arts among them, either in public or private collections."[4] What a humiliation, that such a fantastic new world should care so little about art!

But there was good news. This perceived scarcity could be fixed, it was assumed, with an appropriate level of governmental and commu-nity buy-in through the support of art education and exhibition oppor-tunities. And though slow in arriving, this support did eventually bear fruit. America's first art schools opened in the nineteenth century: the Pennsylvania Academy of the Fine Arts (PAFA) in Philadelphia led the charge in 1805; New York joined the game later in 1825, estab-lishing the Society for the Improvement of Drawing, which morphed into the National Academy of Design.[5] Soon, the first museums in the country opened their doors as well—the Wadsworth Atheneum pioneered the art institution in the United States when it was founded in 1842, but larger entities like the Smithsonian American Art Museum

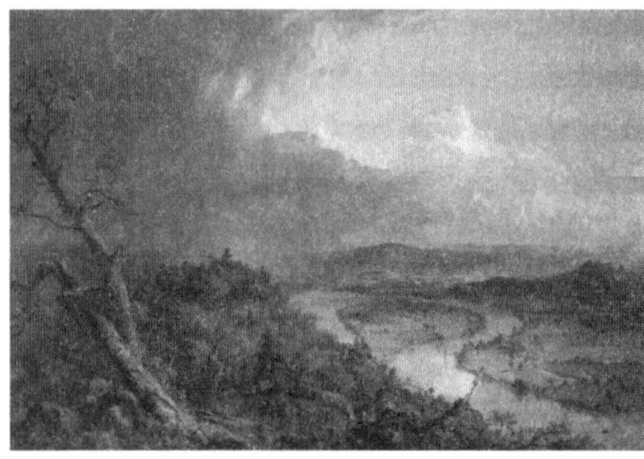

Figure 2.2. *Thomas Cole,* View from Mount Holyoke, Northampton, Massachusetts, after a Thunderstorm—The Oxbow, *1836. Metropolitan Museum of Art.*

followed only a few years later.[6]

Within the first half of the nineteenth century, then, the assertion of *we need art NOW* was accepted by American tastemakers and cultural critics, and institutions had been inaugurated to encourage it. But what was not widely agreed upon was what American art *was,* or what it should be.[7] This tricky question inspired even more press in the post–Civil War era, when the nation grappled with the reality that no singular America existed. Could there be, then, one truly *American* school of art? Perhaps, but only if American art could escape the shadow of European history first.

This was easier said than done. America's preeminent early artists focused their brushes upon the genres of portraiture and history painting,[8] both of which stemmed from the centuries-old conventions of Western art. *That's not American,* the critics huffed. *American art should be unlike anything produced in London, Paris, Rome, or beyond—it must be a celebration of our new country, our unspoiled land.*

That unspoiled land proved to be the ideal subject for American art. It is not a coincidence that the Hudson River School of painting, inaugurated by Thomas Cole's pastoral canvases in the 1820s, gained ascendancy during this period. Landscape paintings, coupling sublime vistas with the occasional imaginings of noble Native Americans or enterprising pioneers, defined American art for much of the nineteenth century, providing a romantic and Edenic view of the nation. Nor is it a coincidence that the reputation of the visual arts improved immensely in the States with the wholehearted adoption of natural beauty (akin to godliness by mid-century) as its centerpiece.

And for most Americans, this was enough: art created about America's staggering beauty by American artists, and produced in an intuitive way that was unfettered by the restricting traditions and training beyond the sea.

Well, at least it was enough for a little while.

IT TOOK A rather public international embarrassment to bring the quality of American art and education to the forefront of national conversation, and the humiliation happened in Paris, of all places. Between 1855 and 1900, the French mounted five *expositions universelles* (world's fairs), each with stunning displays of monumentalism and artistic might (the famed Eiffel Tower, as the most prominent example, was the centerpiece for 1889's exposition). As part of the grand renovation of Paris during the Second Empire, Louis Napoléon declared his intention to present one of these fairs in 1867—an excellent showcase to flaunt his city's transformation to the widest possible audience. And it paid off, too: more than nine million visitors attended the fair during its run.[9]

Though this period's expositions prioritized industrialism and mechanical innovations—such as Samuel Morse's updated design for the telegraph—the arts were prominently featured as well, and the United States was keen to be as good an exhibitor on this front as any other. In the 1867 exposition, U.S. art representatives lined three walls of a small gallery with paintings and sculpture, with special prominence for those epic Hudson River School pictures, to provide a showcase of their country's innate artistry and purity in the face of Old World decadence. America, full of pride and hope, was attempting to burst onto the international art stage.

The exhibition backfired spectacularly. Little did most Americans know, cloistered in their paradise across the Atlantic, that landscape painting—especially empty landscapes without hints of narrative, morality, history, or even titillation—was considered trite and uninspired by European standards. The Parisian press lambasted the U.S. entries, calling them ignorant and childish, noting that "the American school is trailing painfully behind the English," which was a *double* insult, considering that the French thought rather poorly of England's own artistic output.[10]

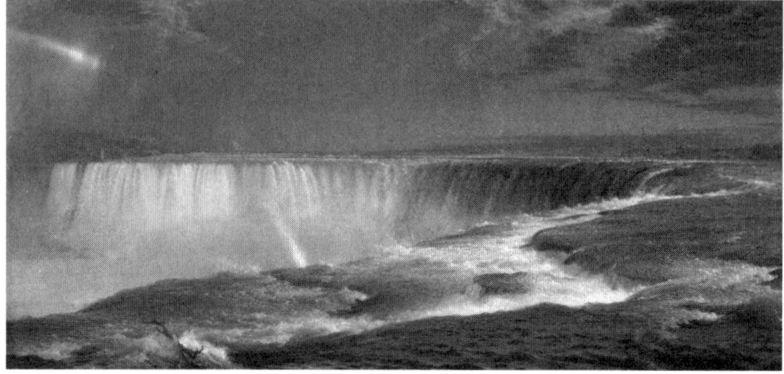

Figure 2.3. *Frederic Edwin Church,* Niagara, *1857. National Gallery of Art.*

What was most injurious, though, was not the opinion of the French but the disappointed agreement of their own compatriots that the American art on display at the exposition was, by comparison, lackluster. The Yankees had witnessed the achievements of European art and were thus humiliated and humbled by the homegrown artwork that they had previously celebrated. "We most failed in our lauded landscapists," art critic James Jackson Jarves admitted. He continued:

> [Frederic] Church's "Niagara" [Fig. 2.3] with no more sentiment, a cold hard atmosphere and metallic flow of water . . . was a literal transcript of the scene [and] taught us a salutary lesson by placing the average American sculpture and painting in direct comparison with the European, thereby proving our actual mediocrity.[11]

It was clear: in its cultural output, the United States had been found wanting. American artists needed to get their act together *fast* to play comparably on the world stage. But how?

The solution seemed like an about-face to some but was obvious to many. To improve the standards of American art, American artists needed to go straight to the source: Europe, especially Paris, where they could learn at the feet of artists like the ones who had upstaged them at the Exposition Universelle. And then, *by God,* those artists would come home and create the best damned schools of art (in both thinking and in literal educational facilities) the world had yet seen.

It was such a good idea that Katherine M. Cohen would take up this recommendation for herself, and would share it with her audience twenty-six years later.

BEFORE THE BELLE Époque, fewer than one hundred American artists called Paris a temporary or permanent home.[12] But that number, which is probably a conservative estimate, soon grew at an astonishing rate in keeping with the city's irresistibility and the general acknowledgment of its art scene as the world's best—even beating Munich, which had previously been a continental hot spot.[13] The growing American ranks were tallied with aplomb by the *American Register*, a newspaper reporting upon anything of interest to the expatriate community, with particular emphasis on their comings and goings. These documents reveal the amazing increase in the American population in Paris. In 1883, the *Register* declared that more than three hundred artists claimed Paris as home. Only five years later, in 1888, the number had magnified, with the *Register* announcing that there were more than "800 American ladies studying art in Paris" that year alone.[14]

Note the specificity of words chosen by the editors of the *American Register*: whereas once they calculated the total number of American artists living (possibly long-term, if not permanently) in the French capital, by 1888 they instead documented the number of *students*—not just established artists already working professionally. More importantly, their tally highlights that an incredible number of these art students were *women*. This substantial increase in female art students crucially reflects the simultaneous increase in studios and art academies available there for women. Though the École des beaux-arts—France's official state-sponsored art school[15]—remained off-limits to women until 1897, an entire network of private academies and ateliers—such as the Académie Colarossi, the Académie Vitti, the Académie Julian, the Académie de la Grande Chaumière, the Académie Delécluse, and others—filled in the gaps, either offering mixed-gender classes or providing separate studios for ladies. It must be noted that while these schools offered a simulacrum of the education offered to male students, most—and

Julian's in particular—charged women double in admission fees while offering half the instruction and criticism. Yes, indeed: for twice the price, women received half the attention of the academy's instructors. Still, any Parisian art education was better than nothing, so American women arrived in droves to partake of its opportunities.

For many, it seemed that the city had transformed overnight, brimming with so many art students that author and artist May Alcott Nieriker, sister of Louisa May Alcott, declared that Paris was ". . . apt to strike the newcomer as being but one vast studio,"[16] one that catered as much to women artists as to their brethren. It was a demographic shift that took many people by surprise—even some women, because only a few decades prior, the rise of the woman artist would have seemed nearly impossible, the phrase itself deemed an oxymoron.[17]

CHAPTER 3

A Good Woman or a Great Artist

*Perhaps you can put it this way. A man who does a man's work is
a normal human being. A woman who does a man's work is a kind of
superwoman. She must be two selves, one who supplies energy for
her part of the world's work, the other the woman who fulfils
the obligations custom has laid upon her.*

—Cecilia Beaux, American artist, interviewed
in the *Boston Herald* (1910)[1]

*Listen, Fräulein: there are two kinds of women painters: the one[s] who
want to get married and the others who also have no talent.*

—Cartoon of an art teacher's advice to his female student,
Simplicissimus magazine (1901)[2]

At the age of twenty-four, Louisville native and future Girls' Club resident Enid Yandell (1869–1934) had already reached heights few could imagine. A remarkable sculptor, she was commissioned to create twenty-four nine-foot-tall plaster caryatids to sit atop the Woman's Building at the 1893 World's Columbian Exposition.[3] That was enough of an accomplishment in and of itself, but Yandell did not stop there:

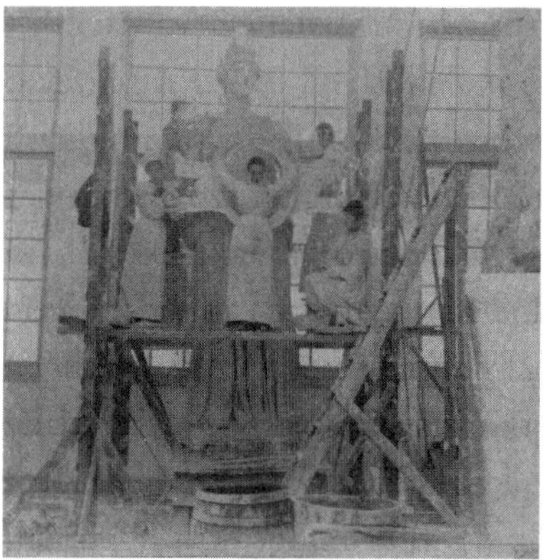

Figure 3.1. *Enid Bland Yandell (center) and Janet Scudder (left) in studio, ca. 1891. The Filson Historical Society Digital Projects.*

she also sculpted a much-lauded life-size rendition of the frontiersman Daniel Boone for the exposition's Kentucky Pavilion, and she nabbed a position as a "White Rabbit," one of the women hired to assist the American sculptor Lorado Taft in his own commissions.[4] For her efforts at the exposition, she was awarded a coveted Gold Designer's Medal, one of only three given to women that year.[5] In short: she was highly sought-after, working professionally, getting paid to be a fine artist, *and* receiving acclaim for it.

Yet not everyone celebrated Yandell's achievements. Upon learning of his niece's success, the artist's uncle, David Yandell—a prominent Louisville physician—shook his head, declaring her to be "the first woman of the Yandell name who ever earned a dollar for herself . . . a disgrace to the family."[6] Even relative strangers opined upon the sculptor's life choices. While in Chicago, Yandell briefly met Julia Dent Grant, the widow of President Ulysses S. Grant, who dismissed her sullenly, saying:

> I don't approve of these women who play on the piano and let the children roll about on the floor, or who paint and write and embroider in a soiled gown and are all cross and tired when the men come home and don't attend to the house or table. Can you make any better [a] housewife for your cutting marble?[7]

Yandell is said to have declared to Mrs. Grant that her work enabled her to "[develop] muscle to beat biscuit when I keep house."[8] That tongue-in-cheek reply may be apocryphal, but the point of Mrs. Grant's diatribe still stands: a career—save teaching or caring for home and children—was not considered an option for a true lady.

~

TO UNDERSTAND THE hard-won journey that American women like Enid Yandell and the future members of the Club undertook to become professional artists, it is first necessary to grasp some details of the theories and assumptions about gender in the nineteenth century. In the United States, the sexes were firmly split into separate binary spheres: men belonged to the wide realm of work, commerce, communication, and, well, the outside world. As a contrast, then, (white, middle- or upper-class) women reigned in the cozy interior of the home as keepers of children, hearth, and the happiness of all. Making this gender split more interesting was a parallel belief in the innate goodness of women, who were viewed as gentle, submissive, and God-fearing. Such thinking enabled wives and mothers to be elevated to a mythical, even spiritual level. This belief, known as the "Cult of Domesticity"[9] (and sometimes also called "the Cult of True Womanhood"), found great traction in the United States, having wafted over the Atlantic from Europe like a soft breeze. Americans, obsessed with the newness and purity of the land around them, particularly glommed on to the metaphorical connection between their Madonna-like women and their new Eden. Indeed, the Cult of Domesticity used nature as its supporting document: *What's more natural than motherhood for a woman? Where else would a woman belong, but in the warmth of the home she provides for her loving family? That's her element!*

For the reason of women's "natural" goodness, the separation of men and women was especially prominent in the early nineteenth century, partially because of a dominant fear of sullying a lady's delicate, innate wholesomeness. Americans and Europeans of this era patently obsessed over the concept of "falling"—moral ruination—specifically concerned with their daughters, wives, and other female family members becoming the much-loathed "fallen woman."[10] If a woman became compromised through

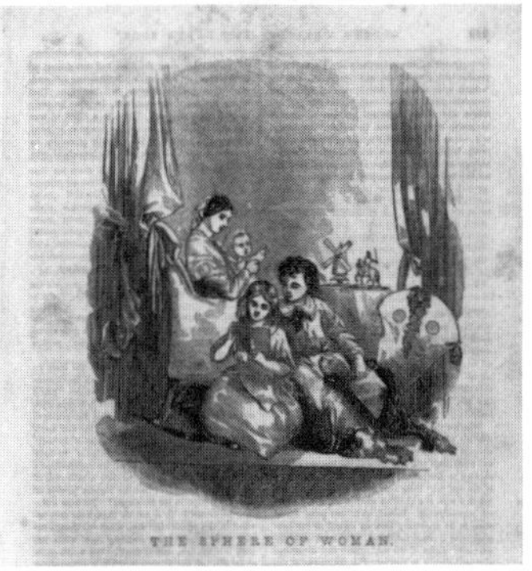

Figure 3.2. *"The Sphere of Woman."* Godey's Lady's Book, *March 1850.*

her own exposure to the Big Bad World, it was deemed disastrous to everyone—herself, her family and friends, even potentially to society at large. The "angel of the house," then, was urged to remain in the safety of the home to avoid the myriad desecrations of the world, wrought by industrialization and war, which threatened to infiltrate the sacred home via temptation after temptation.[11]

It is not as though women had been fully denied the pleasures of partaking in the visual arts while sequestered at home, however. Both girls and women were often encouraged to paint miniatures, produce quilts, embroider tablecloths, or dabble in pastels or watercolors. Such activities not only entertained, but the end product could be used as a decoration for the home, which could then be enjoyed by all— thereby promoting art as a benefit for others and thus a rather ladylike, selfless endeavor. It was, as historian Karen J. Blair calls it, "instruction in arts for domestic training."[12] These pastimes had the additional benefit of being clean—no marble dust, no turpentine, no oil paint splatters—and therefore worthy of ladies, too.

But amateur artists, beware! Too much time spent on a creative project could produce a perceived double threat to the Cult of Domesticity—self-absorption and the neglect of household duties—as illustrated by Julia Dent Grant in her dismissal of Enid Yandell.

IN AN INTERESTING twist, the general idealization of women as the "angels of the house" played a role in establishing greater opportunities for them to pursue the study of the visual arts. As arbiters of all things moral and good, women were tasked with lifting their families—and society in general—into a more dignified, beautiful plane of citizenship. The arts proved a vehicle for this endeavor, one that became increasingly necessary in the minds of many as the modern world imperiled the principles of the naive and innocent. Art was a beacon of hope, the inspiration of virtue. "Drawing may well go hand in hand with music; so may the formation of libraries and the cultivation of reading, etc. Every pure taste implanted in the youthful mind becomes a barrier to resist the allurements of sensuality," wrote education reformer Horace

Mann in 1841.[13] Show a person a lovely painting of a floral still life, and perhaps they will be less apt to stray into less savory mental arenas. Beauty should be taught, then, to beautify the mind.

Just as a mother was expected to curtail the unrefined habits of her children, so, too, was the nineteenth-century art teacher expected to hone the refined artistic tastes and intellectual world views of her students. Indeed, the British artist and critic Pen Dalton connects motherhood with the feminization of education during this era, as teachers (who, for the first time in history, were now mostly women) nurtured their young charges in a manner that mirrored the functions of the ideal bourgeois or middle-class mother.[14] Women accordingly integrated artistic studies, even if on a small scale, into their curricula for the explicit purpose of shaping students into cultured and well-cultivated citizens.

Art education slowly filtered into American schools under the purview of gentle-minded, idealistic female instructors. But what about the girls and women who aimed for more than a career teaching elementary school kids about drawing and ceramics? What about becoming working artists themselves? In the United States, that remained an uphill battle for quite some time. And a lot of that battle can be summarized in two little words: the nude.

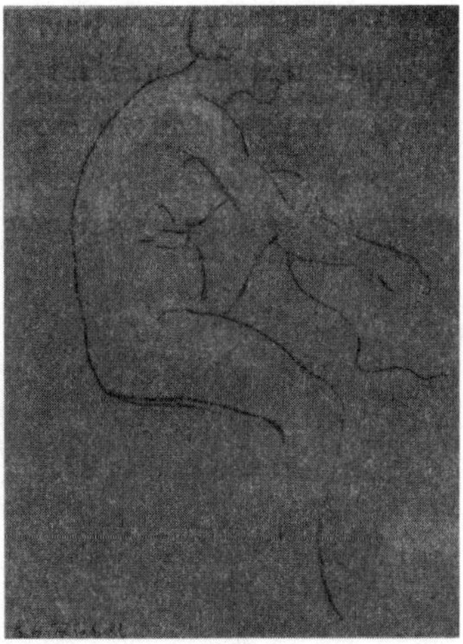

BALTIMORE ARTIST (AND future Club resident) Grace Turnbull (1880–1976) was lucky to have been born into a well-bred family with a dedication to culture and the arts. Her father, Lawrence, was an editor with the literary journal the *New Eclectic*, and the Turnbull family funded a lecture program on poetry at nearby Johns Hopkins University in memory of Turnbull's brother, Percy, who died at the age of eight.[15] Yet just because beauty and the humanities were

Figure 3.3. *Grace Turnbull, Nude, undated.* Chips from My Chisel, *1953.*

appreciated among the Turnbulls did not mean that theirs was a free and easy home. "Ours was a household where law, order and tradition reigned supreme," Grace noted in her 1953 autobiography, *Chips from My Chisel*.[16] There were simply things that *one did not do*, especially as a girl. Turnbull was careful to toe the line, until it interfered with her artistic intentions.

Turnbull had benefited from an excellent art education, one of the best a woman in the 1890s could have secured. She studied "modeling"— sculpting with clay to build a figure up over an armature or structure—in Rome during a family vacation and returned to study painting at the Maryland Institute College of Art in her late teens. She quickly learned, though, that something was missing from her education: a "thorough understanding of the human body."[17] She felt this could only be achieved by sketching from the nude model, known colloquially as attending a "life class." But when she approached her family about this possibility, she was rebuffed. "Father's pious upbringing in a rigid Presbyterian household, coupled with his ever-anxious temperament made him scent danger moral or physical in this as in almost everything," Turnbull wrote. "Mother's objection I felt I could overcome; but she told me solemnly that if I carried out my intention of working in a life class it would kill Father."[18]

Papa Turnbull's imagined reaction might have been extreme, but it was not uncommon. Recall the supposed "innate purity" expected of and inflicted upon women during this period. Exposure to the nude human form (outside of the prescribed domains of marriage and child-rearing) had long been considered a denigration of that purity and a threat to purportedly fragile feminine sensibilities. As such, life classes and nude modeling were explicitly disallowed for

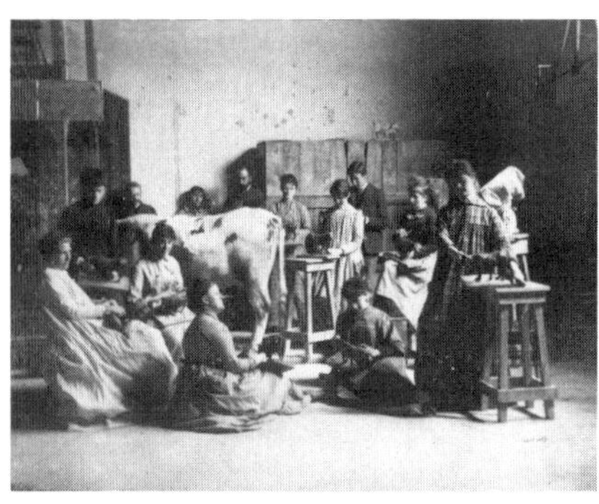

Figure 3.4. *Circle of Eakins,* Women's Modeling Class with Cow in Pennsylvania Academy Studio, *ca. 1882. Pennsylvania Academy of the Fine Arts.*

women students for most of the nineteenth century. Men, however, could study from both male and female unclothed figures. This proved to be a major problem, as the inequality catapulted men into a higher stratosphere of ability: being able to accurately portray the human body, clothed *and* not, had marked an artist as a "true" talent for centuries. Such artists were awarded the most prestigious commissions and garnered the biggest bucks. Denying women the ability to attend life classes effectively barred them from reaching these heights.

As educational opportunities expanded for women artists in the last decades of the nineteenth century, so did the controversy regarding their exposure to the nude and life classes. In one famous instance, the American painter Thomas Eakins—a fervent proponent of life study for *all* students, regardless of gender—provided an eyeful to his female students at the Pennsylvania Academy while lecturing about the anatomy of the pelvis in early 1886. Determining that *showing* was better than *telling*, Eakins casually removed the loincloth of a male model to display the curvature of pelvic muscles. This brief display caused an immediate stir among PAFA faculty, students, and their families. Though Eakins had the support of many students—male and female—he was dismissed from his teaching position at the Academy for his "immoral" actions.[19]

To both appease sidelined students and cater to their concerned families, a few American art schools began offering women-only art lessons wherein artists could participate in life classes with female models within the confines of a single-gendered space, often headed by a female instructor (or, if headed by a male teacher, one who might make himself scarce during modeling sessions).[20] Though this permitted a generation of women to receive a semblance of the experience shared by their male colleagues, it produced at least two negative side effects: first, it promoted an ongoing separation between the sexes, relegating women to their own classes. Yes, they did keep young ladies from the moral danger of being "[exposed] . . . to undraped bodies in mixed company," as historian Laura Prieto writes,[21] but this separation meant that they were taken less seriously than their male counterparts, specified as *women* artists rather than simply *artists*. Second, the stigma associated with life classes for women—even single-sex ones—remained outsize, and particularly vicious critics scrutinized women's work for signs of anatomical accuracy, which would mark them as having partaken in such "indecent" and scandalous courses. The problem was this, as one historian noted: "The aspiring female artist was torn between being 'a good woman' or 'a great artist'—the two being deemed mutually exclusive."[22]

Thankfully, many women felt that these dangers were worth the risk, as it furthered their goals of artistic professionalization. In Grace Turnbull's case, she took her family's reservations seriously, being especially concerned about her mother's statement that her attendance at a life class would "kill" her father. "I was not of an innately murderous disposition, so this announcement naturally gave me pause," she reflected humorously in *Chips from My Chisel*. But her ambition and self-confidence took precedence over her family's fears. "I felt in my bones that [taking life classes] would not really have that sinister effect, and being at the time in my twenties I decided I must take my life into my own hands then or never. As a matter of fact my joining the life class appeared to have no malignant effect whatsoever upon my Father."[23]

The nude might not kill, then; but could the study of art be calamitous in other ways? If a young woman opted to go to Paris, rumor had it that tragedy could befall her at any step.

CHAPTER 4

Starving Artists and Ugly Americans

Never shall I forget the utter desolation of the first night in [Paris]. I washed my face and hands before dinner, but went to bed unwashed, for the water was still standing in the basin, and there was no place to throw it away. It was the same thing the next morning. My bed suggested nothing so much as the tales of the penances of the Middle Ages, for the coarse unbleached cotton sheets had never been laundered, and bristled like horse hair.

—KATHARINE DE FOREST, "ART STUDENT LIFE IN PARIS,"
HARPER'S BAZAAR (1900)[1]

Nothing in the world enrages me so much as to hear people say Paris is no place for young women; that it offers more pitfalls than any other city; that temptations are multiplied there—all of which is ignorant nonsense.

—JANET SCUDDER, *MODELING MY LIFE* (1925)[2]

In the years between 1870 and 1914, dozens—if not hundreds—of stories proliferated describing the dangers sure to befall any American girl who had the audacity to journey to France unaccompanied by a chaperone—especially a girl lacking the built-in safety of a *male* chaperone, like her father or a protective brother. And these stories were not subtle. "FURTHER PROTECTION FOR AMERICAN AND ENGLISH GIRLS IN THE FRENCH CAPITAL IS IMPERATIVE,"[3] one *New York Times* op-ed blared in all caps. "MARTYRS TO ART IN THE FRENCH CAPITAL," screamed another headline in Louisville, Kentucky (Fig. 4.2).[4]

Though communities around the world extolled the many charms and virtues of Paris, there was at least one subsection that loudly proclaimed its awfulness: the fear-driven, overbearing white American mother. In drawing rooms and kitchens throughout the United States, mothers cried over the all-too-probable fates of their headstrong young daughters, the ones eagerly packing their steamer trunks and furtively palming the latest edition of a Baedeker's guidebook behind their backs. It is not difficult to imagine these poor women, sobbing into embroidered handkerchiefs by lamplight. Like good parents should, they only wanted the best for their babies. And they were certain that the best could *not* be found in Paris.

It must be noted that not every American mother mourned a daughter's temporary departure for Europe: many undoubtedly understood the merits of an international sojourn, especially to experience the cultural riches of Paris. But you would not necessarily know this from the many reports in the American press during the second half of the nineteenth century.

As the number of women traveling to Paris rose—whether as tourists or as expatriates planning a much longer stay—so did the number of sordid tales foretelling their inevitable downfall thanks to any number of offenders. Pickpockets proliferated in bustling stations throughout the city; card sharps prowled trains both aboveground and under; anarchists set off

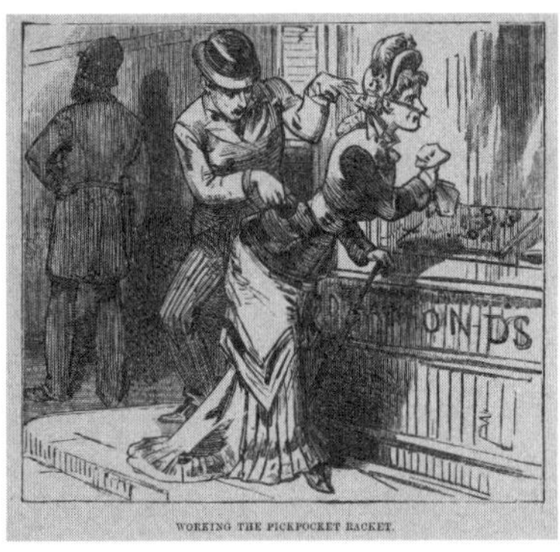

Figure 4.1. *"Working the Pickpocket Racket." From Gustave Macé,* Paris Unveiled, *1888. Library of Congress.*

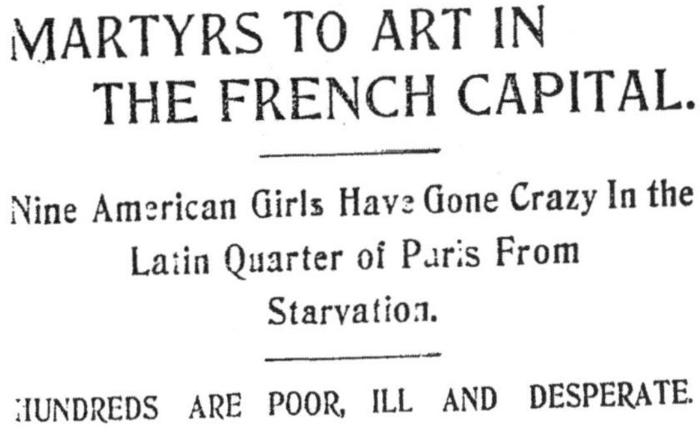

MARTYRS TO ART IN
THE FRENCH CAPITAL.

Nine American Girls Have Gone Crazy In the
Latin Quarter of Paris From
Starvation.

HUNDREDS ARE POOR, ILL AND DESPERATE.

Figure 4.2. *"Martyrs to Art in the French Capital,"*
Louisville Courier-Journal, *December 10, 1899.*

the occasional bomb in cafés and bars frequented by tourists and locals alike.[5] Historian Eugen Weber highlights the dangers even further, writing, "Juvenile delinquency was rampant, shoplifting commonplace (department stores made it easier), assault and murder seemed to be everywhere: poison, acid throwing (this was the heyday of vitriol), hammer blows, knives and hatchets of every kind, canes, cudgels, truncheons, garrotes, lassos, swordsticks, shotguns and revolvers . . ."[6] While Paris was certain to be hazardous for all, women were deemed most vulnerable, and in *Baedeker's Paris* editors began issuing warnings to women regarding the avoidance of specific areas of town, "where they risked being misunderstood and possibly harassed."[7] Paris, it seemed, was anything but safe for a young, impressionable, foreign lady.

Naturally, violence was the worst possible outcome, but death from exposure, malnutrition, and disease was altogether plausible, too, stoking further fears from American parents. The typical American girl, the press crowed, was unprepared for the expense of the City of Light, as well as the amount of time needed for an artist to gain the necessary academic experience there—a double whammy that led to extreme penny-pinching. And penny-pinching begat disaster. An 1899 article in the *Louisville Courier-Journal* announced in a hysterical subtitle that "Nine American Girls Have Gone Crazy in the Latin Quarter of Paris from Starvation," with the author, Bessie van Vorst, painting a rather vivid picture of the typical morning struggle for one of the hundreds she calls "poor, ill, and desperate":

> The winter days dawn cold and damp in Paris and the American
> student has neither a furnace register nor steam heat, nor running
> hot water . . . she makes a fire on rising; she heats water; through
> the door she slips in a small bottle of milk, two rolls, a diminutive
> piece of butter, left on the stairway at an early hour, and with some
> coffee . . . she prepares her morning meal at the cost of seven
> cents . . .[8]

This, van Vorst leads readers to believe, is the *high point* of the American student's day; the rest is spent toiling at whatever work the student has chosen, all while guzzling cups of tea as a substitute for an additional meal. Even if a woman was lucky enough to afford food, it was likely that she'd only settle into the cheapest of cafés for "tough meat and greasy soup from coarse, thick china."[9] Van Vorst's imaginary waif might be considered rather lucky to even have a garret to call her own; in 1896, British journalist William Stevens described the art student's "common practice of sleeping at night on a shelf in the closed studio where they have been working all day."[10] One can nearly hear the anachronistic tunes from *Les Misérables* streaming across the decades; obviously the trope of the "starving artist," an individual pinging between the pillars of overwork and malnutrition, held sway during this era.

While the myth of the starving artist was not gender-specific, it is true that the cost of living in Paris for women was more considerable—sometimes even double—the cost for men. The options for dining in a "respectable" restaurant, lodging in a safe boarding house, or paying fees for a reputable atelier were limited, thus ensuring that a lady, eager to keep her reputation intact nearly as much as her coin purse, would assent to a steep price.[11] As with their entry to the art world in the first place, women artists arrived in Paris already at a disadvantage compared to men.

Speaking of men, if a violent death, starvation, or dysentery were not in the cards for the archetypal American girl, there was still another rather common concern: those suave and sneaky foreign men. In a *Ladies' Home Journal* article from 1906 titled "Is Paris Wise for the Average American Girl?" author Mildred Stapley describes the city's Latin Quarter, that student epicenter, as a veritable den of iniquity, filled with "French, Italians, Russians, Roumanians, Greeks—everything—men whose attitude toward her sex is as unlike an American's (in his own country) as one could possibly imagine."[12] Against this cast of prowling rogues, innocent American girls were assumed to have no chance of withstanding their advances. "There are cases in which innocence is a crime," one writer commented in 1919. "In instances I personally know of, the girls did not realize they were playing with live wires."[13]

Finally, the death knell of a dream: if they even made it back alive, unsuspecting American girls, it was said, would undoubtedly "return home stript of their health, their jewels, their innocence, even their belief in God."[14] Given these frequent and highly publicized warnings, is it any surprise that many were loath to encourage young women artists to continue their studies abroad?

THROUGH THE PRESS and plain hearsay, it was clear to Americans that their daughters would be in dire straits if they were to travel to Paris for their artistic education. Even if they survived the French capital and returned home unscathed (and that was a big *if*), surely these women would have lost valuable time, money, and even their reputations in pursuit of a frivolous dream. These were some of the main reasons that young Americans—but especially women—were strongly discouraged from attending art school in France. But these concerns reflect only one part of the story. Another facet complicating parental viewpoints was the reality that the reputation of Americans traveling throughout Europe in the final years of the nineteenth century was . . . *not great.*

Though the phrase "ugly American" did not enter the vernacular until decades later—after the 1958 publication of the political satire *The Ugly American* by Eugene Burdick and William Lederer—the judgmental sentiment had been fomenting for many years prior, since at least the mid-nineteenth century. In France, a growing resentment toward Americans contrasted sharply with the opinions of previous generations, in which French thinkers—inundated with diplomatic visits from influential politicians like Benjamin Franklin, Thomas

Jefferson, and John and Abigail Adams, to name but a few—often considered Americans, as a whole, to be virtuous and brave (if slightly naive) folks living in an agricultural backwater of a nation. But by the end of the Belle Époque, exposure to a much larger swath of Americans transformed the previously positive outlook. Instead, French descriptions of Americans in the latter years of the nineteenth century tended toward hyperbolic character stereotypes like "heartless American industrialists" and "scheming society girls."[15]

So, yes. The Americans now traveling abroad in greater numbers than ever before were noticeably at odds with their surroundings and the people who lived there. But if the general American reputation was not particularly wonderful, what about the reputation of the so-called "American girl"?

Well, if you can believe it, it was even *worse.*

It feels like a perversion of Newton's third law: for every news article proclaiming the hazards of Paris, there was an equal (if not greater) number bemoaning the actions of the young American women gallivanting there. Freed from the disapproving glares of parents left Stateside, these "New Women"[16]—the term popularized by the American and European press to identify newly independent and free-thinking girls—enjoyed activities that they might not otherwise have back home: staying out late, attending the theater unchaperoned, or—*gasp!*—visiting a café, where any number of uncivilized events could take place. In 1890, a Mrs. John Sherwood published a ten-page screed in the *North American Review,* describing one young lady's observations of other American women in Europe:

> In the cafés she saw certain ladies who sat in a very free-and-easy fashion, one knee over the other, drinking, laughing, perhaps smoking; and she observed that these ladies were very popular with gentlemen: she accordingly made herself as like them as she could, poor, innocent American flower![17]

It is no coincidence that Sherwood's description of the anonymous American here is of a "poor innocent flower," a reminder of both the strict policing of female sexuality and virginity during this era, and the assumption of a woman's propensity to be led astray by any number of bad actors.

This negative "American Girl" stereotype spread quickly in pop culture, with Henry James taking up the mantle in his novella *Daisy Miller* (1879). Daisy is the quintessential woman of this type, flirting openly and acting spontaneously in a manner that scandalizes her family, the narrator (an American man named Winterbourne), and European society at large. One conversation between Winterbourne and American expatriate Mrs. Walker summarizes their shared frustration with Daisy:

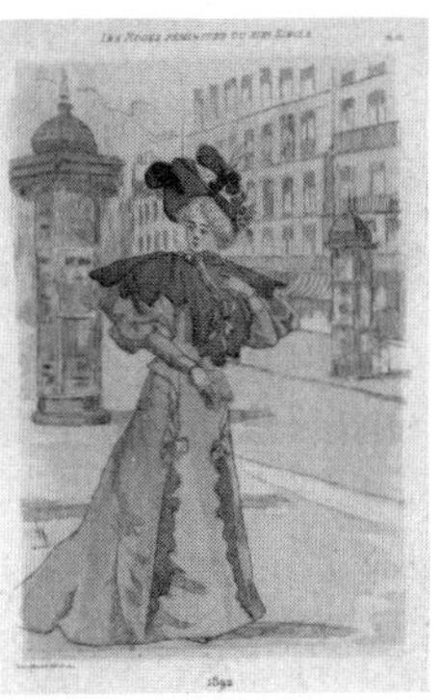

Figure 4.3. *Henri Boutet, "1892, Women's Fashion in Nineteenth Century Paris." New York Public Library Digital Collection.*

"What has she been doing?"

"Everything that is not done here. Flirting with any man she could pick up; sitting in corners with mysterious Italians; dancing all the evening with the same partners; receiving visits at eleven o'clock at night."[18]

In short, Daisy is not behaving well, and *everybody* knows it.

THE IMPACT OF *Daisy Miller* on the opinion of the American girl cannot be understated, and the name itself became a cultural shorthand for their poor behavior. As Harvey Levenstein notes in his marvelous *Seductive Journey: American Tourists in France from Jefferson to the Jazz Age*, writers across the United States bandied about Daisy's name in spectacular fashion, sometimes even comparing Daisy *favorably* to the average American girl abroad, as the editors of the *Springfield Republican* once did:

Daisy Miller was a model of discretion compared with some American girls who, with no home training and no standard of decorum, plunge into the bohemianism of student life . . . There is a giddy, egotistic, reckless type of American girl that ought to be kept out of that environment.[19]

THE AMERICAN GIRL, having been established as the *ugliest* (and most noticeable) subset of the "ugly American" trope, was thus denounced far and wide. Rare was the American mother who wanted to subject her daughter to this difficult double stereotype (let alone all those imminent dangers), so families frequently resisted their children's requests to travel abroad, purportedly to save their delicate reputations as well as their lives. But not every American girl could be deterred from her dreams. In lucky cases, then, willing parents accompanied their daughters across the Atlantic, or sent worthy stand-ins (brothers, maiden aunts, elder cousins, trusted family friends). But those who had no such connections or who could not afford a chaperone's passage: what could they do? Would those parents and guardians simply cross their fingers, praying their child had enough to eat and was not being stalked as a lothario's plaything? Oftentimes, yes. Yet they dreamed, too, just as their daughters did. They dreamed that a kind matron or concierge would take pity on their girls, acting as a maternal stand-in. But how reliable was this dream?

The unlikely answer to this motherly quandary would arrive in late 1893, and not a moment too soon, thanks to the philanthropic gestures of another American mother—and one who had also herself once been an American girl in Paris.

CHAPTER 5

The Minister's Wife

*Prominent among the charitable work done by American women
who reside in foreign countries stands that of Mrs. Whitelaw Reid, who is
regarded by hundreds of American girl students in Paris almost as
their patron saint, for the American Girls' Club . . . filled a crying
need and has more than justified its existence . . .*

—"The American Girls' Club in Paris," Town & Country (1909)[1]

The community of expatriate Americans living in Paris, colloquially known as the "American Colony," was abuzz with excitement, if not a small amount of apprehension. The newly elected U.S. president, Benjamin Harrison, had finalized his cabinet and ambassadorial positions as he took office in March of 1889, and had just announced his minister to France: the politician and journalist Whitelaw Reid.

Though Whitelaw Reid's assignment caused a stir, ultimately his tenure was mostly uneventful (save the removal of a ban on American pork,[2] ending what was known as the "Pork War"—really!). Instead, his wife's impact in France has had a far longer legacy. During Whitelaw's Parisian tenure, Elisabeth Mills Reid (1858–1931) took measures that would eventually change the lives of many—though she certainly could not have foreseen her destiny when she joined Whitelaw, alongside their

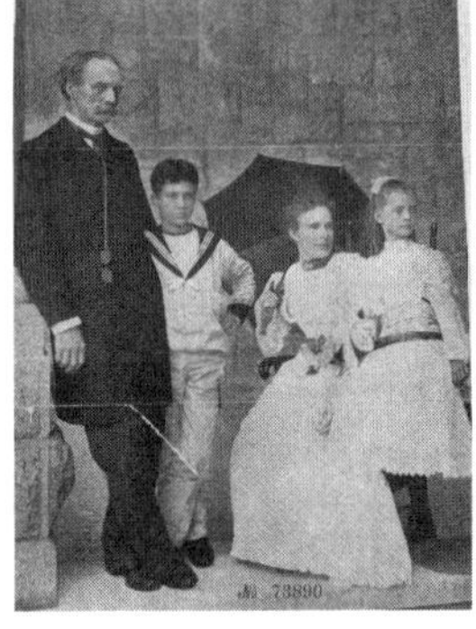

Figure 5.1. *Whitelaw Reid and Elisabeth Mills Reid with their children, ca. 1890s. Reid Family Papers, Library of Congress.*

two children, seven-year-old Ogden and five-year-old Jean, on the eight-day voyage from New York to Le Havre aboard the ship *Bourgogne* in May 1889.[3] At that time, Elisabeth, an affluent yet devoted "angel of the house," concerned herself primarily with supporting her husband's political career and her family's transition to the French capital.

BORN IN OCTOBER 1837 in Xenia, Ohio, to a poor family, Whitelaw Reid embodied a classic "rags-to-riches" narrative. Originally trained as a journalist, Reid honed his writing skills as a correspondent during the Civil War for the *Cincinnati Gazette*, where his coverage of the Battle of Shiloh (1862) garnered national attention. In the years following the war, he joined the *New-York Tribune* as an editor under the aegis of famed journalist and editor Horace Greeley.[4] After Greeley's death, Reid purchased the paper, moving from editor to owner in a savvy career move, one that enabled him to focus on growing the paper's readership and employing new technology, such as the linotype machine, to make printing more cost-efficient and faster. The by-product of this innovation was Reid's steadily accumulating wealth, propelling him into the upper class before he reached his forties. Feeling thus secure in his finances and in his position in the world, Reid made a bold, life-changing decision: he was ready to marry Elisabeth Mills.

The boldness of Whitelaw Reid's decision was not that he decided to marry, but *whom* he decided to marry. Elisabeth Mills, a sweet and shy twenty-three-year-old, hailed from one of the most prominent and prosperous families in the United States. Speaking of a rags-to-riches story: the transformation of Elisabeth's father from store clerk to the wealthiest man in California is a doozy. Darius Ogden Mills, called D. O. Mills, worked as a clerk in both general stores and banks in his home state of New York before following two of his brothers out to California as one of the "Forty-Niners" of the Gold Rush. He quickly amassed a fortune, not simply in gold mining but also in silver ore, as one of the trustees of the celebrated Comstock Lode. D. O. Mills also established the Bank of California and invested heavily in railroads, both of which increased his status to the wealthiest man in California (for a time), but also assisted in establishing the Golden State as an economic juggernaut. Mills and his wife, Jane Templeton Cunningham, made their homes in California and New York, and it was in New York City on January 6, 1858, that their second child—and only daughter, Elisabeth—was born.

Little is known about Elisabeth Mills's early years, save that she spent most of her childhood either in Sacramento (this author's hometown, coincidentally) or at her father's "country place," Millbrae, in San Mateo County, about fifteen miles south of San Francisco,[5] with the occasional respite at the Hudson Valley enclave of her maternal grandparents. Though mostly educated at the hands of governesses, Lizzie, as she was known to her closest friends, attended classes in New York City at the Brackett School for Girls. But one wonders if another educational experience—her time as an *étudiante* in Paris in the 1870s—was even more influential. As a teenager, Elisabeth Mills attended *collège*—the French version of an American high school—in Paris at a school run by Alphonsine-Eulalie Goudeman, known as Aline Valette,[6] who later gained recognition for her feminist publications supporting women's education and the rights of mothers. It is not difficult to draw a direct line from Valette's all-girls school, based in Montmartre, to Elisabeth Mills's eventual interest in women's education. Indeed, it may have developed there with Valette's encouragement and guidance.

During her stint in Paris, Mills enjoyed connecting with the burgeoning American Colony, particularly as a member of the American Cathedral of the Holy Trinity (known today as the American Cathedral in Paris), the most prominent English-language Christian church in the capital. Mills was confirmed into the Episcopalian Church at the cathedral in 1874, alongside confirmation classmate John Singer Sargent, the lauded American painter.[7]

Upon completion of her formal education in New York and in Paris—she did not attend a university—Elisabeth Mills did as was required of young ladies from wealthy families: she dedicated herself to philanthropy. As the consummate "Daddy's girl," she looked to her father as an inspiration for her giving. D. O. Mills had an interest in funding healthcare, and thus Elisabeth followed suit. Mills supported dozens of projects aimed at furthering medical training and care over her long philanthropic career. She established several hospitals, formed chapters of the American Red Cross in multiple locations, opened training schools and dormitories for medical personnel, and even provided salaries for nurses. The dedication to medicine would be a common refrain for Elisabeth Mills, and would essentially function as the heiress's career—the only "acceptable" career for a woman of her social and financial status at that juncture.

Of course, as a well-to-do young woman, she was also required to make a good domestic match. In the late 1870s, Whitelaw Reid, a Republican donor, visited Millbrae to connect with D. O. Mills, also a high-ranking Republican donor. But Reid walked away with more than political camaraderie: he returned to New York sporting a sizable crush on Elisabeth, a five-foot-five, blue-eyed beauty. And it seems that the feeling was mutual. Mills and Reid corresponded long-distance for two years before their engagement, and according to Whitelaw Reid's biographer, their relationship may not have been without its drama. Whitelaw Reid was twenty years Lizzie's senior, and though his purchase of the *New-York Tribune* had made him wealthier, his financial magnitude was nowhere close to that of the Mills family.[8] Still, theirs was a love match, and D. O. Mills was nothing if not partial to his daughter. By February 1881, he accepted Reid's request for Lizzie's hand in marriage—or rather, he accepted *Lizzie's* insistence on the matter. In a letter to her betrothed, Elisabeth Mills wrote of their partnership, "Of course I can not flatter myself that my parents are wildly delighted, but we will make them so in time."[9] On April 26, 1881, Lizzie Mills became Elisabeth Mills Reid, marrying Whitelaw Reid in her family's Fifth Avenue mansion in front of 250 guests.

THE REIDS HAD not intended to find themselves in Paris in 1889. In the years following their marriage, Reid's political connections grew to include many influential figures, such as the soon-to-be American president Benjamin Harrison and the late president James A. Garfield. His clout had only increased with his connection to the Mills family, and the escalating power and influence of the *Tribune* heightened his status within Washington, too. Though he once claimed little interest in holding office, the possibility of supporting his party by occupying a cabinet-level or diplomatic position seemed appealing. He set his sights immediately upon the most desirable option: the ambassadorship to the Court of St. James's, the top diplomatic position to the United Kingdom. It was an appointment, though, that eluded Reid, at least for the time being. Instead, he was offered appointments as ambassador to Germany on two separate occasions, both of which he declined. Feeling pressured to step up on behalf of his nation and his political party, he finally assented to a three-year stint as Minister to France under Harrison, a position considered the second-best option after the Court of St. James's.[10] Somewhat grudgingly, Whitelaw Reid thus relocated his young family to Paris in the spring of 1889.

FROM THE PRESS coverage of the Reids' time in Paris, one might assume that Elisabeth did little but host lavish soirées for all manner of American and international dignitaries. Society pages around the United States reported on every party, every luncheon, and every afternoon tea held and attended by the minister's wife. The *Sacramento Daily Union* described one 1890 evening in glowing terms, the authors proudly crowing of Elisabeth Mills Reid's status as hometown-girl-made-good:

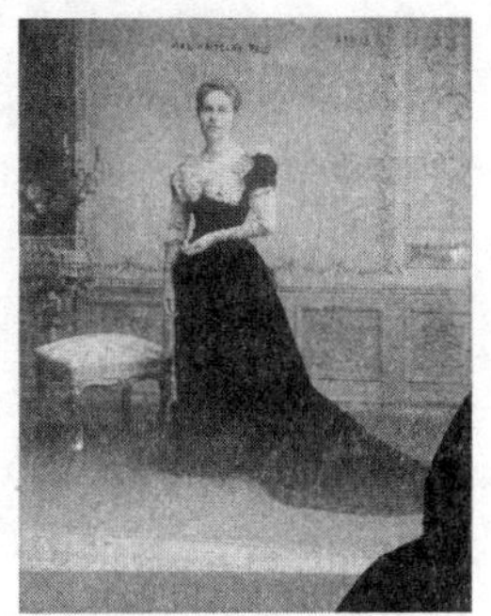

Figure 5.2.
*Mrs. Whitelaw Reid.
Undated photograph,
Bain News Service.
Library of Congress.*

> The sumptuous hotel occupied by Mr. and Mrs. Whitelaw Reid on the Avenue Hoche was ablaze with light last evening, and gay with music and dancing. It was the occasion of a ball given by the Minister's hospitable wife, and was

> designed especially for the pleasure of her young friends, both French and American.
>
> Then, if never before, Columbia's fair daughters sojourning in Paris had an unlimited opportunity for waltzing, flirting and possibly in their delightfully unceremonious fashion snubbing a choice collection of elegant French noblemen who rallied from various aristocratic faubourgs to meet them.[11]

Note the nod to young American women—"Columbia's fair daughters"—as coquettish: a reminder, though somewhat benign here, of the rampant stereotyping of American girls as flighty and whimsical.

Such descriptions of events were fairly common in the nineteenth century, with ample column space dedicated to accounts of the opulent gowns and expensive jewels worn by partygoers and the Who's Who they mingled with on any given evening. Today, chronicles like these are often relegated to the pages of magazines like *Town & Country*, *Vanity Fair*, or perhaps even *People* in the case of celebrities, but in the *fin de siècle*, they passed for news, and practically every newspaper of any city of size contained generous "society" sections. Elisabeth Mills Reid's endeavors and exploits were thus well known and widely reported in both the French and American press.

Though not as extensively publicized, other things besides hostess duties occupied the time of the minister's wife. Elisabeth Mills Reid threw herself enthusiastically into the heart of the American Colony, a community so welcoming to her only fifteen years prior during her *collège* days. Though nowhere close to the populous peak it would reach in the 1920s, the American Colony of the 1890s was extensive enough to be named as one of the largest expatriate communities in Paris, smaller only than the British, which the Americans nevertheless outranked in wealth and spending power.[12] The kernels of the Colony had been planted in the late eighteenth century prior to the French Revolution, especially after the French allied so victoriously with the American colonists—the ones based in the newly formed United States, not its Parisian counterpart—during the American Revolution. By the post–Civil War era, the migration of newly wealthy expats to the French capital created the Colony as it existed during Reid's youth in the 1870s and during her return in the 1890s.

The Colony existed in a bubble of sorts, a close-knit community criticized by Americans as being "too French" and by the French as "too American," because although several clubs and social groups purported to support Franco-American relations, the majority of American Colonists kept to themselves. Colonists congregated on the Right Bank of Paris, in the areas surrounding the Paris Opera (now deemed the Opéra Garnier) and over toward the Champs-Élysées and the place de l'Étoile, in which the Arc de Triomphe is centered.[13] They relished partaking in French cultural events, like several world's fairs and the yearly art exhibitions of the École des beaux-arts and the Société des artistes français, but at the end of the day, Colonists frequented American-run teahouses and restaurants, made appointments with American dentists, shopped at the English-language bookstore Brentano's (still in existence today), read a Paris edition of the *New York Herald* ("friend and guide of Americans Abroad," one description read[14]), and socialized with fellow Yankees at events held by upper-class hostesses like Elisabeth Mills Reid. Even an American baseball club was established, featuring players sourced from (male) art students at the popular Académie Julian.[15] The Colony thus presented the ideal home-away-from-home for a subset of moneyed Americans. As author and activist Annie Adams Fields had noted during a trip through the city in 1859, "It is almost like returning to Boston to come to Paris. At every turn and on every stair we meet Boston friends."[16] Sure, they "engaged with the natives," as historian Nancy Green jocosely writes, but they did so on a shallower level than with their own countrymen.[17]

True to the spirit of America's puritanical, Protestant roots, many of the Colony's most important social connections were made at the two American-run churches, the American Chapel (today called, somewhat confusingly, the American Church in Paris) and the American

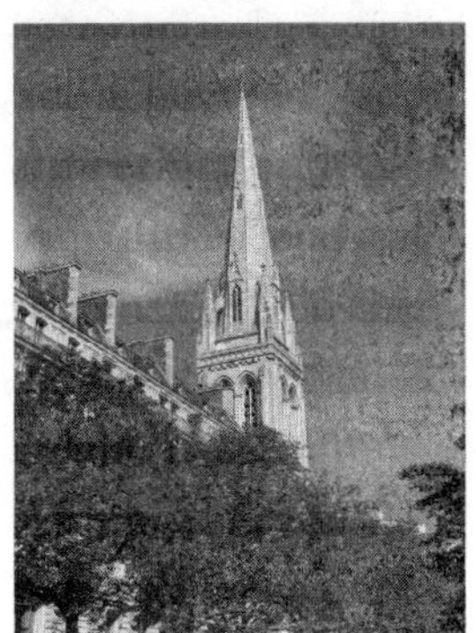

Figure 5.3. *Spire of the American Cathedral of the Holy Trinity, Paris. Courtesy of the author.*

Cathedral of the Holy Trinity, Reid's preferred house of worship. The Cathedral, newly relocated in 1884 onto the avenue de l'Alma (now avenue George V) and only a stone's throw away from the Champs-Élysées, was the far more influential of the two religious institutions. With her original connection to the Episcopalian cathedral, it only made sense that Elisabeth Mills Reid would visit there to attend weekly services. It also had the benefit of being relatively close to Reid's home, based in a luxury hotel on the avenue Hoche just around the corner from the Étoile. In her role as a diplomatic wife, she eagerly formed a kind of ministry of her own, meeting with Cathedral congregants to formulate plans for charitable activities.

It was within this religious environment that Elisabeth Mills Reid became acquainted with a certain Mrs. William Newell, and that she learned about a *secondary* American colony—one with only a tangential link to the American Colony at large and in much greater need of financial and moral support.

THE AMERICAN EPISCOPAL and Presbyterian minister William W. Newell[18] and his wife, Helen Pert Newell (born ca. 1845), bemoaned the spiritual and moral dangers they felt awaited their fellow Americans—many of whom were art students—who lived hand-to-mouth in that bohemian enclave, the Latin Quarter. Reverend Newell, a clergyman associated with the American Cathedral, felt compelled to provide his services to this semi-forgotten subsection of American expats, segregated, as they were, from the epicenter of the Colony flourishing on the other side of the Seine. Newell began small, holding ad hoc services in his family apartment at 87 rue de Rennes in the late 1880s.[19] So successful was this endeavor, however, that it soon caught the attention of several members of the Colony and inspired financial backing from the American Cathedral itself. This popularity likewise enabled Newell to extend his ministerial duties farther into the *Quartier Latin* when he convinced the administrators of the Cathedral to permit church services in the area, ones specifically catering to the student—especially the art

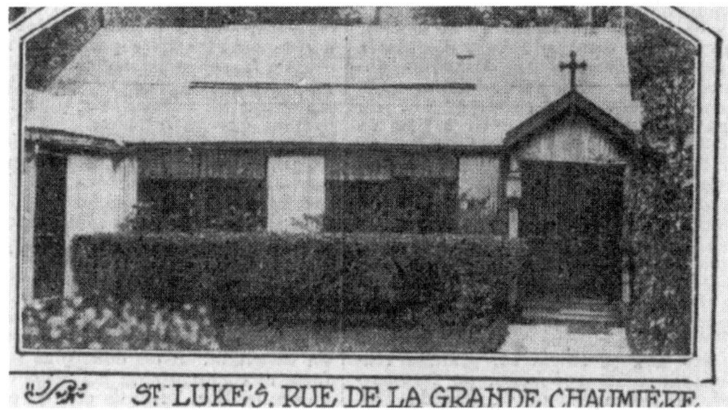

Figure 5.4. *"St. Luke's, Rue de la Grande Chaumière."*
New York Herald *European edition, September 15, 1912.*

student—community. On October 18, 1891, Reverend Newell hosted his first religious service in the Quarter. Serendipitously, October 18 is celebrated as the feast day of St. Luke, the patron saint of artists.[20] What religious figure could be a better connection to the artist-students of the Latin Quarter? In honor of this fortuitous link, this new church began its life as St. Luke's Chapel. A year later, a long-term location for St. Luke's tiny but devoted congregation would be dedicated at 5 rue de la Grande Chaumière. Located in a quiet residential garden, St. Luke's—also called "The Little Tin Chapel" for its petite size and corrugated roof,[21] or "St. Luke's in the Garden" for its locale[22]—abutted an eighteenth-century abode, painted a glowing yellow and sporting one of the most peaceful courtyards of the quarter. In a wonderful coincidence—or perhaps not a coincidence at all—this elegant, tranquil building would soon be adopted as the American Girls' Club in Paris.

Yet church services only provided so much succor, and one wonders if the Pennsylvania-born Helen Newell,[23] in support of her clergyman husband, suggested a secondary offering: a weekly Sunday dinner. Into their home the Newells began inviting American students for much-needed sustenance, conviviality, and—naturally—some gentle proselytization. One early attendee, sculptor Lorado Taft, later recalled the Newell gatherings' early days:

> [Newell] had the happy inspiration to invite the presumably hungry
> art student to his house for dinner on Sundays . . . Soon I was
> bidden to bring others to the hospitable board. Before many weeks
> we were a large and enthusiastic circle. They seemed to enjoy
> having us there, and we had a hearty, whole-souled way of eating
> everything up, which showed our appreciation and made our hosts
> feel more at home.[24]

It is likely that Helen Newell took the lead in the preparations of these dinners, shopping for fresh ingredients and cooking meals for her newly adopted brood of students. Having raised three boys[25]—only one of whom still lived at home with his parents—Helen certainly had practice feeding a rowdy, hungry crowd of artists like Lorado Taft. One evening, however, someone else caught her eye amid the mild chaos of those Sunday suppers: a quiet young woman. This singular event was later depicted in an 1894 article in the weekly magazine *The Outlook*:

> Mrs. William Newell . . . noticed at her reception a lonely girl, and,
> calling upon her soon after, found her in a tiny bare room. "Don't
> loosen your cloak," the girl said. "I took a room without a chimney,
> lest I should be tempted to have a fire." She was an art student
> making a brave struggle to stay in Paris, and her heroism was that
> year rewarded by her picture being accepted at the Salon.
> Mrs. Newell, who had herself been homesick in Paris, has ever
> since been holding in her heart and brain the hope of brightening
> the loneliness that often comes to American girls transplanted to
> this foreign life.[26]

It is fair to note that Helen Newell was shaken by her direct experience with the prototypical suffering girl-artist. Here was evidence that, for all their charitable works, the Newells still lacked the ability to properly serve women within their community. The men, she knew, had greater options, but women struggled more mightily and often in silence. At that moment, Newell made an important decision: she would speak for them.

The first seeds of the American Girls' Club had been sown.

THOUGH SHE IS far less flashy a figure nor as famous as Elisabeth Mills Reid (and indeed, only the scantest of details exist to document her life), Helen Newell must be credited with the conception of the Girls' Club. Newell's comparative lack of glamour—being a clergyman's wife, as opposed to a minister's heiress partner—might be one of the reasons that some later accounts of the Club's founding mistakenly reported that "Mrs. Reid interested Mrs. William Newhall in the project," when it was most certainly the other way around. (Also, note the misspelling of Newell's name here—perhaps this article should never have been taken as serious news.[27])

How and when Mrs. Newell connected with Reid is unclear, but their mutual association with the American Cathedral, and the American Colony as a whole, suggests that their meeting was somewhat inevitable. Indeed, either woman may have requested a meeting with the other: Newell, understanding Reid's position as wife of the Minister to France, was convinced that Reid could pull the right strings to support a large-scale charitable mission; for her part, Reid may have been privy to the Ministry's numerous calls from both struggling young women and their concerned families, and may have known of the Newells' attempts on behalf of their betterment and thus wanted to assist. Regardless, the two women joined together in the early 1890s with a singular goal: "to meet the needs of the increasing number of American girls coming abroad to study."[28]

Initially, the idea behind the organization that would eventually be called the American Girls' Club was a simple one: a small gathering space where any American woman studying art or music[29] in Paris could savor a warm cup of tea and the English-language publications stocked in its meager library. Coed church services, led by Reverend Newell, could also be enjoyed on Sunday evenings, for those who lacked the inclination to trek down to St. Luke's Chapel. The exchange of ideas, embraces, and knowing smiles between like-minded ladies was all part of the package.

For its audience, this space functioned similarly to a social club, a nonresidential locale intended as a community center for those of a particular background or commonality, but one with a somewhat philanthropic or charitable bent, if not a charity per se (after all, though the Club would open its doors to any female American student, its true intent was to help that typical down-and-out artist, like the young woman who had so distressed Mrs. Newell). This is an important distinction for two reasons: primarily, it provides the perfect lens to understand Elisabeth Mills Reid's involvement, as she was widely known and lauded for her charitable giving. Secondarily, the Club's creation aligns within the "women's club movement" of the United States, which experienced its beneficent heyday in the period of 1880–1920.[30]

Until the dawn of the twentieth century, women in the United States of America had few official means of enacting change, being allowed neither to hold office nor to vote. Strength, though, lies in numbers: thus, since colonial times, American women formed a myriad of "women's clubs" to "raise funds, speak publicly, conduct business, demand rights, build community institutions, and educate themselves through their experience in voluntary associations."[31] Clubs, then, became safe—if still resolutely separate—spheres for women to further projects or missions of their own design. Interestingly, in the 1880s and '90s, one of the fastest-growing types of "women's clubs" was the art association.[32]

When Newell and Reid jointly organized the American Girls' Club, which opened in a small apartment at 19 rue Vavin in 1891,[33] their brand-new establishment would have been very *en vogue* and thus familiar to the typical American woman. The 1903 *American Students' Census, Paris* confirmed to its readers a decade later that ". . . the club soon fulfilled the expectations of its generous founders, and became a favorite rendezvous for the students of the *Quartier*, as well as for those more distant ones who were attracted by its reputation for comfort and quiet."[34]

That could have been the end of the story: the formation of a sweet reading room and meeting center for American "girls." But the Club's popularity, as well as the ongoing and varied needs of its primary audience, led to the creation of something much bigger and more wide-reaching. It led to the establishment of the soon-to-be-world-famous iteration of the American Girls' Club in Paris—the version of the Club that was spearheaded predominantly by Elisabeth Mills Reid.

Elisabeth Mills Reid's dedication to the Club may seem to be a strange pivot. Her extensive list of philanthropic donations, projects, and commitments chiefly focused on medicine, as mentioned previously: the American Red Cross and the funding of hospitals and nursing schools took precedence long before the development of the Club and long after. She was also a staunch supporter of several Episcopalian organizations, including the American Cathedral of the Holy Trinity (where she endowed a pew in 1924 in honor of her late husband; the plaque with the dedication "In memory of Whitelaw Reid, American Minister to France, 1889–1892" remains attached there today).[35] Perhaps Reid's interest in the American Girls' Club simply stemmed from this Christian focus on "good works" and, more specifically, from her Episcopalian faith.

And yet Reid's actions in establishing the Club were greater than many would have expected. Why did Reid develop the Club—let alone expand it—when she could have simply supported the mission of the American Cathedral, St. Luke's Chapel, or the work of the Newells themselves? It was surely not an interest in contemporary art that persuaded her, as Reid's tastes, described in profiles of her own art collection, skewed toward historical portraits and landscapes by the likes of Anthony van Dyck, Henry Raeburn, and Canaletto.[36] What else inspired her to go above and beyond to help American girls?

The answer may lie in something as simple as nostalgia. Reid's stint in Paris at Aline Valette's protofeminist Parisian school is an oft-neglected part of her biography, but it surely affected her deeply. It set the stage for a lifelong love of the city and of the French, as well as an understanding of the importance of education and opportunity for women of all ages. Reid may have remembered her teenage years fondly and hoped that her assistance might bring other young American women an experience closer to her own—if not one of elegance and *richesse*, one that could be defined at the very least as affordable and safe. As the mother of two, and especially as the mother of a young girl—Reid's daughter, Jean, was seven years old when the Club was inaugurated in 1891—she also may have sympathized deeply with the American mothers struggling to allow their girls to live and work on their own across the Atlantic. She held the unique position, then, of understanding the student's *and* her mother's perspectives, and she was exceptionally able to help them both.

An additional element of interest for Reid may have been the Club's distinction as being outside her family's philanthropic and business missions. Though it tangentially related to her husband's work as Minister to France, it was solely *Elisabeth Mills Reid's* project, and one distinct from her famous father's concerns, too. D. O. Mills influenced his daughter's interest in medicine, but the American Girls' Club was *hers*, and hers only. Just as women need "a room of one's own," to quote Virginia Woolf, Reid longed for a purpose and a project of her own, and the Club fit the bill—something her lifelong dedication clearly demonstrates. In a handwritten, undated letter likely written in the mid-1920s, Reid noted to an associate that she longed to continue providing "women . . . their chance in life at my Club."[37]

IN ALL LIKELIHOOD, Reid and Newell decided to expand the Club beyond a simple meeting room and library in early 1892. In advance of the United States presidential election in November 1892, Whitelaw Reid completed his duties as Minister to France and the Reid family returned to the States, leaving Paris in the spring to allow plenty of time for Whitelaw's transition into the vice-presidential nominee for the Republican party, which paired him with the incumbent Benjamin Harrison (the ticket ultimately lost to Democrats Grover Cleveland and his vice president, Adlai Stevenson I[38]). Given the family's built-in expiration date for their Parisian residency, it is likely that Elisabeth Mills Reid began her negotiations for the bigger-and-better Club before her departure. At the top of her to-do list was to locate a larger venue, as the Club had outgrown its small space on the rue Vavin. Reid hoped that the Club could become a home base for American women studying abroad—or, rather, to American "girls," as its name would later confirm, possibly as a means of suggesting its services to unmarried women—so it needed a suitable number of rooms in which to house these women, either individually or in groups of two or three. The reading room and library at the rue Vavin could not be abandoned, either, as they were extremely popular among the American Colony as a whole, as was the Club's most famous offering: its afternoon tea. A kitchen and a dedicated *salon de thé*, then, had to be added to the residential club's mix.

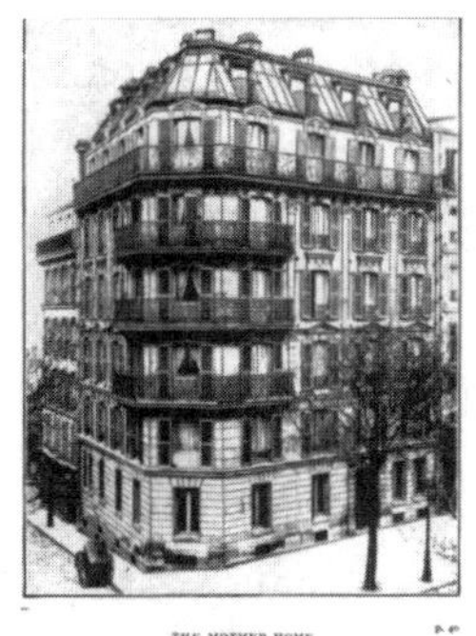

Figure 5.5. *"The Mother Home." Mrs. Travers (Ada Leigh) Lewis,* Homeless in Paris: The Founding of the "Ada Leigh" Homes, *1920.*

Reid and Newell were not alone in their intention to open an institution for the protection of foreign women living in Paris, nor were they the first to do so. That honor goes to Ada Leigh Lewis, a British woman who opened Mission Home for Young English and American Women in 1872.[39] Mission Home had a wider scope, both geographically and generally, than the American Girls' Club, housing women regardless of their occupation or educational status. Still, it was a small residence, housing only twelve women in its early years.[40] With the significant growth of American women traveling to Paris to study art and music, there was enough of a need that both organizations could happily coexist.

In searching for the perfect base for the expanded Club, Elisabeth Mills Reid toured various properties on the Left Bank but left disappointed and frustrated by the condition of some buildings and the lack of amenities in others. However, when the beautiful eighteenth-century home abutting the rear of St. Luke's Chapel became available for rent, it felt like divine intervention. The philanthropist's prayers—and the prayers of many an American girl, her parents, and even her jittery homeland—were soon answered.

A Rambling Old Structure

When the American girl first sets foot in the rue de Chevreuse . . . she begins for the first time to associate narrow streetways with beauty and picturesqueness instead of, as heretofore, with neglect and decay. There is here no filth or squalor, but order, refinement, and, above all—she feels it, the atmosphere exhales it—an unspeakable romance.

—Emily Meredyth Aylward, "The American Girls' Art
Club in Paris," Scribner's (1894)[1]

On the left [of the rue de Chevreuse] is a large four-story building shining in a fresh coat of cream-colored paint. When the great porte opens we catch a glimpse of a sunny court with a garden behind. The house extends around three sides of a paved court; in the center is a large flower-bed filled with scarlet geraniums, hollyhocks, and roses; an old well has been covered over and transformed into a pansy bed, and here and there are boxes overflowing with gay nasturtiums. The tall trees and shrubs in the garden shield the court from the view of neighboring houses, and in the pleasant seclusion the noisy, dusty boulevard seems far away.

—Elizabeth Taylor, "The American Girls' Club in Paris,"
The Churchman (1894)[2]

For artistic expats and students in the Latin Quarter and Montparnasse, the quiet, residential rue de Chevreuse was a perfect home base. Situated in the sixth *arrondissement* and just around the corner

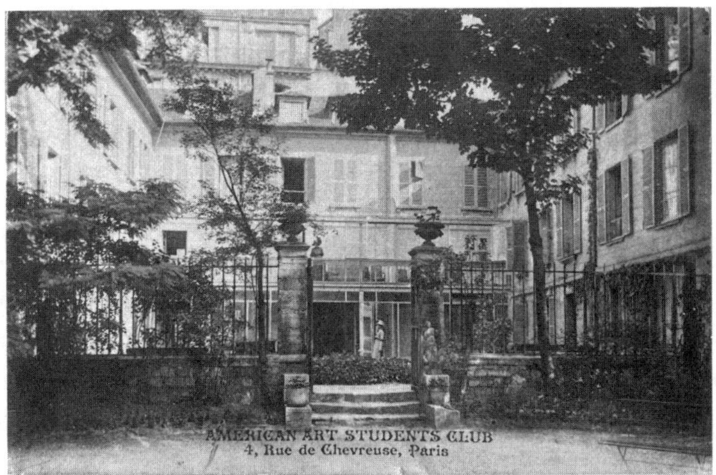

Figure 6.1. *"American Art Students Club." Postcard, ca. 1910. Alice Morgan Wright Papers, Smith College.*

from several art schools and ateliers, the narrow street was close to everything: well-stocked art supply shops; inexpensive cafés and *crémeries*; and the Luxembourg Garden, one of the prime locations in the city for sketching *en plein air*. There was nothing glamorous about the location, though: one 1880s resident recalled it as "an ugly little street that linked the boulevard Montparnasse to the rue Notre Dame des Champs . . . not one bit aristocratic, despite the name of this poor street: a few houses . . . for workers or 'petits bourgeois' and facing n° 4, two wine merchants on the ground floor. The remaining buildings were rather seedy furnished hotels."[3]

Nevertheless, when Elisabeth Mills Reid learned of the availability of the property at 4 rue de Chevreuse adjoining St. Luke's Chapel, its suitability may have come as a lightning bolt of inspiration. Its direct and literal connection to St. Luke's was a major selling point, but it had also been used previously as a boys' boarding school and was thus properly outfitted as a residence for several dozen individuals. It was eye-catching, too. Comprising four stories, the building—described as "a rambling old structure of almost a hundred rooms"[4]—wrapped around three sides of an interior flagstone courtyard, with wisteria-decked balconies and verandas overlooking this splendid space. The property's garden was separated by two stone pillars linked by a wrought iron gate, opening it up to St. Luke's and extending to rue de la Grande Chaumière directly behind it. It is the garden and the courtyard that garnered the most glowing praise during the following years, and it seems to have made a strong impression on Reid, too. She imagined the space as the perfect foil for the purported bohemianism of the Latin Quarter, a semi-secluded place where a young lady could lounge in a hammock in peace with her sketch pads or her French *cahiers*, gossiping with a friend or two.

If the building's appealing aesthetics had not persuaded Reid, surely the artsy atmosphere did. In addition to the numerous art schools of the surrounding Latin Quarter, the neighborhood had already drawn attention from several rather famous (or soon-to-be famous) residents. Paul Cézanne, the noted Postimpressionist, situated his studio directly across the street at 5 rue de Chevreuse; American expat James Abbott McNeill Whistler housed his own practice directly behind the Club's garden.[5]

Most of all, though, Reid's selection ensured that "her" girls, as she would lovingly call them, would be assuredly safe, protected within the building's eighteenth-century stone walls and looked after by a matronly on-site director. It had the right bones for the perfect home-away-from-home for the American girl, and thus, with little hesitation, Elisabeth Mills Reid leased the property, and the next iteration of the Club was under way.

Even prior to the Club's official reopening in 1893, its new location was the subject of much discussion, as the site came with a compelling backstory—and even more myth. The earliest tales of this section of Paris, between what is now the boulevard du Montparnasse and the Luxembourg Garden, suggest a certain notoriety, according to historian Dorothy Louise Mackay, who traced 4 rue de Chevreuse's history in the 1930s.[6] Beginning in the thirteenth century, rumor had it that malevolent ghosts freely congregated there, giving it a rather spooky reputation. This belief so troubled the French king, Louis IX—an extremely devout Catholic, later canonized as a saint in 1297[7]—that he vacated his nearby palace, donating it instead to a monastery of Carthusian monks in hopes that they could expel the spirits.[8] Whether or not the monks were successful is in question, but given that a nearby road was known long after by the forbidding moniker of rue d'Enfer ("Hell Street"), the region's reputation must have held fast for some time.[9]

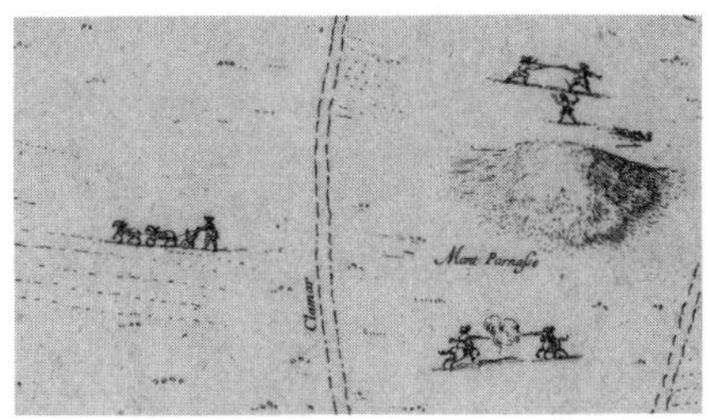

Figure 6.2. *Detail of duelers in Montparnasse, from a 1675 map of Paris by Albert Jouvin de Rochefort.*

The situation had not improved by the mid-seventeenth century. Though talk of ghosts and the underworld had lessened, perhaps, by this era, the streets encompassing the future 4 rue de Chevreuse received an all-new appellation: Coupe-Gorge, or "Cutthroat."[10] Coupe-Gorge, as Mackay dryly notes, "was spoken of as a 'little frequented place which it was not prudent to risk visiting at night,'" and maps of Montparnasse dating from this period were emblazoned with figures engaged in bloody duels or displaying their deadly arms (Fig. 6.2).[11]

At some point around the beginning of the eighteenth century, intrepid landowners braved the infamous region and settled therein, eventually lending an air of respectability to the former wasteland. It was likely during this era that 4 rue de Chevreuse was constructed. As Mackay concludes, the architectural styles popular during the early eighteenth century are reflected in its exterior: "The court with the large cobblestones, the heavy, square, wooden entrance doors, the iron grill in the garden, the open gallery facing it, and the rows of gabled windows all around the house, stamp it with the cachet of this period."[12]

Who built this lovely edifice on the rue de Chevreuse? To date, this question remains unanswerable. Some historians have posited that the street name may correspond to the home's purported use as a hunting lodge for members of the Duchy of Chevreuse, located approximately nineteen miles southeast of Paris. To later inhabitants, the romantic exterior of the building surely reflected an equally romantic past, so this link to nobility was eagerly adopted, leading to more than a few tall tales.

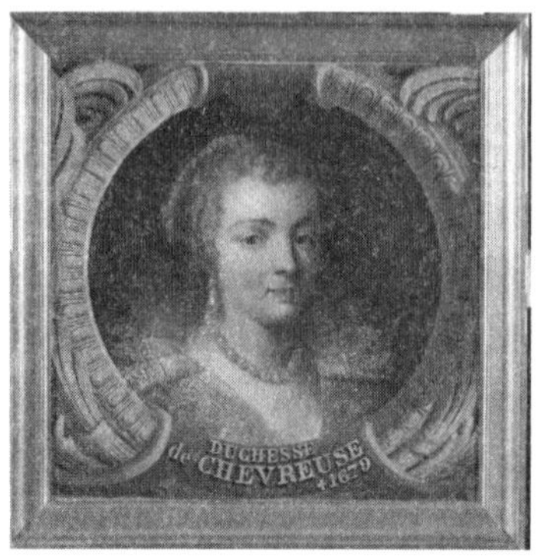

Figure 6.3. *Jean-Pierre Franque,* Marie de Rohan, *1839. Château de Versailles.*

Most intriguingly, 4 rue de Chevreuse was long thought to be the erstwhile home of Marie de Rohan, the Duchess of Chevreuse (also called Marie de Rohan-Montbazon, or simply Madame de Chevreuse), a colorful character whose many courtly intrigues during the reign of King Louis XIII kept gossips chattering.[13] In a biography of the famed Cardinal Richelieu, one of Marie's mortal enemies, she is described wonderfully: "She was everything that Richelieu was not: beautiful, healthy, imaginative, sympathetic, romantic, witty. She cared nothing for crowns or laws but much for individuals and power. She was a brigand with a brigand's code of honor."[14]

Marie's life was the stuff of legend. Born in 1600, she rose to prominence in the French court, eventually befriending Anne of Austria, queen to Louis XIII. The women grew close, often exchanging confidences at the expense of the all-powerful Richelieu—until Richelieu uncovered Marie's involvement in the so-called *Conspiration des Dames,* wherein the women united to thwart the Cardinal's power over the extended royal family. Marie was thus exiled from the court in 1626—but not before she and her English lover, Henry Rich (Earl of Holland), attempted to convince the queen to have an affair with George Villiers, the first duke of Buckingham. Queen Anne demurred but Villiers did not, and he created quite a controversy by openly attempting to kiss her, much to Marie's amusement.[15] These are but two of the early scandals that circulated around Marie de Rohan, and only her *first* exile, mind you.

Several books and biographies have covered Marie's fascinating existence, but even great nonfiction was not enough to contain her: Alexandre Dumas, the eminent French novelist, included her as a character not only in *The Three Musketeers* (1844), where she featured as the mistress of Musketeer Aramis, but also in its sequel, *Twenty Years Later*

(1845), wherein it is revealed that Marie de Rohan secretly bore *Athos's* son[16]—yes, two Musketeers, unbeknownst to one other, had flings with the same intriguing *duchesse* (poor Porthos, he never had a chance).

Adding further excitement to the reputed connection, 4 rue de Chevreuse was long rumored to have been built above a secret tunnel that ran roughly a kilometer in length and connected it to the Luxembourg Palace, one of the many royal strongholds scattered around Paris where Marie de Rohan purportedly held her romantic trysts.[17]

Compelling though these stories may be, they appear to be nothing more than myth, yet they nevertheless stuck around. In her unpublished memoir, artist and American Girls' Club resident Anne Goldthwaite (1869–1944), wrote of 4 rue de Chevreuse, "It was a charming place, supposedly the hotel of the Duchesse de Chevreuse, friend of Anne of Austria, and I see no reason why it should not be true . . . on one side was an opening to an underground passage leading, it was said, to the Palais de Luxembourg. At any rate, it started off in that direction before losing itself in darkness."[18]

The reality is that the earliest days of Number 4 are unknown. The first hints of its existence appear in the 1790s as a small, struggling porcelain factory. The factory transferred hands twice that decade before two brothers, Pierre-Louis Dagoty and Étienne-Jean-Baptiste Dagoty, leased the property in 1800. After his brother's untimely passing late that year, Pierre-Louis took over sole proprietorship of the Dagoty Brothers factory and completely revitalized the site's porcelain output. Under his supervision, 4 rue de Chevreuse transformed into a decorative arts powerhouse, one that would later be called "one of the most brilliant . . . manufactories existing in Paris at that time."[19] By 1804, Dagoty

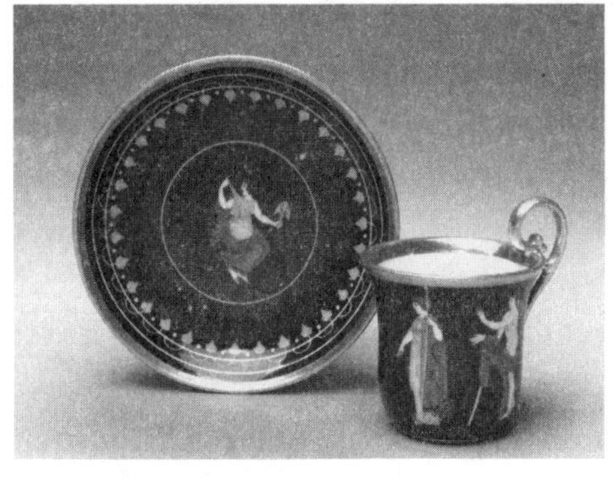

Figure 6.4. *Dagoty, Cup and Saucer, ca. 1810. Metropolitan Museum of Art.*

Brothers employed more than 100 artisans at five separate factories, with the Chevreuse site as one of the primary locations. The high quality of Dagoty products, identifiable per the British Museum via its "attractive ground colours and lavish gilding,"[20] grabbed international attention. Most notably, Empress Josephine, the first wife of Napoléon I, collected Dagoty porcelain, using Dagoty as a supplier for the Palace of Versailles.[21]

After Pierre-Louis Dagoty's retirement in 1823, 4 rue de Chevreuse morphed into something entirely different: for ten years, it became an orthopedic surgery and therapy center, where Charles-Amédée Maisonabe, a doctor, treated various maladies, including "scoliosis, but also . . . club feet, muscular contractures, defects of the sensory organs, and skin diseases."[22] The rue de Chevreuse medical outpost, officially called the Établissement orthopédique et gymnastique du Mont-Parnasse, proved to be an ideal location for recovering patients, who could stay in the residence or enjoy the center's gym, which featured various contraptions, including a trapeze, trampoline, and parallel bars, for both personal use and physical therapy. It would not be the last time the site would be retrofitted for medical purposes.

One of the longest chapters of the history of 4 rue de Chevreuse followed: its usage as a boarding school, run by the Swiss pastor Jean-Jacques Keller. After the closure of the Établissement orthopédique in 1834, Keller, alongside his business partner, the lawyer Valdemar Monod, opened the Institution Keller, a first in France: a Protestant school for boys that accepted students from several countries, including England, Scotland, Germany, Switzerland, French Polynesia, and the United States.[23] The Institution emphasized a curriculum heavy in both classical literature and modern language studies, with German as a particular forte, given Keller's Swiss-Germanic roots. Most important, though, was its Calvinist bent, which Keller admitted in later years: "Our ideal, which we perhaps followed with more zeal than wisdom, was the evangelization of our pupils."[24] Keller instructors expected their charges to attend daily sermons and Bible studies, and several scholars have noted a preponderance of Protestant pastors among the school's alumni listings.

Residents later recalled their coping mechanisms for rebelling against the stifling religious atmosphere of the Institution. At a dinner to celebrate the school's fiftieth anniversary in 1884, one former pupil reminisced, "We were a bunch of rascals. When night fell we would often gather in a secluded corner of the garden and savor a cigarette, all the more delicious, alas, because it was forbidden fruit."[25]

The Institution maintained its position as one of the preeminent boarding schools in Europe for decades, molding the minds of young men destined to achieve high-ranking positions in French, English, and American political circles. Even nonresidents were taught there: André Gide, the future Nobel Prize–winning writer, sought tutoring from Keller's son, Jean-Jacques Édouard (known as Jacob), to improve his chances of readmittance to another nearby school, the École alsacienne.

The École alsacienne may have inadvertently played a role in the Institution Keller's eventual closure in the early 1890s: after the École alsacienne opened in 1874, it pulled prospective students away from the longer-running Institution, leading to slowly decreasing admissions. After the death of Jean-Jacques Keller in 1889, Jacob Keller maintained the school but found the prospect difficult, especially from a financial standpoint, as his son, Gustave, later recalled:

> [F]or months, he struggled, trying to remain afloat, and finally he received an offer to rent the entire house for a project [to accommodate] young American women who had come to Paris to study the arts, and he made a decision . . . to rent the house. We thus left the rue de Chevreuse in August 1893 . . .[26]

With little fanfare, the Kellers departed. It was the end of an era, and the start to a more beautiful one. After a thorough cleaning and with the addition of some feminine touches, the American Girls' Club officially opened its new doors at the rue de Chevreuse only two months later, on October 16, 1893.

CHAPTER 7

In the Midst of Luxury
and Romance

*It is a great misfortune that none of the girls who come abroad, and who would
like to have a home at the club, are unable to do so; the house will
accommodate only fifty students; but it is the center and gathering
point for all American girls studying in Paris.*

—JOSEPHINE BREEKONS, "JOLLY AND BUSY GIRLS,"
THE WASHINGTON POST (1903)[1]

*. . . [The homesick American girl at the Club's restaurant] will be ready to
exclaim, "This is a little heaven on earth. I have sat in the public restaurant
alone with the tears rolling down my cheeks into my soup."*

—CARO LLOYD, "THE CLUB FOR AMERICAN GIRLS
STUDYING IN PARIS," NEW OUTLOOK (1894)[2]

Frances Cranmer (later Frances Cranmer Greenman, 1890–1981)
stepped out of a Renault hackney carriage into the darkest of nights
on the rue de Chevreuse in 1911. Pulling her coat tighter around her
waist, she paused for a moment before knocking at the large double
doors, then painted green, in front of her. Had the driver delivered her

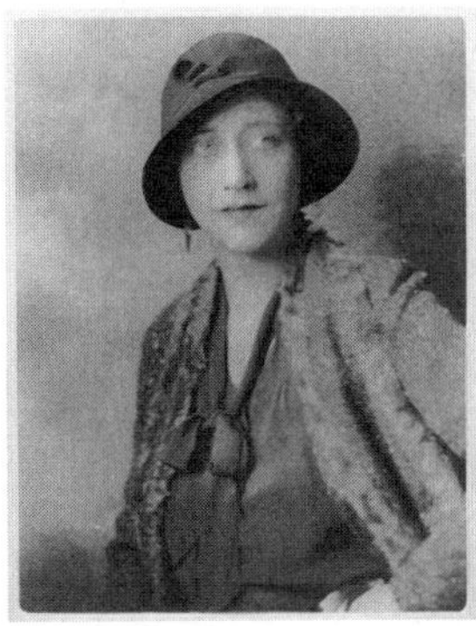

Figure 7.1. Frances
Cranmer Greenman,
*undated. Hennepin History
Museum.*

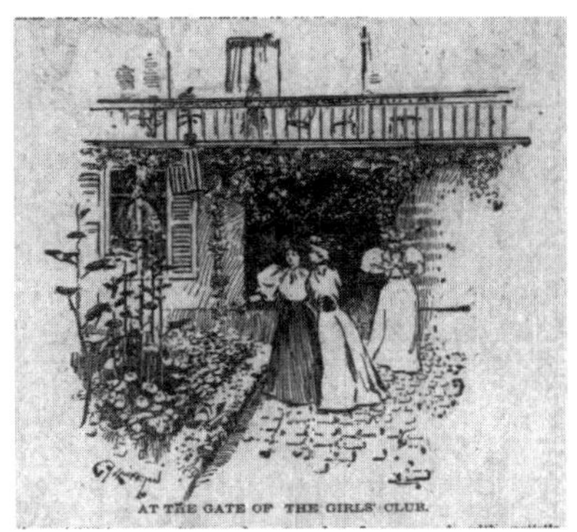

Figure 7.2. *"At the Gate of the Girls'
Club."* Lincoln Nebraska State
Journal, *April 7, 1895.*

to the correct address? The streetlamp nearby only illuminated so much, and the *batîment* appeared so plain and, well, *boring*: was this place truly her new Parisian home?

The only daughter of Emma A. Cranmer, a Midwestern suffragist and temperance activist, Frances Cranmer had been raised to be proud and confident, developing into a woman who rarely hesitated to go after what she wanted. (*Attending art schools in four different states? No problem! Training with two of the top American teachers in New York City? Done!*) At that moment on the shadowed street, Cranmer had little to do but forge ahead as she had always done. She thus rang the bell of her temporary home at the American Girls' Club in Paris with characteristic vivacity. Nerves be damned!

In the quiet of the evening, the Club was still, its garden and corridors empty. The concierge, however, was always on duty, and she "roused with the clang of the bell, popped her head, in its nightcap, out the little window and soon shuffled to a door wide enough to allow a carriage to drive through and opened it," Cranmer wrote in her 1954 memoir, *Higher Than the Sky*. "The headmistress, expecting me, led me through the narrow stone halls to my room. With the bed rocking from the ship's rhythm and my few pennies tied around my neck, I went to sleep."[3] There had been little time for exploration of her new home; she would have to wait until morning.

And oh, *that morning*: the golden dawn washed away any slight misgivings that the typically bold Cranmer secretly carried.

"It was a new world to me, that next morning," Cranmer recalled dreamily. "Breakfast under ancient trees in the old world garden of the club hidden behind high walls and chimney pots. My little yellow table, on a carpet of white pebbles and ivy, shone in the sunlight."[4]

CRANMER'S 1911 ARRIVAL at the Club followed a script that had been repeated by a generation of artists since its opening in 1893: arrival at the Club's doorstep was marked by the uncertainty befitting the start of any new adventure, but once a new tenant passed over the building's threshold, she would typically fall under its spell quickly and deeply. There was a lot to love about the charming, historic structure. "We paid little board but lived in the midst of luxury and romance," asserted resident Anne Goldthwaite.[5]

The rue de Chevreuse property improved upon the Newells' early vision of the Club, just as Elisabeth Mills Reid had planned. To begin with, it was significantly larger: the building's original footprint, little changed since the eighteenth century, housed more than forty rooms, providing enough space for private lodgings, public reception rooms, storage facilities, and on-site accommodations for the concierge. The gentle elegance of the American Girls' Club was naturally situated primarily in those public spaces, particularly its inviting library and reading room. In the Club's earliest days on the rue de Chevreuse, it housed more than six hundred books

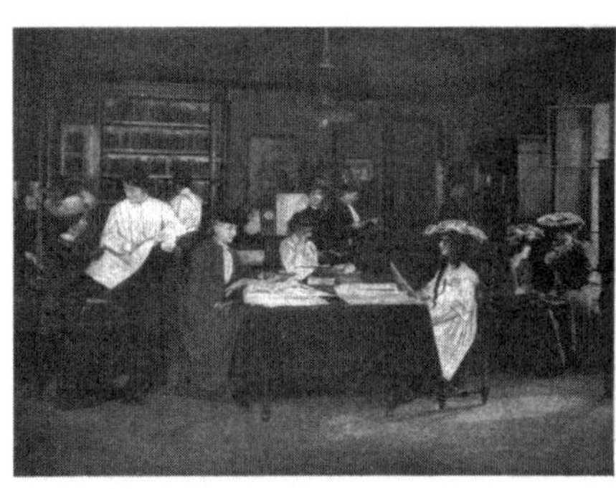

Figure 7.3. *"The Library in the Ladies' Club in the Rue de Chevreuse."* Broadway Magazine, *1905.*

on floor-to-ceiling shelves, forming "a fine and comprehensive library, with two valuable divisions devoted to French literature and art," per a 1909 article in *Town & Country*.[6] It was greatly expanded in the 1910s, but the 1890s version was especially cozy, with a rocking chair placed adjacent to a glowing fireplace. Nearby, the reading room supplied both French and English periodicals across a large central table that women often occupied to take French lessons or pen letters to send home. Not that everyone spent a great deal of time perusing said periodicals. "We have all the American magazines and papers here at the club and a large library but no time to read," resident Alice Morgan Wright (1881–1975) confessed in a letter to her mother in late December of 1909.[7]

Helpfully, the reading room also contained a bulletin board brimming with useful information such as "church services, and summer sketching classes, addresses of doctors, dentists, French teachers, boarding houses, and announcements of the sale of students' furniture," noted resident Elizabeth Taylor (no, not *that* one; this one lived from 1856 to 1932).[8] Members also used the Club as their post office ("I get my mail at the club so don't bother to remember this address," Wright wrote to a friend after she moved away from the Club in 1912).[9] It thus functioned as a hub connecting its members to greater Paris and its communities beyond its walls.

In both private correspondence and news reports, the comfortable, homey atmosphere of the Club's salons and garden were widely extolled. The rented rooms were equally praised for their capacity to house approximately forty to fifty women. The residential rooms' ambience, though, was less appealing. They were not shabby by any means, but they were sparsely furnished and lacked decorative details. Later generations described them as akin to college dormitories, an apt comparison. Upping the ante, male American students jokingly baptized the Club as "the nunnery"[10] for the purported sparseness of the private rooms and the seemingly pious nature of its residents, too (one wonders if this joke went a bit too far, because by 1902, the *New York Herald* incorrectly reported that "Tradition has it that [the Club] was once a convent").[11] Sure, the rented rooms were nothing to write home about, but no matter—they became an artist's blank canvas. "It is left for the taste and purse of the occupant to make them homelike and attractive," Florence Blanchard of the *San Francisco Call* asserted in 1895.

And what attractive rooms they became, scattered lovingly with objects sourced from flea markets and European travel—and far beyond. A fine, if rather unique, example is the room of the Ohio-born Taylor, a fascinating naturalist, artist, writer, and a "true collector of experiences," in the words of her biographer.[12] In 1892—only a year before the Club's opening—Taylor temporarily abandoned her artistic training at the Académie Delécluse to take an extended summer trip through Canada's Upper Northwest Territory to the Arctic Circle. Returning to Paris to resume her studies in late 1893, she sought relief and convenience above all else—no surprise, given that her Arctic excursion had been a difficult one.[13] To her great excitement, she procured a room at the newly opened Club, a move that made her one of its earliest residents. It is evident that Taylor cherished living there. The following year, she composed "The American Girls' Club in Paris" for *The Churchman*,[14] an Episcopalian magazine, delighting readers with glowing descriptions of the still-new facilities, afternoon tea, and one of the bedrooms:

> The room of a student who has been over sometime shows the result of many such expeditions. A gray-greenish net makes misty shadows as it hangs in graceful curves from the ceiling. Photographs and summer sketches are pinned up on the walls, a great Dutch milk can by the window is filled with holly, and by it stands a pair of Breton sabots [clogs]. On a charming writing desk, improvised from an orange box, is a quaintly carved old hour glass; a Botticelli bas-relief and a graceful Tanagra figure catch the light from a side window; a brass kettle is singing, and a huge ladle of Spanish copper gleams like a coal from a dusky corner.[15]

Though she coyly notes that the room simply belongs to "a student," the room described here is undoubtedly Taylor's own, as confirmed when Taylor's compatriot writer, Caro Lloyd, noted, "One of the quietest [residents of the Club] is a passionate explorer, the only woman who has penetrated the lower Mackenzie [River, in Canada]. Her room is adorned with presents from the Eskimo, and a wonderful Norway fishnet."[16] Taylor's room, albeit brimming with items specific to her travels, is nevertheless indicative of the artsy mish-

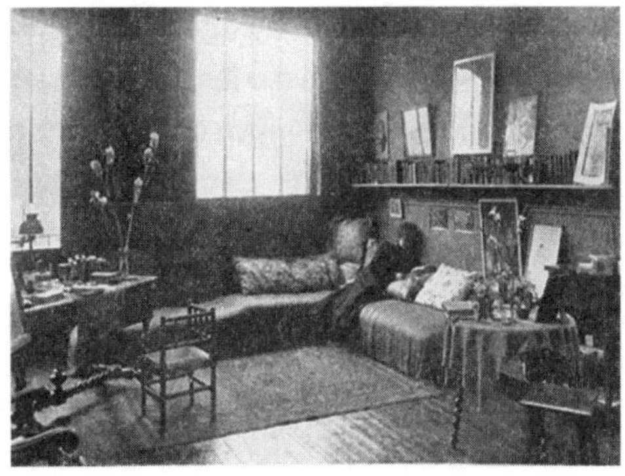

Figure 7.4. *"A Typical Girls' Studio in Paris."* Town & Country, *July 17, 1909.*

mash preferred by Club residents. "Within a couple of weeks every student has provided herself with the few yards of scrim or cretonne, the etchings and the half-dozen little decorative knick-knacks to be had for a song in Paris," author Emily Aylward asserted in her 1894 article for *Scribner's*, "The American Girls' Art Club in Paris."[17] Shabby chic was the order of the day—but some enterprising residents also shopped at Le Bon Marché department store, selling their goods at a markup "to repair the fatal damage to [their] allowance."[18]

The Club's standard-size rooms could be rented for thirty-five francs a month; tiny chambers—the AGCP's version of a bohemian garret, perhaps—were rented for twenty-five francs, while an extra-large space, meant to be shared by two or three women, retailed at sixty francs per month. The average cost of thirty-five francs, per Aylward, equaled just under seven dollars. In a city solidly unaffordable even in the nineteenth century, this was a steal, and such a bargain was widely praised. "When the young American aspirant realizes [this] . . . her courage will begin to ascend," Aylward wrote.[19] Her courage would ascend, that is, as long as she was not placed in one of the Club's cheapest rooms—a small chamber, unidentified today, that was rumored to be haunted by a particularly restless spirit.[20]

Rent at the Club—as is often true today—did not include heat and lighting, nor did it involve water, either, since 4 rue de Chevreuse was not plumbed until later. A "ducking" at a public bath house nearby cost twenty-five cents, however, and a week's worth of wood for a fire could be delivered for approximately six francs[21] (coal was a cheaper alternative at half the price—but it also provided half the heat of a woodstove, nicknamed "the little devil" by Club residents[22]). Those wishing to economize made do with burning coal, taking a sponge bath in their rooms, and investing in a tattered rag rug to warm themselves underfoot.

What little furniture the Club provided was meant to promote multifunctionality. Every bedroom at the AGCP contained a futon-like divan, folded down into a bed at night and back up into a couch during the day, providing seating for friends or greater floor space for impromptu drawing or modeling sessions, depending on the proposed activity and the time of day. Japanese screens tucked artfully into corners hid personal effects and steamer trunks jammed with gloves, veils, the occasional traveling suit, and "old underclothes," according to author May Alcott Nieriker, because "the acid used by all Parisian *blanchisseuses* [would] soon rot and spoil anything delicate and nicely trimmed." Those ragged unmentionables, though, should absolutely be kept, because they were "invaluable as paint rags . . . which artists so often have to buy."[23]

IF THE ACCOMMODATION was bare-bones, two little luxuries formed the central Club experience: its newly inaugurated restaurant and its reinvented afternoon tea. Following the great success of the Club's tea at the Newell residence, a restaurant was opened at 4 rue de Chevreuse to provide its residents more sustenance—breakfast (served from 7 to 9 A.M.), *déjeuner à la fourchette* (lunch, available from noon until 1:30 P.M.), and dinner (served from 6 to 7:30 P.M.). Visitors, too, were welcome to dine. Though room

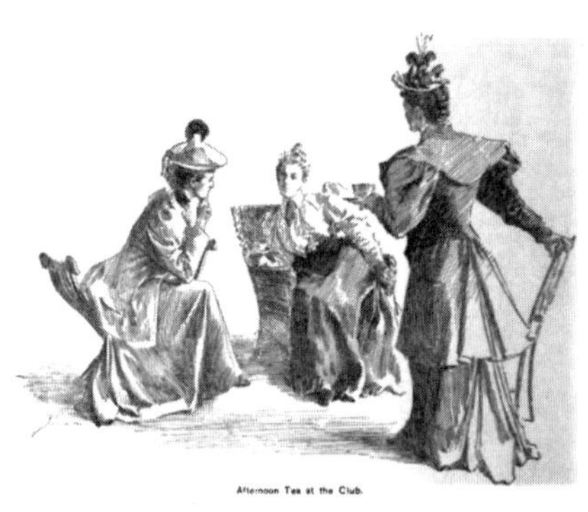

Figure 7.5. *"Afternoon Tea at the Club."* Scribner's, *November 1894.*

rentals were usually off-limits to married women, the Club's restaurant was not, as was reported in 1895: "The restaurant is open to all who wish to avail themselves of the opportunity of obtaining wholesome food at reasonable rates."[24] This wholesome food, served by "trim, spotless women-servants,"[25] was widely described in newspapers and magazines back home in the United States, where journalists relayed entire menus with (no pun intended) relish. In the November 1894 issue of *Scribner's*, journalist Aylward shared sample menus with prices in French francs, including one for the evening of November 30, 1893:

Potage

Julienne. 0.20

Hors d'Oeuvre

Saumon, sauce tartare. 0.35

Entrées

Rôts

Turkey and cranberry sauce . . . 0.40
Salade de saison. 0.20

Légumes

Purée de pommes. 0.15
Céleri. 0.05
Chouxfleurs, nature. . . . 0.20

Desserts

Fromage. 0.10
Fruits, oranges. 0.10
Biscuit. 0.10
Ice-cream. 0.40
Macarons. 0.15
Café noir. 0.15
Thé. 0.15
Bière. 0.40

Vin rouge. 0.80

Chablis. . . . . . . 1.80[26]

The American public understood that this was a fine menu provided at a ridiculously low expense, especially after a Washington, D.C., newspaper provided an exchange rate for additional lunch and dinner prices listed in Aylward's article:

> Veal Stew, 8 cents; beefsteak garni, 8 cents; mashed potatoes, 3 cents; salmon 7 cents (!), and turkey with cranberry sauce, 8 cents! It is the miracle of loaves and fishes. The pious Paris ladies of the library restaurants cannot feed their working girls like one of these. The working girl must eat hash pie at 6 cents, while for 7 cents the Art Club gives its daughter salmon . . .[27]

In contemporary currency, the cheapest item on the menu, whether it be cheese, oranges, or a small cookie, equals approximately thirty-six cents. The chablis, the priciest item—though it is difficult to tell whether the wine on offer is purchased by the bottle or a *verre* (glass)—equals $6.50.[28]

Even nearly two decades later, the Club's restaurant prices remained as affordable as they were in 1893. In 1912, traveler Jane Teal reported her dining expenses back to her hometown newspaper, the *Lompoc Journal*: "The breakfast of coffee, rolls, and butter were only 50 centimes (10c); the luncheons were 25 cents and the dinner of five courses only 30 cents, making only 65 cents for three good meals much better cooked and served than those at some of our American high-priced hotels."[29] And compared to some of the pricier tourist restaurants in greater Paris, the Club was still unbeatable in both taste and company. "[T]he food at the Club was much better," recalled resident Anne Goldthwaite, "and I found little satisfaction in attempting to sit with young men at restaurants."[30]

This is not to suggest that each and every meal at the Club was a culinary delight. Of one breakfast, Frances Cranmer recalled, "They were pouring hot milk, with a scum on it, into my coffee and calling it 'café au lait.' I was spreading unsalted butter on a 'croissant.'"[31]

Though the quality and cost of the Club restaurant's cuisine was its primary draw, American women enjoyed its décor, too, as a little reminder of home. The dining room's most lauded detail was a frieze tacked near the ceiling illustrating a "procession of ducks, geese, strutting gobblers, and every fowl known to be edible, the parade being interrupted at intervals by exhibition pumpkins, grapes, and all matter of dining-room fruit."[32] Painted by a group of American men from the École des beaux-arts, this "turkey frieze," as it was popularly known, was intended to be temporary, either in celebration of an art exhibition or as a decorative thank-you gift to the Club's matron—sources differ[33]—but it remained on view for at least ten years, if not until the Club's closing in 1914.

With such inspiring, homey decorations, it is no surprise that the restaurant became a favorite location for celebrating holidays, especially Thanksgiving—those "strutting gobblers" provided a perfect excuse, after all.[34] The American holiday became one of the Club's most sought-after events, as several residents of the Club asserted. Anne Goldthwaite commented in her memoir that if a potential Club member's behavior or reputation left something to be desired, "they tried to conceal their waywardness that they might be invited to Thanksgiving dinner."[35] Alice Morgan Wright received her invite in 1912 directly from the visiting Elisabeth Mills Reid, an offer that she joyfully reported to a friend, though she was unable to accept it: "Mrs. Ried, notwithstanding our militant persuasions, invited us to thanksgiving dinner and xmas breakfast and dinner at her club, none of which [unintelligible] we were sufficiently unoccupied to attend."[36]

For the holiday, the matrons overseeing the Club went all out, decorating the restaurant extravagantly, including "chairs of crimson satin [that] were hired . . . at a cost of $60 for the evening."[37] The residents, too, took advantage of the holiday to prepare a special presentation: *tableaux vivants*, or "living pictures," wherein participants recreate famous works of art via costumes, poses, props, and more.[38] Typically, the residents of the Girls' Club, with their artist sensibilities and natural attunement to their craft, were excellent reenactors, though there were memorable mishaps, too, including a "travesty" of a recreation of Diego

Velázquez's *Infanta Margarita Teresa* (*Portrait de l'infante Marguerite Thérèse*, 1654, Musée du Louvre) that devolved into "a life-like caricature with red worsted hair, buckram collar edged with cranberries, and parsley bouquet."[39]

And then there was the Club's afternoon tea, carried over from the Club's earliest days at the Newell residence. So lauded was this daily offering that it was mentioned in practically every news article, replete with rapturous descriptions of everything from the delicate blue-and-white china place settings to the large brass samovar standing sentinel in the corner of the "Red Room," so named for its crimson furnishings and curtains, where the tea was served most of the year (in fine spring weather, tea would be offered in the garden). "Young art-nostrils quiver with delight in an atmosphere like this, and in the tea and cake, and bread-and-butter sandwiches find veritable nectar and ambrosia here, over-looking the fair cool garden in the heart of the Quartier Latin," Aylward rhapsodized in 1894.[40] So many visitors enjoyed the tea itself that the samovar required frequent refilling; "three cups [of tea], it seems, is the least capacity of visitors or residents," mused one journalist in 1902.[41]

The tea was the centerpiece of Club life, a civilized little ritual amid an art student's otherwise hectic day. Given the popularity of the daily event and its centrality in the lives of so many, teatime crept into the artworks of several Girls' Club members, including Pennsylvanian Emilie Zeckwer (b. 1877), whose iteration was revealed in a 1904 exhibition, and Ida Sedgwick Proper (1873-1957), who showed her painting *Five O' Clock Tea* at the 1910 Salon des beaux-arts (see Fig. 8.3).[42] The tea also served as the metaphorical town square for the community, as Taylor reported in an 1894 article. "If you want to know what is going on in the student world this is the place and the hour to hear it," she averred. "From the different groups one hears talk of the next salon pictures, exhibitions, and entertainments, studio gossip, and plans for summer travel."[43]

Like its on-site restaurant, the Club's afternoon tea served members, residents, and the general (American) public, providing yet another opportunity for art students to mingle with the Colony, tourists, and visiting family and friends. Its renown even spread into the French

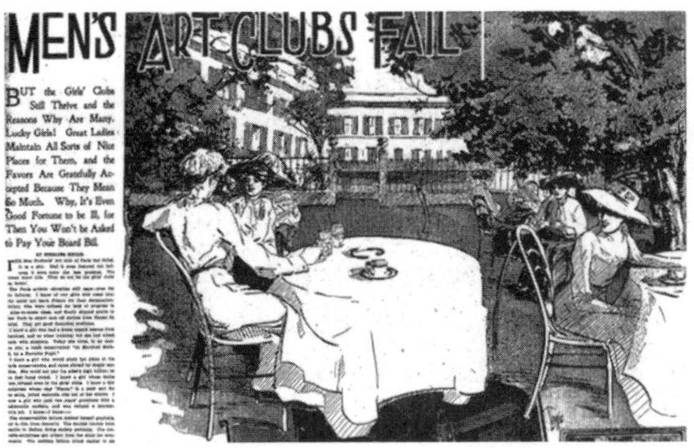

Figure 7.6. *Illustration of afternoon tea at the Girls'
Club, 1910.* Cleveland Plain Dealer, *April 3, 1910.*

community, where it became known phonemically as "feev o'clock
tay."[44] This focus on community—both inside and outside the Club's
walls—was of utmost importance to Elisabeth Mills Reid, so much so
that she funded the teas herself. For more than twenty years, no one,
member or not, was charged a single franc for afternoon tea.

Lest it appear that the Girls' Club was an idyllic wonderland, the
Club asserted a few rules and regulations for its residents. The lights in
the Club's social areas were extinguished every night at ten o'clock, by
which time all guests and visitors must exit (though the Club's matron
could be convinced of a slightly later departure time if given a reasonable explanation and *plenty* of advance warning).[45] That the relaxation
of this particular rule only involved guests of the female sex was unstated
but understood; "male callers," though welcome to visit, were only
allowed to do so at specific times and only in the Club's public spaces—
never in a resident's private room.[46] Room keys, as in most hotels of the
day, were left behind at a desk in the foyer whenever a resident departed,
whether to attend classes around the corner at the Académie de la Grande
Chaumière or to catch the latest dance performance by Isadora Duncan.
One 1902 news article reported that residents could explore Paris's
nightlife to their hearts' content, but only if they were accompanied
by at least one other person *and* if they confirmed their intended destination before departure.[47] These strictures confirm that "good conduct

[was] more thought of than ability to pay one's board," as the *San Francisco Call* declared in 1899.[48]

Most ingeniously, the Club's rules were reproduced in many articles about the Club, a savvy move that further endeared the organization to nervous American parents back home. This guarantee of protection via matronly supervision thus assured 4 rue de Chevreuse's ongoing reputation as an "ark of safety"[49] and the best place for any American girl to stay in Paris, a feat it met easily: in the two decades it was in operation, the American Girls' Club in Paris functioned at or near capacity most of the time. "[A]fter all, the great value of the club is the moral one of 'a place to go to.' American parents know that their daughters can come here and find counsel in getting established, just as though they were sent to an old friend of the family," Lorado Taft confirmed.[50] The Club, then, was viewed as ideal nearly across the board—for American women *and* their concerned families.

CHAPTER 8

Early Reviews

The efforts made by good Christian Americans to preserve the Puritan and moral atmosphere of the American home here in wicked Paris are the most amazing things I have ever seen . . . Of course the effect is to drive any person with any gumption out of the students' hostels and students' clubs.

—RANDOLPH BOURNE, AMERICAN AUTHOR (1913)[1]

Besides these rules there are no restrictions on individual freedom, and yet there are no irregularities. This, no doubt, is because the club presents nothing to appeal to the tastes of other than the refined and serious. Indeed, I think those wishing to leave the straight and narrow path for a gambol on the highway would find the club an appallingly virtuous place.

—GERALDINE ROWLAND, "THE STUDY OF ART IN PARIS," *HARPER'S BAZAAR* (1902)[2]

News articles celebrating the 1893 opening of the American Girls' Club were published in the city's English-language periodicals and distributed in papers across the United States, where they were met with intense interest as "slices of life" unavailable to most readers. Journalists—mostly young female writers like Elizabeth Taylor, Emily Aylward, and Katharine de Forest—reported upon every corner of the

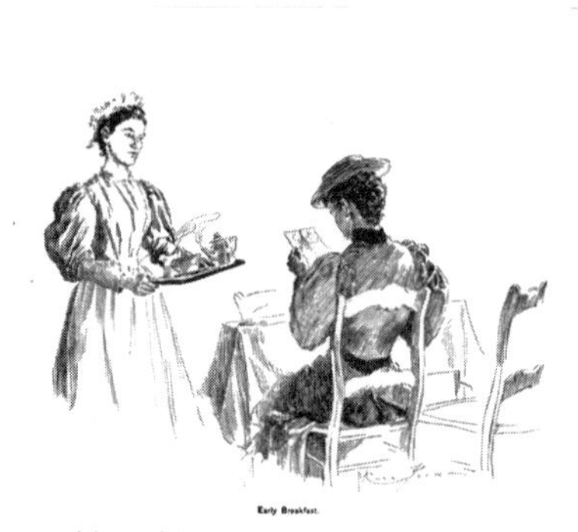

Figure 8.1. *"Early Breakfast."* Scribner's, *November 1894.*

Club in their lengthy dispatches, with long paragraphs relaying praise for the Red Room's samovar and the price of that afternoon's *déjeuner.*

Curiously, though, they contain few descriptions of the American girls who were lucky enough to lodge or take tea at the Club. The rare details that are provided in these missives almost exclusively use fashion as the primary carrier of meaning. "One frequently passes in the Latin Quarter of Paris girls who reveal by their sailor hats and the delicate beauty beneath the brims that they are Americans," noted journalist Caro Lloyd in 1894.[3] Such a chronicle surely meant to paint them as respectable, serious, and wholesome, a welcome contrast to the reigning narrative trifecta of the starving artist, the ugly American, and the rebellious bohemian.

Yet respectability did not equal dullness or banality. Aylward's 1894 article for *Scribner's,* a key document of the Club's first year, is a fascinating contrast to Lloyd's prim description. Though Aylward herself barely mentions the appearance or comportment of American women (she rightly focuses her review on the Club itself), her article is peppered with several pen-and-ink illustrations purportedly commissioned from a Club resident, Minna Brown of Pennsylvania.[4] Brown's drawings resemble fashion plates—no tidy sailor hats here! One image captioned "Early Breakfast" (Fig. 8.1) presents a seated woman shown from behind as she is waited upon by a contemplative (and slightly vacuous?) maid. The diner, hair tightly curled up into a chignon or braid topped with a straw boater, glances down at the morning's menu, her waist delicately belted and cinched, her sleeves puffed and voluminous.

Even more glamorous is the article's first illustration. A demure lady in evening dress—at least it can be assumed to be a more formal outfit, with its fitted bodice and a boat neckline that highlights her shoulders and long neck—is seated, hands in her lap and eyes downcast. Though she is identified in the illustration's caption as "One of the Art Students" (Fig. 8.2), nothing visually identifies her as such—no paint-brush, no palette, and definitely no smock. She could be any upstanding American woman from any state in the union. And that, perhaps, was the point: the evocative illustration functioned like a cipher, a stand-in for the thousands of women who dreamed of being such a glamorous Parisian student, whether or not they ever considered being a professional artist. More importantly, it provided further reassurance to these women's

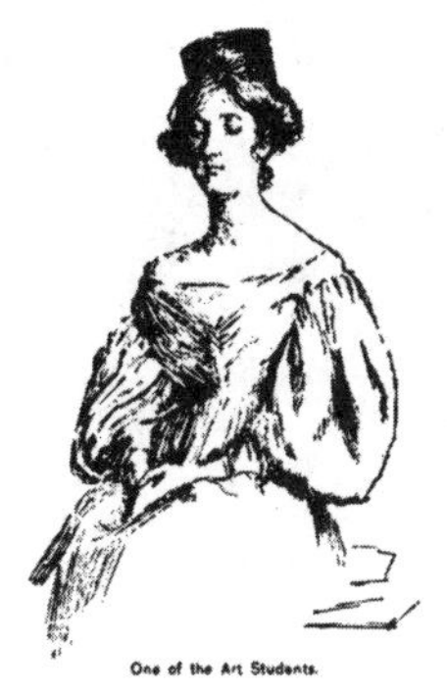

Figure 8.2. *"One of the Art Students."* Scribner's, *November 1894.*

fretting parents, allowing them to visualize their daughters in the role of elegant social butterflies rather than imagining them toiling in stuffy art studios. Like the paragraphs that detailed the Club's virtuous rules and restrictions, Brown's illustrations were surely some of the best press that the Club ever received.

Of course, it must be admitted that not everyone raved about the newly opened Club or its charming residents. The purposeful specificity of its member base—American women studying the arts—begat an early gripe that its community was too insular, a characteristic that also featured heavily in general criticism regarding the American Colony. Coddled and cloistered within the walls at 4 rue de Chevreuse, some women might choose to take every meal, every meeting, and every entertainment there, only leaving the Club, perhaps, to attend their lessons at an *académie* a block or two away. The Club, then, could theoretically act as the near-totality of a member's Parisian experience. An article in the *New England Magazine* called such tendencies a "clannishness," commenting, "[A]ssociating almost wholly with Americans, [a student] may learn comparatively little of the French language and of the French people. But in so doing he will miss many interesting and valuable experiences . . ."[5]

The insulation—perhaps even *isolation*—frequently dovetailed with another common complaint about the Club in particular: its

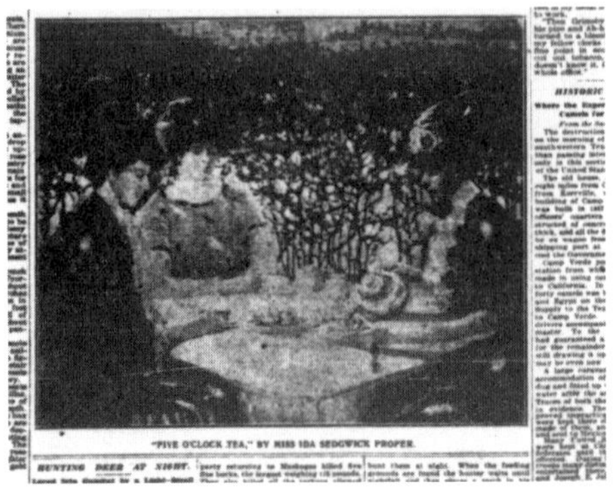

Figure 8.3. *Reproduction of Ida Sedgwick Proper's* Five O'Clock Tea, *1910. New York Sun, 1910.*

cliquishness. "There were cliques and cabals," de Forest admitted, and her assessment was borne out in the memoirs of several women through the Club's tenure. Not long after her arrival in Paris in 1908, for example, sculptor Malvina Hoffman (1885–1966) joined her friend Ida Sedgwick Proper at the Girls' Club for afternoon tea. Hoffman found the women at the Club to be unfriendly and cold, noting that she was snubbed when "it was learned that she only had six months of experience drawing from plaster casts"[6] rather than drawing from the live model. (It was not just the Club that did not pass muster with Malvina: she also found the nearby Académie Colarossi objectionable.[7])

Further criticism of the Club corresponded to its focus on the propriety of its members, especially its inhabitants. Combined with its overt connections to the American Cathedral of the Holy Trinity and the adjoining St. Luke's Chapel, outsiders sometimes sneered that it functioned as little more than a finishing school rather than a community focused on aiding women in their professional advancement.[8] It was thus compared unfavorably to the all-male American Art Association of Paris, which boasted a membership of more than 1,500 by at least 1903[9] and included major players like Henry Ossawa Tanner, Frederick Carl Frieseke, and Edward Steichen among their large ranks. The AAAP was *the* art society for the American artist, providing opportunity and connections aplenty to support its members. That the AGCP did similarly for women was likely diminished by contemporary critics.

The "finishing school" comparison brings to mind another (perhaps more reasonable) critique of the Club: to some, it seemed to be too strict (recall that American men snubbed the Club as "the nunnery"!). The "mothering" on offer there by the ever-watchful concierge, the Club's director, and various employees surely pleased American parents back home, but their daughters likely considered it more akin to "smothering." Though it was written after the Club's closure, a 1926 article's subtitle perfectly captures the frustrations of women artists over previous decades: "They Want to Look Out For Selves and Not Be Bothered by Persons Who Are Nuisances."[10] Being pestered about one's company and destination on a night out in Paris—*constantly*—would surely be tiring, and the stricture for grown women to wrap up an evening's conversation in the Red Room or library before lights-out at ten o'clock could grow similarly irksome. It is unsurprising that many long-term students[11] chose to lodge at the Club for brief periods rather than the entirety of their stay: the freedom of an apartment, whether taken solo or shared with one or two others, was too delectable to ignore.

A SURPRISING TRUTH about the Club's earliest days is that it almost failed. Only months—yes, *months!*—after the Club's opening at 4 rue de Chevreuse, a column in the *Chicago Daily Tribune* lamented, "The American Colony is in dismay over the impending break-up of the Girls' club, organized with an endowment for a library by Mrs. Whitelaw Reid."[12] What happened to nearly derail this much-needed and widely praised institution? While the *Daily Tribune* notes that financial mismanagement played a role, it is just as likely that there were personality issues among the staff, leading to "incessant bickering and heartburning."[13]

Some blame, it appears, may be laid at the feet of none other than Helen Newell, the clergyman's wife who convinced Elisabeth Mills Reid to invest in the health and safety of American girls in the first place, thus begetting the Club. As the *Daily Tribune* reported, "Mrs. Newell, it is said, demoralized the servants and prejudiced the creditors, leaving the matron powerless." Little else is known about Newell's disagreements—indeed, little else is known about Newell herself, as she slips out of the historical record not long after she "withdrew to Plainfield, N.J.," in early 1894.[14]

Newell may have had good reason to be irritated and irritable. According to Parisian death records, her husband of nearly thirty years,

Reverend William Newell, died on January 24, 1894—leaving Helen Newell and their son, Oliver Shaw Newell, on their own.[15] Mrs. Newell did return to the United States only a month after her husband's death: she is listed on the first-class passenger manifest for arrivals at the Port of New York on February 26, 1894, having sailed from Le Havre on the ship *Bourgogne*, the same steamer that originally ferried the Reid family to France five years prior.[16] It is not difficult to imagine that Helen Newell may have struggled with her emotions during this period, as she was likely grieving.

One wonders, too, if handing over the daily management of her pet project—the Club itself—was an added stressor for Newell. The early progenitors of the Club on the rue de Chevreuse were small and contained: the Sunday dinners originated in Newell's own home, while the first version of the Club was headquartered in the small apartment at 19 rue Vavin. The leap from a reading room–cum–teahouse to a full-scale residential club and restaurant was significant, and though this might not have come as a shock to Newell, she may have grown frustrated with her inability to oversee every detail of her newly realized dream. And, not for nothing—she no longer had the in-person support of her partner in this endeavor, Elisabeth Mills Reid.

Regardless, after Newell returned to the States and the Club's first matron, a certain Mrs. Irvine, departed,[17] the management and staff of the Club were overhauled, and the Club found its footing once more. By mid-1894, American magazines were again replete with articles celebrating the Club's warmth and convenience, just in time for a new spate of American women to arrive in Paris for the academic year.

BURGEONING ARTISTS AND their anxious parents were not the only ones keeping a close watch on the early days of the Girls' Club and taking comfort in its eventual success. Other soft-hearted philanthropists were, too. Within a short span of time, the Club spawned several competitors, providing American women with even more options for affordable, secure housing in Paris. Like the Club, most were founded with the purpose of assisting "women of the working and student classes utterly unprotected and in a precarious condition of life," as described in the British journal *The Leisure Hour*.[18]

First to open was Lafayette Home, established in 1894 by the American Colony dentist Thomas Evans.[19] In articles and advertisements promoting the Home, it comes off as more akin to Ada Leigh Lewis's Mission Home, though, than to the Club. "It is open to any American or English young woman, asking for admission, who comes provided with satisfactory recommendations, and who is living in Paris for the purpose of studying music, painting, drawing, design, the languages, or any one of the liberal arts and sciences," noted an 1898 column celebrating the Home's fourth anniversary.[20]

Other alternatives popped up after the dawn of the twentieth century. Trinity Lodge, loosely affiliated with St. Luke's Chapel, followed soon after, opening its doors to English-speaking women in 1905. Much later, one woman spoke of rooming in "a little English convent," so such religious institutions may have offered boarding, at least temporarily, during the Belle Époque.[21]

The closest competitor to the American Girls' Club opened in 1906. In conjunction with the YWCA of Paris, Grace Whitney Hoff, a philanthropist hailing from Detroit, founded the Student Hostel, known today as the *Foyer international des étudiantes*. Like Ada Leigh Lewis's Mission Home, the Student Hostel promised to serve women from many diverse backgrounds, nationalities, and career paths, though the hostel itself was only large enough to accommodate twenty-five lodgers[22]—about half the capacity of the Girls' Club. A 1909 profile of the Hostel, while mostly complimentary, hints at the gentle chaos of a typical day (and reveals how much it owed its inspiration to the Club, too):

> Sometimes as many as 100 or 150 students will call at the Hostel on one day for various purposes such as to use the fine baths, take books from the library, enjoy the reading and writing room, consult the resident nurse or doctor, take afternoon tea or ask any needed advice or help from the noble group of women in charge of the work . . .[23]

If imitation is, as is said, the sincerest form of flattery, then the Student Hostel was the sincerest flatterer of them all.

The Club engendered international imitators, too, the first being the Three Arts Club in New York City, which opened in 1904 and specified the Parisian club as its direct model. "It is designed to give the young women who flock to New York to study painting, music, or dramatic art, all the comforts and privileges which its famous prototype gives to girl students abroad," the *New York Times* announced.[24] There was, however, one major difference: Three Arts purposefully lacked a restaurant. "Those in authority at the American Girls' Club . . . considered a restaurant a mistake in an organization of the kind. It makes many more servants necessary, and increases the trouble and expense of the housekeeping out of proportion to the advantages gained," the article stated, a sentiment that discloses the rare behind-the-scenes feelings about the Girls' Club's popular restaurant[25]—popular, that is, with the residents and guests, but apparently not with the Club's staff.

Overall, though, the reviews were in: the American Girls' Club in Paris was a much-needed and wholly deserving institution, worthy of being emulated across the globe and amiably serving an underserved and growing community. It would continue to receive acclaim for the next twenty years.

CHAPTER 9

A Day in Anna Lester's Life

There are thousands *and hundreds of thousands who do better work than I could dream of—I am always going to do my best, and that is* all *I can do—I might as well cry for the moon as a prize of* any *kind! I never expect to be rich— if I can get any* pleasure *out of my work, I will be satisfied.*

—ANNA LESTER, IN A LETTER TO HER PARENTS, SEPTEMBER 30, 1897[1]

In an 1895 issue of the *Baltimore Sun*, artist Lorado Taft shared a description of the prototypical female American art student in Paris. "She is tall and she is short; she is fat and she is thin. She has a merry face, with a cute little turn-up nose and golden ringlets and a pink shirt waist, or she may be of maturer years and wear a regretful expression." And in a surprising yet hilarious blast of shade, he added, "She always combs her hair prettily, and when she does not she is English."[2]

Taft's article humorously reveals that there was not one singular type of woman who studied art in Paris, but that American girls of all stripes sought a serious creative life there. This diversity does not mean that there were no commonalities among them, however: the overwhelming majority of art students were painters[3] from middle- or upper-class (white) families who prioritized education—whether in art academies, university settings, or both—for their hard-working and talented daughters. Such a

Figure 9.1. *Postcard sent to Anna Lester, postmarked November 1898. From* Tea with Sister Anna, *2005.*

characterization could be used to describe most of the members of the American Girls' Club, and it changed little during the Club's run from 1893 through 1914. Indeed, a young artist arriving in Paris in 1897, like Anna McNulty Lester, enjoyed a remarkably similar experience to that of an artist arriving in 1913.

Anna Lester's documentation of her Paris adventures, in meticulous and humorous letters to her family, allow us to view her as the prototypical "American Girl" in so many ways. In particular, she shared many details of her life as an artist-in-training, describing the intricacies of finding a home base and choosing the right art school, and the everyday travails of a serious student in the French capital on the cusp of the twentieth century.

ANNA LESTER ARRIVED in Paris in the autumn of 1897, lodging not at the Club but at one of the Club's competitors, the Lafayette Home. After she discovered the Lafayette Home's distance from the heart of the Latin Quarter ("Here it takes over an hour by Buss and I could not stand that all winter in bad weather," she commented to her parents on September 30, 1897), she intended to transfer to the convenient and appealing Girls' Club.

Unfortunately, Lester was quickly met with frustration. "They only had one room [available]—and I did not like that," she wrote home, clearly disappointed. But she *did* enjoy the care offered to her there, a sign of the quality of service offered by the Club, even to nonresidents. "[T]he lady in charge asked me if I would like to go to a French family. I told her I would like to see the rooms. And, will you believe it, she got her hat and went with me! Was just as kind as possible," she continued.[4]

After moving into a pension in Montparnasse, Anna Lester immediately went to work to find the best school for study. Within only a few blocks of 4 rue de Chevreuse (and Anna's pension, too), several acclaimed ateliers awaited her: the Académie Delécluse (84 rue Notre-Dame des Champs), the Académie Colarossi (10 rue de la Grande Chaumière), and the Académie de la Grande Chaumière (only steps away from Colarossi, at 14 rue de la Grande Chaumière) are but a few examples; going only slightly farther afield, Lester would have encountered at least three branches of the Académie Julian (passage des Panoramas, 28 boulevard Saint-Jacques, and 31 rue du Dragon), as well as the Académie Vitti (49 boulevard du Montparnasse). And these ateliers were only the beginning: the ability to seek study with a single master—whether it be William-Adolphe Bouguereau, James Abbott McNeil Whistler, Auguste Rodin, or others—was another potential route.

After touring several options, Lester registered at the Académie Delécluse, "where I want to work for 6 months, then I will go to [Académie] Julian for a while."[5] Delécluse was among the most popular art schools for American girls, voted as one of the top two ateliers in a survey of Club members only a few years prior.[6] Lester's note, though, hints at a rather common bias among Parisian art students: while several academies offered top-notch courses for women, it was the Académie Julian that garnered the most attention.

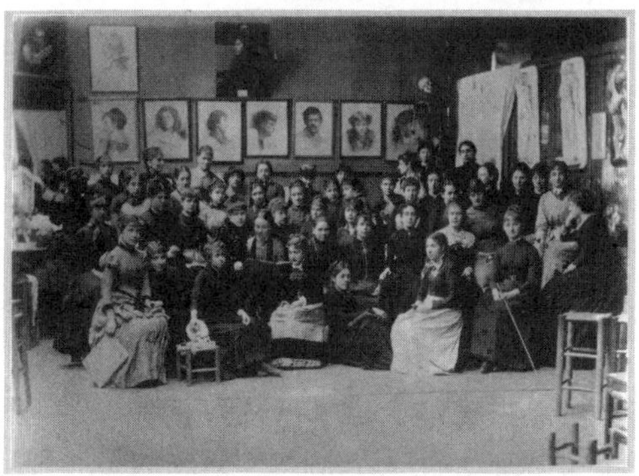

Figure 9.2. *Group of art students, Académie Julian, Paris, ca. 1885. Library of Congress.*

By Anna's time, the Académie Julian was perhaps the most prestigious private art school in the city. Founded thirty years prior by artist and former wrestler Rodolphe Julian, the Académie accepted female students practically from the start, at a time when very few offered space for women's serious study. A capitalist bent—and the lack of competition during that era—likely drove Julian's decision in part, as it provided him with twice the number of students and thus twice the income. Nevertheless, his students later awarded him the title of "father of the feminist movement"[7] for his forward-thinking arts inclusivity, and within its first decade, Julian's Académie was deemed "the only good one for women," as the famed Russian painter Marie Bashkirtseff declared.[8] By the 1890s, Julian had expanded his offerings into a legitimate brand, with nine studios under his purview—five for men and four for women.[9]

Anna Lester's determination to attend the Académie Julian was, then, partially motivated by the atelier's reputation for greatness. "[F]or the *name* of it I *have* to go to Julian's some while here, so I will do so when I am in better practice," Lester confessed to her younger sister in October 1897.[10] The school's reputation was just as prominent across the Atlantic, as she also revealed. "In America, they think Julian's is the only studio here, you know," she wrote the following year.[11] In actuality, Lester hopped among studios, attending not only Julian's and Delécluse but also the Académie Colarossi, another Club favorite. Studio-hopping was quite common among art students, keen as they were to acquire as much experience as possible in their brief tenures abroad, with exposure to different instructors and styles being of paramount importance.

Working at an art atelier was an all-day affair. After awakening in the predawn chill of a Parisian morning, Anna Lester donned the typical *artiste* uniform: a simple long-sleeved, high-necked dress over which she would drape a loose-fitting artist's smock. Breakfast in her pension was a simple matter, consisting of "a *bowl* of coffee and cold light bread"[12]—not quite the pleasing spread available at the Club!—before scampering out the door with plenty of time to spare. And Anna was not alone: she joined hundreds of others in this daily ritual. "Off to the studio, to be there by eight, whether it rained, snowed, or blew a blizzard," wrote

Daisy Brown in the *Corcoran Art Journal,* echoing the experience of every art student in Paris.[13] Even if late arrivals were permitted at an institution, a tardy student would surely be relegated to a dimly lit back corner of the congested studio. Earlier was always better, allowing each woman a bit of extra leeway in arranging her easel close to the day's model. In a letter to her parents, Lester recorded the process of determining the day's hierarchy of placement:

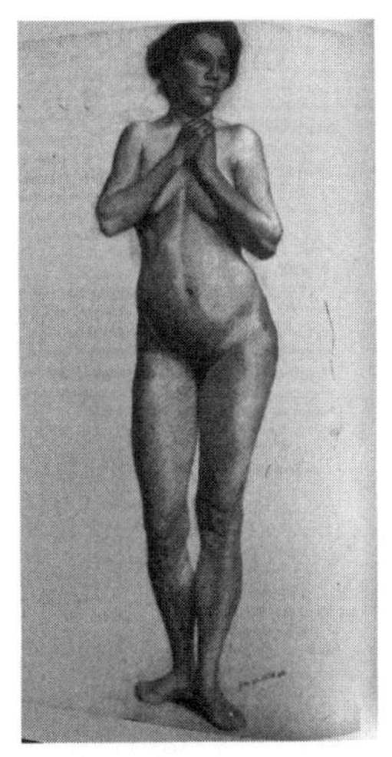

Figure 9.3. *Anna McNulty Lester,* Untitled *[nude charcoal study], undated [1897 or 1898]. From* Tea with Sister Anna, *2005.*

> I got there in time to draw for my place. You see, there is one model and about 30 girls work from the one. So they have numbers and the one who gets one, two, and three, have first choice—and so on—that is about the first time I ever got as good a number and the funny part is when the man in charge called out 3 in French I did not know myself by that funny name—"trois" for 3.[14]

After the drama of placement, artists and model toiled: a model, often selected from the *marché aux modèles* (models' market) at the intersection of the boulevard de Montparnasse and rue de la Grande Chaumière, typically posed for four or more hours per day, nearly every day. "The model poses five days in the same position, then on Saturday a change is made every half-hour!" Lester exclaimed. "My goodness that is hard. I only got two out of the seven [poses] to look at all right."[15] The artist's letters to her family reassert the fact that making art is *work.* "[I]t is no joke to draw a full length figure from Life—models do not stand as still as [plaster] casts, you know, then one has the color to contend with and that all makes it harder to see the lights and shadows correctly," Lester proclaimed in another letter. "I'm going to do my best, however—and that is all one can do."[16]

The effort itself was challenging enough, but the studio's atmosphere did not make it any easier. Described as a "'barny' sort of place,"[17] the environment of Parisian art studios was unpleasant at best: poorly ventilated, filled with scattered rags doused in turpentine and oil paint, abounding with fire hazards. Studios were often overcrowded, too: only a few years prior, early Club resident Elizabeth Taylor left Julian's for another academy after realizing that her class was so packed that artists bumped elbows when seated at their easels.[18] Still, few students complained: a smelly, cramped studio was better than no studio at all.

Anna Lester toiled diligently until noon, when she and her fellow students were allowed a one-hour break. French artists typically lunched at home with their families, but most international *académiciennes* packed baskets of snacks and remained on site, or—if lucky and in close proximity—they enjoyed a simple break at the American Girls' Club for its inexpensive fare and camaraderie. From one o'clock, classes at the Académie continued until five, when the studio typically closed for the day, though the occasional evening sketch might be offered ("In the evenings after dinner we went to Collarossi's Academy and drew from life for three hours; then back again to gather up energy for the next day," sculptor Janet Scudder [1869–1940] would later recall in her memoir[19]). And thus it continued, six days a week; according to articles of the time, Julian would only close his studios on Sunday, and the other academies likely followed suit.[20]

The strenuous effort of sculpting, drawing, painting, and simply *looking* at a model for several hours was exhausting, requiring energetic

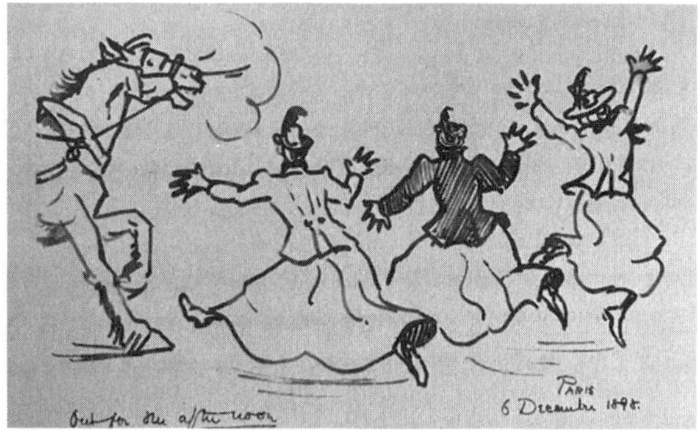

Figure 9.4. *Frances M. B. Blaikie,* Out for the Afternoon, *1898. From* Tea with Sister Anna, *2005.*

focus. The wearied, if determined, letters that Lester wrote describing her travails might lead one to believe that an artist's stint in Paris was more labor than leisure. Yet these artists indicate that they took their play as seriously as their work and wholeheartedly enjoyed the excitement of the Belle Époque. One of Lester's many letters home included a sketch by her friend the Scottish illustrator Frances M. B. Blaikie captioned "Out for the Afternoon" (Fig. 9.4). Blaikie's drawing shows three women—"we, the two Scotch girls and I," as Anna noted— gleefully running about freely, their arms flung wide and with such abandon that they scare a passing horse.[21] Imagine the delight art students must have felt in these moments, spending a rare afternoon indulging in fresh air rather than the stifling confines of an atelier.

This joyful jaunt was about as wild as Anna Lester got, however. By the average day's end, she was more likely to collapse onto her tidy bed at her pension rather than attend the free tea offered at the Club. "I went once and it was good!" she confessed to her parents. "But I felt strange [like a] stray cat."[22] Lester was not the late-night type, either, as she further revealed:

> I have never been out later than 6:30 and I am not inclined to be, but I hear the girls at the studio talk of not being afraid to stay out until 1 A.M. Excuse me from trying that! I am a little too old to begin, anyway I am sleepy and tired before eight, and sometimes excuse myself from the dinner table before the others get through talking and come to my room.[23]

THE DAILY LIFE of an art student in Paris was draining and occasionally hectic. But, as Anna Lester's experience shows, there was one thing that it was *not*, for

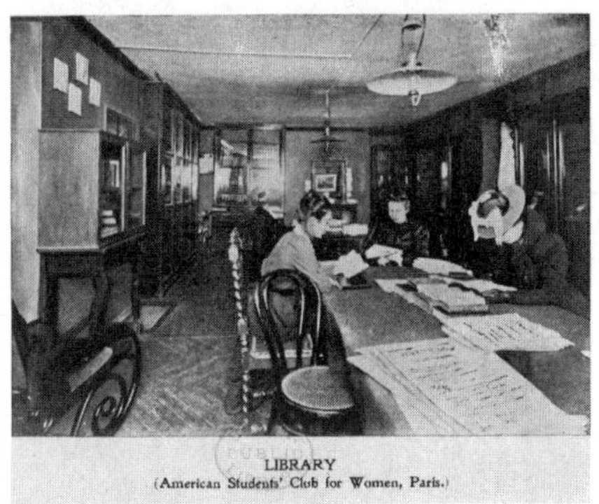

Figure 9.5. *"Library: American Students' Club for Women, Paris." From* American Students' Census, Paris, 1903.

most members of the Club: a bohemian free-for-all. In reality, the girls who frequented the Club rarely behaved like Daisy Miller, and were more apt to be contemplative rather than capricious. After all, these women paid dearly to move to Paris and attend the Académie Julian or the Académie Delécluse—or both—so why jeopardize such a privilege with carelessness? Indeed, few did, opting instead to commit to their education as the worthiest of causes. As Lester's Club compatriot Enid Yandell noted in a missive to her hometown newspaper, the *Louisville Courier-Journal*, "We must have it in ourselves if we succeed. Study and work. These must be the art students' watchwords."[24]

This is not to say that the residents of the Club did not get into the occasional spot of trouble, minimal though it may appear to our modern eyes. Several years after Anna Lester's tenure in Paris, the *Los Angeles Herald* published an exposé about a "lively scandal" wherein AGCP ladies hosted a party with "men guests for thirty girls and the traditional chaperon was uninvited," much to the surprise of the French.[25] The *Herald* further harangued Club members for carrying on past midnight ("the men found it terrible," the article asserted) and—*shocking!*—providing their guests not with chairs or settees for resting upon, but with "red and yellow cushions heaped along the stairway."[26]

True mischief, therefore, was uncommon. Some might consider such seriousness a bit of a shame—*these women, independent for perhaps the first time in their lives, should be gallivanting across Paris and enjoying every moment!* But every sketch, every lesson, and every visit to the Louvre could pave the way toward professional success, the ultimate goal. And nothing proved an artist's success like admission to the most prestigious and exclusive exhibition, the Paris Salon.

CHAPTER 10

What Hopes and Fears, and Triumphs

*There are queer tales told on the inside in the art colony. One is of how a certain
beautiful exhibitor . . . fell to the floor in hysterics of joy when told that
her picture had passed the judges successfully.*

—Margaret E. Handalman, "Artists in Summer,"
San Jose Mercury-News (1897)[1]

In the late summer of 1902—four years after Anna Lester completed
her Parisian lessons—Alabama native Alice Rumph had similarly
finished her own artistic outing, returning to her hometown of
Birmingham after two years abroad. Soon after her arrival, she published
a column in the *Birmingham News* in hopes of concisely explaining the
life-changing experience of studying art in Paris. Or perhaps the article
was a clever way of ensuring that acquaintances would stop pestering
her. "So many of my friends have asked about my sojourn abroad that
I suppose on being again requested, I should try to give them an outline,
at least, of that most delightful and profitable time," she began.[2]

In truth, Alice Rumph might never have studied in Paris at all if it
were not for her strong work ethic and incredibly good fortune. The

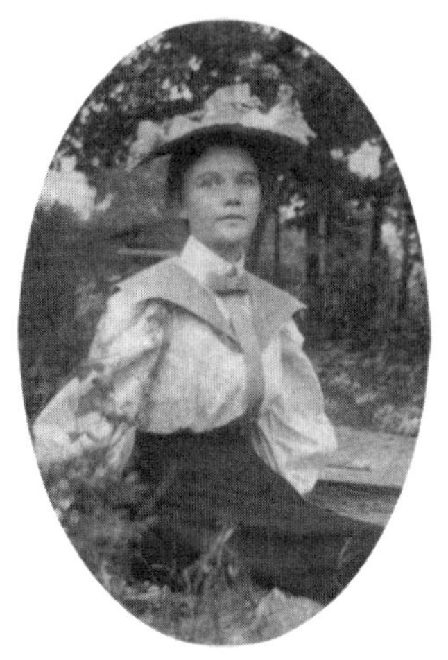

Figure 10.1. *Alice Rumph, ca. 1900. Birmingham Public Library.*

twenty-three-year-old hailed from a working-class family for whom money was often exceptionally tight,[3] so she rarely had anything beyond her everyday necessities. In 1900, though, she won a coveted art scholarship funding two years of study in France—a major coup that thrilled her friends and family as much as the artist herself. Everyone wanted to know the full details of her Parisian life: her work schedule, her favorite restaurants, and her extracurricular activities.

Rumph's recollections read as part memoir and part travelogue, filled with enthusiastic glimpses of a woman's first visions of the "Old World," as she deemed it. After recounting journeys through London, Berlin, and an unnamed "little Dutch village," she arrived, both literally and metaphorically, at the crux of her story: her two-year stint in Paris, where she had lived happily at the Club. The city and its cultural treasures receive the most emotive segments of her prose ("My first impression of the great pictures of the Louvre I shall not tell," she notes mysteriously, and one imagines Rumph shielding her eyes with the back of her hand, her memories too intense to share with her readers).[4] But one bastion of the Parisian artist's life—and indeed, that of many artists in the Western world at that point—is described almost breathlessly. "The annual salons are the climax of art exhibitions in Paris . . . what hopes and fears, and triumphs are embodied there . . ."[5]

MODERN-DAY READERS MIGHT think Rumph a bit over-dramatic, even a little twee in her delivery, but any of Rumph's artistic contemporaries reading her article would have nodded vigorously with understanding. The Salon was *the* pinnacle, the single event awaited by every artist—male or female, French or American, young or old. It was the zenith of a Parisian year, and potentially a career-making one, too. For most of the artists who frequented the American Girls' Club, it was a near-daily conversation topic, the gossip of one's acceptance or rejection from the Salon flitting throughout the Club's restaurant and reception rooms on the lips of every visitor.

To be fair, there was not just *one* salon, though it was often referred to in the singular. By the time Rumph arrived in Paris in 1900, there were actually several salons, with varying levels of attention bestowed upon them and with varying requirements for entry. But when most artists mentioned vying for entry in "the Salon," they meant the "official" Salon with a capital *S*.

The Salon had a long history: the annual exhibition was a holdover from the *ancien régime* and was first held in 1667 under the auspices of the Académie royale de peinture et de sculpture, France's monarchy-sponsored art membership organization and school.[6] The Royal Academy (and thus the Salon) were disbanded during the Revolution, only to be resuscitated in modified formats over the years, ultimately becoming a government-sponsored entity known under the lofty title of the École nationale supérieure des beaux-arts—but most folks shortened the moniker to the simpler École des beaux-arts. As in its earliest conception, the Salon was the École's annual exhibition, a showcase for (French) living artists, featuring works of art selected by a jury and culminating in coveted prizes, including the Prix de Rome, a scholarship that funded a residency in that Italian city. By the 1890s, when the Girls' Club opened, the Salon had long since begun accepting foreign artists into the mix, with Americans showing for the first time around 1800.[7] But things were also more complicated: in 1881, the Salon, in its singular, government-sponsored form, separated amicably from the École and fragmented into *two* separate Salons in a move that is still confusing today. The "Salon," then, could either refer to the Salon des beaux-arts or the Salon des artistes français, both of which were highly regarded.

Scholar Lois Marie Fink, author of an excellent history of the Paris Salon(s), once compared its cultural significance to the Academy

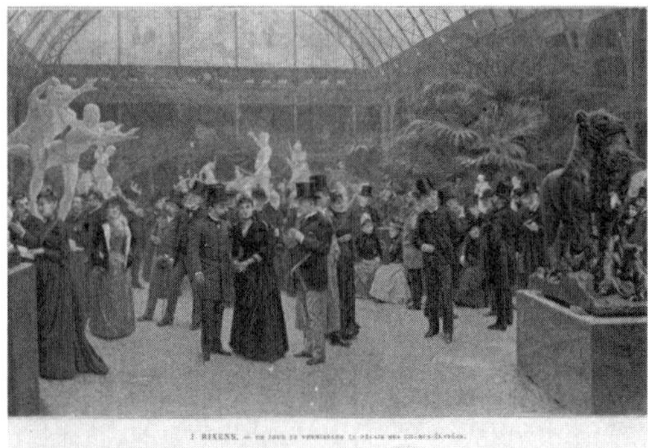

Figure 10.2. *Jean-André Rixens,* Un Jour de vernissage au palais des Champs-Élysées, *1890.* *From* Figaro-Salon 1890.

Awards.[8] Just as the Oscars are presented by the Academy of Motion Picture Arts and Sciences to reward the achievements of its own ilk, the Salon was the great award system for the visual arts of the Western Hemisphere as presented by its most important arbiter of taste, the Parisian art world. Just being included in the exhibition (no need to even win one of its coveted medals!) was a huge accomplishment. A blushing actor might suggest that it is an honor just to be nominated, but in the case of the Salon, it was actually true—no "aw, shucks" humility to be feigned. Having a work of art selected for the Salon was widely considered one of the greatest accomplishments of the era, a tacit acknowledgment that an artist displayed the kind of talent that would lead to a long and successful career buoyed by commissions and sales. The international press coverage of the event, too, conferred a kind of celebrity status upon lucky artists. It was the be-all and end-all experience for contemporary artists, particularly in the nineteenth century.

Consider, then, the unbelievable pressure experienced by Salon hopefuls—which was practically every artist in Paris. The American painter Cecilia Beaux expressed her "blues and anxieties" over submitting to the Salon, because, as she explained in letters home to her family, she felt that so much was "at stake."[9] Most artists understood that acceptance at the Salon signified their "arrival," their inclusion in the rarefied world of art professionals. But think, too, of the personal pressures that many—especially Americans not hailing from wealthy families—placed upon themselves. "I must do very, very well [at the Salon] to pay for the sacrifice of living so far from home," painter Elizabeth Jane Gardner (later Elizabeth Jane Bouguereau) confessed in a letter to her brother in 1867.[10] Admission to the Salon provided clear assurance to worried parents, perhaps, that the expense of sending their beloved child to Paris to study art had not been in vain, and that upon return to the States they would surely be guaranteed a steady income. As Gardner's peer May Alcott Nieriker noted in a 1877 letter to her mother, a Salon acceptance would be "a very great honor, and a fine feather in my cap to start a career with, for color-dealers, picture purchasers, and all nationalities, turn to the Salon catalogue as the criterion by which to judge of an artist whose name is unknown to them."[11] It is thus only with a modicum of hyperbole that the French art historian Adolphe Tabarant later concluded, "Everything revolves around [the] Salon: the satisfaction of pride, reputation, fame, fortune and even one's daily bread."[12]

FOR A VISITOR, the Salon was surely not the most pleasant of experiences. At the height of its influence, huge crowds—up to ten thousand viewers a day!—rushed into the cavernous Palais de l'industrie, on the grand Champs-Elysées, to ogle that year's selections.[13] And that is even if you could *see* the selections at all. "Went to the *vernissage* ["varnishing day," the Salon's official opening] on Saturday at the Salon," artist Alice Morgan Wright wrote to her friend Edith Shepard in 1913. "The place is perfectly huge and it is crowded. Shall have to go again soon to see the stuff."[14]

The crowds were one thing; the way that the Salon was hung—the works of art displayed—was another. A *salon hang* or *gallery hang* in today's design parlance calls to mind clean, artful groupings of paintings, photographs, or ephemera. The Salon's salon hang? It was an absolute mess. Thousands of works of art—yes, *thousands*, with 1880's iteration topping out at a mind-boggling 6,743 works accepted[15]—hung from floor to (very high) ceiling, taking up every inch of space, frames knocking into one another and occasionally overlapping.[16] Sculpture spilled into the center of the galleries on pedestals of varying heights. To maintain some semblance of order, the Salon was typically organized by an artist's surname, which caused further stylistic and subject dissonance: a brushy Impressionist landscape here, a nearly photographic Orientalist scene there, a portrait miniature abutting that. Experiencing the exhibition was likely a headache for many. "My goodness so many pictures," Anna Lester wrote to her parents after attending her first Salon in May 1898. She continued:

> I got so very tired because I tried to see all, and get a general idea
> of what was there so I would know next time just where to go and
> see what I wanted . . . But one afternoon is all I can take in. I can't
> see after three hours of looking. Some things are beautiful, others
> not good at all. I can judge, you know![17]

Regardless of the varied quality and overwhelming quantity of art on view, the Salon was the unmissable art experience of the year, the center around which dozens of events, both official and unsanctioned, swirled. Parties abounded; restaurants overflowed with revelers from across the globe; even Parisian couturiers planned the release of their springtime lines to correspond with its opening.[18] It made a significant impression on Lester, who concluded her letter to her parents by saying that, despite her exhausting visit to the show, "I would be thankful to have something with my name on it there. If I stay and succeed, next winter I will try."[19]

To an American like Lester—and probably her non-artsy family members in particular—the thought that art could play such an outsize role in a modern society must have been somewhat shocking, considering the United States' slow acceptance of the visual arts as a meaningful component of cultural life. Yet they caught on quickly enough. By the final decade of the nineteenth century, the American press made a habit of covering the annual event, much to the delight of stateside collectors (*Lovely, now I know which artist to purchase on my next European buying trip!*) and general readers eager for gossip (*Could you believe the painting that won the top medal this year? What a travesty!*). So integral was the Salon that when the *New England Magazine* published a helpful article in August 1890 documenting the life of a typical (male) American art student, it culminated with several pages detailing the intricacies of the exhibition, including its peculiar slang (peculiar, that is, to the average American reader):

> In admitting a picture, the jury bestow upon it one of three numbers—1, 2, or 3—or no number at all. The number serves as a guide for placing. Number 1 is given the place of honor "upon the line," that is, on a line with the eye, where it can be seen to best advantage . . . and those pictures which receive no number are "skyed,"—an expression which explains itself.[20]

It must be noted that being "skyed"[21] into the upper corners of a gallery was by no means something to boast about . . . but at the same time, it was far preferable to a Salon rejection. Your work might be barely visible, but still: you were *in*.

It is ironic that during the same period that the American press actively began covering the Salon, the exhibition's power had begun to fade. Part of the Salon's purported decline was due to the ample opportunities for artist exposure: independent groups putting on their own "salons," like the aptly named Salon des indépendants, a show first held in 1884 and described proudly as *"sans jury ni récompense"*—no jury and no rewards (or prizes), a truly egalitarian prospect. A Salon des femmes was established, too, by the Union des femmes peintres et sculpteurs around 1882, highlighting solely the works of women and showing their works in—*sacrebleu!*—an aesthetically pleasing, democratic manner, no skying allowed.[22] Smaller groups, including the American Art Association of Paris, held their own exhibitions, too, through which sales could be made, and by the turn of the century dozens of art dealers stood at the ready to showcase their wares as well.

Salon? *What* Salon? (Or perhaps "*Which* salon?")

All of this prompts the question: Why did American artists like Alice Rumph and Anna Lester bother with the official Salon, then, anyway?

The Salon was by no means the final word on "good" art (nor was such a definition monolithic); though many of its exhibition juries tended to veer conservative in their art preferences, the Salon's admissions sometimes lined up with public tastes and sometimes did not. Still, its link to the prime art school of the country connoted a certain level of quality that could set exhibitors apart from the hordes of canvas-wielding hopefuls. When Elizabeth Jane Gardner learned that two of her paintings had been accepted for exhibition at the 1868 Salon, she concluded, "It gives me at once a position among foreign artists and raises the value of what I paint."[23]

Success stories, so deliciously enticing that they were whispered like incantations between struggling artists, only fueled the perception of the Salon's abilities to make or break a career. At the 1872 Salon, American painter Robert Wylie received a second-class medal, an award that immediately netted him an art dealer (the renowned Adolphe Goupil of Goupil et Cie) who provided the American with a monthly stipend to live in France for the remainder of his (too brief) life, all in the name of continuing to paint.[24]

And for the American audience back home—collectors and neophytes alike—the Salon had already become a well-known entity in a country whose promotion of the arts was minimal, if any, and who typically seemed to be behind the times in cultural trends. But *the Salon! That's where the big things happen,* one imagines them concluding. *I read about that in* Scribner's *or in the newspaper.* Its influence may have been declining in Europe, but it was still relevant and meaningful to Americans, and explains why so many articles about Club members include references to it. "Miss Thompson has spent three years studying art in the Latin Quarter of Paris and it is said that some of her work attracted the attention and admiration of well-known French artists. Many of her paintings were exhibited in the salon," a 1912 article proclaimed meaningfully of the successes of Marguerite Thompson (1887–1968), a California-born Club attendee.[25]

A Salon frustration, too, could make the news, as was the case for Tennessean painter and Club resident Willie Betty Newman (1863–1935), a frequent Salon exhibitor who had previously garnered honorable mentions for her work. "I have not given up hope of winning the Salon medal," she sighed to a reporter for the *Nashville American* newspaper after admitting that her paintings in the 1902 Salon had failed to secure her any awards. "[T]hough I am so heartsick with disappointment even yet I am almost too dazed to form an intelligent plan. I hope, however, if I can secure the sitters, to paint portraits of some prominent people, which I will send back to next spring's exhibition."[26]

AFTER HER FIRST year in Paris, Alice Rumph decided that she was ready to give it a try: she was going to produce a Salon-worthy painting. The previous summer, on her tour of Europe before settling into her fall classes in Paris, she had "wandered into Holland," where she had been inspired by the friendly Dutch and the beauty of the natural environment. "There I did my first painting abroad and aided by the pleasant season, accomplished more than I had dreamed of doing," she later wrote.[27] On this trip and later excursions, Rumph enjoyed watercolor, which allowed her to work outdoors with speed; the limited drying time of the wet paint was conducive to travel, so works could be easily moved from place to place. Plus, watercolor was far less fussy than oils, which required a little more finesse (and took far longer to solidify on the canvas or board). *Watercolor—she knew watercolors!* So, a watercolor it would be for her first Salon inclusion.

Considering that, by the spring of 1901, Rumph was only preparing to finish off her first academic year in Paris, it makes sense that she would choose a format that she already knew so intimately; she was still learning some of the basics of drawing, perhaps, and oil painting following that. Rumph chose to play to her strengths, a wise move that could only fill her with confidence. She could always experiment with something newer, riskier, to submit to the Salon the following year—after getting another year of serious Parisian training under her belt.

To that end, she produced *Devant la fenêtre* (*Before the Window*), a watercolor that she submitted for consideration for the 1901 Salon. Unfortunately, this is all we know about her submission, as Rumph did not retain documents. From her single article in the *Birmingham News*, it is clear that she preferred to keep things to herself, as evidenced by her comment about her first impressions of the Louvre. The only public document recording her submission's title and medium is the Salon's 1901 catalogue[28]—because *oui!* Alice Rumph *was* selected for the Salon. She had made it at last.

The most endearing element of Rumph's Salon victory is her affecting excitement for her selection, all contagious joy and can-you-believe-it energy. She shared her thrilling news via letter to a Birmingham friend—and said friend then shared with the *Birmingham News* (no account survives regarding what Alice Rumph thought of this public announcement, or if she was even aware of its publication at that time). In a May 1902 social column, Rumph's letter was reproduced in part:

> My Dear Friend: I am writing tonight to tell you that congratulations are in order, for I am in the "Salon," which is to say, that the "Society of French Artists," who exhibit annually in a big exposition room by name of the "Salon," have accepted one of the pictures I sent them . . . I am duly elated over my success, and all the more because I have absolutely no influence, having none of the prestige that some of the big schools give . . . Everyone is congratulating me and saying how glad they are, because so many have been refused this year. Now I feel that my year's work has been well crowned . . . .[29]

The following year, in her *Birmingham News* column, Rumph took back control of her own narrative. Her descriptions of her two years in Europe—including the generalities of the Salon—brim with sentimentality, but in the single line in which she mentions her own inclusion in the period's most influential art exhibition, she kept things characteristically close to the chest, simply noting, "I shall not tell what my feelings were when I found my modest little picture hanging there among the thousands."[30]

But readers—and, especially, her fellow artists at the American Girls' Club—surely knew better. They understood Rumph's triumph without her having to say anything at all.

CHAPTER 11

An Exhibition of Their Own

. . . [W]e decided to return to our own loved Quartier and see what the women were doing in a sketch exhibition and sale just opened by the Girls' Club. In the other [exhibitions], we had felt the lack of women in art.

—ENID YANDELL, AMERICAN ARTIST (1895)[1]

Altogether the American Woman's Art Association may be congratulated on a most interesting demonstration of their talent and industry, which proves at least this, as compared with previous exhibitions of female art, how swiftly the weaker sex is attaining to executional levels of the stronger, especially among the Americans.

—"ART NOTES," AMERICAN REGISTER (1901)[2]

While the Salon was the central event around which the Parisian student year focused, another art exhibition grew to hold particular prominence for the women of the American Girls' Club. And it is no surprise that it found such popularity with Club-goers. It was *theirs,* after all: a show for American women artists, put together by American women artists.

What would eventually gain such respect began rather modestly, and only a couple of months after the Club's opening at 4 rue de Chevreuse.

In late 1893, a large group of students—around sixty in total—convened at the Club to discuss a compelling idea: the possibility of showcasing their artwork there. After all, they *were* artists . . . what would be more natural than showing the fruits of their labors? Excitement built immediately: perhaps they could invite some of their instructors, or maybe some established professional artists, to critique their work. And how about opening the exhibition to the Parisian public, not simply to the Club's membership?[3] A plan came together quickly: they would produce a small showing of Club members' works, hold a free reception, and even host a dance to follow. Author Emily Aylward extolled the exhibition's December 1893 inauguration:

> All the students' work for the year is hung in the exhibition gallery, a spacious, finely lit room with polished floor, and divans here and there for visitors, for all artistic Paris, male and female is invited . . . To Exhibition Day the girls look forward all year with intense eagerness the informal criticisms made en passant by some of the most prominent French artists being followed and listened for as suggestions of priceless value. In the evening there is a reception, supper, and dance to a good Italian string band.[4]

The exhibition—and, crucially, the artwork therein—was so well received that it was almost immediately declared a cornerstone event of the Club: the annual show of women's art was thus born.[5]

To manage the increasingly complicated logistics of this ever-expanding and ambitious exhibition, the American Woman's Art Association (AWAA) was formed in 1895 and headquartered at the Club. Charged with everything from securing refreshments for the show's opening reception to advertising the exhibition's hours, the AWAA swiftly transformed into one of the busiest art organizations in the city.

The AWAA's membership—like that of the Club itself—grew at an incredible pace, soon including the likes of Mary Cassatt, Mary Fairchild MacMonnies, Lilla Cabot Perry, Anna Klumpke, Gertrude Vanderbilt Whitney, Elizabeth Nourse, and John Singer Sargent's cousin, Anita Sargent, among many others. Several of these artists even held leadership positions in the AWAA. Mary Cassatt served as president from 1898 to 1899, with Nourse taking over the role one year later.[6] In these roles, AWAA officers made frequent visits to 4 rue de Chevreuse for organizational meetings, budgetary reports, lectures, and exhibition planning, further exposing the Club's members and residents to larger segments of the artistic community of Paris, and brushes with such well-regarded and established figures likely led to everything from supportive comments to offers of mentorship.

The AWAA officers in charge of any given year's exhibition made another decision that affected the visibility of the show and its artists: they opted to hire a jury of well-respected artists and instructors to select the show's entries. Several American expatriates juried multiple showings, such as Walter Shirlaw, Walter Gay, and Will Hicok Low. Beloved French and American instructors—like sculptor Jean-Antoine Injalbert and painter Richard E. Miller—participated. Elisabeth Mills Reid, the Club's founder, was an early supporter, too. With her consent—or perhaps it was her idea in the first place—the Club began purchasing one work per year beginning in 1894, housing the selection in its reading room.[7] The chosen piece remained in its place of honor until the following year's exhibition. From the start, the Club's directors were supremely proud of the event and sought to encourage and promote it. Reid herself went even further, eventually offering monetary prizes—growing to 1,000 francs by 1914—for the top works exhibited each year.

Like any administration, the AWAA experienced some minor hiccups. "The American Woman's Art Association has so far been held together by a somewhat fragile thread," declared Katharine de Forest in a 1900 article for *Harper's Bazaar*. "It has no stable organization, it has no permanent officers."[8] Perhaps it is for this reason that in at least one instance, from 1903 to 1904, the officers remained the same: Mary Fairchild MacMonnies as president, Elisabeth Kruseman van Elten as vice president, and Club resident Caroline Minturn Hall (1874–1972) as secretary. Regardless of its purported instability, the AWAA carried on its mission to create meaningful opportunities to support and showcase the work of American women artists at the point in history when the population of American women in Paris had reached critical mass.

Rather confusingly, the term "American" seems to have been loosely applied to the AWAA's annual exhibition, as several Swedish, Danish, English, French, and even New Zealander women were admitted into the show in various years (and lest you believe, dear reader, that this was an irregularity isolated from Club residence, think again: in 1897, Polish painter Casimira Dziekonska [1851–1934] resided at the Club; Canadian artist Dorothy Betts [1890–1964] lived at the Club in 1913; there were surely several more international members).

Early on, the AWAA exhibition functioned as a student art sale—and the reception's timing in these early years coincided perfectly with the holiday season: a benefit to both artists and gift-givers! The December 21, 1897, issue of the *New York Herald*'s European edition included a letter to the editor by an "L.S.B." (probably Kentucky-born artist Laura Sutton Bruce [b. 1853], who served as that year's AWAA president) encouraging the American Colony to support young artists with their spending. "Most of the pictures are on sale," L.S.B. wrote, "and no better encouragement could be given to these young earnest workers than the purchase of their pictures, and buyers would secure some very charming Christmas gifts."[9] By around 1910, the managers of the American Girls' Club determined the need for ongoing sales support for AWAA members and allowed them access to a segment of the rue de Chevreuse property to open a salesroom,[10] further promoting the professionalization of women artists— especially Americans—throughout Paris.

As the AWAA annual exhibition expanded in the final years of the nineteenth century, the press coverage of the event increased, too. Overall, the critical response each year was positive in both the French and American presses: in an article highlighting various Parisian art exhibitions for her hometown newspaper, the *Louisville Courier-Journal*,

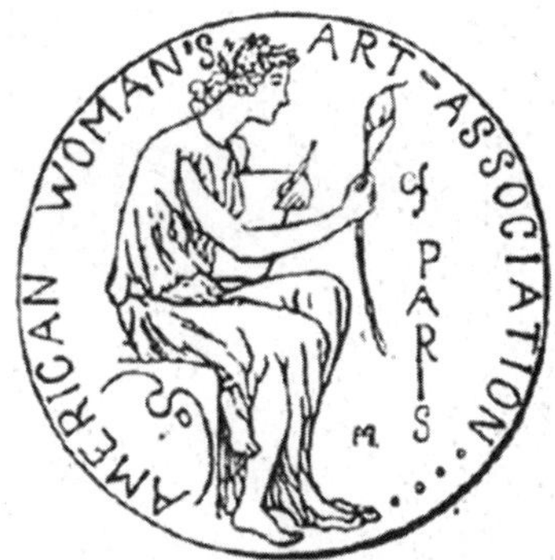

Figure 11.1. *The logo of the AWAA, designed by Club member Marion Holden, ca. 1901. Printed on the cover of the* Catalogue of the American Woman's Art Association, *February 12–28, 1910. Archives of American Art.*

Enid Yandell proclaimed the excellence of an 1895 exhibition of drawings. "It compared not unfavorably with the other [more professional exhibitions and salons]," she wrote. "It showed sincere work and conscientious study. There was a number of decorative panels with an amount of imagination and poetry in them that was delightful."[11] Yandell's positive commentary was echoed ten years later by the reviewers for the *New York Herald*'s Paris outpost, who declared the works on view as of high enough quality to be "quite worthy of the line of vision of the elder Salon"—one of the greatest compliments for an aspiring art student.[12]

With such encouraging reviews, it is unsurprising that women clamored to be juried into the AWAA's presentations. By the turn of the century, several hundred American women submitted their work—pastels, miniatures, oil paintings, marble sculptures—for consideration; when Mary MacMonnies helmed the AWAA in 1902, the jury admitted—not *judged*, but *selected for show!*—more than two hundred pieces for that year's exhibition.[13] And that enthusiasm was contagious, gradually transforming the "modest little show" into a must-see event equally noted for its quality and for the quantity of works on view. In 1898, a reviewer for the *Quartier Latin* reported:

> Not only were the walls of the exhibition room generously covered with pictures, but the hat and cloak room downstairs was also crowded with works of art, which necessarily forced each visitor to be his own *vestiaire* [cloakroom]. For this trifling inconvenience, however, he was more than compensated by the merit and excellence of the pictures that caused it.[14]

By the time Anne Goldthwaite was elected president in 1910, the AWAA exhibition at the Club had reached such acclaim—no doubt owing to its large membership and its successful marketing—that a commemorative catalogue was published,[15] and the American ambassador to France, Robert Bacon, supplied that year's opening remarks. This ministerial tradition continued until the dawning of World War One, when Ambassador Myron T. Herrick "delivered a short address" at the reception of the 1914 iteration, the AWAA's final exhibition.[16] The ambassadorial address likely took inspiration from none other than Whitelaw Reid, who had presided over the May 1890 opening of the American Art Association of Paris—originally called the American Students' Association—during his own ministry days.[17] It is equally likely that the AWAA itself was inspired by the AAAP, the all-male society that predated it by four years. The American *Woman's* Art Association, then, was a critical course correction, a vital centerpiece of artistic life in the American Colony for the half of the population unable to join the exclusive AAAP.

Though always popular with students and visitors and frequently praised by the press, the exhibition had its occasional disparager over its twenty-year history. "What can one say of the 200 artworks exhibited at rue de Chevreuse?" asked a critic for *Le Matin* newspaper in 1897, the same year that Anna Lester arrived in Paris. "Some modest, banal and without character . . . As for the *objets d'art* and sculptures, exhibited imperfectly, it's best not to mention them."[18] Of the 1904 iteration, one foreign correspondent for the *New York Times* reported that the exhibition "contains, of course, examples of that pathetic striving after the unattainable which has ended in irremediable failure, but so do most picture galleries."[19] Most infamously, Storrs Lee, a reviewer for the journal *Quartier Latin*, bashed the 1897 exhibition, deeming most of the paintings "very dead" and "bizarre and dyspeptic." A portrait bust by Jane Hammond (1857–1901), claimed by Lee as the "best piece of modelling," was then dismissed when he added, "It would be more meritorious but for the suggestion it conveys that it was done with an axe."[20] So brutal was Lee's critique that the editors ran an incredible caveat aside it, noting:

> When we sent Mr. Lee to write a "critique" on the recent exhibition at the American Girls' Club, we were not aware (as we now are) that he is a virulent type of the woman-hater. The exhibition being over, it is too late to send around another (and gentler) critic. Therefore we must fain publish Mr. Lee's criticism—in an expurgated form: disclaiming *in toto*, and with emphasis, our concurrence in any and all remarks which may still seem too chilly and severe.[21]

Despite the erratic nature of the exhibitions' quality (and the personal tastes of any given critic), the benefits to the artists shown therein were substantial. Exposure, of course, and sales, yes, but in some cases, it surely provided a confidence boost for very green artists by showing their works in a professional setting for the very first time.

Such an exhibition may have also acted as a mini-Salon, a way of testing out the public reception for a recently completed work. If the piece was well received, it might be deemed worthy enough for submission to the "real" Salon. This appears to have been the case for several Club members, including Cornelia Field Maury (1866–1942), whose sweet pastel composition, *Mother and Child*, was name-checked by a reviewer for the *New York Herald* in the December 1899 exhibition;[22] early the next year, she submitted the work to the Salon des artistes français, where it was accepted *and* hung "on the line": the best an artist could hope for.[23] Conversely, the AWAA show could function as a victory lap for women whose works had already been juried into a previous Salon, and a wonderful opportunity to get more mileage. California-born Susan Watkins (1875–1913), likely proud of *La Communiante*, her portrait of a young girl on her First Communion, which had garnered an honorable mention at the 1898 Salon,[24] presented it at the 1899 AWAA show as well. Even works shown several years before— like Martha Baker's (1871–1911) portrait miniature, *Rayna Simons*,

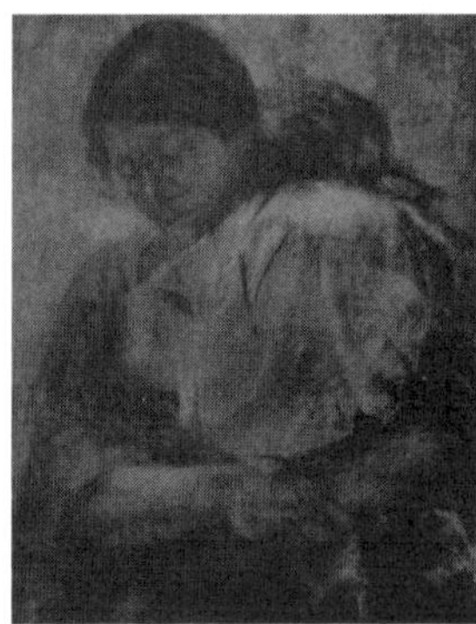

Figure 11.2. *Grace Turnbull,* Mother and Child, *ca. 1913. From* Chips from My Chisel, *1953.*

awarded a bronze medal at the St. Louis Exposition in 1904—received a second life here, lauded again at the 1907 AWAA exhibition.[25]

Resident artists, like Alice Morgan Wright, sometimes took the annual showcase for granted, though they participated whenever able. "The art exhibition you were asking about was just the one here at the Club," Wright told her mother dismissively in an undated letter. "The things we had in it were just little sketches we worked up for the occasion."[26] But others were overwhelmed by the surprise of their inclusion. In the final AWAA exhibition in 1914, Grace Turnbull received an award of 1,000 francs for her oil stain, *Mother and Child* (Fig. 11.2) from 1913. "Why they should have taken it into their heads to single out my insignificant, subdued, old-fashioned Mother and Child in its dull frame to hang in the central position in the Club Gallery seems strange enough," she moaned to her family, "but why to this insult they should add the further injury of awarding to it the first prize of 1,000 francs ($200), remains an unsearchable mystery."[27]

In its final years, the annual exhibition proved so successful that the American Woman's Art Association began adding other small showcases to their yearly calendar, holding media-specific shows for drawings and sculpture, for example. A few artists were given solo exhibitions at the American Girls' Club, but whether these were under the AWAA's purview is unknown, though one can assume that they were.

One curious outlier was the 1912 iteration of the AWAA show. In an interesting move, that year's art exhibition was turned over to the Advisory Board of American Women, helmed by Elisabeth Mills Reid herself and featuring other influential members such as Mrs. Myron T. Herrick—the current French ambassador's wife—and Bessie Springs Smith White, wife of famed architect Stanford White. The women arranged for an exhibition of two hundred works from some of the international art stars of the day and included loans from the Musée du Luxembourg, the key contemporary art museum of Paris during this era. A review of the exhibition in the *New-York Tribune* reads like a Who's Who of Belle Époque artists: Sargent, Whistler, Corot, Millet, Theodore Rousseau, Carolus-Duran, MacMonnies, Frieseke—even Rodin, who presented a "superb and realistic marble group."[28] Unlike the student-heavy exhibitions typically produced by the American Woman's Art Association, this one focused exclusively on established, recognizable artists and was curated (not juried!) by painter George Snowden Howland. But American women of high caliber were not barred: Janet Scudder, Elizabeth Nourse, and Salon darling Florence Esté (1860–1925) were invited to participate.[29] One wonders why AWAA changed formats for this single year; perhaps the attention received from the inclusion of celebrity artists was intended to catapult the

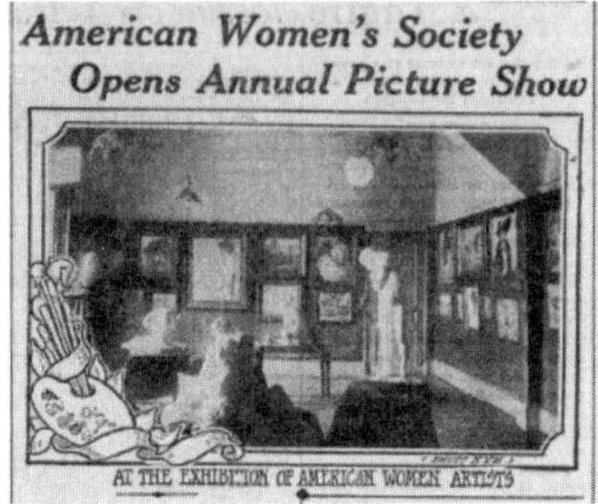

Figure 11.3. *"American Women's Society Opens Annual Picture Show."* New York Herald, *European edition, Sunday, February 19, 1911.*

AWAA and the Girls' Club into a higher artistic echelon, or perhaps it simply documented great American art alongside their French counterparts. Either way, the effect was ravishing: the *New-York Tribune* decreed it to be "the finest loan exhibition of paintings, drawings, and sculptures of the present season," and commended it as "a great success for the American Art Students' Club."[30]

For a generation of women artists, the importance of the American Woman's Art Association, and its annual show in particular, cannot be underestimated. It provided integral support and visibility for hundreds of women, thereby generating sales as well as potential commissions. And the Club's support of the Association was crucial to this success. After all, the willingness of Reid and her AGCP matrons to grant usage of the Club for the annual exhibition surely contributed to the show's longevity and its positive reputation. Though the AWAA and the Club were separate entities, they bolstered each other considerably, the Club as the supportive backbone for the AWAA's meetings and exhibition, and the AWAA as the annual event bringing hundreds of visitors to experience the Club's generous comfort—surely a boon to the growth of both, and for the benefit of American women artists in Paris. Taking home some praise, not to mention 1,000 francs, could not help but put some pep in the step of any struggling painter or sculptor—even one who apparently carves with an axe.

CHAPTER 12

À Notre Regretté Camarade

There is always plenty of human wreckage floating about in the Quarter;
and the tragedy of unfulfilled promise, unaccomplished hopes,
is closely knit with student life.

—CLIVE HOLLAND, "STUDENT LIFE IN THE QUARTIER LATIN, PARIS" (1902)[1]

In June 1897, Massachusetts-born Anna Parkman Osgood (1864–1935) anxiously paced around her painting studio at 152 rue de Vaugirard, an approximately twenty-minute walk west from the American Girls' Club. Osgood, though now living a bit farther afield, was nevertheless still closely tied to the Club, where she resided in at least 1896, according to Parisian art registers.[2] While at the Club, she became excellent friends with fellow American art students, some of whom enthusiastically claimed a new hobby in their off-hours: bicycling. Osgood loved cycling, and according to a "Society" column in the *Boston Sunday Post*, she even completed a "wheeling tour through Europe" in 1895 with another Boston-based friend.[3] But on this fine afternoon in June 1897, Osgood neglected her trusty cycle. Instead, she fretted about the whereabouts of another close confidante and fellow bicyclist: her pal, Gertrude Weil (ca. 1869–1897).

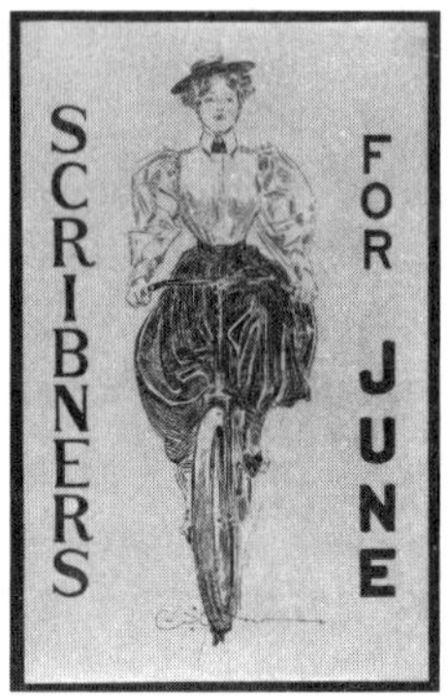

Figure 12.1. *Charles Dana Gibson,* Scribner's for June, *1895. Library of Congress.*

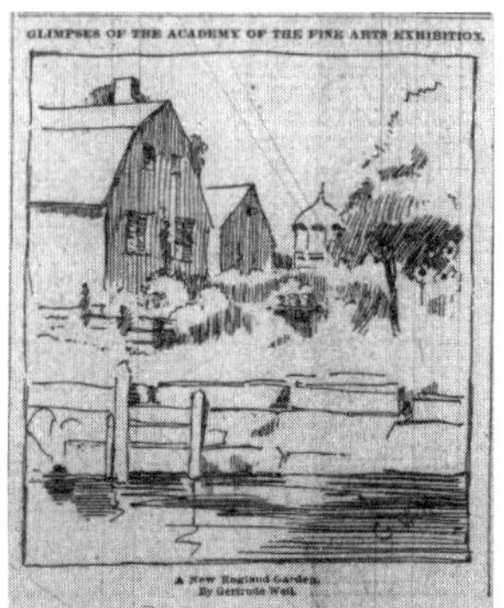

Figure 12.2. *Reproduction of Gertrude Weil's* A New England Garden. Philadelphia Inquirer, *March 2, 1892.*

Weil, a tall, auburn-haired artist from a prominent Jewish family in Philadelphia,[4] had arrived in Paris less than a year prior, in 1896. Her story followed a trajectory similar to that of many American girls during this period: training, achievement, Paris. In 1892, Weil had enrolled at the Pennsylvania Academy of the Fine Arts, one of the top art schools in the nation, where she remained for nearly four years. Her work had caught enough attention that while only in her first year at PAFA, an illustration of one of her paintings, a pastoral New England scene, was highlighted in the *Philadelphia Inquirer* to promote the Academy's latest exhibition (Fig. 12.2).[5]

But art was not only her vocation, it was also her avocation. When she was not at school, she participated as an integral member of Philadelphia's art community, joining the women-only Sketch Club and the Philadelphia Studio Society, where her work was shown alongside the likes of another Parisian expat, Cecilia Beaux.[6]

By 1895, Weil had decamped to New York to attend courses at the Art Students League under the tutelage of the eminent painter William Merritt Chase, but she remained for only one year, as Paris (*bien sûr!*) was an even greater adventure awaiting her.[7]

Few details have survived pertaining to Gertude Weil's brief stint in Paris. Upon arrival in 1896, she took a room at 117 rue Notre-Dame des Champs, a three-minute walk from the Club.[8] This proximity allowed Weil the opportunity to visit the Club often for tea, dinner, or other social activities, and she made friends—like Anna Parkman Osgood—quickly. Weil's studies were going wonderfully, too. She registered at the Académie Vitti to train under the respected French artist Raphaël Collin and quickly soared to prominence, even receiving praise in the otherwise scathing review of the 1897 AWAA exhibition at the Club, in which critic Storrs Lee declared Weil's poster, "composed of several feminine figures, well drawn and placed, and suggest[ing] very much the intellectual American girl abroad," to be the best on offer that year.[9]

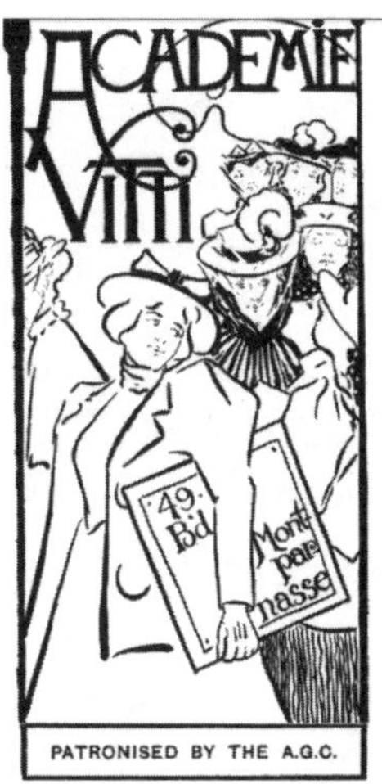

Figure 12.3. *Reproduction of Gertrude Weil's "Académie Vitti" poster. From* Quartier Latin, *January 1897.*

From the outside, her life appeared blissfully calm and was proceeding merrily, as noted in the *Philadelphia Inquirer*:

> She was comfortably situated amid pleasant surroundings and enjoyed perfect health . . . she enjoyed the esteem of her friends for her personal qualities and of her professors for the talent and assiduity with which she pursued her studies.[10]

To Anna Parkman Osgood and her compatriots, then, Gertrude Weil had it all. But did Weil feel the same way about herself?

AFTER A TYPICALLY frigid Paris winter, the late spring of 1897 brought delightfully warm temperatures, tempting art students into the surrounding countryside to enjoy its seasonal beauty. Osgood clamored for the opportunity to escape the city, and Gertrude Weil happily agreed. The pair relished a bicycling trip to Chartres, a town nearly 100 kilometers to the southwest known for its Gothic cathedral.[11] It made such a positive impression on Weil that she confided her wish to continue her cycling explorations, with the intention of following up their trek with a jaunt down to Barbizon—not as far as Chartres, but, at about sixty kilometers, still a significant journey—on a solo ride.

In mid-June of 1897, when Anna Parkman Osgood had not heard from her friend in several days, she assumed that Weil had indeed made good on her promise to visit Barbizon. What she did not know was that Weil had not left Paris—and she would never leave Paris again.

Like most art students, Gertrude Weil enjoyed wandering the city in search of optimal locations for sketching, and on Saturday, June 12, 1897, she was seen drawing atop—or beneath, sources vary[12]—the Pont Neuf, the city's oldest bridge over the river Seine. Her "most intimate friend . . . in Paris," a man named J. M. Gleeson,[13] had spied her there and attempted to call upon her at her studio the following morning, only to find a note affixed to her door requesting that messages be left with the building's concierge. Weil, Gleeson reasoned, had indeed gone to Barbizon, just as Osgood had assumed. But after two further days passed without Weil's return—and when Gleeson's own trip to Barbizon failed to uncover his dear friend—Weil's community grew concerned, and soon enough, the tension spread throughout the American Colony and among its art students. In the tearoom at the Girls' Club, ladies whispered worriedly about Weil's whereabouts and speculated about her mental health. Though she was reported to have been "quite popular among her fellow students, having a cheerful, unassuming disposition,"[14] some Club members nevertheless recalled Weil's "fits of morbid despondency, during which she would speak of suicide."[15] Weil's propensity toward depression was indeed noted by Gleeson, who admitted to the *New York Herald* that he once had threatened to alert Weil's parents to her mental state "unless she promised to cease brooding about such ideas as insanity and suicide."[16] (Indeed, at least one reporter claimed that Weil was dejected because her parents forbade her to marry Gleeson, a Christian—taboo for her Jewish family.[17]) Still, all were loath to believe that Gertrude Weil would have taken her own life, though they had little proof for their convictions, as recorded in the *New York Herald*:

A visit to the Ladies' Art Association, Rue Chevreuse, did not elicit anything of value . . . every one was sure that she could not have committed suicide.

Why?

"Because . . ."[18]

The interviewee's response thus fizzled out.

Driven mad by worry and maintaining the earnest hope that Weil had bicycled out of Paris, Gleeson returned to her apartment and unlocked her door with the assistance of the concierge. Inside, he found her bicycle, adorned with the artist's "sketching apparatus," ready and waiting for that never-taken ride to Barbizon.

The mystery of Gertrude Weil's disappearance was solved quickly thereafter. Her lifeless body was fished out of the Seine on Tuesday, June 15, 1897, and it rested, unidentified, in a morgue for several days. By Monday, June 21, Weil's remains had been identified, and her parents were alerted via cable in Philadelphia; one week later, she was buried at Bagneux Cemetery, just outside the southern portion of modern-day Paris's boulevard Périphérique (ring road). Upon her oak coffin, a wreath of roses was laid by Weil's Club friends and art school colleagues, bearing a note that read, "*À notre regretté camarade—les élèves d'Académie Vitti*" ("To our late friend—the students of the Académie Vitti").

THE DEATH OF Gertrude Weil shook the entire American community in Paris, but it was especially traumatizing to the student population. "It is many years since there was such excitement among the young girl students of the Latin Quarter as has arisen from the suicide or murder of Miss Weil, the young American artist from Philadelphia," the *Chicago Tribune* reported.[19] Part of the horror of the situation stemmed from the fact that one of their own—an American girl—had been cruelly taken away from them. Terrifying, too, was the unanswered question of the cause of Weil's demise. As the *Tribune* noted, some believed that Weil had been murdered, though apparently not for her money—the press made much of the fact that Weil was discovered with $3.20 on her person when she was pulled out of the Seine.[20] This, though, made the conclusion even more awful: *perhaps someone had killed her simply because they could!* girls wondered aloud. Huddled in the Red Room at the Club, young women shuddered together, no doubt imagining themselves in Weil's terrible situation. The effect simultaneously lent credence to all of those disturbing stories about the Latin Quarter and its prodigious dangers—the ones their fearful families continued to insist upon—and reminded them of their gratitude for the American Girls' Club in Paris. How lucky were the residents who sought shelter behind its walls; how much closer to one another the other members should draw together in anxious times like these.

Though Weil's death could have been accidental—and we will surely never know its true cause—most news articles reported it as self-inflicted, which makes a certain amount of sense. While not an everyday occurrence, suicide by art students in Paris was not altogether uncommon. In fact, it happened with enough frequency that Frank H. Mason, the consul general of France, felt it necessary to pen a special report, "American Young Women Art Students in Paris," to dispel rumors of its endemicity. Most deaths by suicide, he reasoned, were due to destitution: as long as a student could afford safe lodging and enough food, she could succeed. But dashed dreams and shattered expectations—a Salon rejection, a dismissive remark from an academician, the struggle to compete with a seemingly endless flood of equally talented artists—might conjure "a rude and often dispairing consciousness of . . . her limitations," Mason admitted reluctantly in his report.[21] That a suicide hit so close to home for the members of the Club is thus not terribly surprising, though it was surely an incredible tragedy. So, too, was the accidental death of Jessie Allen (1868–1899) a mere two years later in 1899.

Born and raised in Albany, New York, Jessie Allen moved to San Francisco at age eighteen, where she became immersed in the city's art scene. Allen trained at the Mark Hopkins Institute of Art and exhibited in California for several years before making the leap to Paris.

Arriving in 1895, she settled into a room at the Girls' Club and enrolled in classes at the Académie Julian and the Académie Vitti, where she studied alongside Gertrude Weil under the tutelage of Raphaël Collin ("He is much pleased with her progress," crowed the *San Francisco Call*).[22] During the academy's summer hiatus, Allen traveled extensively, as reported in a brief but glowing profile in a 1898 edition of Janesville, Wisconsin's *Janesville Daily Gazette*: first, enjoying a sketching trip to Holland in the company of fellow artists in 1896, followed by a stint in London in 1897. Later that year, she opted to leave Paris for several months in order to study

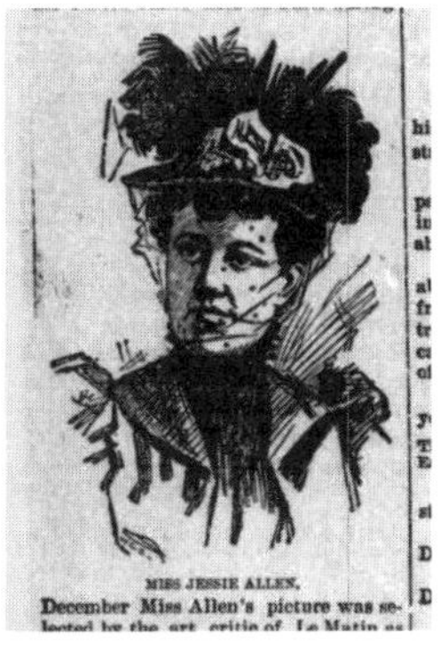

Figure 12.4. *Cartoon of Jessie Allen.* Janesville (WI) Daily Gazette, *February 10, 1898.*

the works of eighteenth-century Venetian artists Canaletto and Francesco Guardi in their home city.[23] For Allen, this sojourn paid dividends: at the American Woman's Art Association exhibition in late 1897, a critic praised her works as standouts in an exhibition otherwise filled with uninspired paintings. In comparison with those unremarkable pieces, "Miss Jessie Allen exhibits a view of Venice which she brings back from a recent trip and which denotes in this young artist a lot of sincerity."[24] To her fellow American girls, Allen was on the rise, soon to become an *arrivée* and, by early 1899, she had reached a significant milestone: her first Paris Salon inclusion—with *two* works accepted, no less!—at age twenty-eight. Jessie Allen was well on her way.

Allen not only worked hard but took her downtime seriously, too. In this way, she proved similar to her acquaintance Gertrude Weil, not only in her chosen profession and in their connection to the Club, but also in pastime: bicycling. In early April 1899, Allen and a "party of friends" undertook a cycling tour of Brittany, but she met with an accident outside of the city of Rennes. She was knocked to the ground by a rogue dog who pounced upon her back, and she sustained a severe injury to her ankle in the process. Though she suffered no broken bones, it was evident that Allen's condition was serious enough to warrant medical help in Paris, and her companions ferried her home. Arriving at the French School of Orthopedic Massage—a recommendation from a doctor in Rennes—she sought the attention of Dr. Paul Archambaud, the school's director.[25] Though his patient suffered from skin and tendon lacerations, Archambaud "subjected Miss Allen to massage treatment," provided without the use of antiseptics.[26] After her release from Archambaud's care, however, Allen quickly developed blood poisoning. Nervously, she consulted the Club's director, Julia H. C. Acly (1851–1932), on her options, of which there were few; she finally assented to admission at Boucicaut Hospital, a fairly new medical institution, for intensive treatment.[27]

Until the very end, Jessie Allen, hospital-bound, remained optimistic about her recovery and her career, penning two letters to her brother in San Francisco describing her cycling expedition, her injuries (including a drawing documenting her ailments), and her recent Salon acceptance. She remained stubborn, too: when doctors at Boucicaut revealed her dire prognosis and recommended a foot amputation, "Jessie said she would rather die," a flippant comment that was ultimately all too prescient.[28] Indeed, Jessie Allen died only a week after entering Boucicaut.

Back at the Club, Julia Acly was equal parts shocked and livid at the loss of Jessie Allen and blamed Dr. Archambaud entirely. "There is no doubt her death is due to improper massage treatment," Acly declared in an article provided by special cable to the *New York World* and the *Chicago Tribune*. "If Miss Allen had applied to me in the first instance, I should have sent her at once to the hospital."[29] As they did with the death of Gertrude Weil, AGCP members found their own way to grieve their lost friend. At the 1899 Salon des artistes français, Allen's two accepted paintings were lovingly draped with black mourning crape, and a painting of Allen herself—done by a fellow Club artist, a "Miss Woodward of Michigan"[30]—hung nearby, a gentle ghost haunting the exhibition that she had anticipated as her greatest achievement.

CHAPTER 13

Why Not Turn Our Art into Food?

Florence Lundborg, the one California girl whom all agree has gotten more out of her three years in Paris than any other art student out of the West . . .

—"The Parisian Café Decorated by a San Francisco Girl,"
San Francisco Chronicle (1900)[1]

Florence Lundborg (1871–1949) was running out of time—and out of cash. Though she hailed from an upper-middle-class family from San Francisco, she pinched pennies to the occasional extreme in hopes of prolonging her studies in the French capital. She had successfully lobbied her parents to extend her time abroad from two to three years, but their permission did not always equal financial support. As her third year approached in 1899, Lundborg had no choice: she needed to find a way to keep herself afloat.

Like many of her compatriots, Florence Lundborg viewed her time in Paris as the last step toward professionalism in art after having spent years in its study and practice. Born in 1871,[2] she attended several art academies in the Bay Area, including

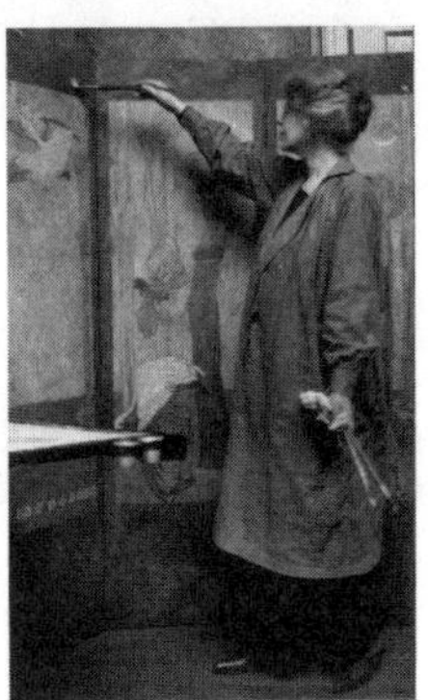

Figure 13.1. *Florence Lundborg in her studio, undated. Library of Congress.*

the California School of Design and—like fellow San Franciscan and likely colleague Jessie Allen—the Mark Hopkins Institute of Art. Lundborg's late teen years and her early twenties were spotted with exhibitions and honors from California to New York, where she gained attention for her painting and printmaking prowess.[3] During this period, she became a member of the San Francisco creative collective Les Jeunes ("The Youth"), whose small-batch literary magazine, *The Lark*, was a West Coast avant-garde touchstone. Lundborg created several covers for *The Lark* during its brief time in print, featuring bold, graphic woodcuts with expertly layered colors. These eye-catching designs— several of which are now part of the collections of the Metropolitan Museum of Art in New York and the Detroit Institute of Arts, among others—proved Lundborg to be one of the Bay Area's most talented creatives, and by 1897, she was ready for that final, all-important step in her career preparation: studying abroad, and doing so as affordably as possible. She departed for Paris alongside a Sacramento-based friend, Mabel Deming (1874–1945), in August 1897, and they soon settled in as residents of the American Girls' Club in Paris.[4]

But a big question remained: how to save those all-important francs and sous? As a tenant of the Club, she already enjoyed inexpensive rent and the ability to order tea and enjoy a discounted meal, but still: money was money. And as a full-time student at the Académie Carmen under the auspices of the American painter James Abbott McNeill Whistler, her time was limited, too. And yet Lundborg was determined to find a way to maximize her savings. She queried Deming and several other students one afternoon over cups of coffee and fresh strawberry tarts at a popular neighborhood haunt, Henriette's.

Henriette's café, a *crémerie* located at 5 rue Léopold Robert, displayed "with French daintiness, the eggs, fresh pots of butter, and cream cheese which, mingled with vivid color in tomatoes and strawberries, the Parisian knows how to make so extraordinarily decorative," in the words of journalist Katharine de Forest.[5] Henriette's was small ("Half a dozen people would perhaps stand with difficulty before the little counter," de Forest quipped[6]), but it featured a lively little restaurant in the back, run by a mother-daughter team, Mme. Paulain and her *jeune fille*, the eponymous Henriette (a striking character, according to Club resident Floy Campbell [1873–1945]: Henriette was "some six feet tall, thin as a pole, and all angles," Campbell wrote in 1904).[7] Even better, Henriette's priced its wares with an eye toward the frugal American students filling the Latin Quarter, charging twenty-five centimes each (approximately five cents in 1900) for a cup of coffee or a bowl of rice pudding, or fifty centimes for heavier fare, including steak, chicken cutlets, or rabbit.[8] "Every Paris visitor should go to Henriette's," Campbell declared.[9]

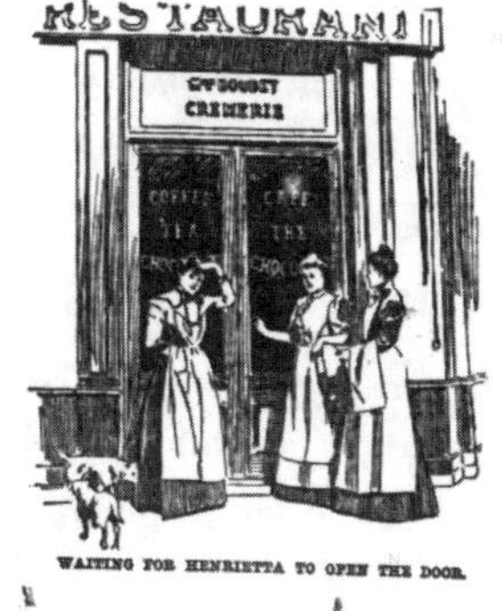

Figure 13.2. *"Waiting for Henrietta to Open the Door."* Louisville Courier-Journal, *December 10, 1899.*

Sitting with her friends at a small wooden table in the back of Henriette's that afternoon, one can almost picture Lundborg, her blonde hair piled high upon her head, squaring her shoulders and surveying her surroundings for something—*anything*—that might inspire a plan to save some cash. Glancing up, she considered the bare walls around her. Turning to Deming and the others, she suddenly lit up.

"Why not turn our art into food?" she exclaimed. "Let's decorate the walls and for our pay—eat."[10]

THOUGH THE GIRLS' Club offered delectable cuisine at reasonable prices, it was certainly not the only restaurant frequented by American women. By Florence Lundborg's final year in Paris, the food scene in the Latin Quarter had positively exploded to meet the needs of the students living there. Even more fascinating, the number of establishments catering to an expressly American clientèle flourished, and it is likely that the Club's founding had a hand in this transformation. In choosing 4 rue de Chevreuse as the new home of the American Girls' Club, Elisabeth Mills Reid not only confirmed the previously established link between the Club and the American Cathedral (particularly via its St. Luke's outpost in the garden), but she also strengthened the

Latin Quarter's connotation as an *alternative* American Colony. As the demographics of the neighborhood changed, so did the shopkeepers and restaurateurs who catered there. An 1896 article from the *Louisville Courier-Journal* describes a typical scene wonderfully, highlighting the ways that the Yankee presence had altered this corner of Paris:

> Surrounded miles deep by Paris . . . a small boy looked up four windows of French architecture and cried: "Baked beans, mamma!" A Frenchman, passing that way, astonished clean out of his politeness, exclaimed "Mon Dieu" . . . But if the Frenchman had been acquainted with the neighborhood he would have known that he was in America at 9 o'clock that morning, that Rue Leopold Robert was not a part of Paris. Paris and France end about four doors from the Boulevard Mont Parnasse and begin about four doors from Boulevard Rospoil. Between is America . . . The small boy was simply telling his mother that day's special dish at the American restaurant across the street.[11]

Rue Léopold Robert, a small road only a two-minute stroll away from the Club, was lovingly deemed "Robert Street" by the American community and provided easy access to greengrocers, butchers, bakeries, and *crémeries* like Henriette's. Most merchants kept their prices low to

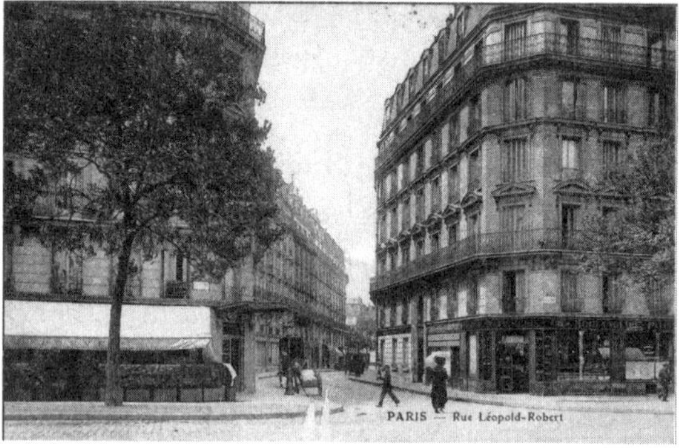

Figure 13.3. *"Rue Léopold-Robert," undated. Postcard, Orville E. Watson, D.D. Postcard Collection, Kenyon College.*

appeal to the budget-conscious students who proliferated in the Latin Quarter. Their cheapness, as much as their geography, led to the development of a devoted clientèle of American girls.

How different things seemed on the other side of the boulevard de Montparnasse! There, the sidewalks teemed with the tables of pricier restaurants and cafés, many of which would become world-renowned (and far more expensive) for their ties to the soon-to-be-famous intellectuals, artists, and writers who frequented their establishments,[12] particularly after World War One. Some of these institutions are still around today, like the celebrated La Closerie des Lilas, the oldest of the grand restaurants in the *quartier*, already almost fifty years old in 1893 when Elisabeth Mills Reid leased the property at 4 rue de Chevreuse. Its darkened, sloping terrace was especially popular on warm evenings, as artist F. Berkeley Smith noted, "with the fresh night air coming from the Luxembourg Gardens."[13] The venerable Le Dôme—famed today for its luxurious seafood towers—opened in 1898, and artsy favorite Café de la Rotonde followed in 1911. But did American girls enter these spaces habitually? Surely some did, requesting a coffee at La Closerie des Lilas or an *apéritif* at La Rotonde before a theater engagement, but Le Dôme? "We almost never went to the Dôme," Anne Goldthwaite later reminisced, though she was quick to point out that gender politics was to blame. "There was a tacit agreement between the American men and the American women—that they [the men] might have one place to themselves beyond the view of their own countrywomen. We would hear of German, Russian, Italian or even English women strolling in and out of the Dôme, but no American woman entered."[14] Or, at least, not during typical night-time business hours. As Frances Cranmer reported in her autobiography, *Higher Than the Sky*:

> I had made a sneak trip to the sinful "Café Du Dome" at six in the morning in the bright sunlight with other students while we took turns getting our pictures taken under that famous sign. The only sin lurking about was a fat charwoman in black sateen sweeping up the litter of last night's revelry.[15]

As a whole, though, the residents and attendees of the American Girls' Club in Paris tended to spend their money more frugally when it came to food, following in the time-honored footsteps of students everywhere. Robert Street and other nearby *rues* provided better deals. Not every inexpensive restaurant was a worthy—or healthy—establishment: "A course of small restaurants is sure to end in dyspepsia, mental and physical," worried Elizabeth Taylor in 1894,[16] while F. Berkeley Smith warned of establishments "whose plat du jour might be traced to some faithful steed finding a final oblivion in a brown sauce and onions."[17]

The good news, however, was that there were several reliable and nourishing favorites. Chez Rosalie, situated on rue Campagne-Première, served humble Italian cuisine at rock-bottom prices and was conveniently located, only a five-minute walk from the Club. Equally beloved and even closer was Henriette's *crémerie* on "Robert Street," which became a student mainstay for its puddings and fried potatoes as much as for its appealing strawberry tarts. But Henriette's played a special role that set it apart from every other restaurant in the Quarter: it served as an artistic stepping-stone in Florence Lundborg's life.

AFTER HER ECONOMICALLY inspired brainstorm—*let's decorate the walls of our favorite café!*—Lundborg and her pals offered their creative services to Henriette and Mme. Paulain, who gladly accepted their proposal. But a question quickly arose: Who would create the artwork for the eatery's walls, and what would it depict? The students knew the power of cohesive design and did not want to enter into their self-commission haphazardly. In a democratic fashion, then, they opted to submit proposed designs anonymously. No details on the competition's "jury" have survived; nonetheless, the winner was clear: Florence Lundborg.

Much of Lundborg's victory, which her hometown newspaper, the *San Francisco Chronicle*, trumpeted in a 1900 article,[18] was due to her subject matter, which nodded cleverly to Henriette's particular delicacy: fruit tarts. Lundborg suggested a design depicting "the old nursery rhyme about the Queen of Hearts who made some tarts . . . for is not

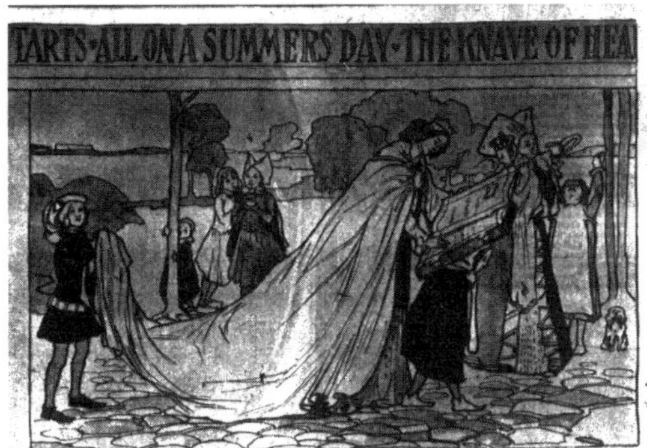

Figure 13.4. *"Queen of Hearts."* San Francisco Chronicle, *September 2, 1900.*

Henrietta the queen of our hearts, and does she not make most excellent tarts?"[19]

The proposed mural at Henriette's would eventually extend across the restaurant's four walls, reaching up to a height of nearly six feet—dimensions that would render the figures life-size. Lundborg wanted to illustrate the entirety of the first stanzas of the traditional English poem:

> The Queen of Hearts
> She made some tarts,
> All on a summer's day;
> The Knave of Hearts
> He stole those tarts,
> And took them quite away.
> The King of Hearts
> Call'd for the tarts,
> And beat the knave full sore;
> The Knave of Hearts
> Brought back those tarts,
> And vow'd he'd steal no more.[20]

The nursery rhyme had grown in popularity after it had been presented in several nineteenth-century works, including Lewis Carroll's

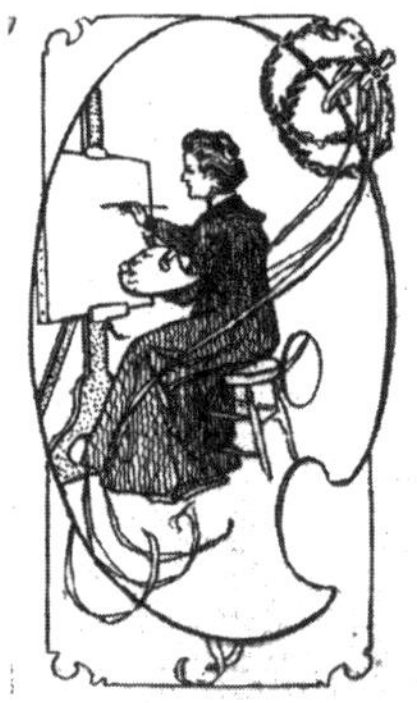

Figure 13.5. *Cartoon of Florence Lundborg. San Francisco Chronicle, September 2, 1900.*

Alice's Adventures in Wonderland (1865) and an extended riff in a poem by Charles Lamb in 1805. Its familiarity was thus widespread, but as an English-language verse it simply meant more to an English-speaking clientèle, like the many American and British students who lived in the quarter and who crossed Henriette's threshold. Lundborg knew her audience (she was one of them, after all!) and sought to please them with a well-known, beloved poem.

One wonders what kind of deal Lundborg struck with Mme. Paulain and Henriette in terms of—what shall we call it?—*nutritional compensation.* From the reports of the *San Francisco Chronicle,* Lundborg and her assistant, fellow Girls' Club artist Alice Mumford (1875–1960), toiled every day to bring the murals to fruition, a process that took almost a year.[21] Did they enjoy a free selection of those tarts upon arrival every morning? Did they receive *carte blanche* access to the day's specials? Those details do not survive. The *Chronicle* did reproduce Lundborg's design for its readers—in print, not photography, though a few low-resolution images do exist—revealing the "story" in eight panels separated by faux pillars with ionic capitals (charmingly and a bit puzzlingly, the *Chronicle* also presents "Lundborg" herself via a fairly generic image of a female painter, palette in hand at a canvas [Fig. 13.5]). Lundborg's style is evident in these reproductions, similar in execution to her illustrations for *The Lark*: her murals are composed in clean, dark lines with an almost cartoonish design reminiscent of both Japanese woodcuts and the sinuous simplicity of art nouveau. Indeed, critics of Lundborg's contemporaneous works, such as her illustrations for a 1900 edition of Omar Khayyam's epic *Rubaiyat,*[22] compared her graphic style to that of the English illustrator Aubrey Beardsley,[23] which makes some sense: as a leading member of the Aestheticism art movement, Beardsley's illustrations would have been familiar to, and potentially shared by, Lundborg's instructor, Whistler, a fellow Aesthete.

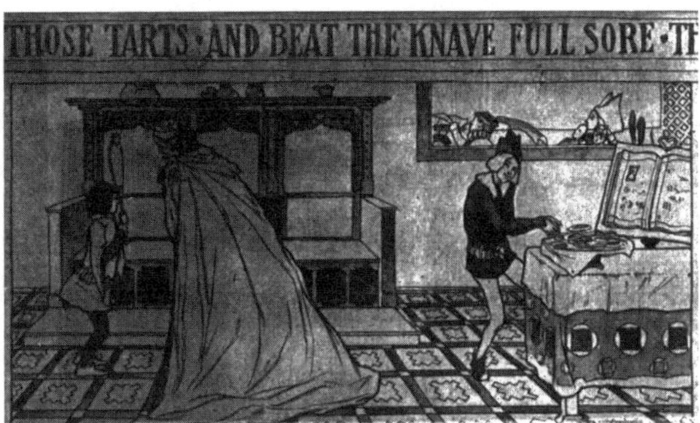

Figure 13.6. *"The Knave."* San Francisco Chronicle, *September 2, 1900.*

In one panel (Fig. 13.4), the Queen of Hearts, donning a flowing cape and a tiny crown, pores over a large book, presumably in search of her recipe; she is accompanied by courtiers and servants, including children, one of whom supports the oversize tome upon her shoulders. In another (Fig. 13.6), she turns away from her finished products, only to have the Knave of Hearts—decked in a tunic and feathered cap, and mischievously smiling at the viewer—snatch them behind her back. What are delightful are the intricate details, many humorous, that Lundborg peppers throughout her mural. From the playful smirk of the knave to an entire panel hinting at the "offscreen" violence the king bestows upon him (a flock of white geese, disturbed by the kerfuffle, scatter, with one's underbelly and tail feathers on proud display; a black cat snoozes indoors, oblivious), Lundborg—and Mumford—enlivened their retelling of the nursery rhyme with true relish and joy. The final designs revealed a color scheme "of soft greens and grays"[24] accompanied by the poem's verses, hand lettered by Lundborg in gold leaf as a frieze above the illustrations.

If Lundborg's goal was simply to produce a pleasing decoration in exchange for some pastries or fresh cream cheese, her finished work proved that she went above and beyond. Nearly every American news article that referenced the popularity of Henriette's among the

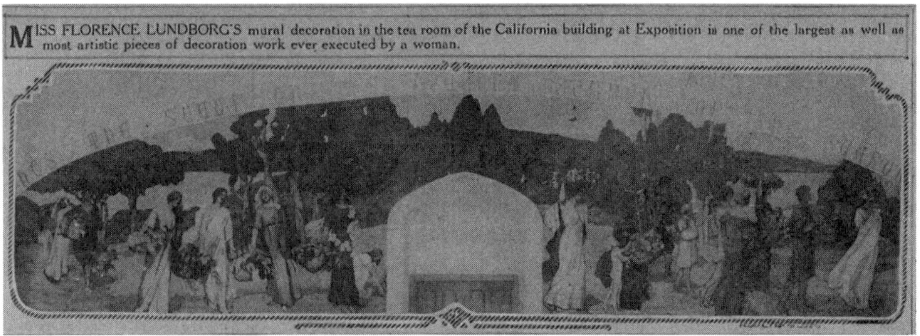

Figure 13.7. *"Miss Florence Lundborg's Mural Decoration."* San Francisco Examiner, *April 25, 1915.*

Americans in Paris also shared the story of Lundborg's and Mumford's creation, which soon became a word-of-mouth sensation, doubling the number of visitors to the tiny *crémerie*.[25] So delighted were the proprietors with the final product that they thanked the two artists with a resplendent banquet for twenty-six guests, featuring several luxuries: "bright, new silverware, the finest of white linens, and trailing roses, which, in Paris, represent a small fortune," crowed the *Chronicle*.[26]

The success of *The Queen of Hearts* had a marked impact on Florence Lundborg's life. Working "in the large" on Henriette's walls was a turning point, inspiring her to continue creating similarly sized works. After her return to the United States in 1900, she worked steadily, producing several murals and large-scale paintings for both private homes and public institutions. Perhaps her greatest accomplishment was a commissioned mural decorating the Tea Room in the California Building of the Panama–Pacific International Exposition, the world's fair of 1915, which was held in Lundborg's hometown in dual celebration of the opening of the Panama Canal and San Francisco's reconstruction after its devastating 1906 earthquake.[27] Her untitled mural, produced atypically on huge canvas panels rather than directly on the wall, spanned fifty-two by fourteen feet and presented a scene described as:

> Symbolical of the wealth of fruit and flowers [of the state of
> California] . . . presenting a procession of figures moving with
> Arcadian joyousness through a typical Californian landscape . . .
> the beauty of the blue sky and the cumulous clouds, rolling hills
> and majestic trees, stretches of sea and a foreground of meadow,
> combined in exquisite beauty of line and glory of color.[28]

The work was widely praised for its quality, finesse, and artistry—the *San Francisco Examiner* declared it to be "OF PERMANENT VALUE" in an all-caps heading to an April 25, 1915, news article. Alas, it was not to be: as with many world's fairs, most of the buildings at the Panama–Pacific International Exposition were constructed to be temporary, and the California Building was no exception. Before the building came down, though, some kind folks removed Florence Lundborg's gargantuan mural, saving it from destruction. The artist's unorthodox choice to create it on canvas in her studio, and not directly onto the California Building's walls, ensured its survival. As of 2015, it was noted as extant, owned by the city of San Francisco and lying dormant in long-term storage.[29]

Perhaps lying dormant, too, is *The Queen of Hearts* at the present-day location of the former *crémerie*, Henriette's. For at least twenty years after Lundborg and Mumford painted their beloved mural, it remained on the café's walls, growing ever more famous—and ever dirtier, too. In 1920, the *Baltimore Sun* published an unexpected request: "Wanted, by Jean Ribaut, of 5 rue Léopold Robert, information as to the present whereabouts of Miss Florence Lundborg, of San Francisco, and Miss Alice Mumford, of Philadelphia. These girls were art students in the Latin Quarter in 1898."[30] Ribaut, who took over Henriette's after Henriette herself won the lottery (!) and departed Paris,[31] acted as chef and proprietor of the café, and had bemoaned the dingy state of the mural on his premises. When he discovered the faded signatures of the artists, he opted to reach out to the American media in hopes of connecting with them to refurbish their student masterpiece. Though dismissed by the *Baltimore Sun* as being "just sentimental," Ribaut refused to paint over *The Queen of Hearts* or to allow another artist to restore it. "Non, it will not be touched unless I can find Mlle. Mumford or Mlle. Lund-borg," he declared. "It is one or the other who must do it. It is their work. It would be sacrilege for another to touch it . . . Some day they will remember Henriette's, and they will come. I am certain they would if I only knew how to find them."[32]

Fascinatingly, and probably coincidentally, Florence Lundborg returned to Paris that same year—in fall 1920—and settled briefly into a studio apartment in the Latin Quarter alongside her friend (and fellow Club alum) Belle McMurtry.[33] Her pied-à-terre was a ten-minute stroll down the boulevard du Montparnasse to Henriette's. It is nearly inconceivable to think that she would not have stopped by to admire her handiwork from years prior. And yet no notes survive to attest to her doing so, nor to the success or failure of Ribaut's outreach attempt.

What does remain, though, is 5 rue Léopold Robert itself, the site of the long-gone Henriette's, now home (at the time of writing) to a small Italian restaurant. Today, its walls are mural-less, painted instead a warm shade of cream, but paint only conceals—it does not remove the traces of its past entirely. Somewhere among its countless striations is Lundborg and Mumford's creation, a quiet memory of the building's connection to the student years of American artists-in-training—proof that American girls affected and contributed to their surroundings, becoming an integral part of the Latin Quarter community, and using their gifts to give back to the places they frequented most.

CHAPTER 14

The Sculptor of Horrors

Mademoiselle, you are a sculptress. Your work is powerful.

—Auguste Rodin to Meta Vaux Warrick, as quoted in Wayman,
"Meta Vaux Warrick (Sculptress)" (1903)[1]

Sculptor Meta Vaux Warrick (later Meta Vaux Warrick Fuller; 1877–1968) disembarked from her train into the bustling Gare du Nord station on a crisp October day in 1899, as Florence Lundborg was likely preparing for another busy day painting at Henriette's. Warrick must have been delighted to have finally arrived in the French capital, because the graceful and lithe twenty-two-year-old's journey had *not* been an easy one. On the ocean liner SS *Belgiumland*, sailing from her hometown of Philadelphia to Liverpool, Warrick's thirteen-day sea crossing in late September 1899 had been fraught with bad luck: unexpected heavy fog, large swells, *two* near-misses with other ships, and a small onboard fire. To cap it all off, her seasickness was severe enough that she stayed in her cabin for half of her trip, confessing in a letter to her brother that she thought her stomach "would turn inside out."[2] Shaken and ill, she opted to acclimate in Liverpool and London before setting out for the French port city of Calais and, finally, Paris. After such a tricky journey, she was ready for something—*anything*—to go smoothly. The difficult part was surely over.

Even the idea of going to Paris had been a challenge for Warrick and her family. Convincing her overprotective, anxious mother to allow her to continue her art education abroad was difficult enough, but Meta herself had needed some serious encouragement, too, because she had found every excuse *not* to pursue her dreams. After her father's death in 1897, the family's financial position felt precarious, and Meta Warrick was loath to disrupt it further. As the baby of the family, she imagined herself to be particularly indebted to her mother and thus intended to play the role of the good and abiding daughter. Art might be her calling, but she could not leave Philadelphia and her family, could she?

Thankfully, Warrick had numerous encouraging art instructors on her side, and they assured her that her sculpture was extraordinary: darkly romantic, symbolic works that stirred emotions and sometimes even shocked viewers with macabre imagery that was "the food upon which my young imagination thrived," as Meta later wrote.[3] *You have a true gift*, they urged her. *You're creating something special here.* And with their gentle prodding, she felt emboldened to pursue a professional career as a "sculptress" via a high-quality education in Paris, where she would stay for almost three years.

After the hard-won fight for her mother's acceptance of her endeavors, Warrick toiled to assuage any lingering worries by doing everything in her power to plan her voyage and her Parisian sojourn meticulously. In the months prior to her departure, the young artist managed every detail of her itinerary, booking her own passage on the *Belgiumland* and even attempting to locate a traveling partner to accompany her on the Atlantic crossing. When her search came up empty, she proposed a thoughtful solution: upon arrival in Paris, a family friend—the famed American painter Henry Ossawa Tanner—would meet her train and shepherd her through the city, where he had lived since 1891. Such escorts for women traveling alone were common and welcome, particularly given the negative reputation of the "bohemian" Latin Quarter, as other American girls noted. "Through the kindness of a friend, the President of the White Star Line sent a protector to the boat at Cherbourg to escort me to the club so that I would, at least, be a virgin until I got under its portals," Frances Cranmer wryly commented in her autobiography.[4]

Most critically for her pre-journey preparations, Warrick wrote a letter to the American consulate in Paris seeking accommodation recommendations, and she received a rather expedient answer to this question with the name of a place touted as the ideal spot for a young lady pursuing a path in the arts: the American Girls' Club on the rue de Chevreuse, already a beloved institution in its sixth year. Without hesitation, Warrick contacted Julia Acly, the Club's director, to request accommodation. She was in luck: of the forty much-coveted rooms at the Club, one would be held for her arrival that autumn. All the pieces had lined up wonderfully and now, in October 1899, Meta Vaux Warrick waited at the Gare du Nord for Tanner's arrival.

Scanning the crowd with her deep brown eyes, Warrick caught no sight of her companion, but she was little concerned. Despite her international journey from London and Calais, she had arrived in Paris earlier than anticipated. Tanner, to be sure, would arrive closer to their prearranged meeting time to escort her to the Club.

And yet the minutes ticked by, moving beyond the point of comfort. Warrick grew nervous. She continued to wait, glancing uneasily around the unfamiliar crowd in an unfamiliar country.

Eventually, to her great consternation, Warrick concluded that Tanner had been unable to meet her and that she now had no choice but to escort *herself* to the Club. Perturbed, she hailed a hansom cab to the sixth *arrondissement*, more than ready to rest in her reserved room after her arduous journey and rather inconvenient wait.

At the double doors of 4 rue de Chevreuse, Warrick was greeted by the Club's concierge, who frowned at her before promptly leading her to Acly's quarters. Warrick recalled what happened next to biographer Sylvia G. L. Dannett decades later:

> I was ushered into the directress [Acly]'s room—this was quite early
> in the morning. She was about to have her breakfast and she was
> having her hair done. She said, "Sit down, child." Well at that time
> it was quite the fashion to wear the heavy veil and I pushed the

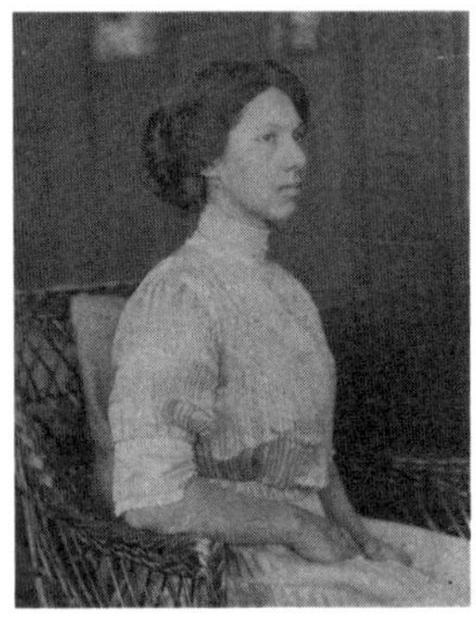

Figure 14.1. *Meta Vaux Warrick Fuller, ca. 1910. New York Public Library Digital Collections.*

traveling veil [up] and she looked at me through the mirror . . . She said, "Why, you didn't tell me that you were not a white girl."[5]

To be sure, the major demographic commonality for women at the Club—especially residents—was their whiteness. Yet Warrick did not feel that her Blackness[6] made any difference—or at least she felt that it *should not* have made any difference—in her position as an art student in Paris, and thus she had chosen not to mention it in her previous letter to Acly upon reserving her room at the Club. On that early morning in Paris in 1899, she reiterated this position, calmly yet firmly responding to Acly, "I was told that the American Girls' Club . . . was here for the American girl students who came to Paris to study and I felt that I, as an American girl, was entitled to come here."[7]

In Warrick's recollections of her meeting with Julia Acly, she described Acly's rejection of her as couched in the classic "I wouldn't want *you* to be uncomfortable" excuse. After her initial shock at seeing Warrick's face wore off, Acly declared, "I would hate to see you ill-treated, discriminated against, and there are Southern girls here [who] might not show you welcome." Warrick, rightly angry, held her ground, arguing, "That doesn't matter to me at all," but it was to no avail. Acly sighed. "If I decide that you should not stay here," she groused, "I wish you wouldn't insist upon it."[8]

TO STATE THAT this was Meta Vaux Warrick's first experience with racism is likely laughable, or at least wishful thinking on this author's part. Though her family belonged to Philadelphia's so-called Black bourgeoisie, they could neither expect nor claim equality with their white bourgeois counterparts. Her family, however, lived in a uniquely privileged realm: Philadelphia was long known as a friendly city for African Americans, boasting ample career opportunities and integrated schools decades prior to *Brown v. Board of Education*. Even more importantly, both of her parents worked in the haircare industry, her mother as a hairdresser and wigmaker and her father as the owner and operator of a barber shop. Both catered to Philadelphia's elite—read: *white folks*—as their primary client base. It is not difficult to imagine that they may have benefited from the familiarity that hairstyling often breeds, a familiarity that may have extended to the Warrick clan as a kind of "pass" not often provided to Black Philadelphians of lower economic status.[9]

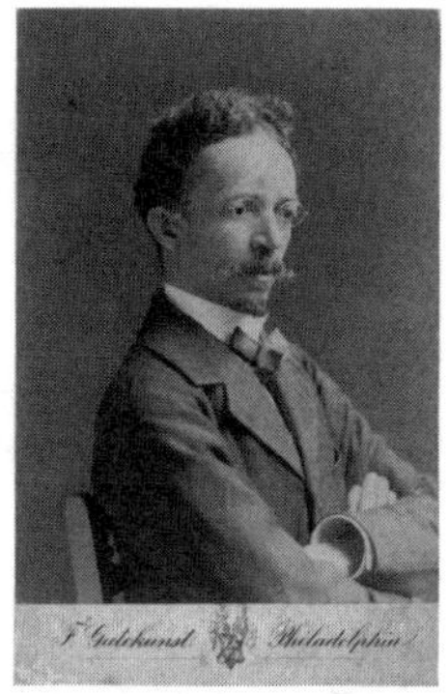

Figure 14.2. *Frederick Gutekunst,* Henry Ossawa Tanner, *1907. Archives of American Art, Smithsonian Institution.*

Fascinatingly, Warrick's recollections of her early life and education contain few remarks about racial discrimination, and indeed, her experience was vastly different than that of Henry Ossawa Tanner, her family friend and late-arriving Parisian guide. Only twenty years prior, Tanner made waves as the first Black student ever admitted to Philadelphia's Pennsylvania Academy of the Fine Arts (PAFA). Though he thrived artistically under the guidance of painter Thomas Eakins, his cohort of fellow artists was not nearly as accommodating. In a 1909 autobiographical article, "The Story of an Artist's Life," Tanner elegantly but excruciatingly recalled his time at PAFA:

> I was extremely timid and to be made to feel that I was not wanted, although in a place where I had every right to be, even months afterwards caused me sometimes weeks of pain. Every time any one of these disagreeable incidents came into my mind, my heart sank, and I was anew tortured by the thought of what I had endured, almost as much as the incident itself.[10]

Though Tanner never specified what "these disagreeable incidents" entailed, they were arduous enough to force him away from

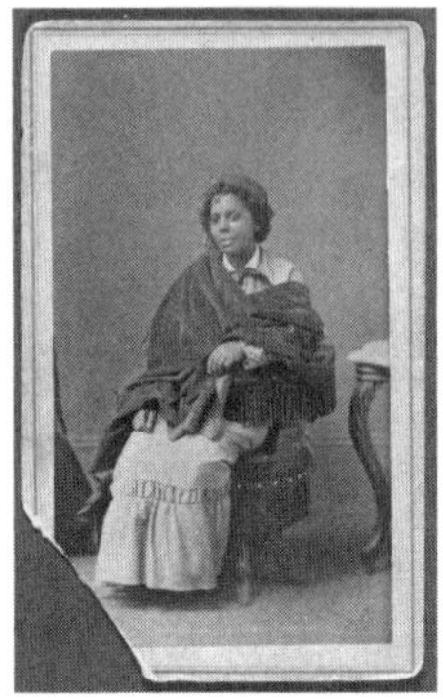

Figure 14.3. *Edmonia Lewis, undated. New York Public Library Digital Collections.*

Pennsylvania altogether. He left PAFA without graduating.

The struggles of Edmonia Lewis, an African American sculptor often described as Warrick's artistic progenitor, were even greater. If accessible training for female artists was in short supply in the United States in the first half of the nineteenth century, access for Black female artists was doubly limited. Though she attended the liberal, desegregated Oberlin College in Ohio, Lewis's experiences with racism there nearly cost both her freedom and her life. In 1862, three years after the beginning of her tenure at Oberlin, she was embroiled in a scandal. After serving two friends mulled wine on a wintry afternoon, her friends—both white—grew severely ill. Lewis was quickly accused of poisoning her friends, though doctors found no evidence of foul play. Thanks to a sympathetic jury and the help of the only Black lawyer practicing in town, Lewis was acquitted of the supposed crime, but not before enduring ongoing discrimination and physical violence. While out on a walk one dark night, Lewis was attacked, dragged into a nearby field, and beaten nearly to death. Though she recovered and soldiered on in her studies at Oberlin, further bigotry kept her, too, from graduating. She left Ohio in 1864.

Both Edmonia Lewis and Henry Ossawa Tanner eventually decamped to live abroad, soothed not only by the strength of European art education but also the comparatively tolerant atmosphere. Of her move to Italy, Lewis noted to the *New York Times* in 1878, "I was practically driven to Rome in order to obtain the opportunities for art culture, and to find a social atmosphere where I was not constantly reminded of my color. The land of liberty had not room for a colored sculptor."[11]

Paris had long been perceived as an especially sympathetic city for Black Americans. Though it reached its height during the jazzy days of the 1920s—think triple-threat Josephine Baker, poet Langston Hughes, and club owner–vaudevillian Ada "Bricktop" Smith, as just a few expat examples—the visitation and migration of African Americans to France, spurred on by the concept of France's color-blindness, had been growing for more than a century. One early visitor, Sally Hemings, the enslaved mistress of Thomas Jefferson, toured Paris alongside the future president in the 1780s.[12] Louisiana, a French colony until its landmark purchase in 1803 under Jefferson's purview, held a substantial population of "free people of color" after France outlawed slavery in its colonies in 1794. When that territory transferred into American hands—sixty years prior to the Emancipation Proclamation—the first large-scale emigration of Black Americans to France accompanied it. Following the Civil War, the movement of formerly enslaved people to Europe spiked again, and it continued to pick up speed during the era when Meta Vaux Warrick landed in Paris.

As it was for so many of the artists making a beeline for the American Girls' Club, Warrick's primary interest in the French capital was its world-renowned art and education scene, but as a Black American, she could not have ignored the seductive concept of a society free of prejudice.[13] As Tyler Stovall notes in his book, *Paris Noir: African Americans in the City of Light*, the reality was far more complex, but when viewed in comparison to the United States, racial discrimination was far less prevalent among the French. "The idea of France as a refuge from American racism had far more to do with conditions in the *United States* than conditions in Paris," Stovall concludes (italics mine).[14] Warrick's rejection at the American Girls' Club in Paris may not have seemed like a good omen, to be sure—but the fact that the beginning of her three-year residency in Paris was marred by racism is unsurprising when considering its source: not French citizens, but *American* women at the *American* Girls' Club in Paris. Active and direct prejudice most frequently spouted from the mouths of her own compatriots.

AFTER DEPARTING JULIA Acly's chambers, Warrick decamped to the Club's library, drafting a letter of complaint to the American consul who had originally recommended the Club to her, stating that her status as an American girl—not a *Black* American girl—determined her eligibility for the Club's services. Coincidentally, her letter-writing was interrupted by the arrival, ridiculously late, of the long-awaited Henry Ossawa Tanner, who commiserated with Warrick's experience, sniffing, "Well, I wouldn't insist on staying here; it's a cliquey place. You can easily find a place to stay and study."[15] As we know, Tanner was not alone in this estimation. Others often remarked on the Club's cliquishness, like Connecticut native Mary Rogers Williams (1857–1907), who, like Warrick, lived in Paris in 1899. In her letters back home, Williams slyly dismissed the Club in her letters as having "too many females."[16]

As one would expect from a tight-knit community, word of Warrick's experience spread throughout the Club and was later reported back to the States. In a 1901 letter to the editor of the *St. Louis Post-Dispatch*, a frustrated writer identified only by the initials "CFM"—likely Club member Cornelia Field Maury—opined upon Warrick's dismissal, though it differed slightly than Warrick's own retelling:

> The case of Miss ______, a colored girl at the American Girls' Club in Paris, is [an] instance of man's inhumanity to man, though here woman's inhumanity to woman. This girl from Philadelphia went to study art as hundreds of other American girls do, bringing good letters [of recommendation], and expected a home at the club. She got board and room there, but when a certain young woman from South Carolina found herself eating breakfast at the same dining room with the colored girl she threatened to leave the club, and Miss ______ was politely asked to go elsewhere. For one year nearly I saw Miss ______ frequently at the club—she was allowed all other privileges of the place—and I know that she was the object of unjust criticism and many a cool snubbing of which she was perfectly conscious, but never openly resented. She couldn't: there were too many against her. And this was done by both northern and southern young women. One could see that she was equal in breeding, education, ideas of dress and politeness to the nicest girls there, but her one sin was the tint of her skin. It would be hard for humanity if God drew the color line across the souls of his children. Yet these same superior Americans, the South Carolinian,

too, went to the little Episcopal chapel [St. Luke's Chapel] in the court every Sunday and thought they were Christians. It seems queer![17]

Though Warrick's name is left out of the letter, she is most certainly its subject.

Julia Acly did, at least, work alongside Warrick and Tanner to find new accommodations for Warrick, escorting them around the Latin Quarter to explore options—a too-pricey pension; a convent with a curfew even stricter than the Club's; a residential hotel whose clientèle Warrick found wanting—until the artist found suitable lodgings, settling first on rue de Bagneaux and later moving to the rue Daguerre.[18] Acly, too, might have introduced Warrick to the American Gilded Age sculptor Augustus Saint-Gaudens, who recommended Warrick join an atelier for several months—advice that the young artist heeded, opting to join morning classes at the Académie Colarossi for sculpture, and anatomy training and additional drawing courses at the École des beaux-arts, which had opened its doors to women in 1897.[19] It is an incredible shame to note that Warrick was not welcomed warmly into the fold of the American Girls' Club, and her rejection there remains one of the biggest stains on the institution's history. But Warrick did not allow her negative early experience to color her stay, and soon enough, she met the artist who would change her Parisian trajectory entirely.

In 1900, Meta Vaux Warrick enjoyed frequent visits to the Exposition Universelle, as did many residents and visitors in the capital. This world's fair was held in Paris every eleven years, and the previous iteration had birthed the Eiffel Tower, a wrought iron masterpiece that not only changed the cityscape but also changed what visitors expected from an event like the fair: grandeur, innovation, and inspiration. At the 1900 exposition, the tower still held massive appeal for visitors, who also appreciated the Grand Roue

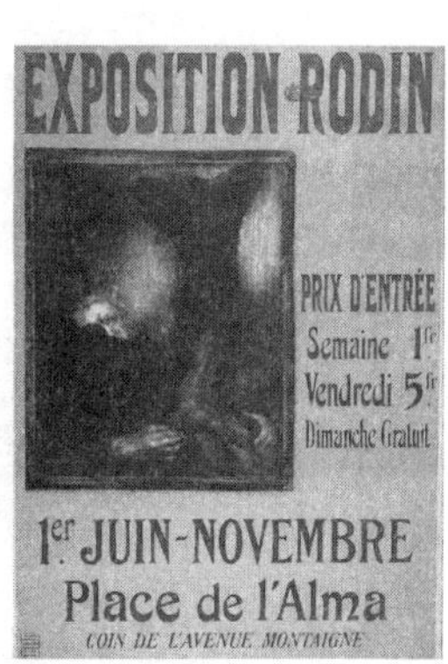

Figure 14.4. *Eugène Carrière,* Affiche pour l'exposition Rodin à l'Alma, *1900. Bibliotheque Forney.*

de Paris—a giant wheel modeled after the groundbreaking ride created for Chicago's 1893 World's Columbian Exposition by George Washington Gale Ferris Jr. The inaugural rides of the Métropolitain—Paris's underground rail system—were held that summer, with its entrances charmingly flanked by curving iron and glass canopies designed by Hector Guimard, a champion of art nouveau architecture and design. The motion picture—pioneered by the Lumière brothers only half a decade prior—was another hugely alluring exhibit. But for Warrick, the exposition's key draw was twofold: the African American–designed "American Negro Exhibit" at the Palace of Social Economy (spearheaded in part by activist and sociologist W. E. B. Du Bois, later a friend to Warrick),[20] and, most critically, the art. And *mon dieu*, what amazing works were on view at the 1900 exposition.

As discussed previously, the visual arts held pride of place at any world's fair. Each fair, too, had its standout pieces, star artists, and controversy—and for the 1900 exposition, all three categories were represented in the singular figure of the French sculptor Auguste Rodin. In a savvy and somewhat scandalous move, Rodin erected his very own pavilion at the place de l'Alma in conjunction with the exposition, a display that he partially funded and filled with dozens of drawings and more than 150 (mostly plaster) sculptures, including some of his now-iconic works: figures for his incomplete monumental project, *The Gates of Hell*, such as *The Kiss* (ca. 1888–98) and *The Thinker* (ca. 1888); elements from his *Burghers of Calais* (ca. 1884–95); and *The Walking Man* (ca. 1889–98). Functioning as a large-scale one-man retrospective[21]—the biggest in the esteemed artist's career at that point—the show captured international imaginations and catapulted Rodin to superstar status, making him one of the world's first celebrity artists. His influence at the fair cannot be underestimated. One exposition attendee, Oscar Wilde, proclaimed, "Rodin has a pavilion to himself and showed me anew all his great dreams in marble. He is by far the

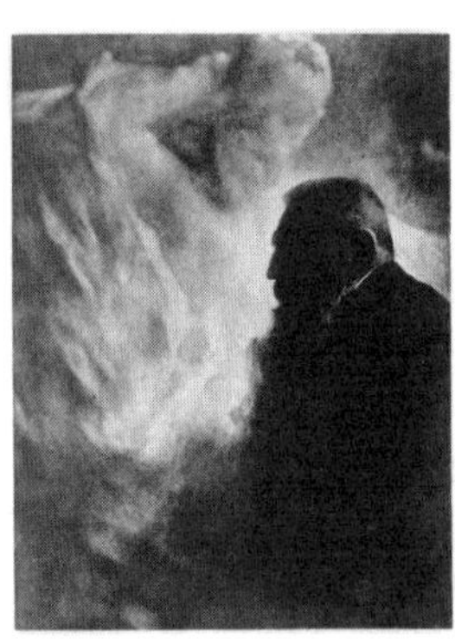

Figure 14.5. *Edward Steichen,* Rodin, *1903. Library of Congress.*

greatest poet in France, and has, as I was glad to tell myself, completely outshone Victor Hugo."[22] Rodin, then and later, boasted many such famous supporters and apologists, including several Americans of note: while Edward Steichen later recalled crowds declaring Rodin's *Balzac* (ca. 1892–97) "a monstrosity" and "a sack of flour with a head stuck on top," he himself understood it immediately as "the very embodiment of a tribute to genius."[23] Dancer Isadora Duncan chastised a grousing crowd at the place de l'Alma, berating them, "Don't you know . . . that this is not the thing itself, but a symbol—a conception of the ideal of life."[24] Whether viewers considered themselves pro-Rodin or anti-Rodin, it cannot be denied that many of them had been introduced to the French sculptor's works by this spectacle at the fair. The exposition's estimated head count, at the end of its seven-month run, exceeded fifty million visitors, and surely a substantial number of those attendees stopped by Rodin's pavilion.

Considered by the international press to be the "most modern among living artists,"[25] Rodin eschewed the idealism of the human figure and denied his sculptures the perfected finish so beloved by academics at the École des beaux-arts and beyond. Rodin literally manhandled his sculptures, leaving traces of his own hand behind on his molds, which, in many cases, would then transfer onto their bronze castings. This—combined with his interest in leaving figures partially incomplete, as if rising from a block of stone or clay, as Michelangelo Buonarroti had done centuries before—lent his works a sense of energy and emotion, a rough and romantic air that contrasted so precisely with the cold perfection of traditional sculpture.

After seeing Rodin's work at the Exposition Universelle, Meta Vaux Warrick was entranced; the elder artist manifested metaphorical and universal themes of grief, love, darkness, and hope in his sculptures unlike any other. Dazzled, she felt an all-encompassing need to understand his inspirations and his techniques. She simply *had* to meet Rodin.

There was only one problem: you couldn't just pop by unannounced to Auguste Rodin's house, or the homes of many, without raising suspicion or ire. In the era of *cartes de visites*, the concept of simply dropping by a Parisian home without announcing your intentions beforehand was absolutely *interdit*. Warrick, then, needed a way in, and thus had to rely on her connections to recommend her to the master. This was easier said than done: Rodin's popularity had increased exponentially in the 1890s, and in the aftermath of the 1900 exposition, his home and studio had become beacons for every passing celebrity, art patron, or wealthy tourist in Paris, let alone the hordes of desperate students seeking his wisdom and attention. Meta Vaux Warrick would have a tough time standing out in such a like-minded crowd, and she knew it. She required a supportive friend to put in a good word for her.

Luckily, her attendance at the Académie Colarossi, on the recommendation of Augustus Saint-Gaudens, had introduced Warrick to several well-connected folks, including artists Paula Modersohn-Becker and Clara Westhoff Rilke. Clara Rilke proved especially useful, as she was a student of Rodin's—as well as the wife of Rodin's personal secretary, the poet Rainer Maria Rilke. It is likely that Rilke combined her efforts with Jelka Rosen, another Rodin student who had befriended Warrick. Together, these women vouched for Warrick's talent and beseeched Rodin to meet with her. An April 1901 letter from Rosen to Rodin survives:

> A young Creole, Mademoiselle Warrick . . . seems to me very gifted . . . She is so poor that she only has this year [left] in Paris and her future in America depends on this . . . Her art is her life and she is so full of enthusiasm that I wish to aid her. Excuse me, master, and if it is inconvenient don't do anything . . .[26]

To Meta Vaux Warrick's surprise and utter delight, Rilke's and Rosen's ploy worked. She was granted a much-coveted meeting with the greatest sculptor of the age.

IN THE SUMMER of 1901, Warrick first set foot at the Villa des Brillants, Rodin's suburban home in Meudon and one of several studios he owned in the greater Paris area. The villa, a striking three-story brick edifice with a steeply pitched slate roof lined with dormer windows, had been the master's home since 1895, and it buzzed with energy stemming from Rodin's myriad assistants and busy bronze casters. Even those who worked on site, like Rainer Maria Rilke, were overcome by the villa's grandeur, especially its main hall, which housed plaster casts of the artist's works in progress. As Rilke noted to Clara, "The effect of this vast hall filled with light, where all these dazzling white sculptures seem to gaze out at you from behind high glass doors, like creatures in an aquarium, is extremely powerful. It makes a huge, a tremendous impression . . ."[27]

Warrick, no doubt, would have been extremely impressed indeed—but she was not the only one. Rodin, too, was quickly affected by viewing Warrick's work. For her audience with the master, the young American had arrived prepared with not only photographs of her recent sculptures, but with a plaster statuette for his perusal, too. *Silent Sorrow*,[28] inspired by the poem "In the Desert" by American writer Stephen Crane,[29] is a masterwork of the grotesque: a naked man, crouched and tangled in his limbs, gnaws on his own heart while staring into space with deep, soulless eyes and barely concealed disgust. Turning the sculpture over repeatedly in his hands, the sixty-one-year-old Rodin displayed a slight hint of approval before rising from his chair and meeting Warrick's tentative gaze. Smiling, he said, *"Mon enfant, vous êtes un sculpteur née. Vous avez le sens de la forme."*[30]—"My child, you are a born sculptor. You have the sense of form."

What a revelation: the greatest living sculptor had just complimented her and her work! Warrick had sought such a recognition of her skill and talent throughout her young life. But for a moment still, her dreams felt just beyond her grasp. When she asked if Rodin would accept her as one of his students, the master demurred, countering, "I already have too many students." Rodin must have seen her crestfallen expression because he immediately clarified that he would *mentor* her regardless: if Warrick were willing to bring her works to him for criticism and guidance, he would happily assist her. Generously, he added that if a sculpture was too large or cumbersome to transport to Villa des Brillants, he would meet her at her Paris studio instead.[31] Rodin quickly sealed the deal by touring her around his property, the pair of them enthusiastically chatting about style and artistic theory while perusing what Warrick later described as "a case with myriads of little hands, feet, legs, and arms,"[32] Rodin's anatomical maquettes on display today at the Musée Rodin in Paris. Understandably, the day held great significance for Warrick, as it represented the beginning of an influential friendship that would define her final year in Paris and her deeper commitment to an expressive, intensely personal style of sculpture. About this commitment, she later recalled, "My heart went out to him, and with clenched fists, I determined to fulfill the fair promise he had bespoken for me."[33] He had acknowledged her as a true artist, and she intended to remain worthy of this highest of compliments.

Beyond mentoring—and even beyond the cachet provided by a connection to such a renowned artist—Rodin's most valuable contribution to Warrick was the boost to her self-confidence. The artist's declaration that she was a "born sculptor" instilled in Warrick a belief in her abilities and talents and convinced her that she was on the right path: creating psychologically rich, expressive, and occasionally jarring figures that grabbed the viewer's attention and would not let go. Under Rodin's influence, she increased her forceful handling of her modeling surfaces, her knuckles creating deeper indentations and fingerprints lingering—physical proof that a human, not an automaton, was behind a figure's creation. While this may have been de rigueur for Rodin, such evidence of the (literal) artist's hand had yet to gain major acceptability in art schools and academies big and small: it certainly was not part of Warrick's curriculum at the Académie Colarossi. For her part, then, Warrick had jumped wholeheartedly into the avant-garde, and she was rewarded for it.

Warrick's final year in Paris was shaped by the recommendations of her mentor. After Rodin asserted the need for her works to be seen by the Parisian art community, she inaugurated private showcases and tours at her studio. This strategy worked: her sculptures soon grabbed critical recognition, and by early 1902 she was approached with invitation-only offers to exhibit her works across Paris. That summer, the art dealer Siegfried Bing, a prominent connoisseur who represented several important artists of the era (including Mary Cassatt, William

Morris, Louis Comfort Tiffany, Paul Signac, Camille Pissarro, and Henri de Toulouse-Lautrec, among others), held an exhibition of Warrick's works at his gallery, called l'Art Nouveau, at 22 rue de Provence.[34] At this show—Warrick's first solo foray—she presented twenty-two pieces that were quintessentially *her*. Take *Oedipus* (1900,

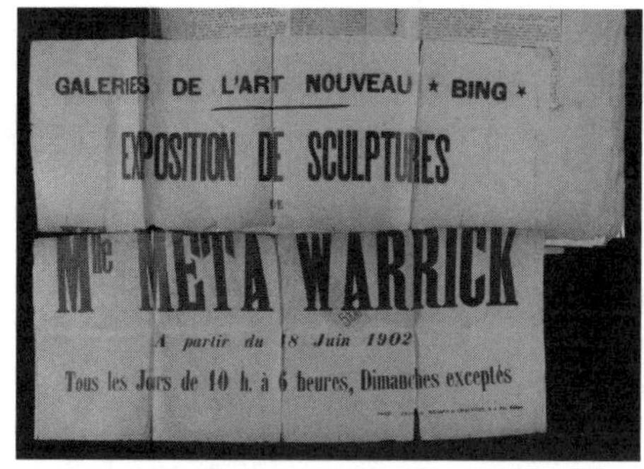

Figure 14.6. *"Exposition de Sculptures de Mlle Meta Warrick," exhibition poster, 1902.*

now lost) as a prime example. The eponymous figure of the famed Sophocles play, long a favorite of artists for its drama, is frozen in Warrick's hands at the moment of his ultimate suffering: his self-inflicted blindness at the story's climax. Kneeling on the ground and clawing at the dirt around him, Oedipus throws his head back in anguish, his eyeless face a mask of horrible despair. As with *Silent Sorrow*, Warrick presents the starkest moment possible and demands that viewers not look away—a bold move at a time when even Rodin, with *The Kiss* and *The Thinker*, still produced pieces that highlighted the beauty of the human form. These works "startled Paris," according to the contemporary press, who made much of the fact that these shocking and graphic sculptures stemmed from a young and proper lady.[35] So surprising was the juxtaposition of the lithe, quiet Warrick with her ghastly imagery that French critics bestowed upon her a new title: "the delicate sculptor of horrors."[36]

It was not just the French who appreciated Warrick's artistic panache. Her Parisian solo exhibition sparked curiosity back home in the States, too, leading a special correspondent to review it for the *New York Times*. In her synopsis, the *Times* journalist cannily noted, "[Warrick's] very great talent, amounting to almost genius, is admitted by the best critics here."[37] By the end of 1902, Warrick's three-year spell in Paris had come to a close, but not before her powerful, arresting sculptures won the acclaim that she—like so many of her fellow artists—so fiercely sought: two of her works were accepted for the 1903 edition of the Salon des beaux-arts, where they were shown alongside pieces by American luminaries like Augustus Saint-Gaudens and Frederick MacMonnies. Warrick was thus anointed as a shimmering American art star, with one critic suggesting that his readers "remember the name Miss Warrick . . . I would be very surprised if, with so many interesting debuts, it does not rapidly become that of a loved and appreciated talent."[38]

Though it had utterly failed Meta Vaux Warrick upon her arrival in Paris, the American Girls' Club—particularly its affiliate, the American Woman's Art Association—eventually reemerged to embrace the artist, if briefly. Prior to her return to Philadelphia, Meta Vaux Warrick received yet another special request: to consider entering the competition for the annual exhibition of the AWAA, then under the aegis of Association president Mary Fairchild MacMonnies.[39] Warrick graciously agreed to participate, and it is fair to say that her artwork made a splash: she was subsequently juried into the show as the only sculptor accepted that year, and an image of her work was reproduced as part of the *New York Herald*'s coverage of the event.[40] Sure, the AWAA exhibition was not a major event like the Paris Salon, but her inclusion was a tacit acknowledgment of Warrick's status as an integral part of both the American Colony and the Parisian art world—and of her primacy therein as one of the city's ascendant artists. It further bolstered her credibility among her fellow American women, too.

One wonders what thoughts fluttered through Warrick's mind when she walked through the doors of 4 rue de Chevreuse to prepare her works for exhibition. Did she feel a modicum of righteous anger, remembering how her repudiation there had given her Parisian sojourn an inauspicious start? Did she feel frustration, knowing that the Club never rectified its inherent racism (no further documentation exists regarding other episodes of discrimination against Black women or any other nonwhite members), and that hers was a stand-alone rejection? Did she mourn her inability to enjoy the conviviality and connection so cherished by Club residents, disappointedly considering what might have been? Perhaps, by that point, Meta Vaux Warrick no longer cared;

she had all of Paris at her feet, and she prepared to return home as a true success story. Perhaps she settled her sculptures there, on their pedestals, with a glimmer of triumph in her eye, because she realized one important truth: she had flourished in Paris beyond her dreams not because of the Club, but in spite of it.

CHAPTER 15

Anne Goldthwaite and the Shock of the New

*Fate gave me several years in Paris at the most exciting time:
during the great reconstruction from art to modern art.*

—ANNE GOLDTHWAITE, AMERICAN ARTIST (1930S)[1]

The community inherent in the American Girls' Club—both for residents and for visitors partaking of the Club's many amenities—continued to be a great selling point for each season's wave of newcomers to Paris after the dawn of the twentieth century. The ability of Club-goers to speak a common language, both literally and metaphorically, eased the pain of adjusting to an unfamiliar land and culture and thus provided women with a near instant social circle. In several fortunate circumstances, an artist's friendships at the Club led to something rare and delightful: accidental brushes with people, places, and art that would propel them into their career's next stage. Such was the case for Anne Goldthwaite during her multiyear residency at the Club, which began in 1906, thirteen years after its opening at 4 rue de Chevreuse.

Born in 1869 in Montgomery, Alabama, only four years after the end of the American Civil War, Anne Goldthwaite was raised in a conservative household as the daughter of Richard Wallach Goldthwaite, a Confederate soldier and attorney. Though groomed to be a typical Southern belle as her mother, Lucy Boyd Armistead, had been, she exhibited an independent streak, bristling against the confines of her home and her family's expectations of her.[2] Rather than remaining cooped up at home playing with dolls, little Anne preferred to roam around her hometown unaccompanied, carrying little but a

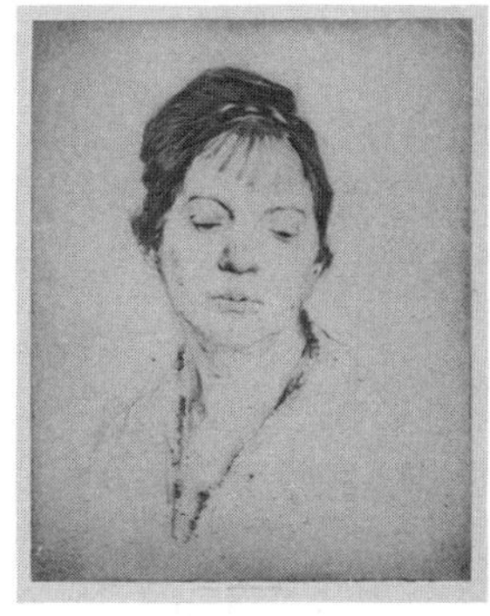

Figure 15.1. *Anne Goldthwaite*, Self-Portrait, *ca. 1918. Amon Carter Museum of American Art.*

sketchpad and a pencil (much to the dismay of her family *and* the good citizens of Montgomery, as this was considered unfitting behavior for a girl of her background).

The Goldthwaite family relocated to Dallas during Anne's childhood, but after her parents' untimely deaths (Richard Goldthwaite died in March 1881 at the age of forty-two, three months prior to Anne's twelfth birthday, and Lucy Armistead Goldthwaite followed in March 1884, also at forty-two), Goldthwaite and her three siblings returned to Montgomery where they were raised by extended family, including, in Anne's case, a stern but loving aunt, Molly Arrington. Research indicates that Arrington may have had contradictory emotions about her niece's early propensity for art. Her primary hope for Goldthwaite was that be-all and end-all for proper ladies: to become a wife. "I was brought up to believe that matrimony was the desired end of a woman's life and a woman's career," Goldthwaite recalled, with Arrington frequently reminding her that "it is better to marry badly than not at all."[3] At the same time, Arrington noted her niece's proficiency in art, and after Goldthwaite took all the "right" steps—"coming out" as a debutante at the age of eighteen, and (halfheartedly, perhaps?) searching for a mate until the age of twenty-three[4]—Molly Arrington assented to her niece's career change: from would-be wife to soon-to-be artist.

Not that Goldthwaite believed she had much of a chance to become a professional artist. In fact, she needed convincing, just as Meta Vaux Warrick had. In a 1915 article titled "How I Discovered Myself," Goldthwaite recalled:

> I never really believed that I was cut out to be an artist. I really had no ambitions and dreamed no visions. I believed that the world was filled with talent and young people far more gifted than I was, and with all the reluctance of youth I refused to come to New York to study. My uncle proposed taking me to New York, and I went, lured by the prospect of a winter in the gay metropolis, rather than by any great urge toward artistic development.[5]

Whether through the encouragement of her instructors, blossoming self-confidence, a passion for creating art, or a combination of all three, Anne Goldthwaite thrived in New York City, where she relocated around 1894.[6] She studied at the National Academy of Design beginning in 1898, where she primarily studied painting. With a practical mindset ("I thought I would learn fashions," she claimed), Goldthwaite intended to use her training as an entrée to commercial illustration, but after six years at the National Academy and at least two years training under the keen eye of painter Walter Shirlaw, she had come to that natural conclusion: "One thing logically followed another and I finally decided to go to Paris because it seemed to me the thing to do."[7]

AS SHE LATER noted in her unpublished memoirs, Anne Goldthwaite headed "straight to Mrs. Whitelaw Reid's Club for American Girls in the rue de Chevreuse"[8] upon her arrival in Paris in 1906. It may be assumed that her reasoning for the selection of the Club as her Parisian home—a place where she would rent a room for at least six of her seven years in Paris—was likely twofold. As indicated by the proliferation of articles in the American press documenting the Club's goings-on, the

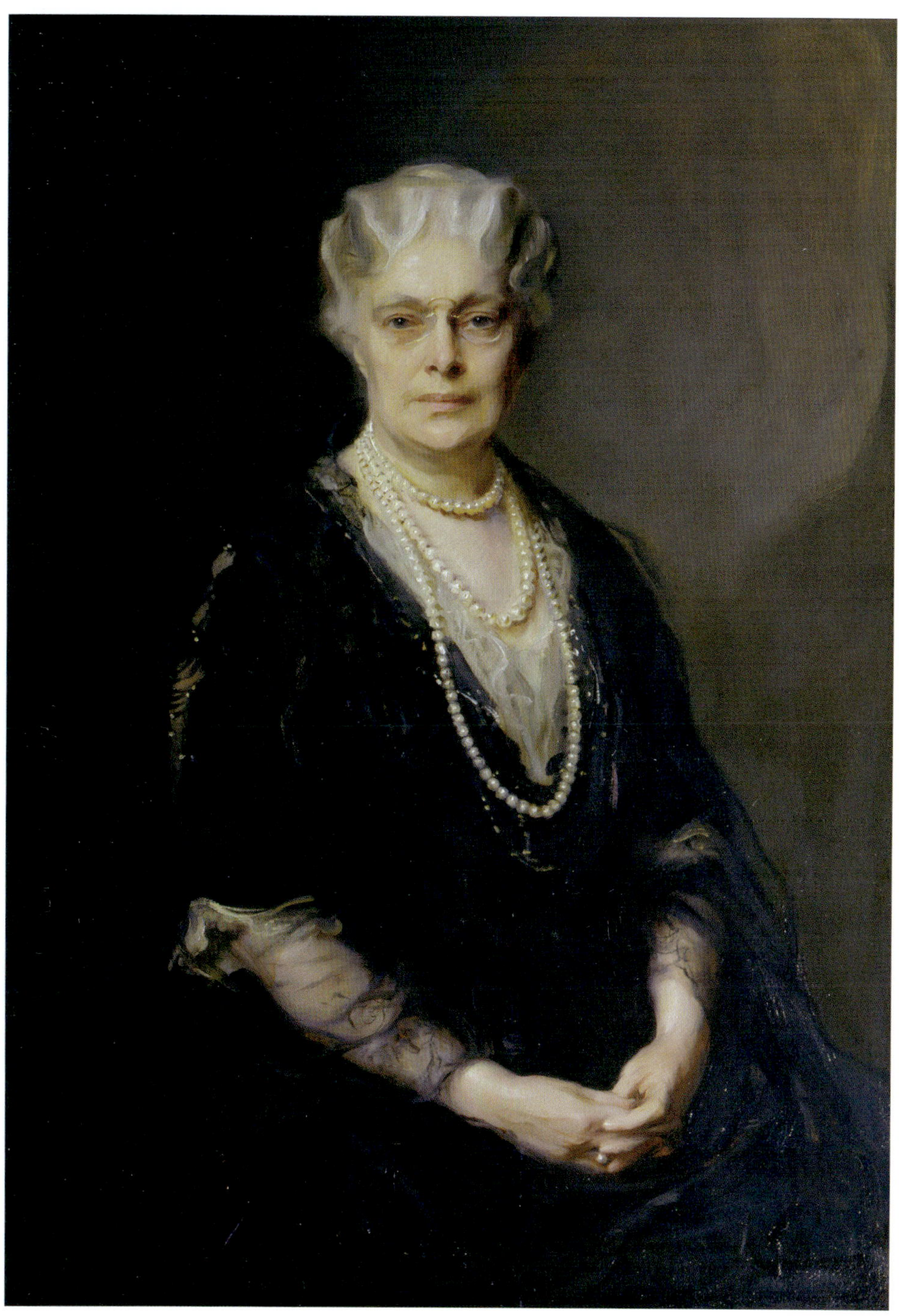

Philip Alexius de László, *Mrs. Whitelaw Reid, née Elisabeth Mills*, 1922.

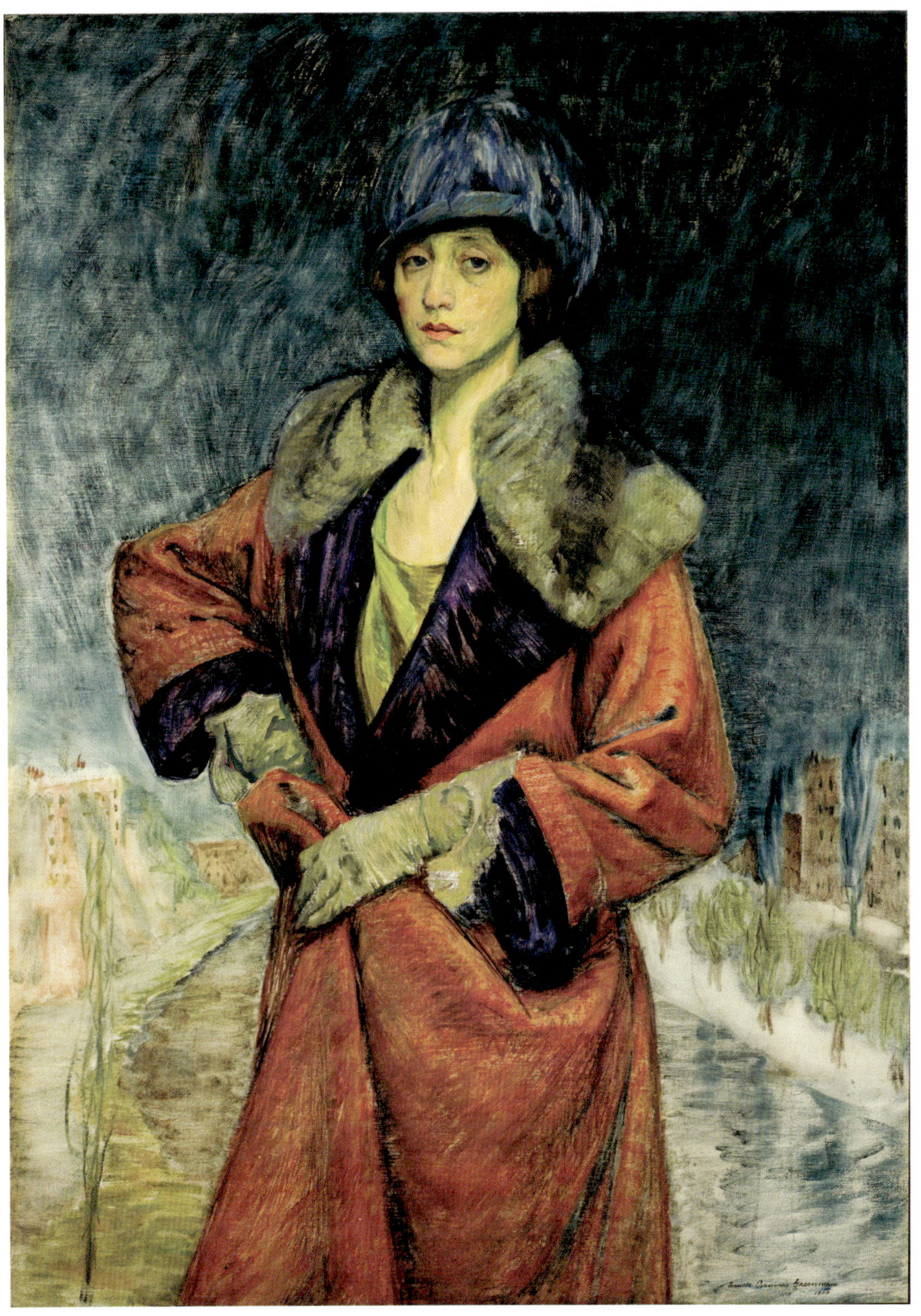

Frances Cranmer Greenman, *Self-Portrait*, 1923.

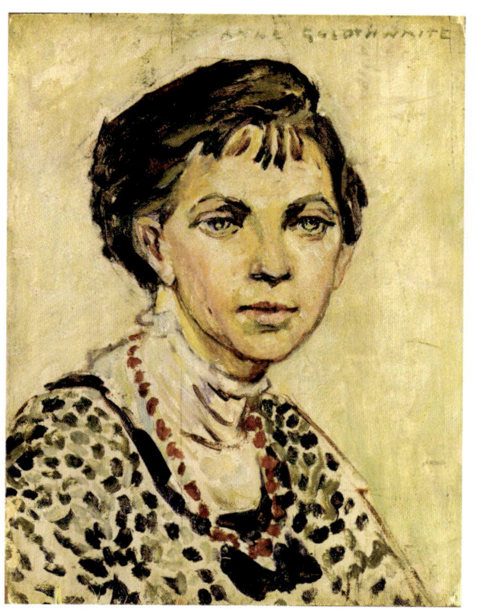

Anne Goldthwaite, *Self-Portrait*,
ca. 1906–1913.

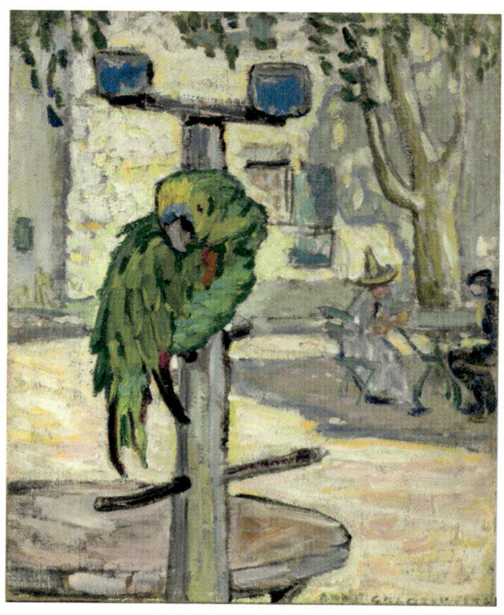

Anne Goldthwaite,
The Green Parrot, ca. 1910.

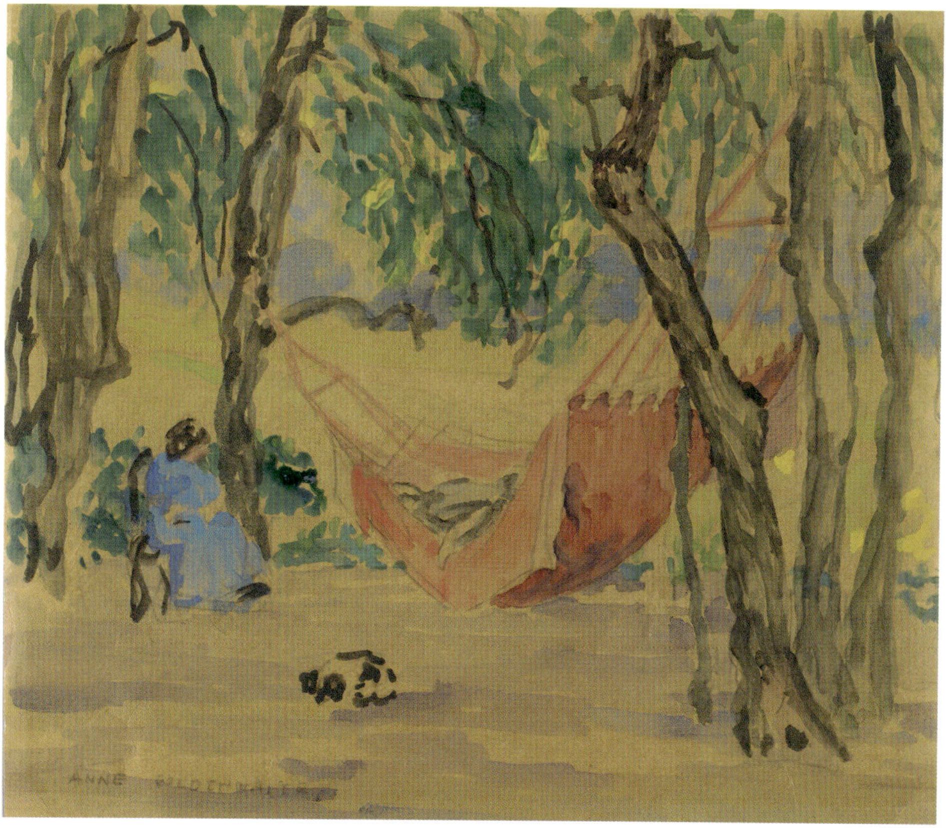

Anne Goldthwaite, *The Red Hammock*, 1913.

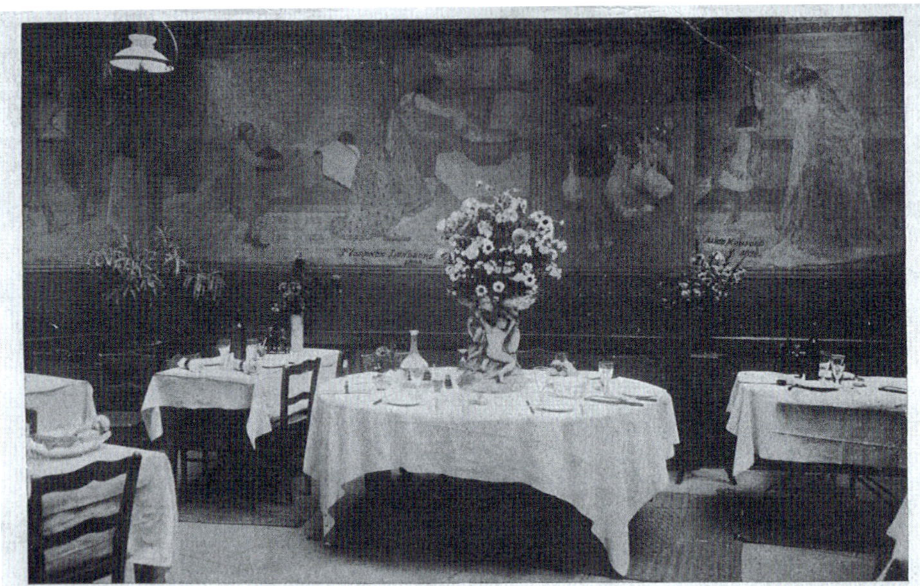

"Crémerie-Restaurant HENRIETTE," undated, postcard. Lundborg and Mumford's names are visible on the murals on either side of the central table.

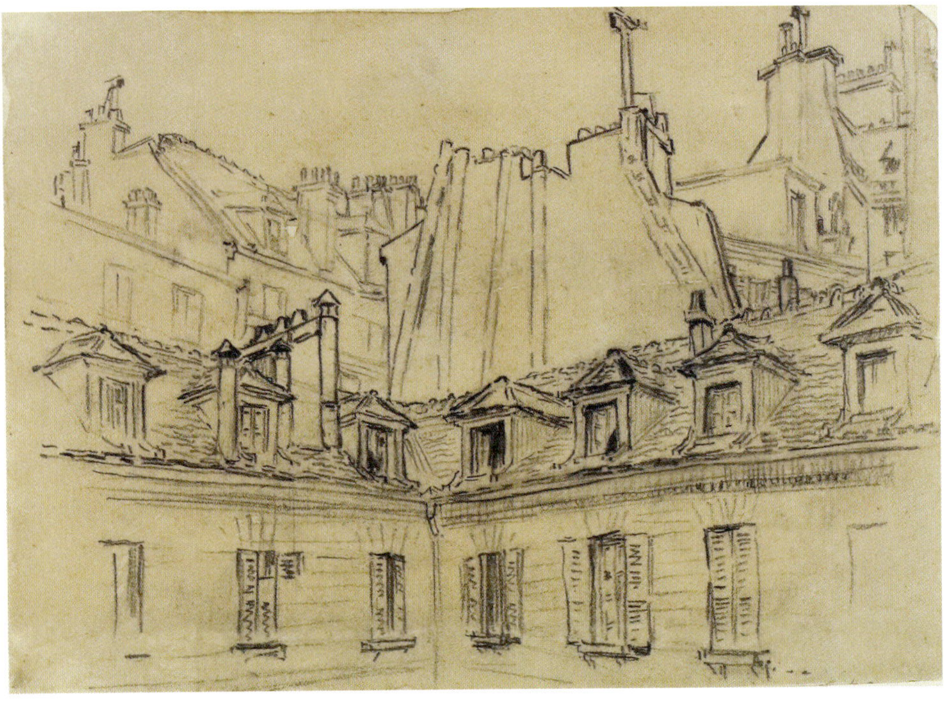

Julia Morgan, *Rooftop of 4 rue de Chevreuse*, undated.

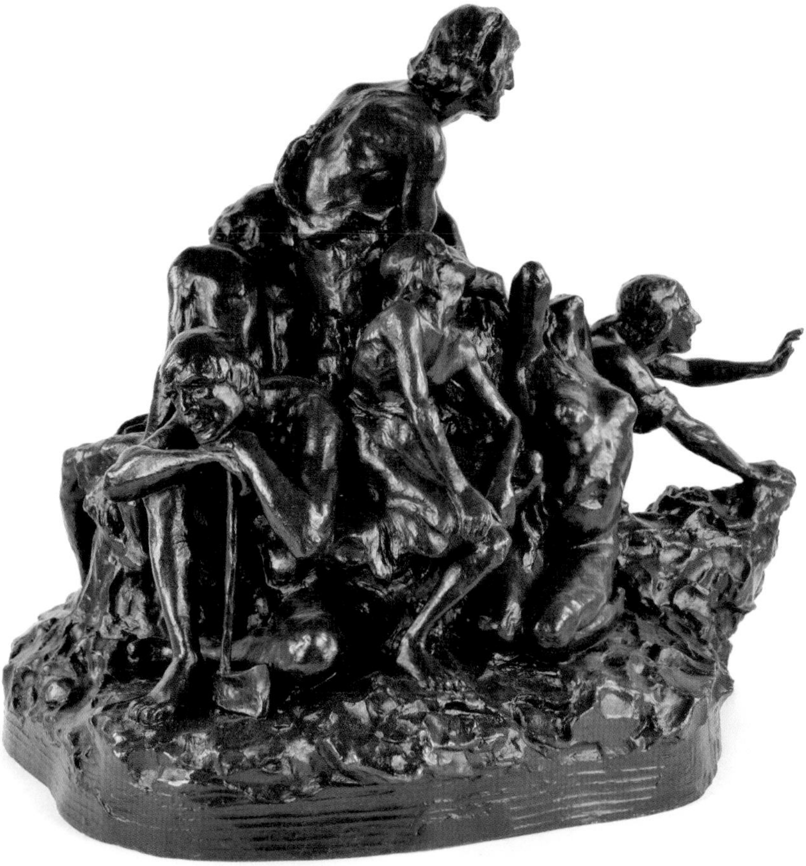

Meta Vaux Warrick, *The Wretched*, 1902.

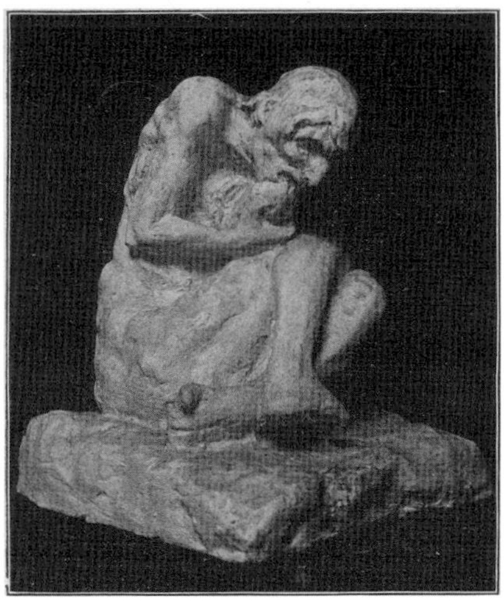

Meta Vaux Warrick, *Man Eating His Heart*, undated.

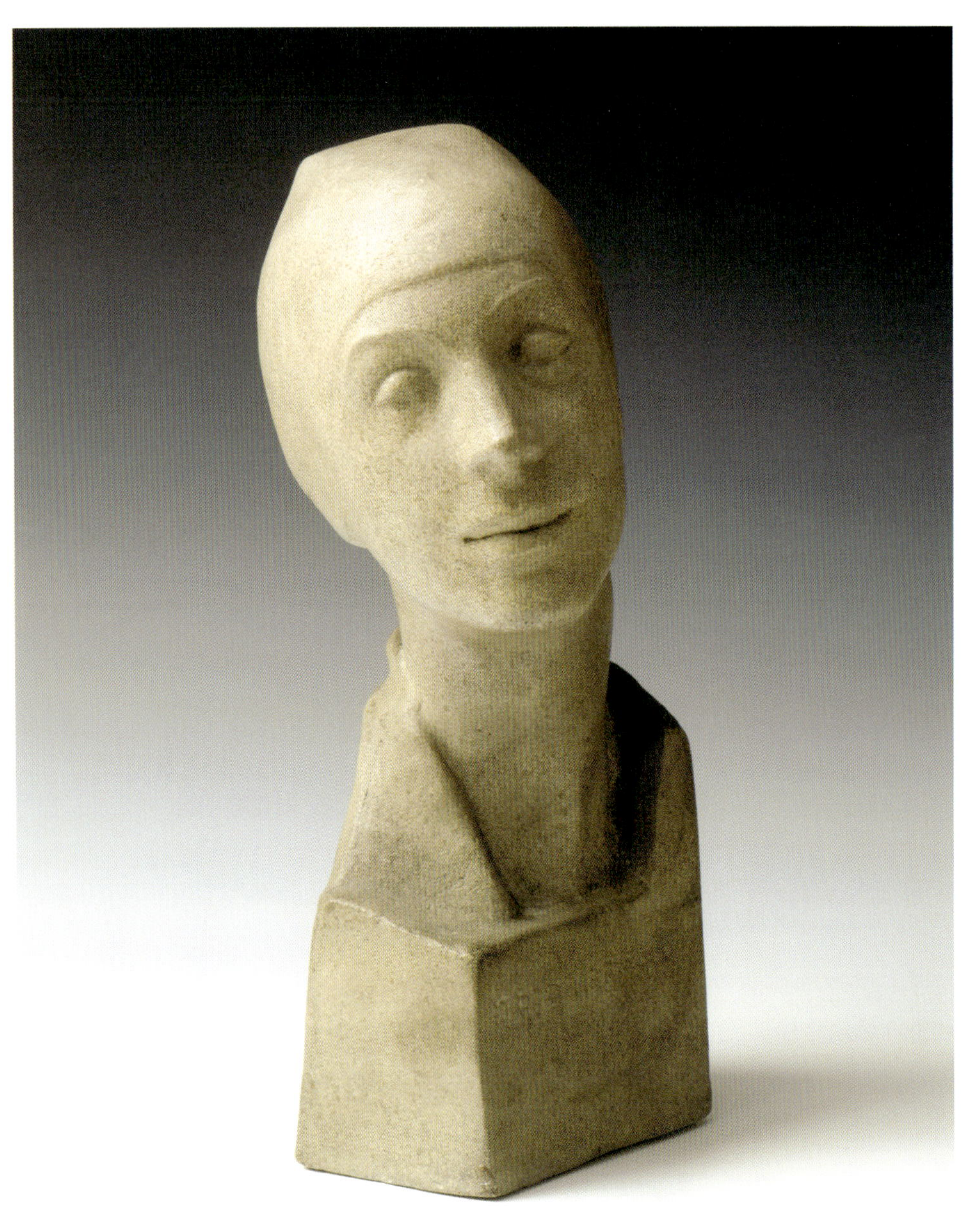

Alice Morgan Wright, *Emmeline Pankhurst*, 1912.

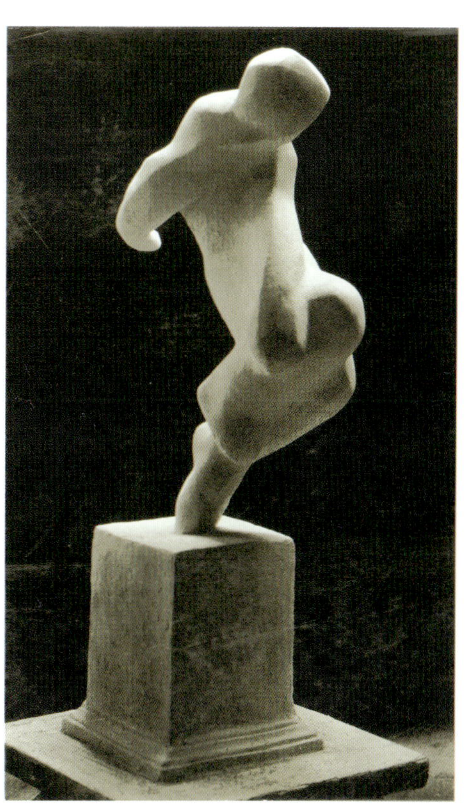

Alice Morgan Wright, *Wind Figure*, ca. 1916.

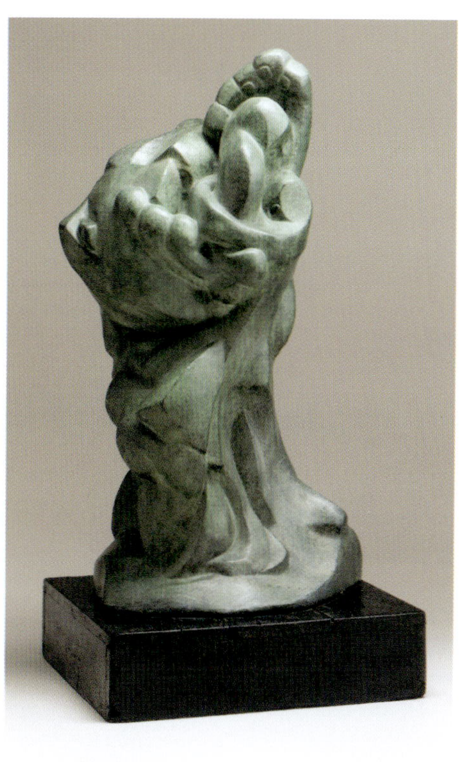

Alice Morgan Wright, *The Fist*, ca. 1921.

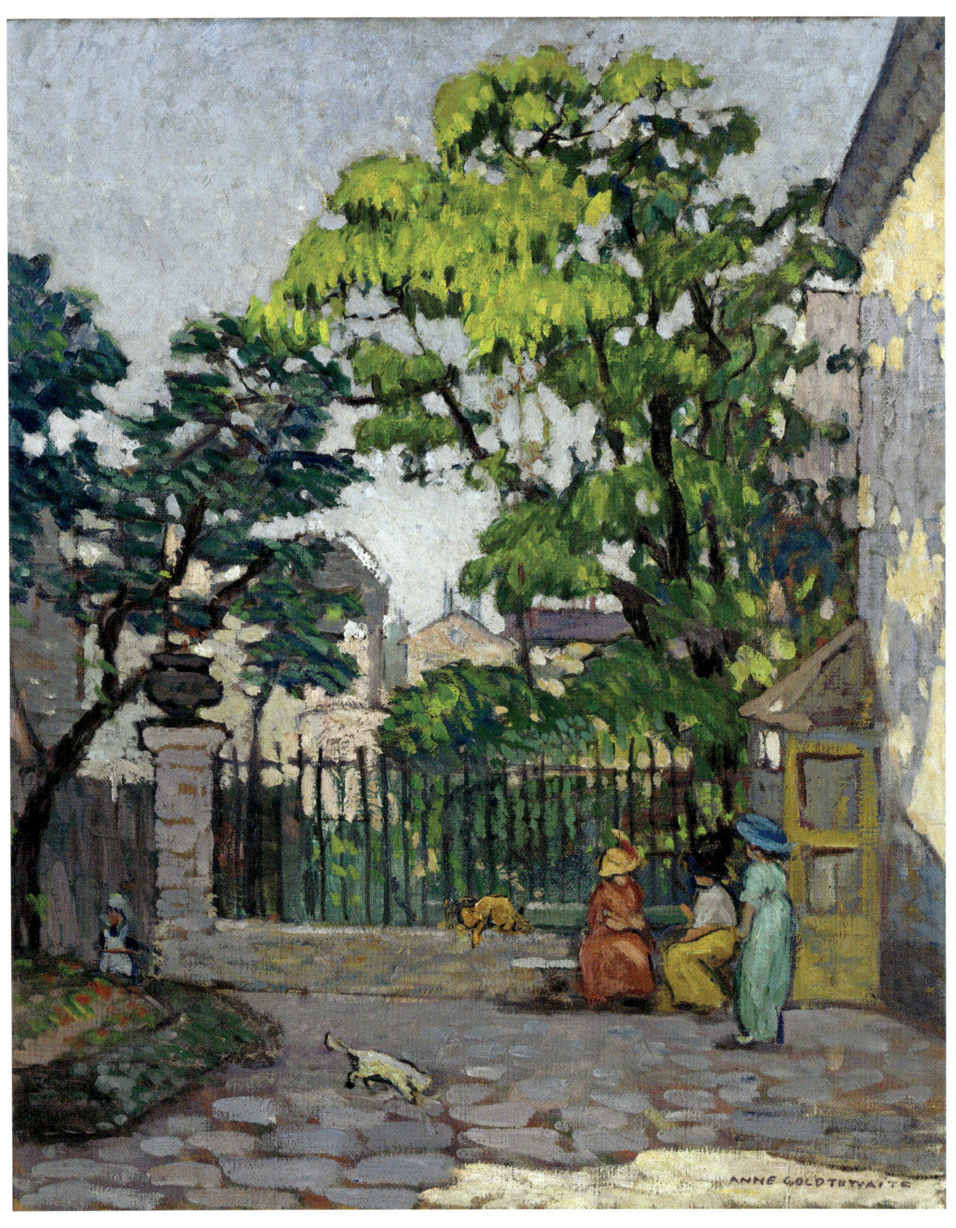

Anne Goldthwaite, *4 Rue de Chevreuse, Paris*, 1908.

Girls' Club was a known entity, and an admired one at that. For Goldthwaite, a young woman from a respected Southern family, the Club's cachet would have assuaged any lingering doubt in the minds of friends and family (and perhaps in herself, too). Just as importantly, though, was the Club's built-in community, a sure draw for the artist, who gravitated toward group settings—especially like-minded, educational ones—throughout her life.

Of the friends that Goldthwaite made during those first few days at the Club, one would play a most fortuitous role: the Arkansas-born painter Frances Thomason (1866–1939). Though Goldthwaite declared that "[t]he club was full of very interesting young women," she took an immediate shine to Thomason, a fellow Southerner.[9] She surely felt secure in the company of an older woman (by three years!) of a similar cultural and geographical background, and one whose artistic reputation had been established in Paris for several years—Thomason was an *arrivée*, as Goldthwaite noted,[10] confirming that she had "made it" in the art world. Thomason was a constant figure in the Parisian art world, showing in multiple iterations of the Salon des beaux-arts and the annual AWAA exhibition, among other art events. Her work was similarly lauded back home in the States, with Thomason having won a coveted bronze medal at the St. Louis World's Fair in 1904.[11] So when Thomason offered to act as Goldthwaite's personal guide to Paris, Goldthwaite assented gratefully. "Artists are very good to young students and Miss Thomason took me under her wing to show me the ways of Paris," she stated.[12]

Only six days after Goldthwaite's arrival, Thomason introduced her to one of the most popular sketching sites in all of Paris: the Jardin du Luxembourg. Designed in the early seventeenth century at the request of Marie de' Medici, the widow of King Henry IV, the Luxembourg Garden—the sixty-acre outdoor space abutting the Luxembourg Palace—has been a haven for Parisians and tourists alike since its inauguration. Filled with a delightful array of fountains, sculptures, and amenities, the Luxembourg was in Anne's day (and is now) a popular escape within the city. For artists, it was especially nice as a free option to study and sketch classically inspired statuary—why pay to visit the

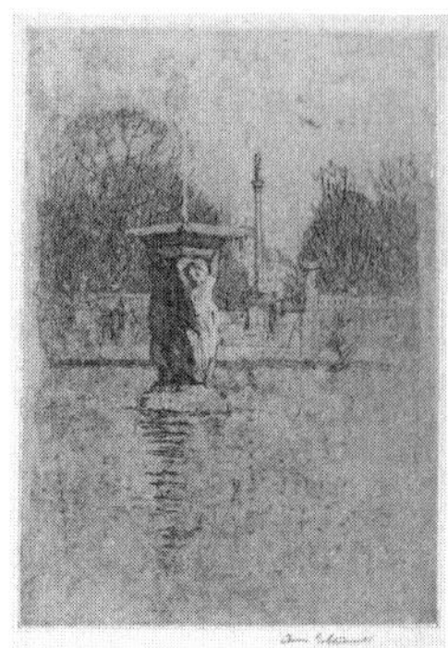

Figure 15.2. *Anne Goldthwaite,* Luxembourg Fountain (No. 2)*, about 1908. Montgomery Museum of Fine Arts.*

sculpture galleries of the Louvre when you could derive equal inspiration from *le jardin*?

Grabbing her sketching pad and pencils, Goldthwaite followed Thomason out of the double doors of the American Girls' Club, walking less than half a mile northeast to the garden's entrance on the rue Auguste Comte. What should have been an ordinary day for her—watching little boys sailing toy boats across the garden's central pond, eavesdropping on the chatter of pedestrians milling about, and reproducing each and every sight with pencil and paper—proved to be anything but. Goldthwaite may not have immediately noticed Thomason standing up and setting her art supplies aside to greet a nearby friend, but when she did, she glimpsed an arresting figure, one who she would vibrantly recall decades later:

> [Thomason] called me over to meet a large, dark woman with whom she was talking and who looked something like an immense dark brown egg. She wore, wrapped tight around her, a brown kimona-like garment and a large flat black hat, and stood on feet covered with wide sandals.[13]

At first glance, Goldthwaite worried that their visitor was indigent, because when the "egg woman" invited them back to her home for tea, Goldthwaite "wondered whether we ought to accept the invitation, whether she could afford to divide her tea with us."[14] Skeptical but following Frances Thomason's lead—and surely wanting to accept the invitation with Southern *politesse*—Goldthwaite exited the garden and ambled due west with her comrades.

She need not have been concerned, however, with the financial status of her new acquaintance. Though not at the same level as a Rockefeller or a Vanderbilt, she was wealthy enough. This American, it turned out, was none other than the famed expat and writer Gertrude Stein.

Upon arrival at Stein's apartment at 27 rue de Fleurus, which Stein shared with her commanding older brother, the art critic Leo Stein, Goldthwaite was taken aback by the sheer beauty of the elegant furnishings and *objets d'art*, especially the Steins' antique Italian furniture. But what really drew her attention was the art adorning every wall—or at least Anne Goldthwaite *thought* she was looking at works of art. "I knew they must be pictures because they were framed and hanging on the walls," she joked years later.[15] These pictures, though, were unlike anything Goldthwaite had yet seen.

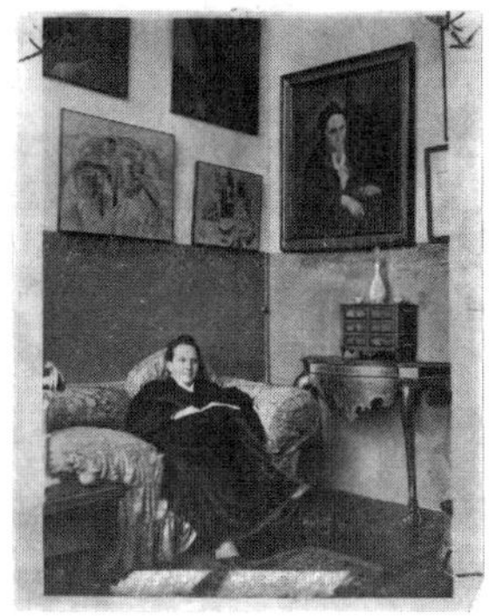

Figure 15.3. *Gertrude Stein at 27 rue des Fleurus, undated. Library of Congress.*

Ever since settling in Paris in 1903, Gertrude and Leo Stein had worked tirelessly to build a collection of art. Their brother Michael, also based in Paris and a great collector in his own right, introduced them to artists and art dealers, including the famed Ambroise Vollard, who sold works by various Impressionist and Postimpressionist artists, like Paul Cézanne, Pierre-Auguste Renoir, Paul Gauguin, and Vincent van Gogh.[16] Vollard also represented some up-and-coming contemporary artists from France and beyond, many of whom were pushing the boundaries of painting. These artists were playing with unnatural colors, toying with abstraction, and jarring viewers with bold outlines and geometric figuration that seemed miles away from their classical brethren ensconced down the road in the Musée du Louvre.

All the Steins—Gertrude, Leo, Michael, and Michael's wife, Sarah— loved the look of these shocking, avant-garde works. Gertrude and Leo, though, especially loved how *inexpensive* they were. Though a family trust provided the siblings with enough cash to maintain their living expenses, not much remained for the purchase of truly priceless works of art, like the Old Master paintings they originally coveted, or even the output of the once revolutionary but now widely accepted Impressionists. And anyway, newer typically meant *cheaper*, so their wallets dictated their earliest purchases. (Vollard later mused nostalgically about them, saying, "The Steins were [my] only clients who collected paintings not because they were rich, but despite the fact that they weren't."[17]) With economy and equally keen eyes, the Steins began amassing a now-legendary art collection, one they delighted in sharing with friends and strangers alike.

Standing in the parlor of 27 rue de Fleurus,[18] Anne Goldthwaite was flummoxed by the art around her, and Gertrude Stein noticed. With a sly grin, Stein asked for Goldthwaite's opinion on her collection. To her credit, Goldthwaite could tell that she was being played: "I knew they were stringing me," she later recalled, "and [I] answered that in that light I could not very well judge them."[19] Nevertheless, Stein would not let the matter slide—perhaps it was simply a matter of point of view?—and she suggested that Goldthwaite climb upon Stein's dining table to better see the paintings. Straightening her staid gray suit, Goldthwaite scrambled up onto the tabletop, and as she paced back and forth over the length of it, she goggled at the works:

> I need not describe the paintings as we have all seen them many times since then. There was what I now know was a head by Picasso, looking like a design made of the backbones of fish; "Le Joie de Vivre," by Matisse; a small grey canvas by Cezanne, and a yellow nude on a peach-colored background, the feet hanging down as in an ascension. It was the only painting whose authorship I do not know. It must have been the one mistake made by Leo and Gertrude Stein![20]

Goldthwaite was saved from sharing her opinions by the arrival of the women's tea, prepared by the concierge of Stein's apartment building. In her unpublished memoir, Goldthwaite, self-effacing and too modest, declared that her company was "probably not . . . interested in my callow opinion" of the art.[21] And yet the act of recalling this moment decades later attests to the strong effect that Stein's collection had on her. "That was my introduction to l'art moderne," she declared with a still-palpable sense of wonder.[22]

Goldthwaite's unexpected visit to the Steins' apartment inspired not only awe, but a fascination to uncover even more about *l'art moderne*—what was it? What could it become? And did Goldthwaite even *like* it? Such curiosity led her to make repeated visits to the Steins' salon and to adopt a new level of experimentation in her own artwork. But it brought frustrations, too, unsettling her classically trained footing and establishing what would become a long-standing personal struggle between traditionalism and modernism. Before she knew it, Goldthwaite was in a bit of a bind: should she play it safe, or should she go modern? The question dogged her ceaselessly, and she frequently replayed that formative

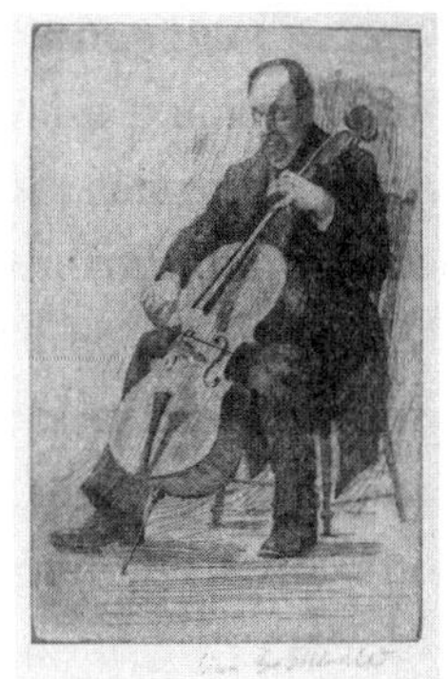

Figure 15.4. *Anne Goldthwaite,* The Cellist—A School Study, *about 1901. Montgomery Museum of Fine Arts.*

moment at Gertrude Stein's home for the remainder of her life. "I wonder if Matisse and Picasso would exist as the artists we now know had it not been for the Steins," Goldthwaite mused.[23] But we may very well ask the same question of Goldthwaite, too, as that fateful afternoon in 1906 may have shaped her own future.

IF HER ARTWORK itself is any indication, Anne Goldthwaite struggled mightily to find her truest artistic style. Her introduction to Picasso, Matisse, Cézanne, and other modernists associated with the Steins shook her academic core. While never photo-perfect in her realism, early graphic works like *The Cellist—A School Study* (ca. 1901, Montgomery Museum of Fine Arts) and *The Potter* (ca. 1902, Montgomery Museum of Fine Arts) retained an interest in representing the "realness" of a figure, as Goldthwaite provided her subjects with the necessary shadowing and foreshortening to suggest depth and weight. Her cellist, for example, is an image of a living person based on direct study, and that realism comes across in her final etching. Not long after her arrival in Paris, however, Goldthwaite's style transitioned to something far looser, suggesting work completed with speed and confidence. Though still representational—and not removed from realism in the same way that a proto-Cubist Picasso portrait would be—Goldthwaite inched ever closer to abstraction with works like *Une Parisienne (No. 1)* (ca. 1912, Montgomery Museum of Fine Arts), which are little more than line drawings of character types rather than portraits of individuals. To go abstract or to stay a realist? This proved to be Goldthwaite's recurring line of questioning.

It is a line of questioning, too, that Goldthwaite's years in Paris bear out. While living at the Girls' Club, she learned of the variety of art schools and private ateliers that her fellow artists attended. During her years in Paris, she bounced between instructors and institutions, seeking, like Goldilocks—or perhaps Goldthwaite's Club precursor, Anna Lester—anything that was *just right* for her. One imagines the artist, her green eyes sparkling with determination, traipsing all around the Latin Quarter in search of the perfect art school. For all we know, Anne Goldthwaite considered each and every choice. What is certain is that she found all of them wanting. She needed another option.

Goldthwaite's memoir, which is spotty at best, lacks many of the major details of her life, and with the exception of her memorable first meeting with Gertrude Stein, her Paris years are neglected entirely (the typescript of her recollections, in the Archives of American Art, skips directly from her tea with Stein and Thomason to 1916, when she resurfaces stateside without fanfare after nearly a decade as an expatriate). What later biographers, such as the historian Adelyn Breeskin, discovered about Anne Goldthwaite during her Parisian stint was her inclination toward leadership. Frustrated with the educational opportunities available to her in Paris—why weren't any of the schools teaching about *l'art moderne*, about the latest styles and methods?—Goldthwaite corralled several compatriots to take things into their own hands. Alongside her lifelong friend the artist (and later, a prominent art conservator) David Rosen,[24] she formed the Académie Moderne.

Scant details survive about the Académie Moderne. Its lack of well-known students and instructors, its independence from the larger art schools, and the disruption of World War One may be contributing factors to its diminished memory.[25] Regardless, what little we do know about the formation of the Académie Moderne is a testament to Goldthwaite's collaborative spirit and drive. The members of the Académie—including a fellow Club member, Ellen Graham Anderson (1885–1970)—gathered at 86 rue Notre-Dame des Champs for their informal classes, with occasional critiques provided by a handful of rotating instructors, particularly Charles Guérin, a student of the Symbolist painter Gustave Moreau and an acolyte of Paul Cézanne.[26] Together, the Académie held a group art exhibition each spring, decamped to the French countryside on sketching exhibitions in the summer, and even presented a selection of their works at the important Salon d'automne, the annual exposition of art that many considered a more experimental and exciting showcase than the more conservative Salon(s) (and where Matisse enjoyed his breakout appearance in 1905). In the catalogue for the 1912 Salon d'automne, Anne Goldthwaite is listed as showing four works.[27] It would not be the last time that she would be included in a major modern art exhibition.

Still, Goldthwaite was not a *fully* modernist painter (and one wonders if she accepted the Académie Moderne's name ironically). She eschewed garish colors and still relied upon the use of linear perspective in her paintings, etchings, and drawings. (One critic praised this aspect of Goldthwaite's works, noting in 1929, "The love of ugliness has failed to touch her, the weight of massive form has not enticed her, nor has she denied normal anatomy in the effort to emphasize freedom from representational taint."[28] Modernism, it must be noted, was not universally loved by the American press.) As such, it is not surprising to learn that her works were accepted at least twice for the somewhat stodgy Salon des artistes français.[29] She also participated in the Salon des beaux-arts, between 1911 and 1914. She fit thusly into both environments, finding admirers within the conventional realms as well as the more innovative ones.

ANNE GOLDTHWAITE'S FINAL year in Paris, 1913, might have been one of her best professional periods. In January, she participated in a small group exhibition at Galerie Max Rodrigues alongside Aline S. Bridge and David Atherton-Smith, British painters who would later marry; in a small note in the Parisian paper *Gil Blas*, Goldthwaite's works—called "interesting etchings"—were praised above the paintings of her fellow exhibitors.[30] Her paintings, too, captured attention: only one month later, in February, she once again participated in the AWAA's annual exhibition at the American Girls' Club, where she was among the four winners who shared the top prize of 1,000 francs offered by Elisabeth Mills Reid herself in celebration of the best painting. Though surviving news reports do not indicate the exact painting that secured Goldthwaite's award—she showed "six excellent portrait sketches," the *New York Herald* notes—it may very well have been a portrait of the eminent Harvard law professor George Grafton Wilson, who acted as an exchange professor in Paris for the academic year of 1912–13.[31] Not only would this portrait of Wilson have exhibited Goldthwaite's winning style and technique, but its subject also suggests the artist's connection to the ever-growing American Colony, a wise business move on her part; portraits often begat portraits, after all, as patrons recommended their preferred artists to friends and family.

Awards, honors, and showings at the official Salon and beyond—all of this was wonderful, but 1913 provided an even bigger coup for Anne Goldthwaite. In February—the same month as her award-winning placement in the AWAA's annual exhibition—two of her paintings, *The House on the Hill* (Fig. 15.5) and *Prince's Feathers*,[32] had been accepted for a group exhibition in New York City.[33] For one month from February 17, 1913, to March 15, 1913, Goldthwaite enjoyed visibility as one of around three hundred artists presented in the International Exhibition of Modern Art, held at the 69th Regiment Armory on Lexington Avenue. Though most likely still in Paris and thus unable to experience the exhibition personally,[34] Goldthwaite would have been keen to follow the press about what would be deemed "the Armory Show." Thanks to the well-stocked reading room and library at the American Girls' Club, she could easily do so, curling up in a chair next to the library's fireplace to peruse reviews from the *New York Times* and beyond (the *Times*'s February 17, 1913, article called the show "great," and noted that "no one within reach of it can afford to ignore it").[35]

By no means could Goldthwaite have known the eventual cultural significance of the Armory Show; with the retrospection of a century, historians have pinpointed it as the singular introduction of modernism and avant-garde art in the United States. Some of the twentieth century's most lauded artists made their American debut at the exhi-

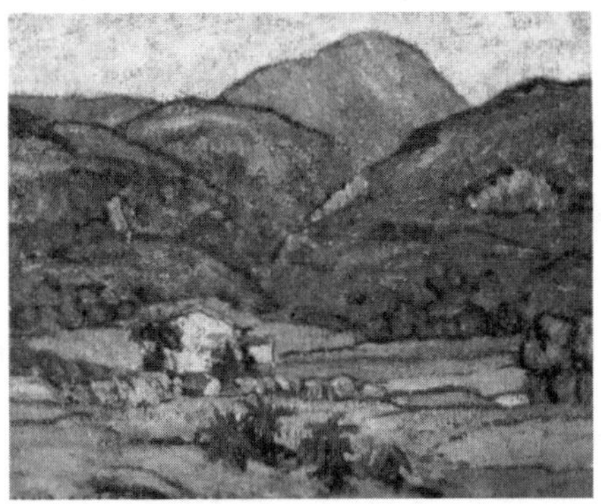

Figure 15.5. *Anne Goldthwaite,* The House on the Hill, *ca. 1910/1911. Blount International Corporate Art Collection.*

bition, including Pablo Picasso, Henri Matisse, Constantin Brâncuşi, Marcel Duchamp, and Wassily Kandinsky; many of their Impressionist and Postimpressionist forebears, like Claude Monet, Mary Cassatt, Edgar Degas, and Vincent van Gogh, were displayed, too. Goldthwaite was one of fifty women[36] chosen for the watershed exhibition, a telltale sign that hers was considered among the best artworks in the Western world, and she would have been rewarded with a record-setting viewership: more than 87,000 visitors attended the hallmark exhibition.[37]

What is funny about Goldthwaite's inclusion in the Armory Show is that it further emphasizes her own ambivalence about modernism. Several journalists, after viewing her 1910/1911 oil painting *The House on the Hill* (also known as *Church on the Hill*),[38] described its kinship to the works of Paul Cézanne. "[I]n the freedom of her outlines, the directness of her touch, and the simplicity of her paint, certainly there is more than an indication that she is a post-Cézanne," one critic commented in 1916.[39] This makes sense when considering that Charles Guérin, one of the Académie Moderne's itinerant instructors, espoused Cézanne's working style; indeed, *The House on the Hill* presents mountainous surroundings with the same golden-green tones and a flatness that recalls many of Cézanne's works in his *Mont Sainte-Victoire* series. Goldthwaite thus may have absorbed some of Cézanne's tenets indirectly. And yet even as one of the three hundred artists accepted into one of the most important modern art exhibitions, she nevertheless balked at the description of her own works as modern, later declaring, "I never got over being surprised each time it happened."[40] Truthfully, Goldthwaite's works have little in common with the Armory's most avant-garde, shocking inclusions, such as Duchamp's infamous *Nude Descending a Staircase, No. 2* (1912, Philadelphia Museum of Art). But within a wider definition of modernism, Goldthwaite assented that she might be included. "I knew I was painting, not according to any school, but according to the way I saw my subject," she concluded. "Perhaps I was modern, but if it were true, I was so innately and not by conscious effort."[41]

ANNE GOLDTHWAITE'S RESIDENCY at the American Girls' Club in Paris coincided with a marked period of self-discovery and self-determination, of taking risks with her artistic direction—and she was rewarded for it with honors and inclusions in significant exhibitions like the Armory Show. As it had done for so many others before—like Alice Rumph, Florence Lundborg, and Anna Lester—the Club provided the perfect home base for Goldthwaite's exploration, a reliable place to land while venturing into uncharted creative territory.

Not that the American Girls' Club provided Goldthwaite with *only* good things. In at least one mildly humorous case, the artist's connection to the Club lost her a profitable award. In mid-1913, not long before her return to the United States, Goldthwaite submitted a portrait (unknown today) to a "concours" held at the Student Hostel (*Foyer international des étudiantes*), the rival association founded by American philanthropist Grace Whitney Hoff for the similar purpose of housing female students. Hoff offered a 1,000-franc award to the best work exhibited at her hostel's exhibition, to be granted by a jury of highly esteemed French artists. The only stipulations Hoff made were that the winning work should stem from an "international woman painter resident in Paris," and that the chosen piece would be retained for the hostel's own collection.[42]

It might not be a surprise to us that Anne Goldthwaite, among the most talented Americans in Paris during her tenure, won this award by a unanimous vote. But for Hoff, it was a travesty. After all, how could the jury *possibly* select a winner affiliated with a competing girls' home (and one with a glowing reputation, compared with the Student Hostel's less beloved one[43])? *Quelle horreur!* Bitterly, Hoff denied Goldthwaite the award, claiming that the winning portrait was too small—at eighteen by twenty-two inches—to be worthy of the 1,000-franc honor, and she thus bestowed the prize upon an artist of her own choosing, who subsequently refused it.[44] The whole event, fascinatingly, made international news and was highlighted in the *New York Times*, with the unnamed author siding strongly with Goldthwaite and the jury and blithely commenting upon the scandal, "It is really doubtful if the Hostel can survive it, and its expositions are, it is said, surely doomed."[45]

Though it was unfair that Anne Goldthwaite was thwarted of her deserved prize, the melee highlights the communal support of the American Girls' Club in Paris above other similar institutions, as well as Goldthwaite's undisputed tie to the Club. It was the quiet center of her world and Goldthwaite was the first to admit it, noting in a handwritten draft of her unpublished memoir that "I was content that it [the Club] should be so, though many of my friends thought that they were not 'living' unless they ate at the Chat Noir on the Rue Odessa, or at least Boudet's Le Duc's."[46] To some, like Goldthwaite's unnamed friends, living at the Girls' Club was unglamorous, a stopgap until more suitable housing could be found (Goldthwaite herself, for at least one point in her sojourn, left the Club in favor of a small studio elsewhere; her address is listed as "216 Boulevard Raspail," in the catalogue for the 1909 Salon, a three-minute walk southwest from the Club[47]). Goldthwaite, though, adored the Club, and wrote lovingly about her time there:

> [I]t was not a club at all, but a glorified *pension* for American women art students . . . The tiled floors and the mansard windows added a zest to the warmth of the living rooms . . . [and there was] so much splendor of living that everyone desired an entrée to the Club . . .[48]

It is no wonder, then, that several of her most enticing creations from her Parisian period portray the Club directly or may have been staged

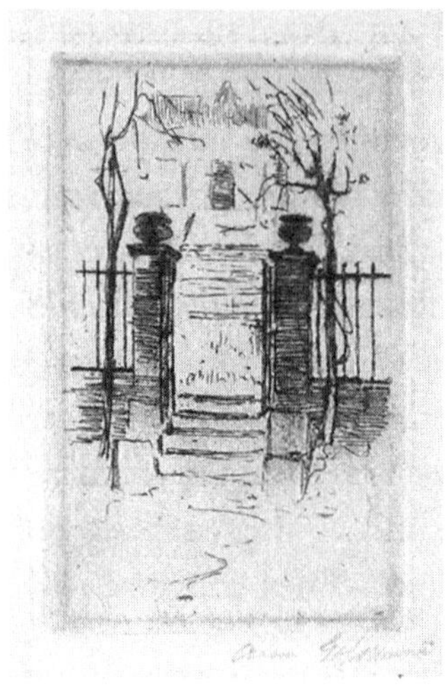

Figure 15.6. *Anne Goldthwaite, Gate at 3 Rue de Chevreuse, about 1907, Montgomery Museum of Fine Arts.*

within its environs. An oil painting, *The Green Parrot* (ca. 1910, Greenville County Museum of Art), showcases the brightly plumed bird of the title seated upon a stand and glancing almost coyly at the viewer. Though the parrot is the undisputed star of the canvas, Goldthwaite takes pains to elaborate the background of her scene. With short, rapidly applied brushstrokes, she conjures a shaded courtyard with rounded tables; one, to the right, features two women in conversation, potentially over cups of steaming tea. This work, along with a delicate watercolor, *The Red Hammock* (1912, Greenville County Museum of Art), might represent the relaxed, intimate atmosphere of the Club, featuring its residents or visitors in much-deserved repose.[49]

In what is quite possibly her most beautiful painting, Anne Goldthwaite does not hint at the Club—she celebrates it wholeheartedly. Her oil painting *4 Rue de Chevreuse, Paris* (1908 [Fig. 15.7]), now in the collection of the Whitney Museum of American Art in New York, is a loving depiction of the inner courtyard of the American Girls' Club, presented as a vision of idyllic student life. Three women, wearing dresses in bright pops of coral, ocher, and teal, and accessorized with attention-grabbing hats, converse in front of the Club's wrought iron gates. Two stray cats scramble through the gate and across the cobblestones; the late afternoon sun on the brushy green trees throws shadows across the stone wall at the right. A fourth figure—a servant in a pinafore—approaches the central garden on the left side. If Goldthwaite ever produced a canvas more dedicated to "the splendor of living" that she experienced at the Club and joyfully recounted in her memoir, it has yet to come to light. In the artist's adept hands, the Club is rendered as the refuge that Elisabeth Mills Reid had dreamed it would be, and that, for Anne, it truly was.

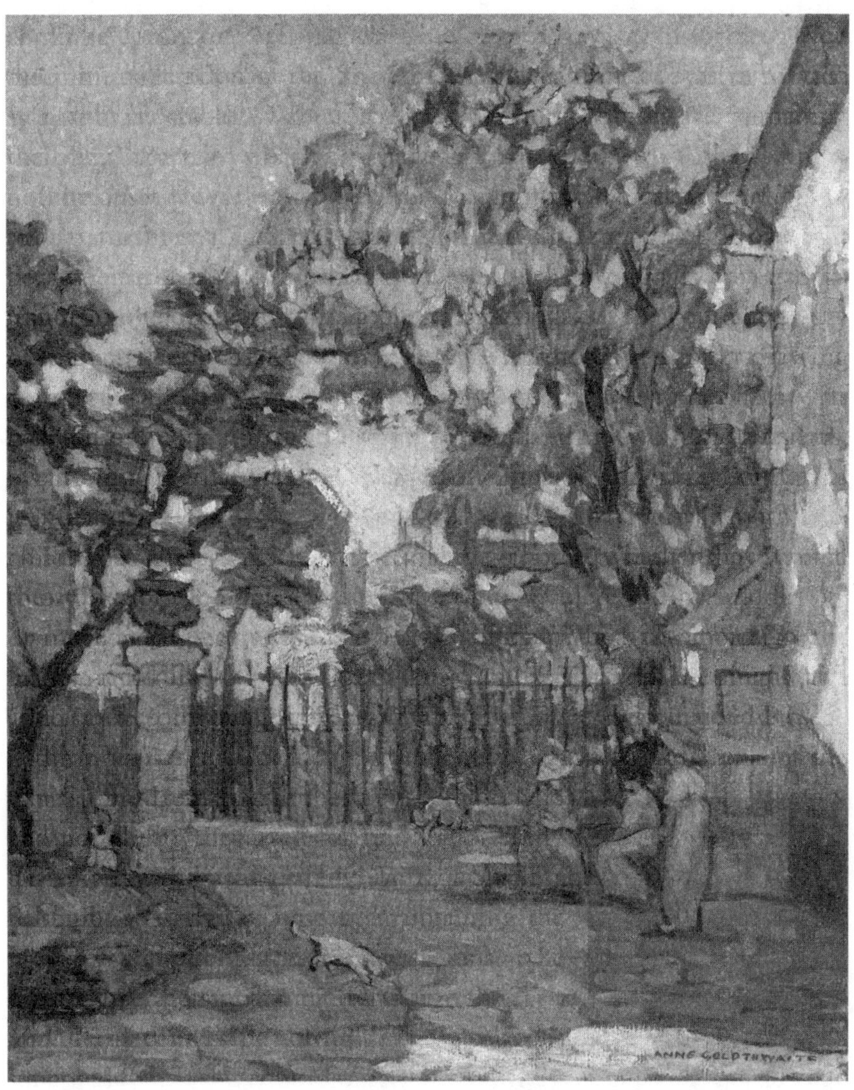

Figure 15.7. *Anne Goldthwaite, 4 Rue de Chevreuse, Paris, 1908. Whitney Museum of American Art.*

Sculpture or Suffrage, or Alice Morgan Goes to Jail

*The proposal of either Sculpture or Suffrage . . . in all my
recollections the two are so involved with each other that
I think I shall not be able to extricate them.*

—Alice Morgan Wright, "Sculpture and Suffrage,"
New York State Business & Professional Women (1947)[1]

Alice Morgan Wright was not one to take "no" for an answer. She would likely be polite to whoever stood in her way, yes, but she would quickly find her own way around any proscriptions in her path. She was nothing if not dedicated to, and passionate about, her goals.

Take, for example, a defining moment in her early art education. While studying at the Art Students League in New York City around 1907 or 1908, Wright—as a woman—was forbidden to participate in life-drawing classes that featured male models. She was angry, naturally—she needed the experience of drawing male anatomy to create realistic pieces!—but more importantly, she was tenacious and resourceful. She would find a way around such silly restrictions.

Within days of her repudiation at the League, a determined Wright began haunting downtown amusement halls that were considered unusual—if not outright uncouth—destinations for a woman from a much-respected, upperclass family. She soon became a regular at athletic clubs (some legal, some not) around the city, taking in dozens of boxing and wrestling matches.[2] Positioned in a seat on the edge of the boxing ring, Wright must have made a peculiar sight, as she was surely one of only a handful of women in the environment—but stranger, too, because she focused little on score-keeping or even the outcome of the bout.

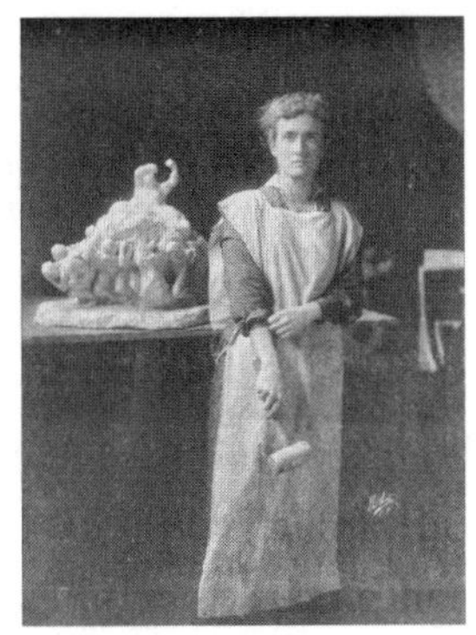

Figure 16.1. *Alice Morgan Wright in her Paris Studio, ca. 1910. Alice Morgan Wright Papers, Smith College.*

Instead, she studied furrowed brows, straining abdominal muscles, and sweat-slicked biceps, reproducing them in her sketchpad with quick flicks of pencil and charcoal. So what if she couldn't join life classes at the League? She could get a similar education from the barechested athletes in her midst instead.

This tenacity led to good things: during her brief artistic career, Alice Morgan Wright became one of the most interesting American sculptors of her time, and her understanding of the human body paid off in her traditional, classically inspired sculptures as well as her modern, abstracted ones.

That same tenacity also nearly derailed her career, stranding her almost 220 miles away from the Club.

ALICE MORGAN WRIGHT'S curiosity and *joie de vivre* revealed itself in her early years. As the only child born, in 1881, to a wealthy Albany family, she was raised to be an independent and free-thinking young woman, though her autonomy and tomboyishness occasionally begat headaches in her household. She recalled how easily she irked her father, Henry Romeyn Wright, an astute wholesale merchant and lifelong

Republican, by engaging in fiery political debates around the dinner table. Henry Wright's political intractability—particularly regarding women's rights—stoked embers of righteousness in his preteen daughter:

> [P]olitical argument was wont to arise between my parents at table. The difference as I grasped it seemed to be that my father was a Republican and my mother a Democrat, so taking the side of the under-dog which I sensed my mother to be, since my father could vote and she could not, I stoutly proclaimed myself to be a Democrat too.[3]

It was only the first of little Alice's social justice actions, which would bloom most fully at the American Girls' Club two decades later.

Almost concurrent with her political enlightenment was her discovery of her enthusiasm for art. Sitting in the stately parlor of her home, Wright spent hours drawing portraits of the family's sleeping cats, the final sketches surprising the adults with their realism;[4] a nascent adoration of sculpture presented itself after she swiped a slab of paraffin (used for waxing hardwood floors) and wielded a jackknife to carve a pint-size figure of an elephant. Proudly displaying the newly minted creation on her living room mantel brought an immense sense of satisfaction, and she later confessed that, in that moment, she determined that she would become a sculptor.[5]

That dream took a brief back seat to a well-rounded education in the liberal arts, as best suited a young woman of her social class. In 1900, Wright entered Smith College in Northampton, Massachusetts, where she established herself as one of the most popular, fun-loving, and active students on campus (Elected to the Committee for Senior Dramatics! Editor of the student newspaper! Captain of the hockey team! Member of the physics, French, philosophical, *and* mandolin clubs—to provide just a selection).[6] For a time, she focused her ambitions primarily on writing, producing reinterpretations and parodies of classic plays for student performances. It was through poetry, though, that Wright expressed herself most freely and frequently; it would be a medium to which she would return repeatedly, even in the midst (or perhaps especially in the midst) of her most trying times. And she was good at it, too: several of her poems were later published in *Harper's*, *The Literary Digest*, and other outlets.[7] A Smith College–issued composition book hand-lettered with "VERSES by Alice Morgan Wright" is archived among her papers, a testament to poetry's continued importance throughout her life.[8]

After graduating Smith in 1904, Wright renewed her commitment to sculpture and settled in New York City to take courses at the Art Students League. From there, her artistic education clicked along in the now-typical manner of talented young students: she excelled under the tutelage of the League's various instructors and won acclaim at local art exhibitions. She distinguished herself in student competitions, too, winning a "general scholarship for best figure in modelling classes" in 1908; her fellow League attendee, Georgia O'Keeffe, was awarded the "general scholarship for still life painting" at the same event.[9]

By 1909, Wright had pursued her education as far as she could within the United States (and even a bit farther, as her unconventional sketching trips to boxing rings attest). If it was somewhat difficult for American women of this era to progress terribly far as painters, gaining prominence as a sculptor was even more complicated. Partially, this was due to unfair gender politics: sculpture had long been considered a determinately masculine medium. To wrangle an implacable material like marble or granite into any form was assumed to require not only brute strength, but also the willingness to get down and dirty with it—a truly unfeminine prospect (imagine all that dust emanating from a chisel!).[10] Because of these assumptions, American educators historically deterred women from following that course of study, though Wright opined, "No prejudice . . . seemed to exist against girls 'taking up' sculpture." Instructors, however, may have been apt to patronize their female sculpture students as trifling and unserious, as Wright continued: "Indeed it was more likely to inspire head-patting."[11]

Even finding appropriate instructors to mentor a budding sculptor was a challenge for a female artist, one made even more tedious by the fact that a significant coterie of the country's most respected sculptors

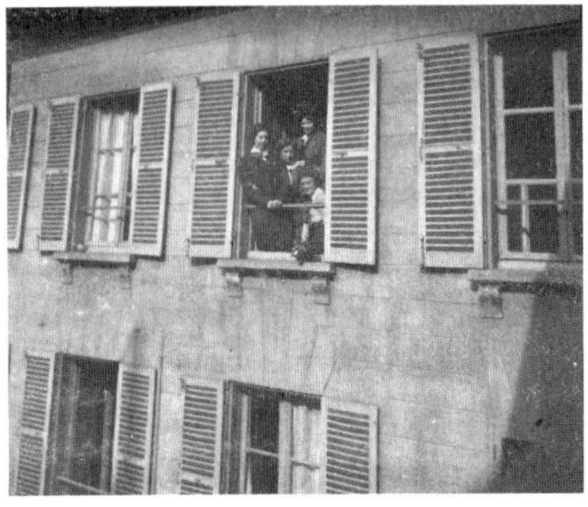

Figure 16.2. *Undated photograph of Alice Morgan Wright (seated, at right) and three women, most likely at the American Girls' Club in Paris. Alice Morgan Wright Papers, Smith College.*

of the era, like Augustus Saint-Gaudens, Frederick MacMonnies, and Daniel Chester French, had decamped to Europe. Alice Morgan Wright, then, made the logical choice: in September 1909—three years after Anne Goldthwaite—she, too, sailed to France. With the exception of the occasional trip back to Albany to visit family, she remained there until 1914.

UPON ARRIVAL IN Paris, Wright immediately secured lodging at the Girls' Club, choosing to live there for three of her five years abroad. Surviving letters suggest that Wright adored Club life and that she was one of its most vocal promoters to friends and family. She mailed postcards featuring charming photographs of its gardens ("Dear Mama, isn't this a nice picture of the club?"[12] [Fig. 6.1]), reserved rooms for them when the Club accepted female tourists in the summer months ("There are nothing but small rooms left . . . but we have nailed one on the same hall as mine, which I consider quite a coup"[13]), and convinced other artists to consider applying for lodging there. In truth, she had not expected to remain stationed at the rue de Chevreuse for so long, as she reported to a friend:

> I had no idea of staying at the club longer than was necessary to look up another abiding place . . . Well, having lived here awhile and comparing our circumstances with those of people we knew who had apartments, we came to the conclusion that we, living here, derived the maximum benefit with the minimum disadvantages obtainable in this part of Paris—and of course we prefer this quarter to all others . . . I don't wish to present the club to you as "<u>all</u> honey and all jam" which it ain't, but I do think that, to a

marvelous extent are eliminated for us there the discomforts which other people in the Quarter have to put up with—the thousand little and big drawbacks which I could not begin to ennumerate and which no one has any idea of, who has not tried living in this semi-civilized section of the globe.[14]

Always industrious and highly motivated, Alice Morgan Wright centered herself in the Parisian art world at a quick pace, enrolling in classes at both the École des beaux-arts and the Académie Colarossi and making a splash at her very first Salon outing, where she presented a life-size plaster statue of the Old Testament figure Cain, now lost. (The work's size, though striking, posed a problem in the artist's small studio: "All beginners feel that this is the way to start out," she later noted of her ambitions. "The drawback is that the statue takes up most of the room and can't be moved."[15] It seems she managed its removal, regardless, as it could not have made its appearance at the Salon otherwise.)

Though she faced few roadblocks in her education and opportunities in France, the memory of her rejection from life-drawing sessions in New York still rankled; as with her fervent championing of her mother at dinnertime debates, it lit a spark of feminist exasperation. So when she met the British suffragist leader Emmeline Pankhurst, she was primed to join the cause wholeheartedly. She had little idea, though, just how much this meeting would alter the course of her life.

BY DECEMBER 1909, THE fifty-one-year-old Emmeline Pankhurst had already garnered international fame as a leading British activist, campaigning for women's right to vote with "deeds, not words."[16] She founded the Women's Social and Political Union (WSPU) in 1903, and by the end of the decade its influence had spread across the Western Hemisphere; she had

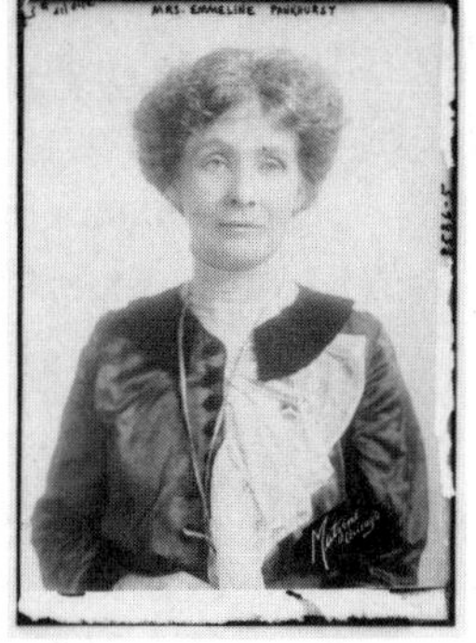

Figure 16.3. *Emmeline Pankhurst, ca. 1912. Library of Congress, Washington, D.C.*

successfully completed a North American lecture tour when Alice Morgan Wright met her aboard a steamship bound for Europe (only months after Wright herself had moved to Paris—possibly she had returned home to visit family for the American Thanksgiving holiday).[17] Given Pankhurst's status, Wright was already familiar with her, and Wright's letters to her closest confidante, Edith Shepard,[18] bubble over with poetic excitement at their formal introduction: "I started out with the sentiments of one who might have [illegible] by the stirrup of Joan of Arc, touching the 'hem of her garment,' you know, feeling the warmth of her halo and the breath of her wings."[19] Stirred by the older woman's grace and determination, Wright became a card-carrying member of the WSPU shortly thereafter, and her Parisian days, once marked by the rhythms of an art student's schedule, morphed. Fewer hours were spent milling about the galleries of the Louvre or the Luxembourg, and she devoted more time to political pursuits.

Wright eventually became one of the most committed suffragists at the American Girls' Club in Paris. While several other residents and Club affiliates, such as Anne Goldthwaite, Ida Sedgwick Proper, Ethel Mars (1876–1959), and Maud Squire (1873–1954), also exhibited interest in the suffrage movement, Wright gradually made it a cornerstone of her life. After attending several disappointing meetings and events organized by French suffragists—"I . . . came away with the impression that the women there were easily led into discussions of their various political preferences and away from any concerted effort toward their own enfranchisement," she later recalled[20]—she took matters into her own hands in true Alice Morgan Wright fashion, successfully manning her own letter-writing campaigns and political gatherings. A highlight of these events was a "big meeting" Wright coordinated at the last minute for Emmeline Pankhurst and her WSPU co-organizer, the similarly named Emmeline Pethick-Lawrence. Wright recalled this coup later in life with sparkling nostalgia, stating that she had arranged the summit "in four days tho' the French suffragists told us that it would take six months to prepare for such a meeting. Well, those were the days!"[21]

A hint of romance tinges the corners of her recollection here because Wright's enthusiasm for Pankhurst may have grown into something far deeper. Historian Wendy L. Rouse has couched Wright's relationship with the British suffragist as "queer adoration,"[22] an infatuation that grew over the artist's Parisian tenure. Though Wright did not clarify her sexual identification or preferences—not surprising given that open acknowledgment and acceptance of same-sex relationships was still decades away during her lifetime—she might safely be identified as a lesbian given that she did have a long-term life partner, a fellow Smith graduate named Edith Goode. With this knowledge, it is possible to read some of Wright's extant Parisian correspondence and poetry in a queer light. Most telling is a brief note Wright shared with Shepard in 1909:

> Well, of course you want to know all that I can tell you about her ladyship [Pankhurst] and glad am I to be at it, though I don't want you to read this to the others—because she has somehow grown so precious to me that I can't talk about her to anyone but you, comprendo-tu?[23]

AS RESIDENTS OF a city long renowned as among the world's most romantic, it is not surprising to note that American Girls enjoyed dalliances and flirtations during their Parisian stays. Several paired up with other artists: Club member Marguerite Thompson met William Zorach in early 1911 at one of the coed courses held at the Académie de la palette, marrying him in New York in late 1912.[24] Likewise, the Georgia-born Lucile Hitt (1877–1927) met painter Cameron Burnside during her studies in the early 1900s and the pair married in 1908, holding their wedding ceremony in the (literal) backyard of the Club in St. Luke's Chapel.[25]

Far more is known about straight couples than their gay counterparts, of course, given the taboos around same-sex relationships at the turn of the twentieth century and the common habit of burning personal correspondence during the same era. There is thus precious little documentation to confirm sexual or romantic interests like Alice Morgan Wright's potential attraction to Emmeline Pankhurst. Even rarer is corroboration of romantic interactions *between* Club members, though they surely occurred. One couple, a pair in Anne Goldthwaite's social circle and likely friendly with Alice Morgan Wright, was Ethel Mars and Maud Hunt Squire, two women assumed to have enjoyed a same-sex relationship.[26]

Mars and Squire, tea-taking members who enjoyed socializing at the Club, might be little known in today's art world (a shame in this author's opinion), but they are perhaps recognized more widely in the realms of modernist literature and in queer American studies as "Miss Furr" and "Miss Skeene," respectively. Around 1910, the couple's friend, Gertrude Stein, lightly fictionalized their relationship in "Miss Furr and Miss Skeene," a prose poem that was not published until 1922 as part of Stein's *Geography and Plays* collection.[27] What is most noticeable about "Miss Furr and Miss Skeene" is Stein's very Stein-ish repetition of key words and phrases (think of her famed "Rose is a rose is a rose is a rose," from the work "Sacred Emily," published in the same volume).[28] In "Miss Furr," one of the most-repeated words is "gay":

> They were quite regularly gay there, Helen Furr and Georgine Skeene, they were regularly gay there where they were gay. They were very regularly gay.

> To be regularly gay was to do every day the gay thing that they did every day. To be regularly gay was to end every day at the same time after they had been regularly gay. They were regularly gay. They were gay every day. They ended every day in the same way, at the same time, and they had been every day regularly gay . . .[29]

In total, "gay" or "gayer" appear 139 times in the 2,000-word text. The repetition is significant, to be sure, but even more important is that Stein's poem appears to be the first known literary use of the coded word to connote a same-sex couple, lending it—and the two women roughly pictured therein—landmark status.[30]

For individuals like Squire, Mars, and Wright, Paris offered an incredible amount of liberty in comparison to the United States. Though women in same-sex partnerships could sometimes pass off their connections as "intimate friendships" in America, the permissive attitudes of the French (and, in the case of Mars and Squire, the support of Gertrude Stein's coterie) enabled these women to enjoy considerable ease and freedom from unwanted attention. Paris thus provided acceptance—or at least benign disinterest—in and for them, just as it had been a more tolerant locale for Meta Vaux Warrick and other Black folks.

IT MUST BE noted that Wright's affection (or more) for Emmeline Pankhurst did not diminish her commitment to their mutual cause; if anything, it enhanced it—to the point where she made a three-month visit to London in 1911 to participate in WSPU activities and, later, coordinated an Albany stop on one of Pankhurst's New York lecture tours. Suffrage and Pankhurst became the two stars around which she orbited unceasingly, the subjects which she discussed most in her letters to her confidantes.

But what about *art*? Was Wright still attending courses at the École des beaux-arts and at Colarossi's during this spate of social action? If so, it was only sparingly. In a July 1912 profile on American women featured in French Salon exhibitions, she was described as ". . . [working] quite independently, under occasional criticism, but with no master."[31] She still showed her work, to be sure, submitting sculptures for the American Woman's Art Association's annual exhibition at the Girls' Club and participating in several iterations of the Salon. But so focused had she become on the suffrage movement that she considered pursuing it as her life's primary work, even dropping her art career in its favor. *Suffrage or sculpture?* The question—like her friend Anne Goldthwaite's concern regarding modernism—boggled her and became an ever-increasing frustration.

It turns out that Emmeline Pankhurst advised Alice Morgan Wright on this matter. In early 1912, Wright confessed her indecision to Pankhurst, who responded unequivocally to the young American's conundrum. "[S]he told me . . . to stick to my sculpting and stay out of causes," Wright recalled. But Wright did not take this advice to heart. "Two months later I was behind bars in Holloway."[32]

THE BRITISH SUFFRAGE movement of the early 1910s was characterized by an increasing fervor for militant demonstrations, following Pankhurst's dogmatic "deeds, not words" decree. Suffragists clashed with the police in protests that often resulted in the arrest of dozens. Once imprisoned, women participated in hunger strikes, a strategy sanctioned and performed by Pankhurst herself. As the tension between suffragists and the authorities escalated, violence grew common: prisoners were brutally force-fed, an inhumane procedure described by suffragist Mary Richardson:

> They fed me five weeks by the nose and at the end of that time my nose what they called 'bit' the tube, and it would not pass into the throat even though they bent it and twisted it into all kinds of shapes. Instead, it went up to the top of my nose and seemed to pierce my eyes . . . Then they forced my mouth open by inserting their fingers and cutting my gums . . . and the lining of my cheeks . . . When I was blind and mad with pain they drove in two large gags. Then the tubes followed and they pressed my tongue down with their fingers and pinched my nose to weaken the natural, and also the purposeful, resistance of my throat.[33]

Such actions shocked and outraged Wright, who remained current on suffrage activities not only through her direct communication with Pankhurst but also via the widespread coverage of suffrage battles in the international press. A report in spring 1912 spurred her to her greatest action yet. As she noted:

> While I was working at my profession in Paris, March 2, I read that the militant suffragettes in London were breaking windows

in order to emphasize their displeasure over the shameful way in which the premier and his ministers had violated their duties and had refused even to permit Parliament to consider the question of equal suffrage. Desiring to take part in the movement, I hurried to London and volunteered my services. My motives are easily explained. I simply desired to share in the protest against the dishonorable treatment of women's demands. Our cause is not merely national: it is universal.[34]

Alice Morgan Wright arrived in London in the early morning hours of Monday, March 4, 1912, stopping only briefly at a hotel in Kensington before jumping into action. Rarely one to shy away from sharing her true thoughts, she informed the hoteliers of her intentions. "She told my wife on her arrival on Monday that she had come specially from Paris to take part in the militant demonstration and promised that if she were arrested she would not give the hotel address," the hotel's proprietor later reported[35] (his interview in the *New York Times*, at least, indicates that he might have been thankful for the press regardless).

That same afternoon, Wright departed her hotel alongside two other suffragists, their pockets filled with stones. As they joined a cadre of several hundred women, one of Wright's friends threw a rock at the window of a nearby post office, smashing it. Another woman attempted to shatter an additional window with a hammer. The scene then erupted in chaos: the police detained two hundred women that day, and though Wright was adamant that the stones in her own pockets had been unused—"I hadn't really smashed anything," she asserted later[36]—she, too, was arrested. Emmeline Pethick-Lawrence and her husband posted Wright's bail, but she was made to appear in a West London court the very next morning on charges of "wilful damage," alongside Pankhurst and several others.[37] Although she fervently admitted her support of suffrage, she nevertheless protested the charges against her and proclaimed her innocence, so she was rather surprised when she was convicted. On March 5, 1912, Alice

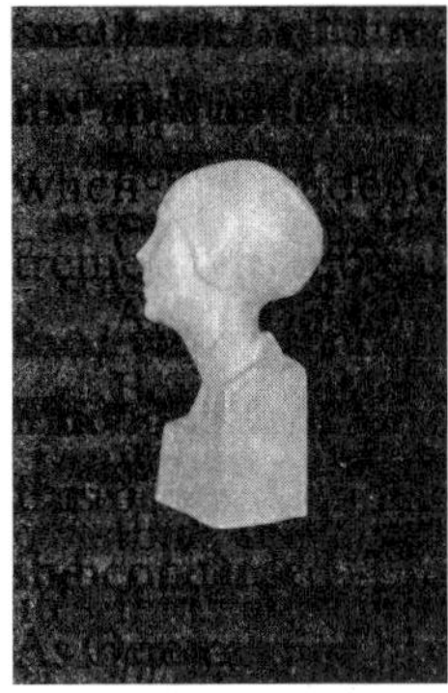

Figure 16.4. *Alice Morgan Wright,* Emmeline Pankhurst, *n.d. (1912). Albany Institute of History and Art.*

Morgan Wright was sentenced to two months at Holloway Gaol, the largest women's and juvenile prison in western Europe.[38]

"Black Marias"—somber horse-driven carriages—ferried Wright and her comrades to Holloway, where other prisoners welcomed their sisters with renditions of WSPU anthems "The March of the Women" and "The Women's Marseillaise." In the crush and confusion of arrival and processing, she smuggled in a few precious objects: pencils tucked inside her stockings, a sketchbook, and—impressively!—"a few pounds of plastoline," or modeling clay.[39] These art materials provided crucial distractions as well as documentation of her brief (if formative) time in jail, which she called "monotonous, but not especially unpleasant."[40] Fascinatingly, the wardresses of Holloway were not irritated by the artist's contraband; they were instead entertained by her creative process, even offering their own hairpins so that she could form armatures for her sculptures (Wright declined; she did, however, squirrel away sugar cubes from her prison tea ration to construct geometric bases for them).[41]

Of Wright's few surviving works from her Holloway imprisonment, several are small portrait busts of Emmeline Pankhurst herself. The most striking iteration (Fig. 16.4), now in the collection of the Albany Institute of History and Art, presents the suffragist as an ageless sylph with smooth, unlined skin and downturned eyes. Her head is tilted in a proud, insouciant manner upon a long and graceful neck. Pankhurst's hair is covered with a wrap or scarf, and her lips look full and soft—she is *beautiful.* Especially in a figure so small, Wright pulls off an incredible feat, elevating her contemporary subject to a timeless heroine suffused with elegance and dignity.

If her small-scale portraits are not clear indications that Alice Morgan Wright spent much of her Holloway internment thinking about

Emmeline Pankhurst, the poems written at Holloway speak even louder. One is particularly emotive and romantic:

What if today and yesterday
Have given me no sight of you
It is enough the whole night through
To think perhaps tomorrow may.

My thoughts all fly to you so fast
Perhaps the beating of their wings
Will warm your cell and drive the things
That bother you away at last.

I think—although you do not know—
Your heart must grow a little gay
Because of me, since day by day
And hour by hour I love you so.

I ache to have the strong sun beat
My hot heart to a shaft of light
And through your bars guide its swift flight
In sunny squares to kiss your feet.[42]

It is possible that Wright's inclusion of the word "gay" here is a coded reference; it had, as Stein's "Miss Furr and Miss Skeene" shows, begun to connote same-sex relationships by this time.[43]

NEWS OF ALICE Morgan Wright's jailing catapulted her to the front page of several American newspapers (though she is intriguingly absent from the Paris edition of the *New York Herald*, and any commentary from her fellow Club members has not been located), with some hysterically inflating the conditions of her stay. "She will be compelled to scrub the floors of the prison, clean the windows,

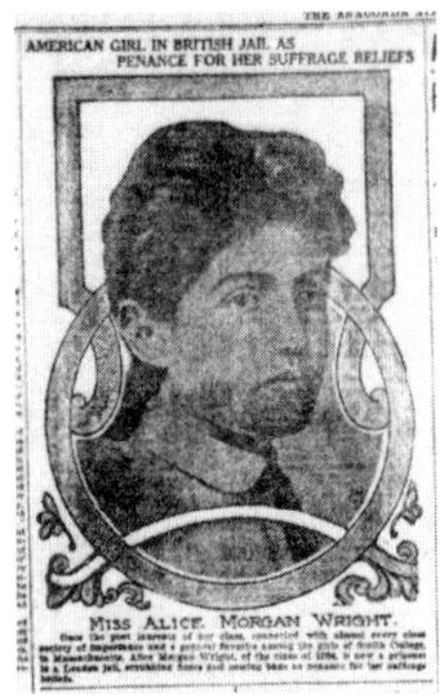

Figure 16.5. *Alice Morgan Wright.* Anaconda (MT) Standard, *March 23, 1912.A*

wash and iron the clothing used in the prison," exclaimed the *Chicago Tribune*, "and when not employed in this way will have to sew on coarse bagging making sacks."[44] "None Can See Miss Wright," declared an Albany paper, giving the impression that she was suffering in solitary confinement. After her release, Wright clarified these assumptions:

> We communicated with our fellow-suffragettes by means of brown paper megaphones through the window gratings. In accordance with a prearranged plan, for the first week I did only the briefest daily exercise and refused either to attend chapel or to work, and no real effort was made to have us do anything. Later I with others did some light work, such as sewing and knitting . . .[45]

Mostly, she occupied herself with sculpture, poetry, and a little light crafting:

> I made an American flag from a handkerchief, getting the red striping by using dye from a book cover and the blue field from portions of my clothing. I placed only six stars in the corner . . . or one for each of the suffrage states of Utah, Colorado, Wyoming, Idaho, Washington, and California. Unfortunately one of the wardresses saw it and confiscated it.[46]

For her family, though, the situation proved to be a nightmare. Wright's parents, who had been enjoying a vacation in the American South, learned of their daughter's arrest and cut their holiday short to lobby for her release. Henry Romeyn Wright was hounded by the press to comment upon the situation, which he did with an air of blustery exasperation:

Of all the stories sent around the world regarding my daughter . . . but one was true and that was her arrest. She is no criminal and committed no crime and was not arrested on a warrant. The stories about her being kept at hard labor, fighting with the guards, and being kept later in close discipline are equally ridiculous. Some newspapers even printed pictures of a woman 60 years old as being my daughter, but the photograph I give you now is a good likeness of her.[47]

As their child was a U.S. citizen being held in a foreign prison, the Wrights sought government intervention in hope of a quick release for Alice, with her mother, Emma, traveling to London to beseech the British embassy in person.[48] In fact, Wright had been offered an exit deal at least once, if not several times, during her incarceration: if she signed an affidavit confirming her guilt and promising not to participate in future suffrage meetings or protests, she could leave Holloway immediately.

Surprising no one, Wright refused to sign.

Alice Morgan Wright was released from Holloway prison in late spring of 1912—oddly, for such an important moment in the artist's history, there seems to be no record of the exact date—and purportedly only days before she had been scheduled to be force-fed, though Wright later dismissed this, saying, "There were too many of us to make abuse on the part of the authorities practical."[49] Returning to Paris with her mother briefly in tow, she settled back into an altered version of her previous role as "Parisian art student." Her suffrage experiences, especially her time in prison, had changed her, and activism thus remained her primary focus.

One wonders if her transformation from art student to imprisoned suffragist had anything to do with Wright's change of home base during this period. By early June of 1912, her postcards bear a return address of 18 rue du Val-de-Grâce, a ten-minute walk east of the Club. "The apartment is perfectly grand," she wrote to her mother, reveling in her new abode.[50] Perhaps she had already planned on living away from the

Club after three years residing under its roof. Or, perhaps, she no longer felt at home in the company of artists far more passionate about their art careers than she now was. A final question: Would the Club have dismissed her for her radical behavior, considering her political conduct problematic?

In her last two years in Paris, Wright continued to promote her political aims, accepting interviews from the American press to highlight the oppression of suffragists and writing letters to British authorities to protest their continued treatment as "common criminals."[51] When Emmeline Pankhurst and Emmeline Pethick-Lawrence were arrested again and sentenced for an additional nine-month prison stay, Wright gathered petition signatures—with several surely gleaned via her connections at the American Girls' Club—and held successful protests demanding that their status be upgraded to that of political prisoners, conferring a higher standard of care.[52] She assumed the role of secretary of the newly formed Paris branch of the WSPU and participated heavily in their events, prodding friends to join her. "I shouldn't be surprised if there would be some wild suffragetting in Paris this winter," she wrote to Edith Shepard in September 1912. "So you would better come down and help. Truly the Lord knows what will happen next in England! One wishes one were an army instead of an individual."[53] In short, she had now committed herself to being an ardent activist, and it was this title—not sculptor, nor even *artist*—that she wore proudly for the rest of her life.

AFTER THE EVENTS of 1912, something interesting occurred: the press started to weigh in on Wright's dual interests of suffrage and sculpture. One newspaper article lamented, "Not only did the recent suffrage campaign impel Miss Wright to forsake literary pursuits engendered by her four years at Smith, but it drew her away from a study of art in which she had already begun to make a name for herself. Only posterity may know how much it lost by the interruption."[54] Another asserted contrarily, "But devoted as Miss Wright is to the cause of women, the main thing in her life is her art."[55] One hilarious interview from 1915, lengthily subtitled "Alice Morgan Wright, Prime Enthusiast, Refuses to Talk About Anything But Votes Until She Has Helped Win Them for Women," presents a delightful exchange between a stubborn Wright and a tenacious reporter:

> "Now please tell me all about your work," the interviewer began brightly.
>
> "You are a suffragist, I hope," responded Alice Morgan Wright, sculptor and suffragist . . .
>
> "Do you do painting as well as sculpture?"
>
> "Do you intend to march in the great suffrage parade on Oct. 23?" parried the artist.
>
> "You studied under Rodin after you finished your course in the League, didn't you?" The interviewer tried to look firm and determined.
>
> "You have seen these notices of the suffrage art exhibit to be opened in the Macbeth Galleries on Sept. 27?" pursued the sculptor.[56]

Further on in the article, Wright responds to an assessment of her artwork by declaring confidently, "I work for suffrage twenty-four hours a day."[57]

Yet Alice Morgan Wright did continue to focus on her artwork for at least a small part of those twenty-four hours a day. Prior to departing Paris to return to the United States in April 1914, she exhibited at both the 1913 and 1914 iterations of the Salon and even participated in 1913's Salon d'automne. Several of her pieces, too, were juried

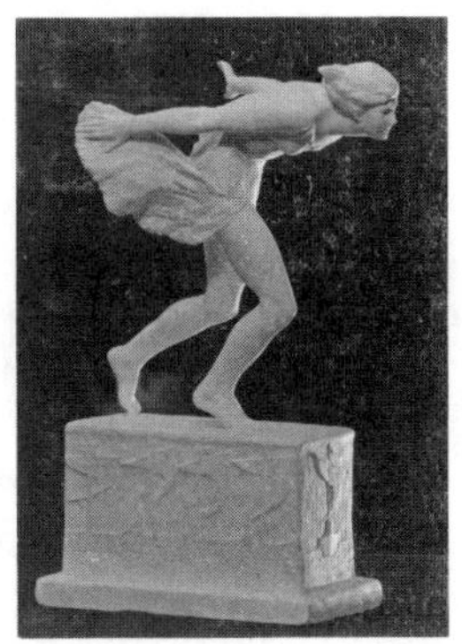

Figure 16.6. *Alice Morgan Wright,* Model for Off-Shore Wind, *n.d. (1919). Photographed by De Witt Ward, Photograph Study Collection, Smithsonian American Art Museum.*

into the AWAA exhibitions for those two years, ensuring her continued presence at the Club. Back at home, where she settled in again in New York City, she completed several commissions, including a project for the decorative façade of the Davenport Theater, an assignment she had won in 1909.[58] Like her fellow Club resident Florence Lundborg, she participated in the 1915 Panama–Pacific International Exposition, where she once again found an international audience.

In New York, her work was presented at the prestigious Modern Art Gallery—an extension of the 291 Gallery helmed by Alfred Stieglitz— where she was shown alongside the likes of Amadeo Modigliani and Constantin Brâncuși. One of her sculptures, *Wind Figure* (1916, 3 versions produced [Fig. 16.6]), was purchased there by the modern artist Arthur B. Davies.[59] All of this is ample evidence of both Wright's amazing abilities and the overwhelmingly positive critical reception of her work. Her inclusion at the Modern Art Gallery further proves that her work was considered an example of some of the best avant-garde sculpture on offer in the United States.

In fact, her artwork, in the opinion of several art historians (including this author), reached the pinnacle of its strength and panache in the late 1910s. By that time, Wright had synthesized the vast number of artistic styles she witnessed during her years in Paris—particularly Cubism and Futurism—and experimented with a very modern direction, creating figures dancing with movement and vigor. While her Paris works were more solidly indebted to Rodin, these pieces echoed no particular master: there is a little bit of Picasso here, some Duchamp-Villon there. Yet Wright never went fully abstract. Her works grew *more* abstract but always retained a reliance on the human body.

And when she applied this aesthetic strength to works of art that reflected her engagement with political issues, the effect was propulsive. *The Fist* (Albany Institute of History and Art), a painted plaster masterwork from 1921, features

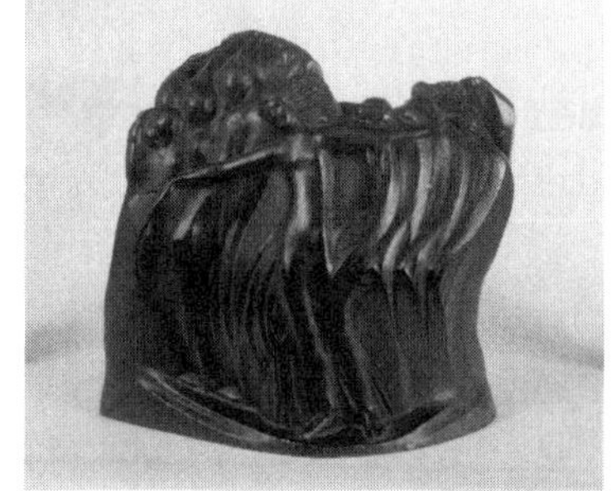

Figure 16.7. *Alice Morgan Wright, Trojan Women, 1927. Albany Institute of History and Art.*

a swirling abstracted hand clenched in triumph. The piece, completed one year after women finally gained the right to vote in the United States, is a victorious celebration of force and fortitude, a powerful testament to the joy the artist likely felt after achieving her hard-won goal. It is a testament, too, to Alice Morgan Wright herself, and an ideal stand-in for the Club's talented and most uncompromising firebrand.

CHAPTER 17

Extending the Club's Sphere of Usefulness

A few days ago a large annex to the original building was completed, almost doubling the capacity and adding materially to its attractiveness.

—"American Art Students' Club House Annex, Almost Doubling Accommodation, Opened," *New York Herald* European edition (1912)[1]

Demand for accommodation in this 'home away from home' has been constant," the *New York Herald* proclaimed about the American Girls' Club in Paris in 1912, during Alice Morgan Wright's tenancy there.[2] Indeed, since the Club's opening in 1893, it had recorded very few vacancies, and the competition for any open room, whether it be single-occupancy or a shared space, was feverish among American women. Prospective residents sent breathless letters to the Club's directors in hope of securing entry, and current residents advocated on behalf of friends and family—or at least they offered advice for gaming the system. "You will write to Miss Moffett [Jeannette Todd Moffett (1868–1946), director from around 1906 through 1910] soon won't you?" Wright beseeched her friend, Edith Shepard, in a 1910 letter from her own room at 4 rue de Chevreuse. She continued:

> The demand for rooms is certainly large—so bring all your force of argument to bear and write with conviction . . . if we are all here together it will be practically the same as having an apartment, only with a bath tub thrown in and all the care + responsibility removed. You know, don't you, that it is ridiculously cheap, being only about $30 a month. And if you shouldn't like it you know you would not have to stay more than a month . . . however don't give Miss Moffett the idea that you might stay . . . less than all winter.[3]

The Club's popularity with nonresidents, too, had increased—not only as a delightful location to enjoy five o' clock tea or a perusal of American periodicals, but as a viable arts center in its own right, as the exhibitions of the American Woman's Art Association continued to draw in dozens, if not hundreds, of visitors. As interest in the AWAA expanded, so, too, did the Association's programming. By the early 1910s, smaller-scale exhibitions were added, including ones specially dedicated to underemphasized media, such as miniatures and prints.[4] Each of these exhibitions had the potential to showcase more than a hundred works of art, dependent on size and medium.

Given these demands and activities, two things became abundantly clear: the Girls' Club was more integral to the American expat and student communities than ever before, and it needed to adjust accordingly. It was time to expand.

ELISABETH MILLS REID had not lived in Paris for nearly two decades, since her family's departure in 1892, but "her girls"—the women who called the Club home—were never terribly far from her mind. And beginning in 1905—the year before Anne Goldthwaite's arrival at the Club—Reid was physically closer to them than she had been in years, too. Much to the Reid family's relief, in 1905 Whitelaw Reid was appointed as ambassador to the Court of St. James's, the official title given to the United States's ambassador to Britain. The post had been Whitelaw's dream—indeed, he had only accepted the position of Minister to France in 1889 as a kind of consolation after being denied the Court of St. James's the first time around.[5] Elisabeth Mills Reid happily reprised her role as an ambassador's wife, settling into Dorchester House, a stately town home in Mayfair that was dubbed "London's finest."[6]

The geographical proximity of London to Paris allowed Reid to visit the Club with relative ease; no longer burdened by multiday transatlantic voyages, her trips to Paris, while never entirely frequent, increased in number. By 1910, she had personally witnessed the jockeying for rooms, the ongoing critical appreciation of the exhibitions held by the AWAA, and the popularity of the in-house restaurant at the rue de Chevreuse, each so feverishly received that Reid quickly determined to grow her Club's meager size. She thus began searching for the appropriate architect to renovate and expand the Club, and ever the champion of Franco-American relations, she found her perfect contractor in Charly Knight.

Charles Meissonier Knight hailed from an artistic family, the second of three sons born to Pennsylvanian painters Daniel Ridgeway Knight and Rebecca Morris Webster.[7] The Knights, Francophiles to the core, had made a permanent move to France in the early 1870s, settling into the town of Poissy on the banks of the Seine thirty kilometers northwest of Paris. Charles—called Charly—grew up shuttling between Poissy and Paris, where he was educated, eventually matriculating at the École des beaux-arts. As a child of American expatriate parents, he was a familiar figure in the American Colony, and it was within the Colony that he won many of his earliest commissions, both as a designer of elegant luxury estates and a renovator of historic structures.[8] To complete the picture, he was also a member of the American Cathedral of the Holy Trinity in Paris, where he must have spent several Sundays worshiping alongside none other than Elisabeth Mills Reid, who maintained her membership in and support of the church while living abroad.[9] For Reid, then, Knight was the ideal candidate for her club's transformation.

Of top importance, Reid alerted her architect, were bedrooms—a *lot* more bedrooms. Since its opening, the Club had maintained several dozen rooms for residential purposes, carried over from its epoch as the

Institution Keller. A couple dozen more beds, Reid knew, could be a blessing to that many more American girls; it would also go a long way to improve morale of her on-the-ground staff, who grudgingly dealt with the frustrations of managing incessant complaints from the would-be inhabitants they continually rebuffed.

Just as important as the Club's prospective residents were its current ones, and Reid keenly understood that 4 rue de Chevreuse had long lacked something essential for flourishing art students: dedicated studio space. Throughout the years, girls who followed their muses into the evening hours had few locations in which to work: they could attend the rare "night life-class" offered at a nearby atelier ("but this is generally found too fatiguing except for a month occasionally," reported journalist Emily Aylward in 1894),[10] or a small group might improvise a drawing club in one of the dormitories:

> Sketching classes are formed in the larger of the girls' rooms, one or more students posing, and in this way some good work is done amid lots of fun. When fun alone is wanted dances are got up, just among the girls themselves, banjos and guitars come forth, refreshments are served picnic fashion, and there is a good time generally.[11]

While a delightful way to practice one's drawing and to bond with fellow Club residents, these makeshift studios were no substitute for the real thing—larger spaces where the women could paint or sculpt (not just draw!) and could even leave their unfinished projects safely ensconced only steps away from their bedrooms.

Out of this dual necessity for bedrooms and studios, the AGCP received an all-new addition.

Running perpendicular to the rue de la Grande Chaumière at the left rear of

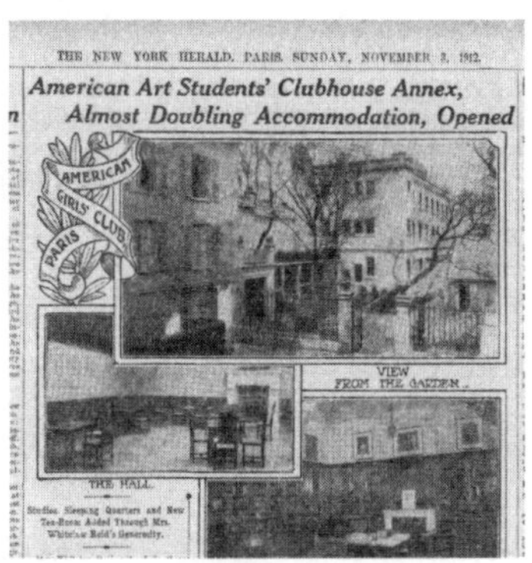

Figure 17.1. *"American Art Students' Clubhouse Annex, Almost Doubling Accommodation, Opened."* New York Herald, *European edition, November 3, 1912.*

the Club's charming garden, the "Annex," as Reid deemed it, was originally conceived as an elegant two-story building in the Renaissance revival style that Knight favored from his days at the École des beaux-arts. With clean lines and simple decorations, the Annex, in extant blueprints, comes across as grand, if slightly severe. The simplicity, though, was a smart move on Knight's part, deftly linking the new addition to the preexisting structure rather than distracting from it. "The annex is, in reality, an extension of the south wing of the original club building," a reporter for the *New York Herald* commented.[12] Knight configured the art studios on the ground floor with windows overlooking the garden and placed bedrooms above them on the second floor. Reid approved of the design—likely from London, where she had lived for the last half-decade—and construction began in either late 1910 or 1911.

At some point, however, the plan changed, though updated blueprints do not survive attesting to this fact. The building itself, though, is confirmation enough that an entire third story was added to the Annex. Upon the conclusion of construction in late October 1912, the Annex, outfitted in buff-colored brick, consisted of twenty new bedrooms, six private studios with tall glass windows, and "one club studio, large enough to permit of six or eight girls painting in it at one time . . ."[13] To further comfort and delight, new bathrooms (with "hot and cold water at all times,"[14] what luxury!) and a small rooftop terrace completed the picture. In the span of nearly two years, the AGCP had almost doubled in size, acting as ample proof of Reid's ambitions for the Club and her dedication to providing the very best amenities to visitors and occupants.

It is curious to note that though residents Anne Goldthwaite and Alice Morgan Wright each lived on-site during these years, neither left comments about the construction in their extant correspondence. To be fair, both women had likely relocated to separate apartments by the project's completion; newer residents, like Baltimore-born Grace Turnbull, reaped the benefits of this new and improved Club. Turnbull, in fact, rented one of the private studios at the Club during her stay in 1913. In a humorous letter to her parents (whom she called "Poder" and

"Moder"), she provided a glimpse of her struggles wrangling models in her Club studio:

> But if the Poder and Moder will peep into my studio . . . they will see ole grace with her hair in disarray, an apron over her old green dress, working before an easel on which is a canvas already spoilt with a Mother and Child. An Italian mother with shabby black hair and years too old for the infant she holds is vainly trying to silence its howls by turning it upside down, this side and that, thumping it, smothering it with kisses . . . Finally the nozzle of a bottle is inserted and its cries die to a gurgle. But by this time . . . not a vestige of the pose remains, and the despairing artist watches the level of the milk slowly lowering as her only hope.[15]

THOUGH THE ANNEX was a much-welcomed inclusion, it was perhaps overshadowed by another addition conceived by Charly Knight and his team: the Grand Salon, also called the *Salle d'exposition* or *la Grande Salle*. Seated between the Annex and the original eighteenth-century structure at 4 rue de Chevreuse, the Grand Salon functioned as a multipurpose space. With some reconfiguration, it could become a larger tearoom whose doors could be flung open into the garden, with small tables spilling out into the courtyard, or it could transform into a music room for community concerts, complete with a brand-new grand piano ("an importation from America," crowed the press;[16] for an American Girls' Club, nothing less than an American instrument would do). The Grand Salon operated as lecture hall for guest speakers and student presentations alike; it even served as a ballroom for special events and, most crucially, it provided a dedicated exhibition hall for the ever-expanding number of art shows held on the premises. From all accounts, it was a gorgeous space: its plastered upper walls were tinted a golden beige, while the lower portion was paneled in honey-hued waxed wood—a nod to the pervasiveness of the Arts and Crafts movement that had, by the 1910s, filtered across mainland Europe from Britain (and was markedly different from earlier French styles, which favored painted wood).[17] A frieze of carved grapevines recalling the style of William Morris crept along the extra-tall ceiling, crowning the structure two floors above.

And oh, that ceiling: it was a marvel, a metal armature supporting great panels of frosted glass that filtered sunlight and enhanced the Salon's welcoming glow. Such ceilings were very *en vogue* at the time, recalling the glass dome of department store Le Bon Marché designed in the 1870s by Gustave Eiffel (yes, *that* Eiffel).[18] Knight may have taken additional inspiration from the nearby Hôtel Lutetia, one kilometer north of the AGCP on boulevard Raspail. The hotel—later a magnet for the likes of James Joyce and Ernest Hemingway—was constructed the same year that Knight received Reid's commission and was topped by a similarly frosted cupola.[19] In the evenings, incandescent globes illuminated the space just enough without diminishing the feeling of intimacy.

Atop these two commissions, Charly Knight added one more project: a relocation of the Club's library, which now abutted the Grand Salon at its upper heights on the second floor. With similar paneling and bookshelves conceived in the "wood 'Gothic' style," it was the salon's aesthetic sibling, its inviting atmosphere making it an immediate hit with residents. It also functioned as the perfect location for some good-natured eavesdropping: one of the library's defining features was a set of French windows that opened directly over the salon below.[20]

A final useful, if less flashy, building was added to the rear of the garden at Reid's request: a small medical clinic, open to any American student living in Paris.

Did Elisabeth Mills Reid visit from London to inaugurate the updates to her Club in a grand manner? No, she did not. In humble fashion, she forewent an ostentatious gala and instead focused upon the daily lives of the residents. "Mrs. Reid desired that the routine life of the club should proceed without any interruption, which might call attention to her latest large contribution," confirmed the *New York Herald* on November 3, 1912. Club members instead celebrated with a small reception without the presence of their benefactor. "The members hope for a visit from her some time during this month," the *Herald* concluded.[21]

Sadly, they would have to wait for some time longer for Reid to come calling. Not long after the *Herald*'s article ran, Whitelaw Reid had begun experiencing severe health issues, which blossomed into "bronchial trouble in an aggravated form."[22] Elisabeth likely remained with him in London during his illness, and she was by his bedside when he died on December 15, 1912, at the age of seventy-five.

THE BUILDING PROJECT on the rue de Chevreuse, by all accounts, was a great success, and Elisabeth Mills Reid's foresight was appreciated in the *New York Herald*:

> In the erection of the annex the club feature has been emphasized, but not at the sacrifice, in any degree, of the "homey" atmosphere which has always pervaded the house. It is Mrs. Reid's purpose to extend the club's sphere of usefulness throughout the American girls' colony in Paris, to make the clubhouse in very fact a centre of activity of the American student life in this foreign capital.[23]

But the philanthropist had one more major surprise in store. In 1911, nearly twenty years after signing the lease on 4 rue de Chevreuse, Reid finally purchased the property from the Keller family.[24] The American Girls' Club, freshly renovated, redesigned, and officially in Elisabeth Mills Reid's hands, was ready to enter a new and glorious era.

CHAPTER 18

A Bolt from the Blue

I walked all the way home along the Boulevard Montparnasse and saw in the expressions of all who passed that the dreaded monster WAR was at large— indeed, had his fangs deep in the hearts of every living soul.

—Malvina Hoffman, American artist, *Yesterday Is Tomorrow: A Personal History* (1965)[1]

After the war began, there was no art. There was nothing but agony and sorrow and a great striving to help.

—Enid Yandell, American artist, quoted in Rubenstein, *American Women Sculptors* (1990)[2]

Sunday, June 28, 1914, dawned clear and warm and with a great frisson of excitement swirling throughout France: it signified the arrival of the long-awaited Grand Prix de Paris, the prestigious annual thoroughbred horse competition declared "the richest race in the world."[3] The Grand Prix was the event of the summer, breathlessly anticipated in reports splashed across the front page of newspapers throughout France, as journalists named their favorite colts, predicted the finest of weather, and presented would-be visitors with the best routes to the Longchamp racecourse to the west of Paris, whether they be fashionable ("to drive or automobile through the leafy avenues of the Bois du Boulogne") or scenic ("a pleasant and inexpensive way of reaching the course is by the numerous steamboats which run to Suresnes").[4]

In groups of threes or fours, American girls departed the Club in the relative cool of the morning, eager to experience race day festivities. Those who opted out of taking the affordable steamboats caught special trains departing from either the Gare Saint-Lazare—a bustling station in the city's eighth *arrondissement* celebrated by the Impressionists, particularly Claude Monet—or the Gare des Invalides, situated on the Seine's left bank—a closer option for Montparnasse dwellers.

They would not have been alone in seeking economical ways to participate in race day. Though it was primarily attended by the moneyed classes and well-heeled tourists, those with tighter purse strings still welcomed the Grand Prix like a holiday, and hundreds flooded the Bois to soak up the ambience with afternoon picnics replete with bottles of *vin blanc* or rosé. "Every class celebrates it," trumpeted the *New York Herald*. "To the Parisian, it is not only the great race day, but also a pretext for an afternoon in the woods."[5]

And even if they could not glimpse a horse, visitors could still enjoy an eyeful of the latest summer fashions, especially as this year's *mode* was determined to be "sufficiently remarkable—chiefly on account of their flimsiness," as one writer sniffed.[6] Such shocking raiment occasionally inspired bad behavior *and* the occasional mild ailment, as Frances Cranmer had experienced at the 1911 event: "I got my leg pinched by strangers and had a sunstroke the day of the Grand Prix and there went another two of my precious dollars to the doctor!" she recalled in her 1954 autobiography.[7] But the indignations and inconveniences were nevertheless worth the trouble of enjoying the race and its sundry events, and the 1914 iteration was no different. The Grand Prix—and the name of its eventual winner, Baron Maurice de Rothschild's bay horse, Sardanapale—was thus on everyone's lips.

The next day, however, another's name was spoken everywhere and in far more solemn tones: that of the Austro-Hungarian heir apparent, Archduke Franz Ferdinand.

News of the assassination of the archduke and his wife, Sophie, the duchess of Hohenberg, in Sarajevo shifted all coverage of the Grand Prix to the interior of Parisian newspapers, where race details were presented in smaller font and with few pictures: a drastic swing from the days and weeks prior, when it had been zealously anticipated. Did journalists and politicians foresee the change about to seize all of Europe—and soon enough, the world as well? Some, at least, witnessed a growing unease. Charles Inman Barnard, the Paris correspondent for the *New York Tribune*,[8] noted in his volume *Paris War Days: Diary of an American*:

> My friend, Mr. Edward Schuler, was dispatched by the Associated Press to Vienna, and when he returned, I readily saw, from the state of feeling that he described as existing in Vienna, that war between Austria and Servia [*sic*] was inevitable, and that unless some supreme effort should be made for peace by Emperor William, a general European war must follow.[9]

For most Paris residents, however, the declaration of war—proclaimed by the Austro-Hungarian Empire on July 28, exactly one month after Franz Ferdinand's assassination—nevertheless arrived "like the traditional Bolt from the Blue!"[10] as Barnard exclaimed. Within days of the announcement, the mood in the city had shifted rapidly; on Sunday, August 2, Barnard recorded in his diary that the ambassador to France, Myron T. Herrick, had organized a fact-finding committee to advise on the safety of American Colonists; the committee concluded that "there is no cause for alarm on the part of those who remain in the city for the present," though he suggested caution.[11] The next day, August 3, Germany declared war, and France mobilized immediately. American painter Elizabeth Nourse noted the immediate change in the city's mood as she stood at the windows of her apartment-cum-studio at 80 rue d'Assas, glancing worriedly across the Luxembourg Garden. In a diary entry on August 4, she scrawled, "Even the great rolling clouds have a sinister look, and last night the heavens were lighted by searchlights . . . Only a week ago all was calm—how things have precipitated themselves!"[12]

In the early weeks of August, the city forced a curfew upon its residents, shuttering *café-concerts*, restaurants, and theaters in a move that extinguished the City of Light in an instant. Any available building that could be commandeered for wartime purposes was transformed: even the inimitable salon of the Société des artistes français was retrofitted as a military stable. "Where the pictures hung, horses are munching their hay," Barnard wearily inscribed in his diary.[13]

The onset of war was equally shocking for the American Girls' Club and its members. The once-vibrant Latin Quarter, like all of Paris, became nearly unrecognizable in the evenings, devoid of laughter trickling from the open doors of La Closerie des Lilas or the contented buzz of students assiduously sketching from a live model at a night drawing course on the rue de la Grande Chaumière. Even the Club—its welcoming main edifice still standing solidly after two hundred years, overcoming revolution and the fall of an empire—no longer comforted its inhabitants.

For the American girls, it was time to go home, whether they wanted to or not.

Indeed, it appears that the Club's residents had no choice in the matter; according to a report from the *New York Tribune* in late August, the Club's director during this period, a Connecticut native named Roselle Lathrop van Allen Shields (1877-1966), hastily ordered the exit of the Club's thirty remaining inhabitants—those who had not already departed for the States—only days after war was declared.[14] Part of Shields's reasoning was the expense of maintaining the property without visitors to rent rooms, take tea, or dine at its restaurant—a charge the *New York Times* dismissed, noting that "the place is supposed to be provisioned for several months."[15] Regardless, with little notice women were turned out of their rooms, and the American Girls' Club in Paris effectively shut down.

Six women, it should be noted, initially refused to leave the comforts of the Club. For a

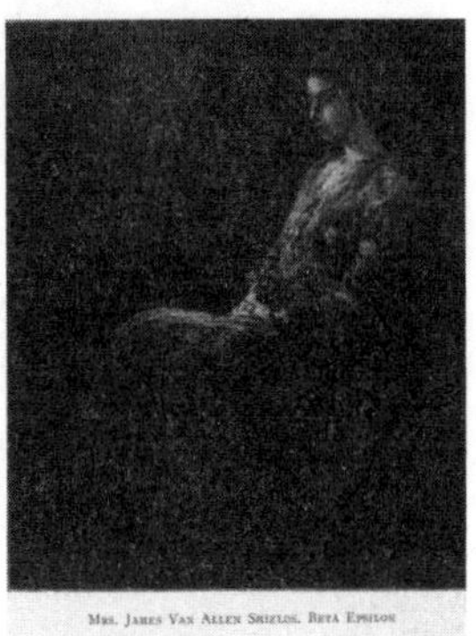

Figure 18.1. *Kate Edwards,* Roselle Lathrop van Allen Shields. The Key, *February 1915.*

brief period, these scrappy ladies had the attentions of twelve maids and four assistant managers, and the comparative luxury of fifty bedrooms, all to themselves[16]—as well as, it must be assumed, ample glares directed at them from Roselle Shields.

In addition to dispelling what residents she could, Shields also denied entry to several "refugees," including former Club members. One woman, thirty-one-year-old Brooklynite Ethel Traphagen,[17] arrived in Paris after a thirty-hour train ride from Switzerland. After Shields refused to admit her to one of the many vacant rooms at her disposal, Traphagen requested a brief rest to enjoy a bath before seeking accommodation elsewhere.

"EVEN A BATH WAS REFUSED," bellowed the subheading of the same *Times* article, in which Traphagen was interviewed (from, thankfully, a transatlantic steamer, the *Espagne*; Traphagen was on her way back to New York at the time of her interview).[18]

As the above connotes, Shields's actions caused a stir on both sides of the Atlantic. "The blame is placed on the preceptress, who, it is declared, should keep the place more widely open now than at any other time," one journalist demanded.[19] Ire further blossomed when rumors surfaced that Shields—after kicking out paying guests—had welcomed her own friends through the doors of 4 rue de Chevreuse.

Though surely frightened, Roselle Shields most likely made the decision to shutter the Club on her own. "It is said that Mrs. Reid knows nothing of present conditions," the *Times* reported. Geography may have been partially to blame here—though it is not entirely certain, Reid likely stayed in the United States after the December 1912 death of Whitelaw Reid in London, when she sailed back to New York with her son Ogden to prepare for Whitelaw's early January 1913 funeral.[20]

FOR AMERICAN EXPATS, returning to the United States was easier said than done; getting out of Paris at all proved to be an awful struggle, as Barnard witnessed:

> The Embassy is literally besieged by hundreds of . . . unfortunate travelers. There were so many of them, and their demands were so urgent, that the Military Attaché, Major Spencer Cosby, had to utilize the services of eight American army officers on leave to form a sort of guard to control their compatriots.[21]

Some were luckier than others. Mildred Burrage (1890–1983), a Maine-born Club alumna who had decamped at Giverny for the summer of 1914, was shuttled to London by her father, making her escape relatively easy, though it was not without its inconveniences: "He [Henry Burrage] motored from Giverny to Dieppe, and was held up every few miles by French soldiers. At Boulogne he was obliged to show his passports no less than 10 times before he cleared the city limits."[22]

Several American women, undeterred by the early days of battle, remained in Paris and joined the small ranks of those who opted to stay behind to bear witness to the war and to assist with relief efforts. Ethel Mars and Maud Squire, for example, stayed in France until late 1915, with Mars chipping in as an ambulance driver during the war's first year. Enid Yandell returned to Paris and worked as one of the founding members of two wartime groups, including the Société des orphelins de la guerre, an American-run relief organization providing aid for war orphans—an organization that she hoped Elisabeth Mills Reid would head as president, but that did *not*, as she confirmed to the *New York Herald*, include the participation of Club director Roselle Shields.[23]

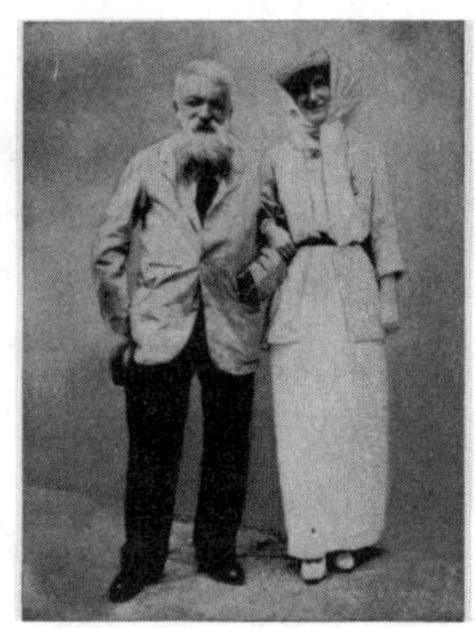

Figure 18.2. *Malvina Hoffman with Auguste Rodin, 1914.* Heads and Tales in Many Lands, *1937.*

Yandell's colleague, Malvina Hoffman, had returned to Paris just prior to the war with her mother in tow, and the two had rented an apartment on the boulevard du Montparnasse for an indefinite stint in the city ("just how indefinite . . . we never suspected!" she recalled in 1965).[24] Hoffman intended to split her time between creating new sculptures and functioning as an assistant to Auguste Rodin; indeed, Hoffman was already quite adept at the latter role, having acted as Rodin's representative when the master fell ill and was unable to attend a London showing of his work earlier that summer.[25] So dedicated was Hoffman to these dual intentions that Rodin himself had to push the American to flee France for her safety and for the health of her fragile mother.[26] The Hoffmans' escape was not any easy one:

> Mother and I, at Rodin's urging, had tried to get booking [to the United States] from France. Impossible. Desperate, we went with light luggage to London and there we found [Russian prima ballerina Anna] Pavlova and her manager, who schemed that I be put in charge of delivering artists' drawings and new stage settings to their New York offices. In this way we were able to get a cabin— Mother and I—and after a rough voyage (many passengers slept on mattresses in the ship's hallways), we arrived safely home.[27]

England's multiple transatlantic connections to the States secured its position as the top destination for Americans fleeing Europe like the Burrages and the Hoffmans. To her credit, Roselle Shields funded the voyage to London for half of her thirty expelled charges, though they were forced to leave their baggage behind;[28] what happened to the erstwhile residents after docking in England, however, is unknown. The hopeful assumption is that they made their own way back to the security of the United States.

AFTER THE CLUB emptied of its artists and musicians (and, supposedly, after Shields vacated her "wealthy friends," too), the buildings at 4 rue de Chevreuse did not remain uninhabited for long. Elisabeth Mills Reid, long a champion for healthcare, jumped into action and offered her property to the French Red Cross to use as an auxiliary hospital, allowing the now-defunct Girls' Club to enter an entirely new phase of its existence upon the hospital's opening in November

1914. Number 4 rue de Chevreuse was not alone in this radical, wartime transformation: many institutions both big and small were repurposed for similar emergency means. The upper floors of the Louvre were likewise reallocated as hospital wards, and the American Cathedral of the Holy Trinity, Reid's spiritual home in Paris, became a temporary dorm

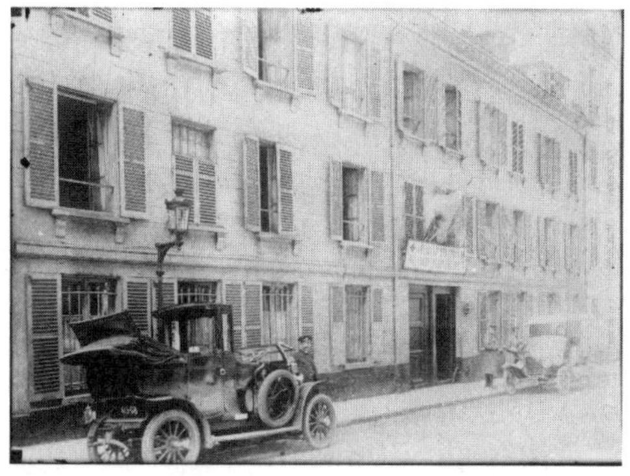

Figure 18.3. *American Red Cross Military Hospital number 3, rue de Chevreuse, Paris. Library of Congress.*

for stranded Americans waiting to flee Europe.[29] The former Club, though, stayed a hospital for far longer than either of these other locations, first becoming Hôpital Auxiliaire number 53 under the purview of the Chambre des notaires de Paris, before transitioning into an American hospital in 1917 with the entry of the United States into World War One.

Elisabeth Mills Reid, when possible, liked to go the distance: for her philanthropic projects, she threw every ounce of her heart and soul (and her financial support) into her most precious ventures. Just as she had renovated 4 rue de Chevreuse prior to the war so that it could better accommodate the needs of artists, she backed an entirely new renovation project to reshape her building into a safe and sanitary hospital. The process, fully funded by Reid, only took a few months: she hired French architect André Vincent (probably on the recommendation of her previous Club architect, Charly Knight[30]) to oversee several critical alterations to the former Club.

Most notably, Vincent tackled the still-new art studios—in the Club's 1913 addition abutting the rue de la Grande-Chaumière—and converted them to suit multiple needs: four of the private studios became sickrooms, while two others became a sterilization room and a pharmacy.[31] The larger "club studio" now housed an operation room. The elegant Grand Salon, with its wood-paneled walls and its frosted glass ceiling, was transformed into a home for wounded soldiers, with enough room to house fifteen beds; a storage area adjoining the salon was retrofitted with a new bathroom and toilet—several washing spaces were added for the sake of sanitation—and rooms above the library became additional patient dormitories.[32] The library itself, as well as the Club's various sitting rooms, functioned as offices for administration and as a socializing space for officers.[33] All in all, the hospital made space for at least fifty beds.

The transition from a French *hôpital* to an American one in 1917 necessitated further change, once again at Reid's behest. In a letter to Colonel Alfred Bradley, head of the medical corps of the American Expeditionary Forces, Reid noted her plans, writing, "I want it to be thoroughly cleaned and the kitchens painted, which will take about a fortnight . . . I am having a lift put in, and shall add a good X-ray plant, and, of course, the Hospital will be fully equipped as to beds, furniture, and everything of that kind."[34]

Reid's efforts certainly paid off. A description of the hospital, now titled the American Red Cross Military Hospital number 3, was submitted to the *Congressional Record* in 1918:

> After the entry of the United States into the war Mrs. Reid offered the buildings and grounds for use as a hospital of officers of the allied armies. The hospital was opened and received its first patient on the 12th of December, 1917. At this time there were accommodation for 50 patients in single and double rooms. It was beautifully and artistically, even luxuriously, furnished, has ample recreation facilities, a large, well-equipped library and reading room, which is kept well supplied with American, English, and French magazines, periodicals, and daily papers. In addition, there is a large reception room containing a Steinway concert grand piano, and a lounge room provided with games, card tables, pianola, and Victrola. Every effort has been made and no expense has been spared to equip all parts of the building comfortably and in a home-like manner . . . Mrs. Reid has spared neither time nor money to bring this about . . .[35]

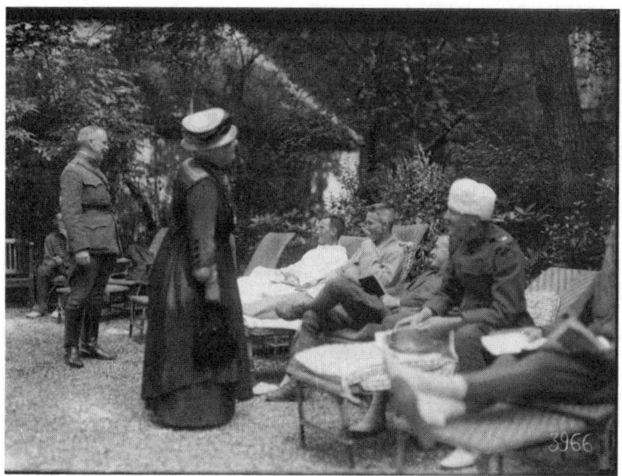

Figure 18.4. *Lewis Hine, "Mrs. Whitlaw Reid and Colonel Gibson, A.R.C., visiting Hospital number 3," 1918. Library of Congress.*

So coveted was Military Hospital number 3 that some servicemen added special instructions to their dog tags: "If I am wounded please send me to Mrs. Reid's hospital in Paris."[36]

On at least one instance, Elisabeth Mills Reid visited 4 rue de Chevreuse (which she now referred to as "her" hospital, just as the AGCP was always "her" Club, and just as infantrymen confirmed it as "Mrs. Reid's hospital") to survey the patients themselves, no doubt to be sure that they were provided with every comfort while recuperating. A series of images (Fig. 18.4), held in the Library of Congress as part of the American Red Cross photograph collection, depicts Reid, wearing a black gown, a flat-topped hat, and gloves, chatting with wounded soldiers stationed on lounge chairs in the garden, their feet covered in slippers, one mustachioed man's head wrapped in bandages. For her wartime services, Reid was awarded France's Cross of the Legion of Honor in 1922.[37]

As necessary and charitable as Reid's efforts were, it was no doubt shocking to anyone who had experienced the building in its previous iteration as the Girls' Club. One such individual, the sculptor Grace Turnbull, visited the premises in 1918 while in France as a volunteer

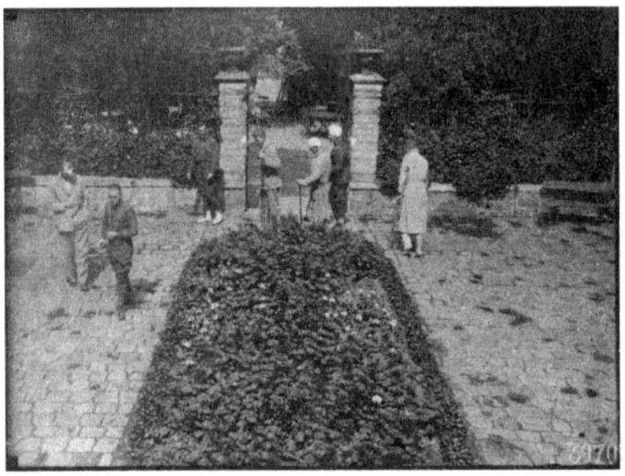

Figure 18.5. *"First Attempts at Exercise," ca. 1918. Library of Congress.*

for the American Red Cross. She recorded her experience in her journal, later published in her 1953 autobiography:

I went yesterday to our dear old American Arts Students Club to learn how it was being used. There, as everywhere, khaki men were swarming; a khaki man in the concierge's lodge, khaki men on beds in the garden where we used to have breakfast; in the ballroom where we had our fancy-dress balls; in the chapel; in *my* studio where I used to paint the mothers and babies! The ballroom had suffered the greatest transformation—the tapestries had been covered with cheesecloth and the white beds were packed like sardines, not in rows with alleys, but as close as could be in all directions; many of them had wooden frames attached so the poor wounded limbs could be drawn up as required.[38]

Turnbull, though, likely assumed in 1918 that the Club's tenure as hospital was only a brief one, and that it would return to its beloved iteration as the center of art and educational life for American women as soon as it could be safely managed. Surely it would be resurrected once again, as it had proved so beneficial to a generation.

Turnbull was right on the first account—Number 4's stint as a hospital was only a few years long. Alas, neither she, nor any other American, not even Elisabeth Mills Reid herself, could have foreseen that the American Girls' Club in Paris was resolutely a thing of the past.

CHAPTER 19

Reestablishing Usefulness to American Girls

During a brief sojourn in Paris recently, I went over No. 4 Rue de Chevreuse with Mrs. Shields and talked with her at length about our plans for use of the building. I am writing to tell you how delighted I was with the whole place.

—Virginia Gildersleeve to Elisabeth Mills Reid, July 6, 1921[1]

After the Armistice in 1918, ongoing relief work and the rebuilding of communities across France and beyond necessitated that the American Red Cross maintain its headquarters in Paris during the postwar period. Though the organization was already based on the place de Rivoli (near the gilded statue of Joan of Arc at today's place des Pyramides),[2] facilitators sought an upgraded and more spacious locale. Naturally, they already had an ideal space in mind: 4 rue de Chevreuse. After all, the Red Cross had established its hospital there in the sixth *arrondissement* nearly a year prior, and with Elisabeth Mills Reid's refurbishments, it was now a top-of-the-line medical facility with a restful atmosphere to boot. It would have been a folly to relocate elsewhere, and thankfully Reid agreed. With little deliberation, she leased her

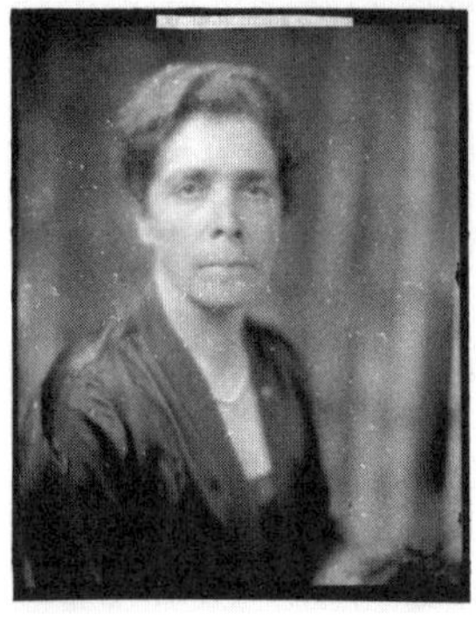

Figure 19.1. *Virginia Gildersleeve, undated. Library of Congress.*

building once again to the American Red Cross, who operated there beginning in mid-1919 and into 1922.

Yet the signing of this new lease sparked some concern in Reid's mind. Though always passionate about medicine and healthcare, the philanthropist had never intended the former Club to remain a hospital or an American Red Cross office forever. *When the lease expires, what shall I do with my Parisian outpost,* she wondered. She knew at least one thing: she wanted to reestablish its usefulness to American girls, that unloved and underserved community to whom she had long committed herself. But should she resuscitate the American Girls' Club? Or should she extend her mission to a larger subset of Americans?

The future of 4 rue de Chevreuse was not only on Reid's mind: it was on the minds of many. The jockeying for use of the building began around the same time that the American Red Cross transferred its headquarters there and remained ongoing for its three-year tenancy—and even beyond. "Many people have been bothering me about the transfer of my building," Reid wrote Virginia Gildersleeve (1877–1965), dean of New York's Barnard College, in late 1920. "It seems that property in Paris has appreciated very much in value."[3] The Red Cross, naturally, wished to remain there, and the dean of the American Cathedral of the Holy Trinity, Frederick Beekman, tugged at her charitable heartstrings when he implored Reid, "I can think of nothing [better than] the conversion of the Studio property into a Reid Memorial or Foundation, carried out as you direct by that branch of Christ's Church which has made the strongest and most intimate appeal in the Student Quarter."[4] Everyone wanted access to the former Girls' Club. The question was: on whom would Reid bestow the honor?

The popularity of the American Girls' Club in Paris, and its twenty-plus-year history, guaranteed that many women felt nostalgic about their time spent in its august library, its cozy tearoom, and their own rented, *brocante*-filled dorms therein. Such nostalgia assured a strong wish that 4 rue de Chevreuse be returned to its former glory as a club for art and music students. An early advocate for a renewal of the Club was Katherine S. Dreier (1877–1952), an artist and key figure in the support of modern art in the United States. Alongside Man Ray, Marcel Duchamp, and others, Dreier founded the Society of Independent Artists and, later, the Société Anonyme, two groups that produced exhibitions, lectures, and literature about Modernism. She lived in Paris for a brief time, studying painting with Raphäel Collin for three months in 1907.[5] Though

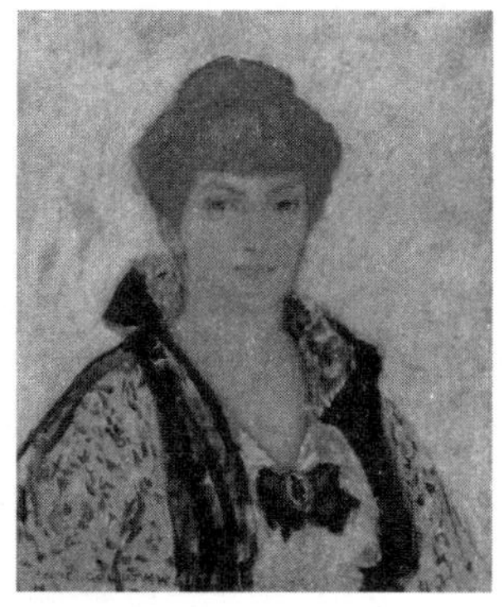

Figure 19.2. *Anne Goldthwaite*, Portrait of Katherine S. Dreier *(1877-1952), 1915–16. Yale University Art Gallery.*

short-lived, Dreier's spell in France—and her visits to the Club in particular—held special significance to her, as she disclosed in a March 1920 letter to Elisabeth Mills Reid, writing, "Ever since my student days in Paris I have kept my interest in the Club, for I realized what it meant to the girls who would go over, and even to such as I, who had the privilege of dropping in and making friends."[6] Dreier went on to suggest the Club's revival and even recommended one of her colleagues as a potential director.

Dreier's wishes were echoed by other former Club members, including Constance Drexel (ca. 1884–1956), who shared her support of a reinstated Girls' Club that same year in an interview with the *New-York Tribune:*

[The Club] was ideal; and when things have quieted down a bit and the high cost of living comes down enough to make it safe for the artistic temperament to abandon stenography and book-keeping, book agent jobs and other war-time makeshifts, and get back to the appointed metier of showing up the beauty spots in this mussy old world, everybody hopes that the American Girls' Club in Paris will resume its place in the Latin Quarter as the center around which the lives of American girls revolved, an oasis in Bohemia.[7]

The most solid proposal for the future of 4 rue de Chevreuse was offered by none other than Virginia Gildersleeve and her cohort, members of the Association of Collegiate Alumnae (ACA, which was soon renamed the American Association of University Women, or AAUW). The ACA sought to establish a residence for female college graduates continuing their educations in Paris. Similar organizations for men had thrived in the years after the war, and achieving parity in this sphere was key for Gildersleeve as the chair of the ACA's Committee on International Relations. In 1919, Gildersleeve sent M. Carey Thomas, president of Bryn Mawr College and a member of the Committee on International Relations, to Paris to scout potential locations for a women-only graduate residence. Upon the recommendation of others, Thomas requested a meeting with Roselle Shields, Elisabeth Reid's Parisian deputy and the Club's former director, to tour 4 rue de Chevreuse. For Thomas, the site's suitability for the ACA's use was immediately evident: "The club house is made to our hand in Mrs Whitelaw Reid's Girls' Club which is excellently situated in the university quarter," Thomas reported.[8] In other words: it was perfect for their purposes, just as it had been for Reid herself in 1893.

Elisabeth Mills Reid found the ACA's proposal interesting and especially admired the option to cater to the needs of a broader audience of American women, but she moved forward cautiously. Naturally, she was apprehensive about the cost of maintaining the aged property, and—as in the Club's early years—she worried that her Club would be downgraded to a boarding house rather than an institution supporting serious students. Virginia Gildersleeve reassured Reid in a February 1921 missive, writing:

It has been our idea that the clubhouse should be open only to college women—that is, those holding degrees from recognized American colleges or undergraduates especially recommended by their colleges. We plan to have testimony regarding the character and personality of all applications before admitting them to residence in the clubhouse for the winter.[9]

Reid's personal correspondence further reveals her wish to maintain some semblance of the Club. A handwritten, undated draft of a letter exists in Reid's papers, wherein Reid queries her unknown recipient (probably Virginia Gildersleeve):

> Would the Club be open to <u>Art</u> and music students of recognized ability . . .? It seems to me it should be, for I still have in mind the various well-known women who were given their chance in life at my Club before the war—the 3 Klumke sisters, Janet Scudder, Malvina Hoffman, Miss Bowie, and others.[10]

Note that Reid specifically capitalized and underlined the word "art."

To Reid's likely disappointment, Gildersleeve replied that, should the ACA take over Reid's buildings, "it would not be well to try to mix art and music students with those studying at the Sorbonne."[11]

Still, in 1921, Reid agreed to lease the property to the (renamed) American Association of University Women for a period of five years, beginning in mid-1922. The AAUW determined that it would use the property—now deemed the American University Women's Club—"to further the educational interests of American university women studying in France . . . by bringing them into contact with the university women of all nations," according to a *New York Times* article.[12] In her letters to Reid, Gildersleeve bubbled over with enthusiasm for Reid's verdict, writing, "There could not be a more admirable place in which to make a center for American college women in Paris. It seems so perfect!"[13]

The news, however, was also met with disappointment. Certainly, those hoping to rent Reid's property were discouraged; the American Red Cross even countered that "the College women should carefully reconsider their decision in the light of existing conditions" in postwar Europe, though neither Reid nor Gildersleeve was persuaded.[14] The most heartbreaking reactions, though, came from those who had experienced the Club's heyday. In her memoir, sculptor Janet Scudder commented, "I regret deeply that this delightful club for art students has now been taken over by university scholars; and especially at a time when art students need such a place more than ever, due to the tremendous increase in the cost of living in Paris."[15] Anne Goldthwaite, too, wrote that the AAUW's takeover "changed [the building] very much for the worse," though she did not elaborate on her reasoning for this belief. "Thank God for its beauty and liberty, as it was in my day," she concluded.[16]

One cannot blame Elisabeth Mills Reid for her decision to change course. In offering her former Club to the AAUW, she had responded to the shifting needs of the expatriate community in the postwar years. By the early 1920s, more women began traveling to Paris to further their collegiate, not artistic, educations. Fewer female artists, too, braved an Atlantic voyage to attend a Parisian art academy, like Julian, Colarossi, or Vitti (and Vitti, in fact, had permanently shut down with the outbreak of the war). In reality, this demographic shift was a good thing for American artists, as it reflected a vast improvement in art education and resources to be found stateside. The absolute *need* to visit Paris to complete one's artistic training no longer held sway. Transforming the former artist's club into a center for university women was, then, the objectively correct move.

Yet that choice, as all do, came with a cost. By the early 1920s, it was official: the American Girls' Club in Paris—and any hope of its art-specific reemergence—the paint-spattered studios, sketch-filled bedrooms, stylistic debates in its sitting parlors, late-night painting sessions, and even its restaurant's salmon with tartar sauce—was well and truly dead.

CHAPTER 20

Through the Vision and Generosity of Elisabeth Mills Reid

*John Ruskin once said that the Ideal Woman did not find roses in her path,
she left them there. The fact that Elisabeth Mills found her path
rose-strewn only aided her to leave many more behind.*

—"Women: Death of a Great Lady," *Time* (1931)[1]

*[Reid Hall] has in a thousand well-planned ways facilitated the comprehension of
French life by American women, guarded against the misunderstandings which dog
the first stages of every attempt to share another national life, opened the right
doors and closed the wrong ones.*

—Dorothy Canfield Fisher, educator and activist (1947)[2]

Handing over use of the former Girls' Club property to the American Association of University Women was, as the *New York Herald Tribune* later noted, "an experiment."[3] Elisabeth Mills Reid entered this new phase with wary optimism, hopeful that the experiment would work out nicely for all involved. Nevertheless, she was likely relieved to know that she could cancel her lease after completion of the AAUW's five-year term if she deemed their usage unsatisfactory.

Indeed, there appears to have been a brief phase in which the relationship between the AAUW and Reid was tenuous. In June of 1926, Reid drafted a letter to Virginia Gildersleeve, recounting the results of her now-yearly visit to 4 rue de Chevreuse:

> Each year I have hopefully gone to see the Club and learn how things were going, and each year have found it dingier and more run down, and have come away disappointed and discouraged. It has not made the place I pictured for it in Paris, nor does it come up to the high standard we all set for such a fine and fully equipped plant. It is little at the moment but a cheap hotel. It is cheaper than any other hotel in Paris, ridiculously so when one considers the comforts supplied and the cost of the franc.[4]

All was found wanting: the peeling paint, the shabby dining room, and even the clientele, whom Reid dismissed as "women who are here simply for travel and pleasure."[5] Her letter, surely a humbling read for Gildersleeve and her team, ended with a stark reminder of the interest so many others maintained in the covetable Montparnasse property. "The church people [from the American Cathedral of the Holy Trinity] have been approaching me on the subject, and I think will make me an offer," she warned. "Perhaps by the end of another year things may be improved and I may feel differently toward it, but at the moment, I cannot see that the Club stands for much in the community, or that it is fulfilling our high hopes and ideals for it as a center of student life and activity."[6]

To the great relief of all involved, the AAUW pulled through, and Reid's exacting standards were met. After seeing the care that the AAUW—under the purview of the inimitable administrator Dorothy Leet (1894–1994), who took the reins in 1927—took in improving her Paris compound, Reid redoubled her efforts to support them. In 1928, she further committed her property for the AAUW's use,[7] and—because she was nothing if not a dedicated philanthropist—she financed another round of major renovations to the aged property. Through 1929, Reid spent more than $100,000 to shore up the Club's roof, update its plumbing and electrical facilities, and expand its footprint a second time. In appreciation, the AAUW renamed 4 rue de Chevreuse Reid Hall, to commemorate Elisabeth Mills Reid's vision and services. A bronze plaque was produced to celebrate both the name change and the patron herself, and it still holds pride of place in the building's foyer today. It reads:

REID HALL
ESTABLISHED IN 1922
AS A CENTRE FOR UNIVERSITY WOMEN
OF THE UNITED STATES
AND THE OTHER NATIONS OF THE WORLD
THROUGH THE VISION AND GENEROSITY OF
ELISABETH MILLS REID

During this latest spate of renovations, one of the most direct vestiges of the building's former life as the American Girls' Club—the ground-floor artist studios in the "Annex"—were repositioned onto the building's brand-new but lesser-trod fourth floor, and the ground floor was redesigned into a dining room. Yet even this reshuffling could not fully dampen the location's connection to its artistic history. Small traces—and people!—remained. The Minnesota-born Lucy Fairfield Perkins (later Ripley, 1875–1949), a painter and sculptor who had trained with Rodin and had shown her work at an AWAA exhibition on-site in 1905,[8] maintained her art studio on the AAUW's premises well into the 1930s. One can imagine the clinking of Perkins's chisel echoing through Reid Hall into the night, a rhythmic accompaniment to the university students' chattering, writings, and toil over French grammar. Perkins must have enjoyed the nostalgia engendered by her studio usage: in a city filled with suitable artist spaces, she nevertheless chose Reid Hall, preferring its familiar, ideal location. To Perkins and many others, the Club was still home.

～

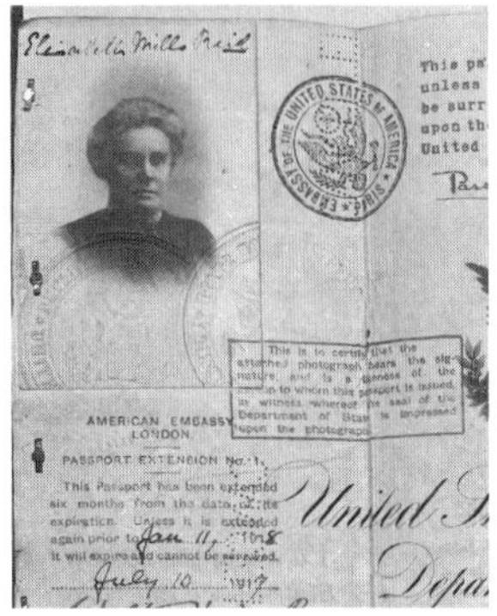

Figure 20.1. *Detail of Elisabeth Mills Reid's diplomatic passport, ca. 1917. Reid Family Papers, Library of Congress.*

AS EACH YEAR passed, the memory of the American Girls' Club faded. The new generation of American women lodging there likely knew only snippets of their university club's history, if at all. Fewer women remained who had bridged the gap between the two eras; former Club director Roselle Shields likely left the property in the early 1920s, and with the exception of Perkins and a handful of former Club members who maintained studios nearby (like sculptors Malvina Hoffman and Janet Scudder), nearly every American Girl had returned home to the States. In 1931, the community of what was once the American Girls' Club in Paris suffered its biggest loss yet: Elisabeth Mills Reid herself.

In mid-April 1931, Reid boarded a ship bound for Cherbourg, having recently vacated her country home, Ophir Hall, a manse nestled near Purchase, New York, in Westchester County. Six months prior, she had offered the house to King Prajadhipok and Queen Rambai Barni, the rulers of Siam (now Thailand), who planned a visit to the United States to seek treatment for the king's myriad eye problems, particularly cataracts.[9] Ophir, filled with plush eighteenth-century brocades, antique Chinese porcelain, and Louis XV furniture, was considered appropriately opulent for the Siamese royals, who gladly accepted her generous proposition.[10] The loan of her favorite home that spring provided Reid with the perfect opportunity to depart the States and travel to France, where she planned a stopover in Paris before making her way south to visit her daughter at her home on the Mediterranean.

Upon disembarking in Cherbourg, the seventy-three-year-old Reid complained of a slight cold, assuming she had contracted a bug during the Atlantic crossing. No matter—Reid did not allow a minor ailment to slow her down as she attended both personal and business engagements, including an hours-long inspection of a brand-new printing plant for the *Paris Herald*,[11] the newspaper then under her son Ogden's jurisdiction. As always, she likewise made it a priority to stop by 4 rue de Chevreuse to confirm that it lived up to her exacting standards.

Standing in the midst of its welcoming courtyard, she took it all in: the scent of freshly bloomed spring flowers, the covered well still standing in the corner, the glinting glass ceiling of the Grand Salon, the iron tables dotting the garden. Somewhere a woman laughed, and Reid smiled, enjoying the knowledge that she had established this place that had served as *home* for so many women over the previous four decades. She "satisf[ied] herself that all went well at Reid Hall," *Time* later reported,[12] and thus she exited the property without looking back. She could not have known that it would be her last visit.

By the time Reid arrived at the villa of her daughter, Jean, in idyllic Saint-Jean-Cap-Ferrat, her affliction had worsened with frightening intensity. A bronchial infection progressed rapidly into double pneumonia, and Jean summoned Dr. Robert Louis Levy, chief of the cardiac department of New York's Presbyterian Medical Center, who had been stationed in Paris. "[B]ut oxygen and his skill were no match for pneumonia and an aged heart," as it was later reported.[13] On April 29, 1931, Elisabeth Mills Reid—champion of American girls in Paris—died, with her daughter and son-in-law by her side in her final moments.

In the days and weeks that followed Reid's passing, a great outpouring of grief-laden affection for her filled American and international newspapers and journals. President Herbert Hoover called Reid's death "both a personal and a national loss";[14] the president of Columbia University, Dr. Nicholas Murray Butler, recalled, "[Reid] had been a tower of strength and a centre point for all that was best and most becoming in our social life and conduct."[15]

Reid's charitable work was lauded frequently in the op-eds extolling her life, the majority involving her connection to the American Red Cross and various hospitals. Her "Franco-American co-operation and friendship," as Walter E. Edge, American ambassador to France, confirmed, had remained a lifelong priority, as had helping the less fortunate. Yet one of the most poignant dedications to Reid's life was an anonymous letter published in the *New York Herald Tribune*, signed

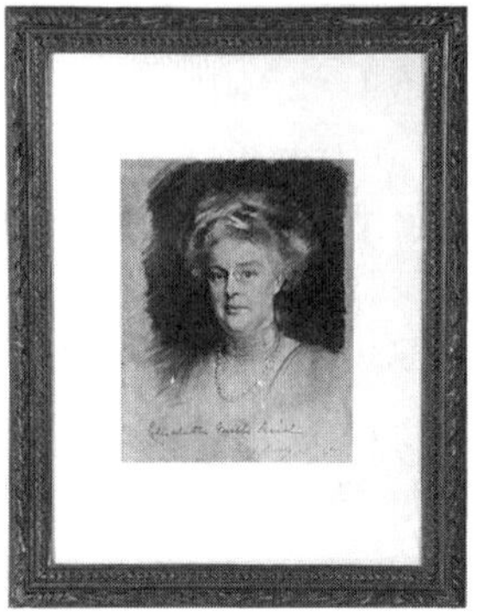

Figure 20.2. *John Singer Sargent,* Elisabeth Mills Reid, *ca. 1912.*

"One of the Obscure." In it, the author gratefully recounted her experiences at 4 rue de Chevreuse:

One of the most delectable of Mrs. Whitelaw Reid's gifts deserves a more personal mention than it has thus far received in the public prints . . . I spent a few weeks at the fine old town house in the rue de Chevreuse, Paris . . . For years this spacious home . . . Mrs. Reid devoted to the housing and care of artist students. During the war all the offices, ballroom, library, the old part and the later addition were given over by the owner to the Red Cross. Since the war the rooms are filled during the winter with students of all ages . . . The fact that so generous a series of benefactions, several decades of immense advantage to young American artists, to the Red Cross, to university women from more than half a hundred nations, can receive only passing notice in the vast number of selfless, wise gifts from a great woman, brings poignantly home the knowledge that "there never was any one like her."[16]

REID HALL HUMMED along through the 1930s after the disbelief at Elisabeth Mills Reid's death had passed, even when the Great Depression brought the occasional hardship to French shores. Sadly, though, a greater challenge arose in 1939: the imminent approach of the Second World War. After Hitler's invasion of Poland, Virginia Gildersleeve—coincidentally in Paris when French mobilization began against the Nazis—met with Reid Hall staff to face the looming crisis calmly and rationally. This was a true blessing, as Gildersleeve wrote in her 1954 memoir, *Many a Good Crusade.* "Unlike World War I, in which the actual outbreak of war came as a shock to many people, World War II hung over us before it broke, a visible, hovering menace."[17] In other words, they had time to act. Reid Hall evacuated its students methodically and safely before closing its doors in the autumn of 1939.[18]

As during the First World War, 4 rue de Chevreuse was once again repurposed during the early 1940s. Several proposed uses were floated to Reid Hall leadership and to Helen Rogers Reid (1882–1970), Elisabeth Mills Reid's daughter-in-law, who accepted responsibility for the Paris property

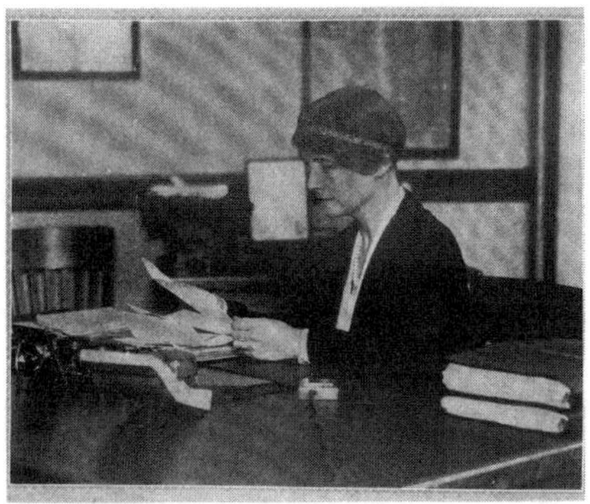

Figure 20.3. *Helen Rogers Reid, undated photograph. Reid Family Papers, Library of Congress.*

after her mother-in-law's death. As before, the Red Cross requested to operate it as a base for soldiers on leave,[19] but the center was instead provided as an alternative location for the École normale de Sèvres, a girls' school that had been destroyed during an air raid. Those girl students, in an attempt to stay warm during Paris's chilly winters, burned many of Reid Hall's original wood furnishings.[20] These "Sévriennes," as they were called, maintained use of Number 4 until after the liberation of Paris in 1944.

Reid Hall did not reopen for its intended purpose of fostering Franco-American relations for university women until September 1947, at which point the building's focus had changed yet again: this time, it became a residential and social hub for university undergraduates—not simply recent graduates or those pursuing further degrees, and not simply for Americans, either. The Hall quickly became a go-to location for academic conferences, colloquia, and guest speakerships for the international educational community. But there was certainly fun to be had, too. Dorothy Leet, now acting as Reid Hall's president, engaged her community with concerts, dances, and art exhibitions that showcased student work.[21] A particularly beloved event was an annual Thanksgiving dinner, which drew lauded speakers and esteemed guests, like Eleanor Roosevelt, who attended the 1951 celebration.[22] One wonders if the beloved "turkey frieze," with those "strutting gobblers," still remained, perched above the attendees of this midcentury feast. In events like these, the spirit of the Girls' Club lingered on.

Behind the scenes, Helen Rogers Reid pondered the future of 4 rue de Chevreuse. Like Virginia Gildersleeve and Dorothy Leet, Rogers Reid considered Franco-American relations—with an emphasis on education—to be the best use of the property. After World War Two, the educational component had become even stronger as Reid Hall became linked to a vast American study abroad program, deemed the "junior year abroad." The students who now resided temporarily under its roof journeyed there from schools like Middlebury College, Sweet Briar College, the University of Pennsylvania, Smith College, and—most crucially—Barnard College, an independent women's college connected to Columbia University. Helen Rogers Reid hoped to maintain this mission for the Paris compound now under her purview.

This educational mission was not a guarantee, however. Interestingly, discussion about 4 rue de Chevreuse remaining within the educational sector was still in question into the early 1960s, when Virginia Gildersleeve suggested to Helen Rogers Reid that the space might be offered to President John F. Kennedy for consolidation of—yet again!—Franco-American cultural relations, thereby "building on the foundations so long and so well established there."[23] Indeed, if it had ever been offered, such a proposal might well have been accepted by the president, being that his wife, Jacqueline Bouvier Kennedy, had studied at Reid Hall during the academic year of 1949–50 for her own junior year abroad with Smith College and harbored great affection for France and for Reid Hall itself.[24]

Still, the Barnard–Columbia link prevailed, and in 1964, 4 rue de Chevreuse was officially gifted to Columbia—a natural fit, given the educational component, but one that also made sense personally, since Helen Rogers Reid had graduated from Barnard in 1903 and later served as a member of the school's board of trustees.[25] "I shall be proud of having Columbia University enabled to have a headquarters in Paris and I feel sure it will be useful for this country in years ahead. It carries out the ideas of my mother-in-law, Mrs. Whitelaw Reid, as well as myself to have the property continue in an educational channel," wrote

Helen Rogers Reid.[26] Columbia maintains control of the property to this day.

As her generous gift showed, Helen Rogers Reid was a passionate philanthropist who dedicated herself to the betterment of others. In this way, she proved herself a worthy successor to Elisabeth Mills Reid, whose own charitable spirit led her to establish the American Girls' Club alongside Helen Newell back in the 1890s. It is thus fitting to learn that Rogers Reid lovingly displayed a portrait of Elisabeth Mills Reid in her office for many years, with the elder Reid's visage gazing down upon her, in the words of one author, like "a guardian angel benevolently watching."[27]

CHAPTER 21

The Hard Work of Remembering

Hundreds of students come to Paris annually and for all possible excuses or reasons, and out of one hundred, perhaps, one has enough grit and a steadfast purpose and a steady head sufficient to win and accomplish greatness . . . Even the strongest striking this tide forget their hard-earned rules and principles, and are lost. In the eagerness to do, they accomplish such which is valueless, unless personal, social or political influence can make their "manner" the fashion; then for a time they "arrive" and sell and are envied, but, oh, where will it all be twenty years hence?

—Enid Yandell, American artist (1895)[1]

The best praise that women have been able to command until now is to have it said that she paints like a man. But that women have a valid place as women artists is both obvious and logical . . . We want to speak to . . . an audience that asks simply—is it good, not—was it done by a woman.

—Anne Goldthwaite, American artist (1934)[2]

To consider the true importance of the American Girls' Club in Paris, we must focus not upon 4 rue de Chevreuse itself, but on the American Girls it received there. The women who crossed its threshold, like Anne Goldthwaite, Alice Morgan Wright, Meta Vaux

Warrick, Florence Lundborg, and Anna Lester, as well as philanthropist Elisabeth Mills Reid herself, were shaped by their experiences at the Club, mostly for the better (Warrick's story is probably the most notable exception). After their Parisian sojourns ended, many Club members returned to the United States with a great sense of achievement: they completed that pivotal final step in their artistic education while gaining international exposure, professional connections, lifelong friendships, and indelible memories. Yet almost all the women associated with the Club are unlikely to be familiar names to readers. Why?

Well, it's complicated. Yet by examining the post-Club years of some of these artists, we can glean some answers. Let us take the talented Anne Goldthwaite as an example.

In 1913, Goldthwaite returned to the United States after living at the American Girls' Club in Paris for several years. Fresh off her inclusion at the landmark Armory Show as well as her achievements in various Salons and gallery exhibitions, she finally considered herself an *"arrivée,"* as her old pal Frances Thomason had been when Anne had first set foot in Paris. Her pride in her blossoming career is evidenced by the fact that she joyfully announced her return to the staff of her alma mater, the National Academy of Design. She must have expected to be welcomed with much of the same support and enthusiasm that her work had received in Paris and with a proposed camaraderie equal to that of the Académie Moderne, or even the Girls' Club itself.

What she received instead could only have emphasized just how singular her experiences in Paris truly had been and how incredibly encouraging her life as an art student at the Club had been. Rather than boisterous acclaim and offers of exhibitions, or even suggestions for available teaching positions, as she had hoped, Goldthwaite was met with dismissive suggestions that she was not a *true* artist: as a woman, academy administrators noted, she should consider her work to be appropriate within the realm of "lady hobbyists."[3] It was an odd response to receive from an educational institution that purportedly aimed to support the professionalization of both women and men, and one whose instructors surely should have been pleased to hear of the successes of

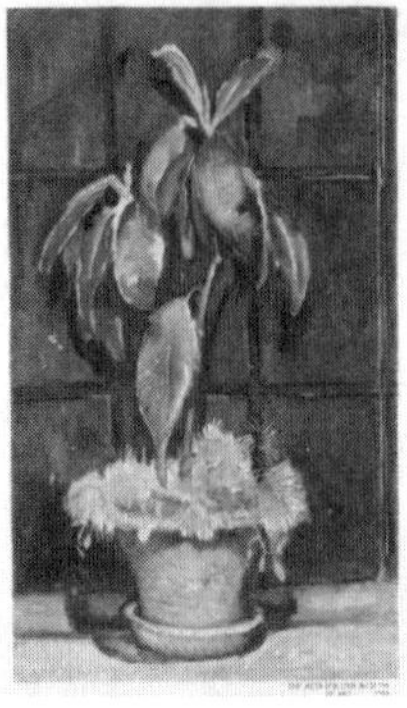

Figure 21.1. *Anne Goldthwaite,* A Window at Night, *ca. 1933.* Metropolitan Museum of Art.

any former student. Goldthwaite must have been extremely disappointed to be so callously brushed aside.

And yet she did not allow the dismissal to dissuade her. She continued to excel, becoming a much-beloved instructor at the exemplary Art Students League in New York and nabbing portrait commissions from the likes of Kate Wehle, the wife of Harry B. Wehle, the distinguished curator of paintings at the Metropolitan Museum of Art,[4] and Katherine S. Dreier, Goldthwaite's friend and fellow artist (see Fig. 19.2). In 1938, Harry Wehle himself added Goldthwaite to the Met's esteemed collection, purchasing *A Window at Night* (ca. 1933 [Fig. 21.1]), an oil painting of a potted tropical plant seated in front of the titular window. For a contemporary artist to be added to the Met's holdings during this period—while still alive, no less!—was a supreme coup, an honor not even awarded to one of the most acclaimed artists of midcentury America, Jackson Pollock.[5]

And yet to most Americans, Goldthwaite's name has been forgotten.

WHILE THAT IS certainly a shame, Goldthwaite's legacy—or, more accurately, the overlooking of her legacy—also makes a sad kind of sense: women artists worldwide have largely faded from memory over the centuries, barred and brushed aside in favor of their male counterparts. In 1971, art historian Linda Nochlin famously detailed the complexities of this practice in her now-iconic essay, "Why Have There Been No Great Women Artists?" The various reasons for these omissions have already been made clear in this history of the Club: a minimum of high-level artistic training available to women; reduced access to exhibition opportunities; the rampant dismissal of female artists as dilettantes or hobbyists rather than potential professionals. "The fault lies not in our stars . . . but in our institutions and our education," Nochlin affirmed.[6]

Some of the blame for the forgetting of the artists of the American Girls' Club may be placed, additionally, at the feet of America herself. From the start, the United States had been rather slow to accept the visual arts as a worthwhile career path for *anyone*, let alone women. Recall that early puritanical Americans looked upon the fine arts as needless frivolities; by extension, those creating works of art were viewed as equally trifling. These perceptions took an incredibly long time to diminish and directly influenced the popularity of Paris as a destination for expat artists, not only because of the city's breadth of academies and ateliers but equally due to the French's general disposition toward taking the arts (and artists) seriously—a distinction Anne Goldthwaite made quickly after her return to the States:

> I found that the great difference between the life of an art student here and in Paris is that in New York nobody is conscious of the fact that such individuals exist, nobody thinks of them as a class; each student is seen as a strange person who happened to go astray in a labyrinth called art. In Paris, on the other hand, they are a class whose existence is acknowledged as important and scarcely abnormal.[7]

Goldthwaite's realization is one that many Parisian-trained women shared. Her predecessor Mary Cassatt opted to settle permanently in France in 1874 for this exact reason, declaring, "After all give me France—women do not have to fight for recognition here, if they do serious work."[8]

But America and its institutions are not solely to blame for the forgetting of the women of the American Girls' Club in Paris. Though prejudices about gender and a general lack of encouragement of the visual arts played pivotal roles in the fortunes of these artists, we cannot overlook the influence of changing trends fueled by the massive shift of the center of the art world from Europe (particularly Paris) to North America (particularly New York). The term "midcentury art" immediately conjures mental images of overlarge canvases splattered with paint, à la Cy Twombly or Jackson Pollock (Pollock's own mentor, Thomas Hart Benton, was a colleague of Goldthwaite's at the Art Students League), or mesmerizing washes of color by Mark Rothko or Morris Louis. Though a handful of women, like Helen Frankenthaler and Joan Mitchell, gained prominence in American art during this period, the majority of acclaimed artwork in mid-twentieth-century America reflected a predilection for hyper-masculine abstraction. Imagine Pollock, flinging his paint as he trod across the surface of his canvases, which he splayed across his studio floor; he *dominated* them, sometimes leaving literal footprints in his wake. Imagine, too, Willem de Kooning and his haphazard figures—especially his women— paintings so thick with heavily applied pigments that his sitters resemble monsters rather than human beings, serving as portraits of possible internalized misogyny.[9] These works, more than anything, have come to symbolize midcentury American art and their artists: expressive, brash, abstract, physical, hard, controlling, even a bit brutish. (This overt midcentury predilection for championing male artists did not go unnoticed by their female peers. "The whole painting says in bold and aggressive tones: 'My name is Helen Frankenthaler—and goddammit, I know how to paint just as well as the boys,'" noted one contemporary review.[10])

In short: the work that came to define America during its most influential period in art history was the *opposite* of the intimate works produced by the majority of women who resided in, or frequented, the Club. Historian Whitney Chadwick described it perfectly when she wrote, "Valorizing stylistic innovation and monumental size, Modernist mythologizing leaves little room for the modest, stylistically consistent paintings" of most female artists of the twentieth century.[11] Just as the genre of history painting had long been viewed as the purview of men, so, too, followed Abstract Expressionism, Pop Art, and other midcentury art movements. Thus, through no fault of their own, women artists were once again left behind.

At the same time, we must not forget that when World War One forced the closure of the Club, avant-garde art was not yet widely accepted in either Europe *or* North America—and this was a fact of which the women of the Club were very aware. Cubism, for example, was still relatively new, and even some of Picasso's own friends—including other avant-garde artists—thought that his breakthrough painting, *Les Demoiselles d'Avignon* (1907, Museum of Modern Art, New York), was a joke.[12] Twenty-first-century readers might take for granted the radicality of these works of art, inured as we are by decades of exposure to them. But when new artistic styles are adopted, the viewing public is typically a step behind, slow to accept any change, let alone to trumpet something as "the next big thing in art." Even artists can be skeptical, as evidenced by Alice Morgan Wright in a 1910 letter to a friend: "The work of Matisse . . . is the most screamingly funny stuff that I ever laid eyeball on. Wait till you get over here and see it. Not by any possibility could you imagine anything so perfectly nutty."[13] (Wright's neighbor at the Club, Mildred Burrage, had a more generous opinion, recalling that the artist's now iconic *Dance* and *Music* [both 1910 and in St. Petersburg's Hermitage Museum] displayed "[n]o shading—no modeling—no anything—just red and green and blue. They were most extraordinary."[14])

Wright's offhand comment about Matisse brings up another point, one that art curators and historians struggle with today: supporting and purchasing contemporary art is a gamble, not a guarantee of financial appreciation and long-term critical acclaim. Though art professionals do their best to make educated decisions about which artists or works will stand the test of time, none of us are fortune tellers. To Wright, the Fauvist paintings of Henri Matisse were an absurd fad, worthy of little but ridicule. Neither she, nor Matisse himself, nor his collectors and dealers could have foreseen the vast effect his canvases would have on redirecting the path of modern art (alas, not even icons like Matisse and Picasso were soothsayers).

So: Why gamble at all, then? Why experiment with avant-gardism if gallerists and buyers might look the other way? Setting aside philosophical responses (*Can a creator ever stop creating?*), one essential answer remains: artists like Matisse and Picasso could *afford* to fail. This does not necessarily suggest a financial cushion, though that would have been helpful. More importantly, as men, they had the ability to follow an unconventional path with fewer consequences and with far more support than a female artist could. For artists like Goldthwaite and Wright, some experimentation was critical, but too much could be risky. It was a safer bet to stay closer to realism than to flirt too heartily with abstraction.

In truth, most of the artists associated with the Girls' Club in Paris, if they intended to return home to the United States to work professionally in the visual arts, assumed that a traditional or conservative style would net them the most commissions from both private and public institutions. A realistic portrait or a classically inspired fountain would likely appeal to a larger portion of the moneyed population than an experimental work. *That work looks like it was painted in quite a hurry,* collectors sometimes sneered at modern creations. Then there's the "my kid can do that!" argument lobbed often at the works of Pollock, Twombly, and their cohort even today. For early abstractionists, it was even riskier. To the wider early or mid-century public, "messy" works connoted a lack of care, precision, or even talent, all of which could reflect poorly on the appreciation of a work's value.[15]

A conservative approach to artmaking was thus deemed to be a safer bet, and the press—if there even *was* press coverage of early female-focused exhibitions in the States—supported this view. Of one such show in Boston in 1928, a complimentary critic noted, "It is all perfectly sane work—nothing eccentric, nothing meretricious about it."[16] A work's conservatism proved it worthy of acclaim during the early decades of the twentieth century. It was only later that the narrative shifted from underneath the feet of those creating such "perfectly sane work."

It is no mistake that the women whose names might be the most recognizable among Club members and residents are Marguerite Thompson Zorach

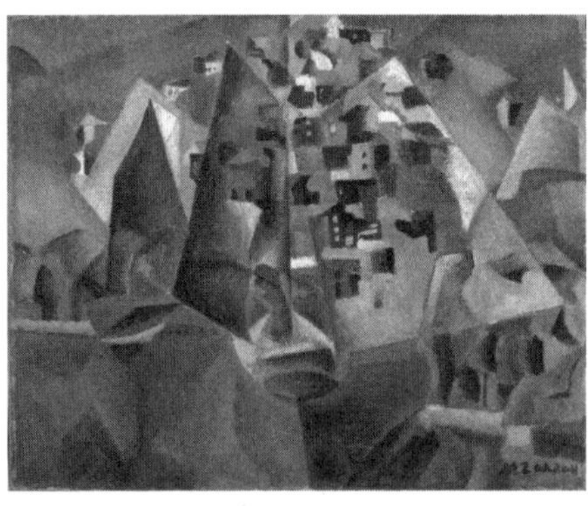

Figure 21.2. *Marguerite Thompson Zorach, Ships in the Harbor, 1917. Smithsonian American Art Museum.*

and Meta Vaux Warrick Fuller, two artists who experimented and adopted modernist styles both in Paris and back home. Their works more closely follow that narrative arc of twentieth-century art and thus are included in more of the history books devoted to this period. The "safe" artwork that a great number of late nineteenth- and early twentieth-century women (and men, too!) produced were moved instead to the basements of many museums and art associations, if not deaccessioned and removed from collections entirely.

This, by the by, is not to suggest that women who edged closer to the avant-garde had it much easier: Mary Cassatt, an AWAA member and one of the early adopters of Impressionism, was dismissed as a painter of "female subject matter"—mothers and children primarily. And Georgia O'Keeffe, with her intense oversized flowers, was similarly snubbed by some as producing metaphorical images of female genitalia, an interpretation that always angered the artist.[17] Gender biases remained, and remain, at play throughout the art world.

Just as artistic styles fall out of favor, so too do specific media. Printmaking—especially etchings—had long been viewed as an inexpensive way to distribute one's work widely, as opposed to, say, the unique singularity of a painting, which can only be owned by a particular individual or institution. At the end of the nineteenth century and even into the early decades of the twentieth, etchings still sold decently, and artists like Alice Rumph and Anne Goldthwaite supplemented their teaching salaries through print sales of their own work. But as historians have pointed out, by the 1940s, the market for prints had dried up.[18] Compared to painting and to the astronomic rise in the popularity of photography, demand for these works on paper remains niche, even now.

Recall, too, that a not-insignificant number of women associated with the Club in Paris produced miniatures—another medium that rapidly fell by the wayside in the twentieth century. And then there was the scourge of the stereotyping of works such as pastels, watercolors, garden sculpture, botanical illustrations, and portraits of children; being identified as the height of appropriate subjects for (amateur, of course) female artist throughout the centuries equaled an easy dismissal as insignificant.[19]

As difficult as it is to admit, another major reason that numerous—or dare we say *most*—Club artists have been lost to history is because many gave up their artistic careers after marriage, particularly if they went on to raise a child or several. Whether or not this abdication was by the artist's own choice is always a question and a complex one at that; suffice it to say that the nineteenth century's Cult of Domesticity, promoting the home as a woman's natural realm, still permeated the new century. Within creative circles, marriage and motherhood were typically considered the death knell of a woman's promising career. One story about the American sculptor Augustus Saint-Gaudens—who taught or hired several Club affiliates—reveals that the artist wept when he learned that one of his favorite female students was engaged to be married. "I suppose there'll be lots of festive children," Saint-Gaudens moaned, saddened by what he viewed as an automatically wasted talent.[20]

Even if an artist chose to continue her career after marriage and motherhood, she likely found it rather challenging. After marrying Solomon Fuller, a psychologist originally hailing from Liberia, in 1909,[21] Meta Vaux Warrick struggled to find the time and energy to sculpt—a difficulty that only grew after she gave birth to three children. Like many parents of young kids, Warrick Fuller found herself stymied by the endless demands of their care and its deleterious effect on her profession. "I am sticking to work as well as I can against all obstacles," she confessed in a letter to a friend. The pressure to be viewed as a "proper" mother, though, forced her to couch her note in a conciliatory and upbeat tone, continuing, "The obstacles are not, however, the dear little children. I would not have anyone think I held them as anything but a joy in spite of all their mischief."[22] One wonders, though, if it is a coincidence that her most professionally productive and inspired period occurred prior to her marriage.[23]

Conversely, female artists who remained unmarried and childless— Elizabeth Nourse, Janet Scudder, Malvina Hoffman, Florence Lundborg, Alice Rumph, Anne Goldthwaite, and others[24]—more easily pursued their artistic goals of creating and exhibiting their work. At the Armory Show in New York in 1913, fifty women were shown, and more than half of them were (and *remained*) unmarried,[25] in many cases choosing to stay unpartnered for the express purpose of forwarding their careers unabated. The epitome of the "great woman artist," Rosa Bonheur, succinctly summed up her philosophy, saying, "I wed art. It is my husband, my world, my life dream, the air I breathe. I know nothing else, feel nothing else, think nothing else."[26] It is not difficult to imagine that at least a segment of the Club's population likely felt the same.[27] But such dedication to one's work had its trade-offs, as Enid Yandell noted to a Louisville reporter in 1905. "Get married, girls," she advised readers. "Success in other lines is hard won—too hard."[28]

Of course, there are wonderful, if scant, examples of women who straddled career and motherhood with skill and aplomb. A particularly inspiring story is that of Pennsylvania-born Austa Densmore Sturdevant (1855–1936). Sturdevant was forty years old—and married with two children—when she opted to seek professional art training in Paris at the studio of the popular Raphaël Collin. Undeterred by middle age or family needs, Sturdevant packed up her daughters and moved to Paris from around 1895 until 1903,[29] when she returned to the United States and acquired the Cragsmoor Inn, an elegant hotel associated with the Cragsmoor artist colony in Ulster County, New York.[30] During her Paris period, Sturdevant established herself as a highly competent painter, exhibiting at least one AWAA show and two Salon des beaux-arts exhibitions and winning an honorable mention at the 1895 Salon for a portrait of her sister.[31]

These complicating and complicated factors—a woman's chosen style or medium, her subject matter, her marital status, her family's needs, and their level of support—*all* of these played heavily into the lives of a large segment of the population of the American Girls' Club in Paris, and may have contributed to their erasure from art history. But those artists that can be named today as Club residents and affiliates are, in some ways, extraordinarily lucky simply because evidence of their Parisian experiences and careers has survived. A fair number of women who showed their work as part of the American Woman's Art Association, for example, were only identified as "H. Edwards"[32] or "Miss Gaspell"[33]—and no other traces of their lives and works have (yet?) come to light.

JUST AS WOMEN from the Club have fared poorly in the retellings of the history of art, the Club itself also disappeared as a place of importance to a generation of women artists. Again, several factors could be at play here. The Club no longer exists—at least not as a club for female art students—though 4 rue de Chevreuse itself, as well as the Club's memory, survives. Yet it may be difficult to conjure excitement for a place whose existence has all but been forgotten or shared with only a select few. This forgetting began in the wake of the First World War when access to the site was shuttered in favor of emergency and health services. Even during the interwar years—when Montparnasse reached its pinnacle as an internationally renowned literature and art center (think Picasso, Dalí, Hemingway, the Fitzgeralds, Josephine Baker, Simone de Beauvoir, and Jean Paul Sartre, as a brief selection of those who flocked there),[34] the Girls' Club was already a decade gone. We can, though, appreciate that the Club was perhaps ahead of its time: when Elisabeth Mills Reid chose Montparnasse as the location of "her Club," she could not have foreseen its avant-garde potential, but it was nevertheless appropriately placed to be at the geographical center of Western art, if the Club had survived the war.

Further adding to the issue is the very group the Club protected and promoted: American women. Again, as a comparison: readers are more likely to run across the all-male American Art Association of Paris in Belle Époque histories because—well, because *men*. That the Club housed *only* women was one of its selling points to both art students and their parents or benefactors, but such female-only spaces are sometimes overlooked as inconsequential.

Adding fuel to this fire: the Club's own name, for goodness's sake. It does not help that everyone—from Elisabeth Mills Reid to the foreign press, from American Colonists to students of all stripes—referred to 4 rue de Chevreuse as the "American Girls' Club," instead of the more mature sounding "American Women's Club." "Girl," a sometimes[35] infantilizing term, invites neglect if not outright disdain. A girls' club in our contemporary era evokes trite imagery of playhouses, games, perhaps even dolls[36]—not a community focused on the comfort and professional lives of women.

And a final complaint: some may argue that the Club did not produce any "big-name" artists. Mary Cassatt and Elizabeth Nourse were involved in the American Woman's Art Association, sure—but how much were they *really* involved at the Club itself? It is, perhaps, a fair question. But these are *exactly* the reasons why the Club deserves a second look in the history of American art. It singularly harbored a large and continually rotating community of independent, talented, and driven young women who were among the first to actively seek professionalization in the visual arts. In a 1916 article about Anne Goldthwaite, the *International Studio* reviewer A. D. Defries commented, "In spite of isolated women artists in the past it is not too much to say that this generation is the first to develope the fine arts in women."[37]

Club members were not just important as part of the first generation of professional women artists; they were incredibly influential to the next generation of artists, too. A sizable portion of these women, if they continued as artists in their post–World War One years, became respected and lauded teachers, introducing many others to the pleasure and profession of the visual arts. Consider the timing of these women's return to the States, too: as instructors beginning their (artistic and/or teaching) careers in the 1910s or '20s, they had the ability to train and influence another impactful generation: the mid-century artists who helped transform the United States into the center of the art world and beyond. Returning to Anne Goldthwaite as a wonderful example: while at the Art Students League in the 1930s, she taught, according to the League's 1931 course booklet, "still life and antique for children." This class appears to have been the only one available to kids in this era.[38] Yet there is evidence that Goldthwaite's kiddie class made a significant impression on many youngsters, including one boy who attended one of her children's classes and enjoyed it so much that he returned to enroll in her watercolor course.[39] That boy, Stanley Kubrick, grew up to be one of the most important and foundational film directors of the twentieth century—and certainly one with an undeniable artistic flair.

The women of the American Girls' Club in Paris, and the understanding of their contributions, major and minor, to the development in American art, is a subject that is long overdue for reconsideration, and now it is up to us to do the hard work of remembering their lives and efforts. It is equally meaningful to shine a new light on the importance of a singular space to the development and nurturing of these women: the stately old building at 4 rue de Chevreuse that provided them safe and creative spaces to call their own, where they could find comfort, common ground, and the ability to forge paths that had not previously existed for them. We owe them that much and more, for no greater reason than this: to honor the courage it took to follow a previously unattainable star.

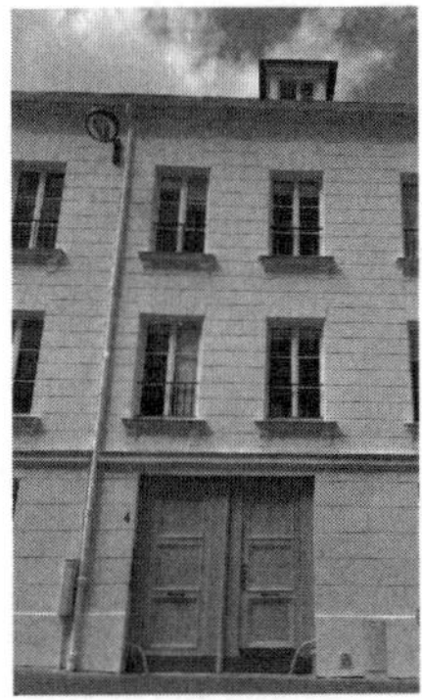

Figure E.1. *Façade of 4 rue de Chevreuse, September 2022. Photograph by the author.*

Sometimes, to step back into history, you simply have to ring the doorbell. In 2022, I stood on the doorstep of the former American Girls' Club in Paris, now Reid Hall, several intersections east of the Vavin Métro station and steps from the Rue Notre-Dame des Champs, waiting for the *réception-niste* to buzz me in. Around me, students came and went freely, unlocking the blue double doors with their *cartes d'identité*. Once inside, I met Krista Faurie, operations manager for Reid Hall and Columbia Global Centers, the linked organizations that now occupy the property. A petite brunette with an impeccably tied scarf (a dead giveaway of an American expat's assimilation into Paris), Faurie graced me with a tour of the property—"Over here is where the 'Little Tin Chapel' stood, and here was the restaurant"—before unlocking the door to my lodging for the evening. Here was one of the primary reasons I had made the trip to Paris in the first place: to stay in the studio apartment that now occupies a section of Reid Hall's second floor, where I could absorb firsthand the "luxury and romance" that I had previously only read about. The apartment is hidden behind a white door to the right of the building's iconic inner courtyard—a door that I immediately recalled as the mustard yellow one so lovingly rendered by Anne Goldthwaite in her 1908 painting *4 Rue de Chevreuse, Paris* (Fig. 15.7). During Goldthwaite's time, this space was likely used as a maintenance room or gardening shed, but in the recent past it has been converted into a suite to house visiting lecturers, faculty, and other short-term guests—like, say, a curious author. I rushed to fling open the studio's large windows to the courtyard, allowing in the crisp

September breeze. After all of this time, here I was, standing in what is the last remaining residence at 4 rue de Chevreuse.

At midday, Reid Hall hummed with activity: in the classrooms surrounding the inner courtyard, students discussed coursework, participated in lectures, and hunched over stickered laptops. I could just make out smatterings of conversation in both English and French. Laughter trickled across the cobblestones. And nearby, in the Grand Salon, a conversation of another kind was being had, one between saws and hammers. After more than a century, this structure, famed as the Club's exhibition and performance space since the early 1910s, was approaching the final stages of a much-needed restoration. This intensive project would be completed and inaugurated in June 2023, nine months after my visit.[1] On my next visit, or yours, we will be able to view its original, famous glass ceiling, which Faurie confirms to be utterly spectacular.

Roaming Reid Hall's interiors today, it can be challenging to suss out its previous iterations. Like many older Parisian buildings, this one has been retrofitted and renovated to serve the needs of its modern-day inhabitants. But this is not an anomaly in Reid Hall's history, as it was altered several times during Elisabeth Mills Reid's heyday and during the AAUW's takeover in the post–World War One years.

Undoubtedly, the largest change is that Reid Hall no longer houses students—male or female, artists or otherwise (as is the case with many

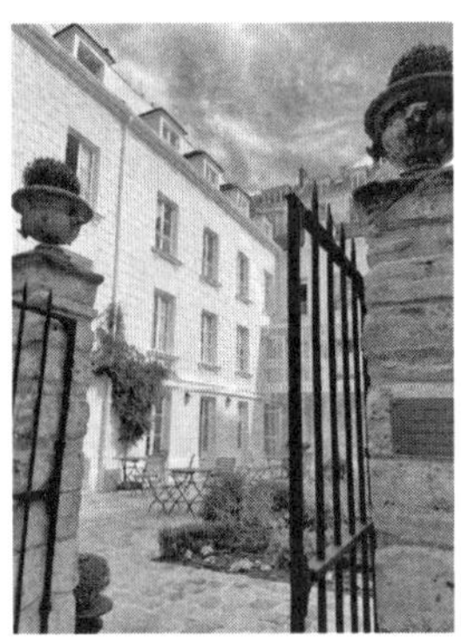

Figure E.2. *Entrance to courtyard of Reid Hall, September 2022. Photograph by the author.*

study abroad programs, students are frequently placed in home stays with local families instead). Today, Reid Hall's spaces instead accommodate classrooms, student lounges, and study nooks. Two of its four stories hold the daytime offices of Reid Hall staff and research fellows. It is now less dainty and more academic—a space replete with whitewash, modernist furniture, and glossy flyers announcing upcoming student exhibitions and faculty conferences.

Yet hints of Reid Hall's unique past are revealed if visitors keep their eyes open. For example, in the reception area immediately upon entry is a black-and-white reproduction of a 1922 portrait of Elisabeth Mills Reid by the Hungarian painter Philip Alexius de László, created when Reid was sixty-four years old.[2] In de László's treatment, she comes across as a slightly dour doyenne, white-haired, bespectacled, and enrobed in black organza and pearls. Displayed nearby is a complementary image, a smiling photograph of Helen Rogers Reid, the Hall's Columbia-era benefactor. The building, and its links to these two influential women, are made manifest here.

Even better, though, are the locations where the spirit of the place remains intact, little changed since the Belle Époque. Reid Hall's library, on the building's third floor adjoining the old "Annex," is just as warm and inviting as it was a hundred years ago. Today, it is dominated by a long, lamp-lit wooden table and more of the utilitarian furniture found throughout the Hall, but its wood-paneled bookshelves echo its storied past.

So, too, does an original work of art hung over the fireplace, a painting by Club resident Blondelle Malone (1877–1951). Malone, a native Southerner, had established herself as an adept painter of landscapes and garden scenes (she was later dubbed the "garden artist of America" by one critic[3]). Here, Malone played to her strengths and produced an engaging oil of the Club's garden in a bright autumnal palette (Fig. E.3).

Indeed, nowhere is Reid Hall more romantic and unchanging than in this garden and courtyard. With its wrought iron gate and stone walls, it is the place most deliciously evocative and awash in memory of past times, and it is where I chose to linger as the afternoon progressed into a dusky evening. By seven P.M., the Hall was nearly deserted, though I spied one or two individuals—fellows,

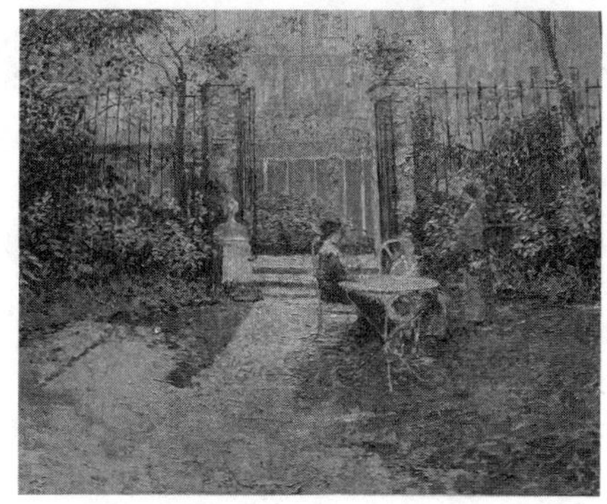

Figure E.3. *Blondelle Malone,* Gardens at 4 Rue de Chevreuse, *1913. Reid Hall collection.*

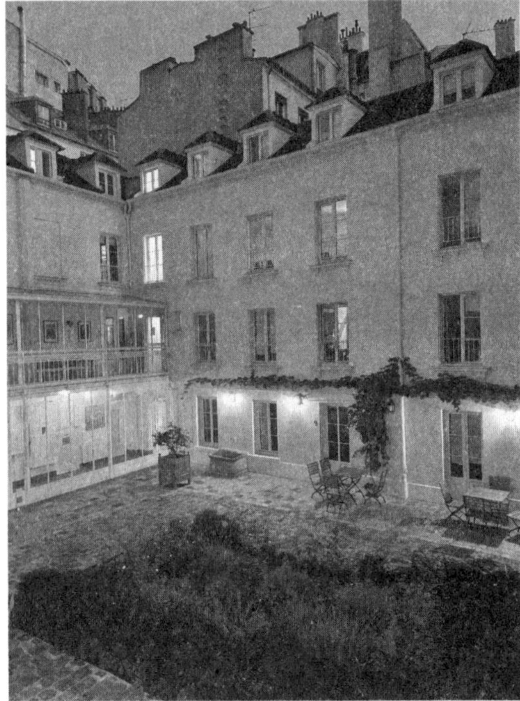

Figure E.4. *Interior courtyard of Reid Hall,*
September 2022. Photograph by the author.

perhaps—hastening to their workspaces above. Their overhead office lights blinked on and off in time with the traffic noise and police sirens of the nearby boulevard du Montparnasse but were soon extinguished. Except for Reid Hall's resident pet, a sweet black cat named Youki who has full reign of the place,[4] I was alone.

But, of course, I did not feel alone, not really. In this former Club, I was surrounded by the memory of the hundreds of women who visited here, lived here, began careers here, and spent their best days, months, or years here. I recalled the beneficence of Elisabeth Mills Reid, her prescience in choosing this "rambling old structure" and transforming it into a club, a tearoom, a library, an exhibition hall, and, above all, a home. Reid intended her Club to nurture, support, and shelter the women who sought comfort there during its decades-long tenure. That today it still does this, albeit in a different capacity and for a broader collection of travelers, is a testament to her vision and to the Club's lingering success.

Gazing around the darkened courtyard—the one where Alice Morgan Wright glanced out from a second-story window, where Anne Goldthwaite strolled on her way to afternoon tea, where Grace Turnbull paused for fresh air between studio sessions, where Meta Vaux Warrick carried her sculptures to install them at an AWAA show, and where a generation more were sheltered from the Parisian night—I lifted a glass of *vin rosé*, obtained earlier from a local wine shop. A sigh of contentment, a glance up to the stars, and I raised a toast—to the American Girls' Club in Paris, and to all the American girls who once called it their home.

AFTERLIVES

ANNE GOLDTHWAITE

Within a few years of her return to the United States, Anne Goldthwaite's works had been lauded in publications across the country; her representation in art exhibitions, too, grew with every year. In 1921, Goldthwaite secured a teaching position at the Art Students League in New York City, where she primarily taught drawing and painting classes on Saturdays. She quickly established herself as a beloved and sought-after instructor at the League, a position she held for more than twenty-two years. Teaching provided the artist with a consistent income as she pursued other ventures, including portrait commissions, mural projects with the Works Progress Administration, and a yearly stint at the Dixie Art Colony in Wetumpka, Alabama, where she often taught during her annual summer visits to family in Montgomery.[1] Many of her most renowned works were produced on these summer jaunts, and Goldthwaite became prized as a regional painter for her images of the American South.

Anne Goldthwaite died at the age of seventy-four on January 29, 1944, after a prolonged battle with cancer. In October of that year, a memorial retrospective of her work was displayed at the famed (and now defunct) Knoedler Gallery, for which curator Holger Cahill provided a brief biography. About the artist, he wrote that she was "one of the two or three leading women painters in this country, and . . . the leading painter of the South."[2]

ANNA MCNULTY LESTER

Anna Lester, who documented Parisian days in memorable letters to her family—detailed by her grandniece, Susan Gilbert Harvey, in her book *Tea with Sister Anna: A Paris Journal* (2005)—cherished her time studying in Pais at the Académies Julian and Delécluse, and elsewhere. Reading those letters more closely, though, reveals repeated references to her ill health, which precipitated her early return to her family home in Rome, Georgia. When she left Paris in December 1898, her days were already numbered. For nearly two years, Lester taught private painting lessons with optimism and good cheer, but her illness progressed rapidly until, in October 1900, she "faded away like a flower," dying of tuberculosis at the age of thirty-eight.[3]

FLORENCE LUNDBORG

Florence Lundborg, who triumphed as the painter of the "Queen of Hearts" mural at Henriette's, was lauded as among the best artists of early twentieth-century California, highly sought after as both a graphic designer and, most critically, a muralist. Before and after her stunning achievements at the Panama–Pacific International Exposition in 1915, she received commissions from wealthy private patrons not only in her home state, but beyond, too, completing projects in Portland, Chicago, New York, and elsewhere.[4] For nearly three decades after her sojourn in Paris, Lundborg remained a renowned figure in muralism. In 1932, she won a prestigious commission to create a mural, titled *The Quest for Knowledge*, at a high school in Staten Island; the work, restored in 1999, is still a celebrated centerpiece of the borough's artistic life.[5] After the early 1930s, though, little has survived regarding her final years.

Florence Lundborg died in New York City on January 18, 1949, at the age of seventy-seven. Though still rather unknown—especially outside of California and New York—her work has been slowly gaining in appreciation for the last few decades. An op-ed in the *Sacramento Bee* in 1979 added Lundborg's name to a list of California residents deserving of entries into a cultural hall of fame,[6] and in 1991, she was one of a half-dozen women exhibited in an acclaimed show at the

M. H. de Young Memorial Museum, "Viewpoints XV: A Time of Change—Northern California Women Artists, 1895–1920."[7]

ALICE RUMPH

Scholarship winner Alice Rumph dedicated her life to teaching, especially instructing women and girls in art. After her return to the United States in 1902, she opted to further her training, as so many did, by moving to New York. She attended the Chase School in 1903 (founded by American painter William Merritt Chase), before transferring back down to Alabama. In Birmingham, she taught at a private girls' school and reconnected with the city's art scene—so much so that when Birmingham formed its "art club" in 1908, Rumph was elected as its first vice president.[8] Like Anne Goldthwaite, Rumph was integral to not only training the next generation of women artists, but also supporting her hometown's cultural life.

Having enjoyed a taste for travel and exploring new locations, Alice Rumph became a bit peripatetic in the second half of her life. She traveled around the South, accepting teaching roles in Roanoke, Virginia, and Asheville, North Carolina, before moving north. Teaching painting, drawing, and etching, Rumph was beloved as an instructor in girls' schools up and down the East Coast. In 1942, she retired after twenty years at a school in Orange, New Jersey. She died at age eighty in Birmingham after "a long illness," according to her obituary; though the article does not specify her ailment, it does hint at a possible cause or precipitating factor: "The family requests that no flowers be sent, but that contributions be made to the Alabama Assn. for Mental Health."[9]

Alice's years in Paris had a lasting effect on her life: not only did her experiences there secure her prestigious teaching positions in multiple private schools, but they also enabled her to supplement her income at those institutions by teaching French, too. More importantly, Birmingham historian Vicki Leigh Ingham has noted that records survive indicating that Rumph took a group of students to Paris every summer, ostensibly to further the girls' art education. "She may have had difficulty adjusting to Paris originally, but once smitten, she apparently couldn't stay away," Ingham writes.[10]

ELIZABETH TAYLOR

Though she suffered from a lack of confidence while attending various Parisian art academies ("I shall never be a real artist," she complained in her letters[11]), Elizabeth Taylor eventually found her stride as a writer. As her journey to the Arctic Circle elucidates, she was not afraid of adventure, and Taylor used her exotic excursions as opportunities to produce illustrated articles about her exploits for such outlets as the *Atlantic* and *Popular Science*. These articles enticed readers as armchair travelogues but were equally enthralling for being written by a "lady adventurer." She managed to get herself into some fascinating predicaments: most famously, she was marooned in the Faroe Islands—now part of Denmark—for the entirety of World War One, an episode she recounted in her 1921 article "Five Years in a Faroe Attic."[12] Such experiences made Taylor a sought-after public speaker, too, so she often lectured to receptive crowds upon visits to the United States between trips.

Since her earliest days as an art student in Paris, Elizabeth Taylor claimed no permanent residence. After more than thirty years of itinerant adventure, she retired, in her late sixties, to a small cabin in Vermont. She died there at the age of seventy-six in 1932.[13]

GRACE TURNBULL

After spending the final year of the Great War in France as a volunteer for the American Red Cross, sculptor Grace Turnbull returned to the United States, settling home in Baltimore and reestablishing herself as a painter. Like her fellow Club alumna Elizabeth Taylor, Turnbull was an extensive traveler and found particular delight in depicting the scenery of her journeys (from the West Indies to the Grand Canyon, from Egypt to Mexico, and beyond). She presented these paintings in gallery exhibitions throughout the eastern United States.

Most interestingly, as she approached her fiftieth birthday, Turnbull made a major career pivot. "I ceased altogether to paint and took instead to sculpture which I believe is my more native bent," she noted in her autobiography, fittingly titled *Chips from My Chisel* (1953).[14] Critics, too, seemed to agree: "It was with sculptures of single nude figures—and of single animal figures as well—that Miss Turnbull was to achieve her best works," noted one *Baltimore Sun* reviewer of a post-humous exhibition in 1980.[15] Indeed, these single-figure works are the ones most frequently found in museums today, like the Baltimore Museum of Art and the Metropolitan Museum of Art.

In addition to her dedication to the visual arts, Turnbull was an active writer, publishing several books, from a novel (1954's *The Uncovered Well*) to a screed on the dangers of alcohol (1950's *Fruit of the Vine*), as well as volumes on art theory and a translation of the Greek philosopher Plotinus. She died in 1976 just two days before turning ninety-six, and was later commemorated in a small exhibition at the Baltimore Museum of Art, where she was claimed as a hometown hero ("Baltimore's Grace Turnbull," 1996).[16]

META VAUX WARRICK (LATER FULLER)

Meta Vaux Warrick's return to Philadelphia in the fall of 1902 was characterized by elevated expectations: hers, her family's, and those of the American press, too. All seemed bright: the *Philadelphia Tribune*, a local African American newspaper, announced her return as a triumph, calling her "the youngest and best sculptress of the race" and "the only colored woman sculptor in the world."[17] Buoyed by her Parisian successes, Fuller established her own studio in Philadelphia with the financial backing of her aunt and her mother.

Success stateside, though, remained somewhat elusive. She struggled to find exhibition opportunities and artistic representation at art galleries, potentially due to Warrick's doubly "negative" status, in the words of historian Renée Ater: as both female and Black, the American art cognoscenti may have dismissed her. Fuller would never reach the same pinnacles in the United States as she had in France.

Despite these obstacles, Warrick garnered several important projects, particularly after she followed the advice of her friend W. E. B. Du Bois and pivoted to become a ". . . [specialist] of Negro types."[18] The support she received from the African American community included a commission of twelve dioramas of "the progress of the Negro in America" for the Jamestown Tercentennial Exposition in 1907.[19] By the time of her death in 1968 at the age of ninety-one, she had acquired a quiet, underground acceptance as an adopted member of the Harlem Renaissance. Today, she is lauded as an original, daring artist whose mature works emanated a positive and celebratory vision of Black identity and artistic perseverance.

ALICE MORGAN WRIGHT

Some might argue that the story of Alice Morgan Wright begins and ends with activism—with a little sidestep into sculpture in the middle. While Wright found acclaim for her art career in the States, it often fell by the wayside in favor of other interests, as her political action depicts. After the ratification of the Nineteenth Amendment in 1920 granted American women the right to vote, Wright's sculpture career picked up speed, but only briefly. Returning home to Albany that year after several years in New York City, she established an art studio on the top floor of her childhood home, but she mostly ceased creating new work by around 1930; after 1940, she no longer exhibited.[20]

Alice Morgan Wright's animal activism is what she—and her life partner, Edith Goode—is most known for today. In her final decades, she was named chairman of the International Relations Committee for the National Humane Education Society (NHES), and in that capacity she led several initiatives for animal welfare at the United Nations.[21] Closer to home, she and Goode purchased 135 acres in northern Virginia, where they founded Peace Plantation, an animal refuge they funded in association with the NHES.[22] Her love of animals was a passion she pursued until the very end. After her death at age ninety-three on April 8, 1975, the majority of Wright's $3 million estate was given to the care and protection of animals.[23]

Alice Morgan Wright's sculptures continue to grow in esteem among curators, historians, and museumgoers. A cache of her works may be viewed at the Albany Institute of History and Art, where special exhibitions are occasionally dedicated to her; she is also represented in the collections of the Smithsonian American Art Museum and the Folger Shakespeare Library, both in Washington, D.C. A bronze cast of one of her Holloway sculptures of Emmeline Pankhurst is held in the Museum of London. A rather personal touch also greets visitors to the National Humane Education Society, both in person and online: the society's logo, designed by Alice Morgan Wright, features her self-portrait; she is seated in profile, tending to a dog while a cat bathes comfortably behind her.[24]

ACKNOWLEDGMENTS

I truly lucked out when writing my first book, *ArtCurious: Stories of the Unexpected, Slightly Odd, and Strangely Wonderful in Art History* (2020). By that, I mean that the writing process was (relatively) painless. Each chapter was its own discrete story, and though each required ample research, this format lent itself to generalities, pithy explanations, and the occasional glossing-over of an artist's life events in favor of a chapter's plot.

The Club is *not* the same as *ArtCurious*. It took a whole lot more work to bring it to fruition, and it was a bit of a beast at times if I am honest.

And more than anything, I cannot describe how utterly grateful I am to have been handed the opportunity to research, compose, and share such a sprawling story. What an incredible gift this project has been, and I am so delighted with it.

My boundless gratitude goes, first and foremost, to my literary agent, William Clark. Not only is he the greatest agent I could ever hope for, but he is also one of the kindest and most genuine people I have ever met. I am in awe of his unflappability, and I strive to be as generous and thoughtful as he is. Thank you, William!

Next up, the inimitable Grace McNamee, my editor at Bloomsbury. Grace just *got* the Girls' Club tale immediately and she made me even more excited to share it, knowing that I had such an incredible partner in this process. Grace, thank you for choosing me and the Club—what an honor it has been to work with you! A big thank you, too, to Hattie LeFavour for her additional editing expertise.

My additional appreciation goes out to the entire Bloomsbury team, including Kenli Manning, Callie Garnett, Suzanne Keller, Janet McDonald, Katherine Kiger, Lauren Ollerhead Fries, Lauren Wilson, and Katie Vaughn. I felt your enthusiasm for this book from day one, and I am still buzzing on it. Thank you to Patti Ratchford for designing The. Perfect. Cover.

The nature of this project meant that not only did I utilize hundreds—*really*! check out that notes section!—of sources to educate myself and to establish a foundation for this story, but I had to undertake some serious on-the-ground archival research. Shout-outs to the many staff members and researchers at the following institutions, who aided me in my journey: the Archives of American Art, Smithsonian Institution, Washington, D.C.; the Sophia Smith Collection, Smith College, Northampton, Massachusetts; University Archives, Rare Book and Manuscript Library, Columbia University Library, New York; the Library of Congress, Washington, D.C.; and the Bibliothèque Nationale, Paris. Thank you to W. Douglas McCombs, PhD, for the behind-the-scenes access to the Alice Morgan Wright collection and archives at the Albany Institute of History and Art—what a treasure trove! Crucially, I send my great appreciation to the administration of Reid Hall, particularly director Brunhilde Biebuyck, operations manager Krista D. Faurie, and senior HR and finance manager Adriana Samaniego. Reid Hall's comprehensive website is a wealth of knowledge on this one-of-a-kind place. And finally, a special nod to Margie White, who clued me in to the Club's existence in the first place.

Large chunks of this book were completed while enjoying two wonderful writing residencies. My thanks to the Weymouth Center for the Arts & Humanities (Southern Pines, North Carolina), for housing me for two wonderful weeks, and *merci*, Angie Tally, for recommending Weymouth to me. Thanks, too, to the Writers' Colony at Dairy Hollow (Eureka Springs, Arkansas) for a blissful week's stay. Not having to think about meals was such a treat.

Speaking of writing residencies: I still required a quiet getaway to do some solid work after those residencies concluded. When Diane Beckman and Douglas Harned offered the no-strings-attached, repeated use of their lakeside cottage, it was an answered prayer. Diane and Douglas, I cannot thank you enough for providing the space I sorely needed to think, write, and rest.

Lots of love and gigantic thanks to Shannon Johnstone, who—yet again!—delivered a truly spectacular set of author photos. Her photography skills have no bounds, and believe me when I say that she makes me look *way* better than I actually do.

In the initial days of preparation for *The Club*, I benefited from the research capabilities of several *ArtCurious* podcast volunteers. Brittany Ashley helped me wrap my mind around the vast history of American expatriates living in Paris; Anna Kienberger and Holly Sauer tracked down an immense amount of information about Anne Goldthwaite and Alice Morgan Wright; Kate Sippey provided great summaries of nineteenth-century educational opportunities for women artists. Most importantly, Savannah Hubbard tracked down dozens of newspaper and journal articles for me, establishing much of my earliest body of research and saving me from a massive headache in the process.

For her generosity, I send thanks to Jenny Rossberg of NYU Press for providing me with several (free!) books that aided in my understanding of certain topics, especially suffrage. Eric J. Segal, PhD, granted me access to his fantastic article "The Ghost of Reid Hall," which lent further color to the already delightful descriptions of the American Girls' Club. Lisette Fischer, a former sales assistant at Mary Ryan Gallery, New York, sent me a copy of an excellent catalogue on Ethel Mars and Maud Hunt Squire.

To the dozens of staff members at Wake County Public Libraries (including one of my besties, Megan Marshall Kaiser!)—thank you for tirelessly fulfilling my repeated requests for interlibrary loans over the course of two and a half years. Thank you to *all* librarians out there, for that matter. I truly cannot imagine life without my local library, nor would I ever want to.

Many friends and family members cheered me on throughout the entire research and writing process, with extra-special appreciation to Rizza Abuan, Laura Finan, Sean Fitzgibbon, Laura Hart, Elaine and John Loyack, Molly Matlock, Sujata Mody, Veronica Roman, Carrie and Ben Sigrist, Steve and Judy Spiro, and Juli Kempton-Woodward. I love all of you!

How can I properly thank my beautiful and amazing parents, Elizabeth and David Ward? I won the kiddo lottery when I was born to them, and I will never forget it. Thank you, Parentals, for the millions of things you have done—large and small—to bring us all to this point in time. I love you so incredibly much. Thanks, too, for putting up with all of my ramblings about our beloved "art crap" over these past twenty-five years. I think it has all turned out pretty well.

My little man, Felix. When we named you, your daddy and I thought that it was extra-cool that your name means "fortunate" and "happy," with hopes that those little words might act as totems for your bright future. Now I know that we—your parents—are the truly fortunate and happy ones. How lucky am I to be your mama. My life became bigger and better when you came into it. *Je t'aime pour toujours.*

And most of all, to Josh, always. There was not a single moment during the writing of this book that you were not right there beside me with assurances and confidence, with a shoulder rub and a negroni (or two), and with unfailing support and love. Thank you for believing in me at every turn, for always lending a listening ear, for suggesting solutions when I was stuck, for reading early drafts, for tackling bedtime duties when I was in the flow, for queuing up *Better Call Saul* (again) when you knew I needed a Kim and Jimmy fix, and for never complaining that I was scheduled for yet *another* writing getaway. I love you more than I can say, but I will spend the rest of my life trying to say it.

Last but not least: to you, dear reader. Authoring a book is a long and mostly solitary process, and to know that it would eventually end up in your hands was a balm that carried me through. Thank you for picking up this copy and know that I so appreciate you.

IMAGE CREDITS

Figure P.1: "Garden of the Art Club." In Emily Meredyth Aylward, "The American Girls' Art Club in Paris," *Scribner's Magazine* 16, no. 5 (November 1894): 601.

Figure 1.1: Photograph of Anna Lester, undated. In Susan Gilbert Harvey, *Tea with Sister Anna: A Paris Journal* (Rome, GA: Golden Apple Press, 2005).

Figure 1.2: Gustave Caillebotte. *Paris Street; Rainy Day*, 1877. Oil on canvas, 83½ × 108¾ in., Art Institute of Chicago, Charles H. and Mary F. S. Worcester Collection, 1964 (1964.336).

Figure 1.3: Edouard Baldus. *Paris. Panorama* / E. Baldus. Paris Île de la Cité France, between 1851 and 1870. Washington, D.C.: Library of Congress. https://www.loc.gov/item/94503987/.

Figure 2.1: Photograph of Katherine M. Cohen. In Mary Kavanaugh Oldham Eagle, *The Congress of Women: Held in the Woman's Building, World's Columbian Exposition, Chicago, USA, 1893* (Chicago: Monarch Book Company, 1894).

Figure 2.2: Thomas Cole. *View from Mount Holyoke, Northampton, Massachusetts, after a Thunderstorm—The Oxbow*, 1836. Oil on canvas, 51½ × 76 in. Metropolitan Museum of Art, Gift of Mrs. Russell Sage, 1908 (08.228).

Figure 2.3: Frederic Edwin Church. *Niagara*, 1857. Oil on canvas, 40 × 90½ in. National Gallery of Art, Washington, D.C., Corcoran Collection (Museum Purchase, Gallery Fund), 2014 (2014.79.10).

Figure 3.1: Enid Bland Yandell (center) and Janet Scudder (left) in studio, ca. 1891. Enid Bland Yandell Photograph Collection, the Filson Historical Society Digital Projects, Louisville, KY (987PC52X.071).

Figure 3.2: "The Sphere of Woman." In *Godey's Lady's Book* 40 (March 1850): 219.

Figure 3.3: Grace Turnbull. *Nude*, undated. In Grace H. Turnbull, *Chips from My Chisel* (Rindge, NH: Richard R. Smith, 1953), plate 16.

Figure 3.4: Circle of Eakins. *Women's Modeling Class with Cow in Pennsylvania Academy Studio*, ca. 1882. Albumen copy print, 3 ¹¹⁄₁₆ × 4 ¹⁵⁄₁₆ in. Pennsylvania Academy of Fine Arts, Charles Bregler's Thomas Eakins Collection, purchased with the partial support of the Pew Memorial Trust, 1985 (1985.68.2.801).

Figure 4.1: "Working the Pickpocket Racket." In Gustave Macé, *Paris Unveiled* (New York: R.K. Fox, 1888). Washington, D.C.: Library of Congress. https://www.loc.gov/item/04021513/.

Figure 4.2: Headline from Bessie van Vorst, "Martyrs to Art in the French Capital: Nine American Girls Have Gone Crazy in the Latin Quarter of Paris from Starvation," *Louisville Courier-Journal*, December 10, 1899: 26.

Figure 4.3: Henri Boutet. "1892, Women's Fashion in Nineteenth Century Paris." New York Public Library Digital collections, the Miriam and Ira D. Wallach Division of Art, Prints and Photographs: Art & Architecture Collection. https://digitalcollections.nypl.org/items/510d47da-3993 -a3d9-e040-e00a18064a99.

Figure 5.1: Whitelaw Reid and Elisabeth Mills Reid with their children, ca. 1890s. Washington, D.C.: Reid Family Papers, Library of Congress.

Figure 5.2: Mrs. Whitelaw Reid. Undated photograph, Bain News Service. Washington, D.C.: Library of Congress. https://www.loc.gov/item /2014681154/.

Figure 5.3: Spire of the American Cathedral of the Holy Trinity, Paris, September 2022. Photograph courtesy of the author.

Figure 5.4: "St. Luke's, Rue de la Grande Chaumière." In "Holy Trinity, First American Church in Paris, Holds Anniversary Celebration," *New York Herald* European edition, September 15, 1912: 6.

Figure 5.5: "The Mother Home." In Mrs. Travers (Ada Leigh) Lewis, *Homeless in Paris: The Founding of the "Ada Leigh" Homes* (New York: Macmillan, 1920), 40.

Figure 6.1: "American Art Students Club." Postcard, ca. 1910. Alice Morgan Wright Papers, Sophia Smith Collection, Smith College, Northampton, MA.

Figure 6.2: Detail of duelers in Montparnasse, from a 1675 map of Paris by Albert Jouvin de Rochefort. Wikimedia Commons: https://commons .wikimedia.org/wiki/File:Paris_map_1672_(Jouvin_de_Rochefort)_1 -4_reduction_-_Gallica.jpg.

Figure 6.3: Jean-Pierre Franque. *Marie de Rohan*, 1839. Oil on canvas, 20½ × 20½ in. Versailles, Châteaux de Versailles et de Trianon, MV7827. https://www .photo.rmn.fr/CS.aspx?VP3=SearchResult&VBID=2CMFCI60VITPFR &SMLS=1&RW=1536&RH=703.

Figure 6.4: Dagoty, Cup and Saucer, ca. 1810. Hard-paste porcelain, 3 ¼ in. × 5 in. Metropolitan Museum of Art, gift of Alfred Duane Pell, 1902 (02.6.76, .77).

Figure 7.1: *Frances Cranmer Greenman*, undated. Hennepin History Museum. Image from HHM Archives.

Figure 7.2: "At the Gate of the Girls' Club." In "The Girls' Art Club," *Lincoln Nebraska State Journal*, April 7, 1895: 10.

Figure 7.3: "The Library in the Ladies' Club in the Rue de Chevreuse." In C. T. Mason, "American Artists in Paris," *Broadway Magazine* (1905): 6.

Figure 7.4: "A Typical Girls' Studio in Paris." In "The American Girls' Club in Paris," *Town & Country*, July 17, 1909: 16.

Figure 7.5: "Afternoon Tea at the Club." In Emily Meredyth Aylward, "The American Girls' Art Club in Paris," *Scribner's Magazine* 16, no. 5 (November 1894): 604.

Figure 7.6: Illustration of afternoon tea at the Girls' Club. In "Men's Art Clubs Fail," *Cleveland Plain Dealer*, April 3, 1910: 64.

Figure 8.1: "Early Breakfast." In Emily Meredyth Aylward, "The American Girls' Art Club in Paris," *Scribner's Magazine* 16, no. 5 (November 1894): 603.

Figure 8.2: "One of the Art Students." In Emily Meredyth Aylward, "The American Girls' Art Club in Paris," *Scribner's Magazine* 16, no. 5 (November 1894): 599.

Figure 8.3: Reproduction of Ida Sedgwick Proper's *Five O' Clock Tea* (now lost). In "Pictures by American Artists Exhibited at the New Salon Which Opened Last Week in Paris," *New York Sun*, April 17, 1910: 36.

Figure 9.1: Postcard sent to Anna Lester, postmarked November 1898. In Susan Gilbert Harvey, *Tea with Sister Anna: A Paris Journal* (Rome, GA: Golden Apple Press, 2005).

Figure 9.2: Group of art students, Académie Julian, Paris, ca. 1885. [Printed Later] Photograph. Washington, D.C.: Library of Congress https://www .loc.gov/item/2001697170/.

Figure 9.3: Anna McNulty Lester. *Untitled* [nude charcoal study], undated [1897 or 1898]. In Susan Gilbert Harvey, *Tea with Sister Anna: A Paris Journal* (Rome, GA: Golden Apple Press, 2005).

Figure 9.4: Blaikie, Frances M. B. *Out for the Afternoon*, 1898. In Susan Gilbert Harvey, *Tea with Sister Anna: A Paris Journal* (Rome, GA: Golden Apple Press, 2005), 199.

Figure 9.5: "Library: American Students' Club for Women, Paris." In Laura McProud, *American Students' Census, Paris, 1903* (Paris: Laura McProud, 1903).

Figure 10.1: Alice Rumph, ca. 1900. Birmingham Public Library. Hill Ferguson Papers, Historical Collection; Collection #56.6, Archives Department.

Figure 10.2: Jean-André Rixens. *Un Jour de Vernissage au Palais des Champs-Élysées*, 1890. In Albert Wolff, *Figaro-Salon 1890* (Paris: Goupil & cie., 1890), 66.

Figure 11.1: The die or logo of the AWAA, designed by AGCP member Marion Holden, ca. 1901. Printed on the cover of the *Catalogue of the American Woman's Art Association*, February 12–28, 1910. Archives of American Art.

Figure 11.2: Grace Turnbull. *Mother and Child*. Oil stain, ca. 1913. In Grace H. Turnbull, *Chips from My Chisel* (Rindge, NH: Richard R. Smith, 1953), plate 12.

Figure 11.3: "American Women's Society Opens Annual Picture Show." In *New York Herald* European edition, February 19, 1911: 6.

Figure 12.1: Charles Dana Gibson. *Scribner's for June*, 1895. Washington, D.C.: Library of Congress. https://www.loc.gov/item/2002720198/.

Figure 12.2: Reproduction of Gertrude Weil's *A New England Garden*. In "Glimpses of the Academy of Fine Arts Exhibition." *Philadelphia Inquirer*, March 2, 1892: 4.

Figure 12.3: Reproduction of Gertrude Weil's "Académie Vitti" poster. In Storrs Lee, "The Sketch Exhibition of the American Girls' Club," *Quartier Latin* 2 (January 1897): 166.

Figure 12.4: Cartoon of Jessie Allen. In "A California Artist," *Janesville* (WI) *Daily Gazette*, February 10, 1898: 7.

Figure 13.1: Florence Lundborg in her studio, undated. Washington, D.C.: Library of Congress. https://www.loc.gov/item/2002722922/.

Figure 13.2: "Waiting for Henrietta to Open the Door." In Bessie van Vorst, "Martyrs to Art in the French Capital: Nine American Girls Have Gone Crazy in the Latin Quarter of Paris from Starvation," *Louisville Courier-Journal*, December 10, 1899: 26.

Figure 13.3: "Rue Léopold-Robert," undated. Postcard, Kenyon College, Orville E. Watson, D.D. Postcard Collection. 972. https://digital.kenyon .edu/watson_postcards/972.

Figure 13.4: "Queen of Hearts." In "The Parisian Café Decorated by a San Francisco Girl," *San Francisco Chronicle*, September 2, 1900: 26.

Figure 13.5: Cartoon of Florence Lundborg. In "The Parisian Café Decorated by a San Francisco Girl." *San Francisco Chronicle*, September 2, 1900: 26.

Figure 13.6: "The Knave." In "The Parisian Café Decorated by a San Francisco Girl," *San Francisco Chronicle*, September 2, 1900: 26.

Figure 13.7: "Miss Florence Lundborg's Mural Decoration." In "S.F. Woman Triumphs in Work of Art." *San Francisco Examiner*, April 25, 1915: 38.

Figure 14.1: Portrait of sculptor Meta Vaux Warrick Fuller, ca. 1910. New York Public Library Digital Collections, Schomburg Center for Research in Black Culture, Photographs and Prints Division.

Figure 14.2: Frederick Gutekunst. *Henry Ossawa Tanner*, 1907. Photograph on board, image: $5\,7/8 \times 4\,5/16$ in.; board: $6\,11/16 \times 4\,5/16$ in. Henry Ossawa Tanner papers, 1860s–1978. Archives of American Art, Smithsonian Institution.

Figure 14.3: Photograph of Edmonia Lewis, undated. New York Public Library Digital Collections, Schomburg Center for Research in Black Culture, Photographs and Prints Division.

Figure 14.4: Eugène Carrière. *Affiche pour l'exposition Rodin à l'Alma*, 1900. Color lithograph. Bibliothèque Forney, Paris.

Figure 14.5: Edward Steichen. *Rodin*, 1903. In *Camera Work* 2 (April 1903), plate I. Washington, D.C.: Library of Congress, https://www.loc.gov/pictures/item/2003663003/.

Figure 14.6: *"Exposition de Sculptures de Mlle Meta Warrick,"* exhibition poster, 1902. 13×18 in. From the scrapbook of Meta Vaux Warrick Fuller. Collection of the Danforth Art Museum at Framingham State University, gift from Carnel Hoover. Photo: Danforth Art Museum.

Figure 15.1: Anne Goldthwaite, *Self-Portrait*, ca. 1918. Etching on paper, $9\,3/4 \times 7\,7/8$ in. Amon Carter Museum of American Art, Fort Worth, Texas, gift of Adelyn D. Breeskin, 1982 (1982.14).

Figure 15.2: Anne Goldthwaite. *Luxembourg Fountain (No. 2)*, about 1908. Etching on paper, $8\,1/8$ in. $\times$ $5\,13/16$ in. Montgomery Museum of Fine Arts, gift of Adelyn D. Breeskin, 1982 (1982.0016.0035).

Figure 15.3: Gertrude Stein sitting on a sofa in her Paris studio, with a portrait of her by Pablo Picasso, and other modern art paintings, hanging on the wall behind her, undated. Washington, D.C.: Library of Congress. https://www.loc.gov/item/2011645501/.

Figure 15.4: Anne Goldthwaite, *The Cellist—A School Study*, about 1901. Etching on paper, 8 15/16 in. × 5 13/16 in. Montgomery Museum of Fine Arts, gift of Adelyn D. Breeskin, 1982 (1982.0016.0005).

Figure 15.5: Anne Goldthwaite. *The House on the Hill*, ca. 1910/1911. Blount International Corporate Art Collection, Birmingham, Alabama.

Figure 15.6: Anne Goldthwaite. *Gate at 3 Rue de Chevreuse* about 1907. Etching, 4 11/16 in. × 2 15/16 in. Montgomery Museum of Fine Arts, gift of Adelyn D. Breeskin, 1982 (1982.0016.0017).

Figure 15.7: Anne Goldthwaite. *4 Rue de Chevreuse, Paris*, 1908. Oil on canvas, 28 13/16 × 23 3/4 in. Whitney Museum of American Art, gift of Gertrude Vanderbilt Whitney, 1931 (31.218).

Figure 16.1: Alice Morgan Wright in her Paris studio, ca. 1910. Alice Morgan Wright Papers, Sophia Smith Collection, Smith College, Northampton, Massachusetts.

Figure 16.2: Undated photograph of Alice Morgan Wright (seated, at right) and three women, most likely at the American Girls' Club in Paris. Alice Morgan Wright Papers, Sophia Smith Collection, Smith College, Northampton, Massachusetts.

Figure 16.3: Emmeline Pankhurst, ca. 1912. Bain News Service. Washington, D.C.: Library of Congress. https://www.loc.gov/item/2014691830/.

Figure 16.4: Alice Morgan Wright. *Emmeline Pankhurst*, n.d. (1912). Cast stone, 10½ in. (height). Albany Institute of History and Art, gift of Elinor Wright (Mrs. Clark) Fleming, cousin of the artist, 2004 (2004.1.27).

Figure 16.5: Cartoon of Alice Morgan Wright. In *Anaconda* (MT) *Standard*, March 23, 1912: 4. https://newspaperarchive.com/anaconda-standard-mar -23-1912-p-4/.

Figure 16.6: Metropolitan Museum of Art Study Collection of American Sculpture Photographs, Smithsonian American Art Museum.

Figure 16.7: Alice Morgan Wright, *Trojan Women*, 1927. Painted Bronze, 23 × 12 × 22 in. Albany Institute of History and Art, gift of Elinor Wright (Mrs. Clark) Fleming, cousin of the artist, 1978 (1978.21.3).

Figure 17.1: "American Art Students' Club House Annex, Almost Doubling Accommodation, Opened." *New York Herald* European edition, November 3, 1912: 6.

Figure 18.1: Kate Edwards. "Mrs. James van Allen Shields, Beta Epsilon." In Susan Myers, "Mrs. James van Allen Shields, Beta Epsilon," *The Key* 32, no. 1 (February 1915): 32.

Figure 18.2: "Rodin and M. H. in August 1914, at Châtelet en Brie, near Fontainebleau." In Malvina Hoffman, *Heads and Tales in Many Lands* (New York: Charles Scribner's Sons, 1937), 50.

Figure 18.3: "American Red Cross Military Hospital number 3, rue de Chevreuse, Paris." Washington, D.C.: Library of Congress. https://www .loc.gov/item/2017674351/.

Figure 18.4: Lewis Wickes Hine. "Mrs. Whitlaw Reid and Colonel Gibson, A.R.C., visiting Hospital number3, 4 rue Chevereux [sic], Hospital for Officers." Washington, D.C.: Library of Congress. https://www.loc.gov /item/2017682161/.

Figure 18.5: "First attempts at exercise. Convalescent American officers in the garden of American Military Hospital number 3, rue de Cheveruse [*sic*], Paris." Washington, D.C.: Library of Congress. https://www.loc.gov /item/2017667934/.

Figure 19.1: Harris & Ewing, photographers. Virginia Gildersleeve, undated. Washington, D.C.: Library of Congress. https://www.loc.gov/item /2016862354/.

Figure 19.2: Anne Goldthwaite. *Portrait of Katherine S. Dreier (1877–1952)*, 1915–16. Oil on canvas, 22 × 19 in. Yale University Art Gallery, gift of Collection Société Anonyme, 1941 (1941.486).

Figure 20.1: Detail of Elisabeth Mills Reid's diplomatic passport, ca. 1917. Washington, D.C.: Reid Family Papers, Library of Congress.

Figure 20.2: John Singer Sargent. *Elisabeth Mills Reid*, ca. 1912. Charcoal on paper, 9¾ × 7½ in. https://www.mutualart.com/Artwork/Portrait-of -Elisabeth-Mills-Reid/.

Figure 20.3: Helen Rogers Reid, undated photograph. Washington, D.C.: Reid Family Papers, Library of Congress.

Figure 21.1: Anne Goldthwaite. *A Window at Night*, ca. 1933. Oil on canvas, 44 × 26¼ in. Metropolitan Museum of Art, George A. Hearn Fund, 1938 (38.48).

Figure 21.2: Marguerite Thompson Zorach. *Ships in the Harbor*, 1917. Oil on canvas, 16⅛ × 20⅛ in. Smithsonian American Art Museum, gift from the collection of the Zorach children, 1970 (1970.65.7).

Figure E.1: Façade of 4 rue de Chevreuse, September 2022. Photograph by the author.

Figure E.2: Entrance to courtyard of Reid Hall, September 2022. Photograph by the author.

Figure E.3: Blondelle Malone. *Gardens at 4 Rue de Chevreuse*, 1913. Oil on canvas. Reid Hall collection, photograph by the author.

Figure E.4: Interior courtyard of Reid Hall, September 2022. Photograph by the author.

PLATE SECTION

Page 1 (left): Roy Fox Fine Art Photography © de Laszlo Foundation.

Page 1 (right): Courtesy of the Minneapolis Institute of Art.

Page 2: Courtesy of the Smithsonian American Art Museum.

Page 3 (top): Courtesy of the Greenville County Museum of Art, museum purchase with funds raised through the 2020 Art for Greenville campaign and a generous donation from the United Community Bank Foundation / Photography credit: Jamie M. Stukenberg Fine Art Photography, Rockford IL.

Page 3 (bottom): Courtesy of the Greenville County Museum of Art, Greenville, SC, gift of Richard W. Goldthwaite in memory of Anne Goldthwaite / Photography credit: Jamie M. Stukenberg Fine Art Photography, Rockford IL.

Page 4 (top): Courtesy of the author.

Page 4 (bottom): Julia Morgan Papers, MS0010, Special Collections and Archives, California Polytechnic State University San Luis Obispo.

Page 5 (top): Collection of Maryhill Museum of Art.

Page 5 (bottom): Meta Vaux Warrick, "Man Eating His Heart," in H. Harrison Wayman, "Meta Vaux Warrick (Sculptress)." *Colored American Magazine* 6, no. 5 (March 1903): 326.

Page 6: Courtesy of the Albany Institute of History & Art.

Page 7 (left): Courtesy of Metropolitan Museum of Art Study Collection of American Sculpture Photographs / Smithsonian American Art Museum.

Page 7 (right): Courtesy of the Albany Institute of History & Art.

Page 8: Digital image courtesy of Whitney Museum of American Art / Licensed by Scala.

NOTES

PROLOGUE

1   As noted, the American Girls' Club in Paris has been known under various names: as a few examples, it was called the Girls' Club (*Chicago Tribune*, 1894, and *Town and Country*, 1909); the American Art Students' Club (*New York Times*, 1894, and *San Francisco Call*, 1908); the American Girls' Club for Artists (*Washington Post*, 1903); the Ladies' Club (*Broadway Magazine*, 1909). Even the current Reid Hall website, associated with Columbia University, refers to this period of its building's history as the "Girls' Art Club." I have chosen to follow in the footsteps of the artists who frequented or resided at the Club, like Alice Morgan Wright, who often called it "The Club" in her correspondence. See Alice Morgan Wright Papers, Sophia Smith Collection, Smith College, Northampton, MA.

CHAPTER 1: THE SPLENDOR OF PARIS

1   Katharine de Forest, *Paris as It Is* (New York: Doubleday, Page, 1900), 3.

2   Susan Gilbert Harvey, *Tea with Sister Anna: A Paris Journal* (Rome, GA: Golden Apple Press, 2005), 4. Like many small colleges in the United States, Augusta Female Seminary has undergone several name changes: it became the Mary Baldwin Seminary in 1895 before being renamed Mary Baldwin College in 1923. In 2016, the institution renamed again, this time to its current title of Mary Baldwin University.

3   Ibid., 15.

4   Rupert Christiansen, *City of Light: The Rebuilding of Paris* (London: Apollo, 2018), 44.

5   Quoted in Christiansen, *City of Light*, 59.

6   Quoted in Adam Gopnik, ed., *Americans in Paris: A Literary Anthology* (New York: Literary Classics of the United States, 2004), 7–8.

7   Christiansen, *City of Light*, 14.

8   Ibid., 86; Harvey Levenstein, *Seductive Journey: American Tourists in France from Jefferson to the Jazz Age* (Chicago: University of Chicago Press,

1998), 86. This urban project was not without its downsides, particularly for the lower classes. Thousands were displaced from their soon-to-be-dismantled tenements and shoved out to the margins of the city, as frequently occurs in a region's transformation and gentrification. In addition, rent in the city's center doubled between 1851 and 1857, and continued to rise astronomically through the end of the nineteenth century. See also Julie Anne Johnson, "Conflicted Selves: Women, Art, & Paris 1880–1914" (doctoral dissertation, Queen's University, 2008), 40–41. For an excellent in-depth discussion of Haussmann's process, as well as his collaboration with Louis Napoléon, see Christiansen, *City of Light*.

9   Alice Rumph, "Miss Alice Rumph Tells of Her Work and Travels While Two Years Abroad," *Birmingham* (AL) *News*, August 2, 1902, 3.

10   Quoted in *Americans in Paris: A Literary Anthology*, 108–9.

11   Joseph Harriss, *The Tallest Tower: Eiffel and the Belle Epoque* (Boston: Houghton Mifflin Harcourt, 2004), 151.

12   Charles Emmerson, *1913: In Search of the World Before the Great War* (New York: PublicAffairs, 2013), 49.

13   Ibid., 154.

14   Nancy L. Green, *The Other Americans in Paris: Businessmen, Countesses, Wayward Youth, 1880–1941* (Chicago: University of Chicago Press, 2015), 18.

15   Levenstein, *Seductive Journey*, 90.

16   Ibid., 93.

17   Ibid., 91.

18   Ibid., 129.

19   Ibid., 126–7.

20   Ibid., 114–5.

21   Charles Carroll Fulton, *Europe Viewed Through American Spectacles* (Philadelphia: J. B. Lippincott, 1874), 181. This experience—of finding Paris difficult to quit—was a common one throughout the first decades of the twentieth century, as evidenced by the popularity of the post–World War One song "How Ya Gonna Keep 'Em Down on the Farm (After They've Seen Paree"). See Green, *The Other Americans in Paris*, 18.

22   While several cities in Germany (particularly Düsseldorf and Munich) also produced internationally renowned art schools, and Rome was famed in the mid-nineteenth century as a draw for sculptors, Paris remained the most popular with foreign art students.

23 Lois Marie Fink, "American Artists in France, 1850–1870," *American Art Journal* 5, no. 2 (November 1973), 32.

CHAPTER 2: TRAILING PAINFULLY BEHIND

1   Quoted in Annie Cohen-Solal, *Painting American: The Rise of American Artists, Paris 1867–New York 1948* (New York: Knopf, 2001), 39.
2   Charlotte Streifer Rubenstein, *American Women Sculptors: A History of Women Working in Three Dimensions* (Boston: G. K. Hall, 1990), 136. Cohen showed her work at the American Girls' Club as part of the American Woman's Art Association (AWAA), though she never resided at the Club. See Chapter 11 for more on the AWAA.
3   Quoted in Cohen-Solal, *Painting American*, 16.
4   "Plan for the Improvement and Diffusion of the Arts, Adapted to the United States." In Sarah Burns and John Davis, eds., *American Art to 1900: A Documentary History* (Berkeley: University of California Press, 2009), 64–65.
5   Laura R. Prieto, *At Home in the Studio: The Professionalization of Women Artists in America* (Cambridge, MA: Harvard University Press, 2001), 26.
6   Art galleries, it must be noted, arrived earlier on American shores. But galleries focused on commerce rather than edification, thereby little affecting the development of both American artists and art appreciation.
7   Though it might be obvious to some, it must be noted that the Americans having these kinds of conversations had their roots in Europe as the descendants of colonists. Indigenous art and traditions of Native Americans were not considered in this context, and Native Americans were not included at all save as "exotic" peoples to be included as subjects in the works of (white) artists.
8   "History painting" does not only refer to paintings illustrating scenes from history but also those presenting stories or elements from classical mythology, religious tales, and literature, among other subjects.
9   According to Harvey Levenstein, one of the main motives behind the 1867 Exposition Universelle was to draw *American* visitors to Paris. See Harvey Levenstein, *Seductive Journey: American Tourists in France from Jefferson to the Jazz Age* (Chicago: University of Chicago Press, 1998), 104.
10 Cohen-Solal, *Painting American*, 6.
11 Quoted in George Hardy, ed. *Americans in Paris 1850–1910: The Academy, the Salon, the Studio, and the Artist's Colony* (Oklahoma City: Oklahoma

City Museum of Art, 2003), 198. Adding insult to injury, the poor showing at the Exposition Universelle inspired some collectors (including William T. Walters, whose collection begat the Walters Art Museum in Baltimore) to sell off their American paintings—and to buy French paintings instead. See also Cohen-Solal, *Painting American*, 7.

12 Lois Marie Fink, "American Artists in France, 1850–1870," *American Art Journal* 5, no. 2 (November 1973), 34.

13 Ibid., 34.

14 Charles Pearo, "Elizabeth Jane Gardner and the American Colony in Paris: 'Making Hay while the Sun Shines' in the Business of Art," *Winterthur Portfolio* 43, no. 4 (Winter 2009), 280. The number of women residing as part of the "American Colony" (see Chapter 5) also grew during this period, and by 1901, more women than men—between 56 and 59 percent—resided in the capital. See also Nancy L. Green, *The Other Americans in Paris: Businessmen, Countesses, Wayward Youth, 1880–1941* (Chicago: University of Chicago Press, 2015), 144.

15 The École is still active today, in the same location on the rue Bonaparte in the sixth *arrondissement*.

16 Quoted in Julie Anne Johnson, "Conflicted Selves: Women, Art, & Paris 1880–1914" (doctoral dissertation, Queen's University, 2008), 127.

17 The phrase "woman artist" (and its plural, "women artists") is somewhat controversial today. Some critics find the modifier "woman" to be unnecessary (its counterpart, "male artist," being rarely used in comparison to the gender-neutral "artist") and feel that it ghettoizes female creators into a separate category, thereby marking them as other. I do not disagree with this argument, but the arguments for and against this phrase are too numerous and complicated to elucidate here. I therefore choose to use the phrase for the sake of ease in this book, considering that it is primarily about women who happen to be artists.

CHAPTER 3: A GOOD WOMAN OR A GREAT ARTIST

1 "Cecilia Beaux, Artist, Her Home, Work, and Ideals," quoted in Sarah Burns and John Davis, eds., *American Art to 1900: A Documentary History* (Berkeley: University of California Press, 2009), 841.

2 J. Diane Radycki, "The Life of Lady Art Students: Changing Art Education at the Turn of the Century," *Art Journal* 42, no. 1 (Spring 1982), 12.

3 "Miss Yandell, Sculptor, Dies," *Boston Globe*, June 13, 1934, 5; Diane Helenman, "Louisville's 'Bachelor Maid,'" *Louisville Courier-Journal*, September 26, 1993, 100.

4 Taft's "White Rabbits" also included fellow Club associate Janet Scudder, seen alongside Yandell in Figure 3.1.

5 Juilee Decker, *Enid Yandell: Kentucky's Pioneer Sculptor* (Lexington: University Press of Kentucky, 2019), 49. Yandell, alongside Jean Loughborough and Laura Hayes, lightly fictionalized her experiences of the lead-up to the World's Columbian Exposition in an 1892 book, *Three Girls in a Flat*. See Laura Hayes, Jean Loughborough, and Enid Yandell, *Three Girls in a Flat* (Chicago: Press of Knight, Leonard and Co., 1892).

6 Charlotte Streifer Rubenstein, *American Women Sculptors: A History of Women Working in Three Dimensions* (Boston: G. K. Hall, 1990), 116; Decker, *Enid Yandell*, 13.

7 Jeanne Madeline Weimann, *The Fair Women: The Story of the Woman's Building at the World's Columbian Exposition, Chicago 1893* (Chicago: Academy Chicago Publishers, 1981), 163.

8 Ibid., 163.

9 Laura R. Prieto, *At Home in the Studio: The Professionalization of Women Artists in America* (Cambridge, MA: Harvard University Press, 2001), 34–35.

10 Ibid., 70.

11 Whitney Chadwick, *Women, Art, and Society* (New York: Thames and Hudson, 1997), 205.

12 Karen J. Blair, *The Torchbearers: Women and Their Amateur Art Associations in America, 1890–1930* (Bloomington: Indiana University Press, 1994), 16.

13 Arthur D. Efland, "Art and Education for Women in 19th Century Boston," *Studies in Art Education* 26, no. 3 (Spring 1985), 133. Women's dedication to the betterment of American society has also been linked to the social reform movements of the mid-nineteenth century, including abolitionism, suffrage, and the temperance movement. See Blair, *The Torchbearers*, 23–24.

14 Pen Dalton, *The Gendering of Art Education: Modernism, Identity and Critical Feminism* (Buckingham [UK] and Philadelphia: Open University Press, 2001), 57.

15 Grace H. Turnbull, *Chips from My Chisel* (Rindge, NH: Richard R. Smith, 1953), 3.

16   Ibid., 10.

17   Ibid., 20.

18   Ibid., 20.

19   Prieto, *At Home in the Studio*, 95.

20   There is a blatant lack of acknowledgment in this era that homoerotic relationships between women could ever exist. See Prieto, *At Home in the Studio*, 93.

21   Ibid., 2.

22   Jane Silcock, "Genius and Gender," *British Art Journal* 19, no. 3 (Winter 2018–2019), 20.

23   Turnbull, *Chips from My Chisel*, 20–21.

CHAPTER 4: STARVING ARTISTS AND UGLY AMERICANS

1   Katharine de Forest, "Art Student Life in Paris," *Harper's Bazaar* 33, no. 27 (July 7, 1900), 628.

2   Janet Scudder, *Modeling My Life* (New York: Harcourt Brace, 1925), 111–2.

3   "Warns Girls Here of Dangers in Paris," *New York Times*, January 13, 1911, 7.

4   Bessie van Vorst, "Martyrs to Art in the French Capital: Nine American Girls Have Gone Crazy in the Latin Quarter of Paris from Starvation," *Louisville Courier-Journal*, December 10, 1899, B2.

5   For an in-depth look at a spate of anarchic bombings during this period, as well as a general overview of Paris's safety, see John Merriman's *The Dynamite Club* (New York: Houghton Mifflin Harcourt, 2009).

6   Quoted in Julie Anne Johnson, "Conflicted Selves: Women, Art, & Paris 1880–1914" (doctoral dissertation, Queen's University, 2008), 43-44.

7   Charles Emmerson, *1913: In Search of the World Before the Great War* (New York: PublicAffairs, 2013), 52.

8   Van Vorst, "Martyrs to Art in the French Capital," B2.

9   Ibid., B2.

10   William Stevens, "Homes and Clubs for Women in Paris," *Leisure Hour* (March 1896), 333.

11   "At some of the most desirable ateliers the fees are double those of men, and where there are twenty cheap restaurants that men can go to, there is but one for women . . . increase [the expenditures of men] by

one-third and she will find she has to exercise the strictest economy to keep within her allowance." See Boston Art Students' Association, *The Art Student in Paris* (Boston: Boston Art Students' Association, 1887), 23. See also Clive Holland, "Lady Art Students' Life in Paris," *International Studio* 30, no. 129 (December 15, 1903), 225–6.

12   Mildred Stapley, "Is Paris Wise for the Average American Girl?" *Ladies' Home Journal* 23 (April 1906), 54.

13   Leonora Raines, "Says American Girl's Innocence Often Led Her into Difficult Situations During Study Abroad," *Musical America* 29, no. 24 (April 12, 1919), 34. It should be noted that the occasional screed regarding the assumed lack of safety for male American art students also popped up in the press from time to time ("I say openly that I know the majority of the leading studios for men in Paris to be hotbeds of immorality"), though far less frequently than worrisome op-eds regarding the safety of women. See "Shall Our Young Men Study in Paris?" *The Arena* 13 (June–August 1895), from which the above quote is taken, as an example.

14   "Defending the American Girl Student Abroad," *Literary Digest*, February 7, 1914, 259.

15   Nancy L. Green, *The Other Americans in Paris: Businessmen, Countesses, Wayward Youth, 1880–1941* (Chicago: University of Chicago Press, 2015), 360.

16   For more on definitions and tropes of the "New Women," see Einav Rabinovitch-Fox, "New Women in Early 20th-Century America," *Oxford Research Encyclopedias: American History*, accessible online: https://doi .org/10.1093/acrefore/9780199329175.013.427.

17   Mrs. John E. Sherwood, "American Girls in Europe," *North American Review* 150, no. 403 (June 1890), 686.

18   Henry James, "Daisy Miller: A Study," in *The Novels and Tales of Henry James* (New York: Charles Scribner's Sons, 1908), 305.

19   Harvey Levenstein, *Seductive Journey: American Tourists in France from Jefferson to the Jazz Age* (Chicago: University of Chicago Press, 1998), 208. Although multiple works of fiction and nonfiction—including several written by women!—popped up in the 1880s and later with the express purpose of refuting James's characterization of erratic, Daisy-ish American girls, few American critics and readers took heed of these books; for examples, see Lucy Hamilton Hooper, *Under the Tricolor: Or, The American Colony in Paris* (Philadelphia: J. B. Lippincott, 1880), and

Lizzie W. Champney, *Three Vassar Girls Abroad: Rambles of Three College Girls on a Vacation Trip through France and Spain for Amusement and Instruction. With Their Haps and Mishaps* (Boston: Estes and Lauriat, 1883).

CHAPTER 5: THE MINISTER'S WIFE

1   "The American Girls' Club in Paris," *Town & Country* 64, no. 18 (July 17, 1909), 16.

2   Bingham Duncan, *Whitelaw Reid: Journalist, Politician, Diplomat* (Athens, GA: University of Georgia Press, 1975), 139.

3   Ibid., 116.

4   In 1924, Reid's son, Ogden, facilitated the merger of the *New-York Tribune* and the *New York Herald*, bringing about the *New York Herald Tribune*, which remained in circulation until 1966.

5   D. O. Mills named his country estate "Millbrae," as a semi-portmanteau of "Mills" and the Scottish word "brae," meaning "rolling hills." The modern-day town of Millbrae developed from this parcel of land and was officially incorporated as a city in 1948. A quick perusal of Google Maps provides many nods to the city's links to the Mills family: examples include Mills High School, Mills–Peninsula Medical Center, and Mills Estate Park, among others.

6   Edward T. James, Janet Wilson James, and Paul S. Boyer, eds., *Notable American Women, 1607–1950: A Biographical Dictionary, Vol. 3* (Cambridge, MA: Belknap Press of Harvard University, 1971), 132; Cameron Allen, *The History of the American Pro-Cathedral of the Holy Trinity, Paris (1815–1980)* (Bloomington, IN: iUniverse Press, 2013), 453. Note that *Notable American Women* misspells Valette as "Vallette."

7   Sargent, many years later, would create a sympathetic charcoal portrait of his classmate. The original, long assumed to be lost, turned up at an auction in Sarasota, Florida, in January 2023, and sold for more than $69,000. See Figure 20.2 in Chapter 20.

8   Duncan, *Whitelaw Reid*, 85–86.

9   Ibid., 86.

10 According to Whitelaw Reid's biographer, a loose hierarchy of diplomatic positions existed: "Berlin was looked upon as equal to Rome or The Hague and a cut above St. Petersburg, Madrid, or Vienna. Only Great Britain or France could be thought of as fitting . . ." See Duncan, *Whitelaw Reid*, 112.

11 "Entertaining Her Friends," *Sacramento Daily Union*, May 30, 1890, 1.

12 Nancy L. Green, *The Other Americans in Paris: Businessmen, Countesses, Wayward Youth, 1880–1941* (Chicago: University of Chicago Press, 2015), 17; Harvey Levenstein, *Seductive Journey: American Tourists in France from Jefferson to the Jazz Age* (Chicago: University of Chicago Press, 1998), 100.

13 As others have noted, the growing importance of the American Colony in the last two decades of the nineteenth century can even be mapped across the city of Paris itself. This was the era that begat the replica of Bartholdi's *Statue of Liberty*, installed on the Île aux Cygnes in the Seine, as well as the rededication of a large park in the sixteenth *arrondissement* as the place des États-Unis. See *Americans in Paris 1860–1900*, 105.

14 Green, *The Other Americans in Paris*, 73.

15 "Paris Local," *American Register*, April 6, 1889, 6.

16 Levenstein, *Seductive Journey*, 102.

17 Green, *The Other Americans in Paris*, 334.

18 William Whitney (or Whiting) Newell, not to be confused with his contemporary, William Wells Newell (1839–1907), another American minister, known best as a folklorist.

19 Unlike most of the Cathedral's members and affiliates, the Newells lived on the Left Bank, though farther north of the Latin Quarter. Their geography made them the perfect witnesses to Left Bank student life and its associated hardships.

20 The *Catholic News Agency* presents a rather detailed list of St. Luke's patronage. In addition to artists, it also includes "bachelors, bookbinders, brewers, butchers, doctors, glass makers, glassworkers, gold workers, goldsmiths, lacemakers, lace workers, notaries, painters, physicians, sculptors, stained glass workers, surgeons." See https://www.catholicnewsagency.com/saint/st-luke-the-evangelist-23.

21 Floy Campbell, "Sunday on the South Side of Paris," *International Official Journal of the Brotherhood of Painters, Decorators, and Paper Hangers of America* XVIII, no. 1 (January 1904), 542. See Campbell's article for descriptions of this intimate, lovely religious space.

22 Emily C. Burns, "St. Luke's Chapel, US Artists' Communities and Protestantism in Paris, 1891–1914," *Artistic Migration and Identity in Paris, 1870–1940*, eds. Federico Lazzaro and Steven Huebner (New York: Peter Lang, 2020), 143. St. Luke's Chapel was demolished in 1934.

23 Details about Helen Pert Newell's life are few. Much of what I have gathered comes from the following sources: the 1850 United States Federal Census; the 1880 United States Federal Census; New Jersey State Archives, Trenton; New Jersey Birth, Marriage and Death Records, 1711–1878; and Essex County, Massachusetts, Probate Records and Indexes 1638–1916, Author: Massachusetts Court of Insolvency (Essex County).

24 Lorado Taft, "In French Studios: Lorado Taft's Estimate of Lady Art Students," *Baltimore Sun*, September 14, 1895, 7.

25 The Newell children were G. Kennedy (born 1866), William (born 1868), and O. Shaw (born 1872). Shaw, a teenager in the late 1880s, lived in Paris with his parents during this period. See Presbyterian Historical Society, Philadelphia; US, Presbyterian Church Records, 1701–1907, Book Title: 1846–1874, Ancestry.com.

26 Caro Lloyd, "The Club for American Girls Studying in Paris," *New Outlook* 50, no. 2 (July 14, 1894), 60.

27 "Generosity of Mrs. Whitelaw Reid: In Establishing a Club for Women," *Nashville American*, August 15, 1909, A6.

28 Josephine Breekons, "Jolly and Busy Girls," *Washington Post*, February 8, 1903, 38.

29 Of the several hundred Club members and residents confirmed as of this book's writing, an overwhelming majority—98 percent!—were active in the visual arts. Though the Club accepted both art and music students, far fewer musicians, save the occasional opera singer or pianist, are known to have had Club ties. Two key factors could skew the data here, however: First, women's fascination with careers in the visual arts positively exploded at the end of the nineteenth century, as previously mentioned—there were simply more artists, rather than musicians, traveling to Paris for further study. Second, and perhaps more crucially, the majority of the sources that have allowed art historians (like your friendly author) to pinpoint these Club ties are exhibition records for the American Woman's Art Association and the various Parisian Salons. Clearly, musicians would not appear in such data. They show up instead in rare extant personal letters or in newspaper articles.

30 Anne Ruggles Gere, *Intimate Practices: Literacy and Cultural Work in U.S. Women's Clubs, 1880–1920* (Champaign: University of Illinois Press, 1997), 3.

31 Laura R. Prieto, *At Home in the Studio: The Professionalization of Women Artists in America* (Cambridge, MA: Harvard University Press, 2001), 109.

See also Estelle Freedman, "Separatism as Strategy: Female Institution Building and American Feminism, 1870–1930," *Feminist Studies* 5 (Fall 1979), 512–29.

32 Ibid., 123.

33 Laura McProud, *American Students' Census, Paris, 1903* (Paris: Laura McProud, 1903), 77.

34 Ibid., 77.

35 Confirmed and photographed by the author, September 12, 2022. Reid also funded a chancel window in New York City's Cathedral of St. John the Divine, again in honor of Whitelaw Reid; she likewise contributed to the building of an Episcopal cathedral and clerical residence in Manila near the end of her life. See "A Notable Career: The Scope of Mrs. Reid's Activities World-Wide," *New York Times*, April 30, 1931, 23.

36 Barbara Sicherman and Carol Hurd Green, *Notable American Women: The Modern Period: A Biographical Dictionary* (Cambridge, MA: Harvard University Press, 1980), 132–33.

37 Undated letter, Reid Family Papers. Library of Congress, Washington, D.C.

38 Not to be confused with his grandson, Adlai Ewing Stevenson II (1900–65), who was the losing Democratic nominee for president of the United States in 1952 and 1956.

39 Mrs. Travers (Ada Leigh) Lewis, *Homeless in Paris: The Founding of the "Ada Leigh" Homes* (New York: Macmillan, 1920), 38. A later branch of Lewis's home, the Governesses and Artists' Institute, tailored itself more specifically to its eponymous careers, with the "artist" segment probably added on as a reflection of the AGCP's popularity as much as the need to cater to that particular student body.

40 Ibid., 38.

CHAPTER 6: A RAMBLING OLD STRUCTURE

1 Emily Meredyth Aylward, "The American Girls' Art Club in Paris," *Scribner's Magazine* 16, no. 5 (November 1894), 598.

2 Elizabeth Taylor, "The American Girls' Club in Paris," *The Churchman* 70 (October 20, 1894), 489.

3 Gustave Keller, "Extrait de 'Souvenir de Famille,' 2 cahiers rédigés durant la première guerre à l'intention de ses enfants," Reid Hall,

Columbia University in the City of New York: https://reidhall .globalcenters.columbia.edu/content/keller-institute-1834-1893.

4 "An Art Students' Club for American Girls," *New York Herald* European edition, January 19, 1902, Supplement, 1. The "hundred rooms" declaration here is an exaggeration: the main structure, before its prewar renovation, contained nearly half that number.

5 William W. Davenport, *An Old House in Paris: The Story of Reid Hall, 4 Rue de Chevreuse, Paris VI* (Paris: Reid Hall, 1975), 10.

6 Dorothy Mackay, "Reid Hall: A Relic of Old Paris," *South Atlantic Quarterly* 30, no. 3 (1931), 264.

7 "Louis IX," *Oxford Dictionary of Saints*, fifth edition (Oxford [UK]: Oxford University Press, 2004), 326.

8 Mackay, "Reid Hall," 264.

9 "Rue d'Enfer" no longer exists in Paris, but there is a "passage d'Enfer" located only a third of a kilometer to the south of 4 rue de Chevreuse.

10 Mackay, "Reid Hall," 264.

11 Ibid., 264.

12 Ibid., 264.

13 For more, see Dorothy de Brissac Campbell, *The Intriguing Duchess: Marie de Rohan, Duchesse de Chevreuse* (London: John Hamilton Ltd.,1900) and H. Noel Williams, *A Fair Conspirator: Marie de Rohan, Duchesse de Chevreuse* (New York: Charles Scribner's Sons, 1913).

14 Louis Auchincloss, *Richelieu* (New York: Studio, 1972), 75.

15 Williams, *A Fair Conspirator*, 36.

16 A. Scott Veitch, "The Sweetheart of Aramis," *Australian Woman's Mirror* 13, no. 31 (June 29, 1937), 13.

17 Laurie Lalla Wisdo, "'Je Suis Americaine'—Especially in France," *Columbia, The Magazine of Columbia University* 9, no. 2 (November 1983), 22; "American Women's Club Names Its Paris Centre Reid Hall," *Paris Times*, December 15, 1928, 3.

18 Anne Goldthwaite, *Memoir*, ca. 1910–39, Anne Goldthwaite Papers, Box 1, Folder 1, Archives of American Art, Smithsonian Institution Washington, D.C., unpaginated.

19 Régine de Plinval de Guillebon, *Dagoty à Paris, la manufacture de porcelaine de L'Impératrice* (Paris: Somogy Editions d'Art, 2006), 26.

20 "Dagoty's Factory." www.britishmuseum.org/collection/term/BIOG 68060.

21 Ibid.

22 "Orthopedic Center, 1823–1833," Reid Hall, Columbia University in the City of New York: https://reidhall.globalcenters.columbia.edu/content/orthopedic-center-1823-1834.

23 Davenport, *An Old House in Paris*, 8.

24 Mackay, "Reid Hall," 259–71. In a wonderful coincidence that perhaps portended its future as an entity of Columbia Global Centers, Columbia College president Charles King (1789–1867, presidential term 1849–64) enrolled his son at the Institution Keller. See also Wisdo, "'Je Suis Americaine,'" 22.

25 Davenport, *An Old House in Paris*, 7.

26 Keller, "Extrait de 'Souvenir de Famille.'"

CHAPTER 7: IN THE MIDST OF LUXURY AND ROMANCE

1 Josephine Breekons, "Jolly and Busy Girls," *Washington Post*, February 8, 1903, 38.

2 Caro Lloyd, "The Club for American Girls Studying in Paris," *New Outlook* 50, no. 2 (July 14, 1894), 60.

3 Frances Cranmer Greenman, *Higher Than the Sky* (New York: Harper & Brothers, 1954), 82.

4 Ibid., 82.

5 Quoted in Adelyn D. Breeskin, *Anne Goldthwaite: A Catalogue Raisonné of the Graphic Work* (Montgomery, AL: Montgomery Museum of Fine Arts, 1982), 25.

6 "The American Girls' Club in Paris," *Town & Country* 64, no. 18 (July 17, 1909), 16.

7 Alice Morgan Wright to Emma Morgan Wright, December 30, 1909, Alice Morgan Wright Papers, Sophia Smith Collection, Smith College, Northampton, MA.

8 Elizabeth Taylor, "The American Girls' Club in Paris," *The Churchman* 70 (October 20, 1894), 489.

9 Letter from Alice Morgan Wright to Edith Shepard, January 24, 1912, Alice Morgan Wright Papers.

10 Florence Blanchard, "The American Art Association of Paris," *San Francisco Call*, November 17, 1895, 24.

11 "An Art Students' Club for American Girls," *New York Herald* European edition, January 19, 1902, Supplement, 1.

12 Elizabeth Taylor, *The Far Islands and Other Cold Places: Travel Essays of a Victorian Lady.* Edited by James Taylor Dunn (Lakeville, MN: Pogo Press, 1997), editor's foreword, 7–8.

13 Ibid., 8.

14 See Taylor, "The American Girls' Club in Paris."

15 Ibid., 489.

16 Lloyd, "The Club for American Girls Studying in Paris," 60.

17 Emily Meredyth Aylward, "The American Girls' Art Club in Paris," *Scribner's Magazine* 16, no. 5 (November 1894), 599.

18 Lloyd, "The Club for American Girls Studying in Paris," 60.

19 Aylward, "The American Girls' Art Club in Paris," 599.

20 Eric J. Segal, "The Ghost of Reid Hall: Early Days at the American Girls' Club in Paris," *Columbia University Institute for Scholars, Reid Hall—Paris Newsletter* 10 (2009/2010), 7.

21 Blanchard, "The American Art Association of Paris," 24; Aylward, "The American Girls' Art Club in Paris," 600, 605.

22 Elaine C. Tillinger, "The Lure of the Line; Influences, Tradition and Innovation in the Education and Career of a Woman Artist: Cornelia Field Maury (1866–1942)" (doctoral dissertation, St. Louis University, 1995), 204.

23 May Alcott Nieriker, *Studying Art Abroad and How to Do It Cheaply* (Boston: Roberts Brothers, 1879), 9.

24 Mildred Madison, "The Girls' Art Club," *Birmingham* (AL) *Age-Herald,* April 6, 1895, 15. Whether this also included men and non-Americans is not clear but it can be assumed, as AGCP residents wrote letters describing their "callers" taking meals with them at the Club.

25 Aylward, "The American Girls' Art Club in Paris," 600.

26 Ibid., 602. In translation and in order of item, the menu reads: Soup, a Julienne (a soup featuring thinly sliced vegetables); an hors d'oeuvre of salmon with tartar sauce; a main course featuring a (rather American) turkey with cranberry sauce and seasonal salad; vegetables, including, somewhat inexplicably, applesauce, as well as celery and raw cauliflower; and dessert, includes options such as cheese, oranges, cookies, ice cream, macarons, as well as black coffee, tea, beer, red wine, and—the biggest splurge on the menu—chablis.

27 "Worship of Food: The French Can Live on What Americans Waste," *Evening Star,* January 26, 1895, 16.

28 Author's note regarding currencies and calculations: in acknowledging the complications involved in converting historical currencies (particularly the French franc, which is no longer actively used), I have turned to the capable work of others and instituted a multiple-step process in order to estimate these prices in today's currencies, a possibly ridiculous act. First, I accessed historical conversions of one French franc in the year 1900 to the euro per this site: https://www.histoire-genealogie .com/De-la-valeur-des-choses-dans-le-temps?lang=fr, which returned one franc = €2,37 on March 7, 2006 (and is the best information I was able to locate). Next, using an inflation calculator (https://fxtop.com/en /inflation-calculator.php), I tracked the inflation of the euro from March 7, 2006, to the day of this note's writing, October 30, 2023. According to the European Union Eurostat index (EUCPI2005), the inflation rate over this period is 43.33%. At this rate of inflation, €2,37 in 2006 would equal €3,40. On October 30, 2023, €3,40 was the equivalent of $3.61. Thus, one French franc in 1900 is akin to $3.61, and 0.10 francs—the cost of oranges or biscuits here—is $0.36. It must be noted these mathematical gymnastics and conversions are my own (a risky undertaking, as I am an art historian and not a mathematician or an economist, after all) and are meant as rough guidelines and not exact, comparable costs.

29 Jane Teal, "In the Heart of Paris," *Lompoc Journal*, February 17, 1912, 6.

30 Quoted in Breeskin, *Anne Goldthwaite: A Catalogue Raisonné of the Graphic Work*, 25.

31 Cranmer Greenman, *Higher Than the Sky*, 82.

32 Breekons, "Jolly and Busy Girls," 38.

33 Aylward, "The American Girls' Art Club in Paris," 605. Aylward also notes that the frieze was composed of "common brown paper" and not canvas, as Breekons asserts.

34 According to a 1911 interview with Alice Morgan Wright, the Club held festive celebrations for many different occasions: "The American patriotic holidays we made much of. On Christmas Eve we, like all Paris, attended midnight mass. On Fourth of July and Washington's birthday we made ice cream." See "Sculptures by Talented Daughter of Albany," *Albany Argus*, December 10, 1911, 9.

35 Quoted in Breeskin, *Anne Goldthwaite: A Catalogue Raisonné of the Graphic Work*, 25.

36 Alice Morgan Wright, letter to Edith Shepard, December 29, 1912, Alice Morgan Wright Papers.

37 Quoted in Breeskin, *Anne Goldthwaite: A Catalogue Raisonné of the Graphic Work*, 26.

38 For modern-day pop culture references to *tableaux vivants*, see television shows *Gilmore Girls* ("The Festival of Living Art," 2003) and *Arrested Development* ("In God We Trust," 2003). Apparently 2003 was a big year for *tableaux vivants*.

39 Aylward, "The American Girls' Art Club in Paris," 605.

40 Ibid., 603.

41 Geraldine Rowland, "The Study of Art in Paris," *Harper's Bazaar* 36, no. 9 (September 1902), 758.

42 Sedgwick's painting is thought to be lost, though its image was recorded in an April 1910 article in the *New York Sun*. See figure 8.3 and "Pictures by American Artists Exhibited at the New Salon Which Opened Last Week in Paris," *New York Sun*, April 17, 1910, 36.

43 Taylor, "The American Girls' Club in Paris," 489.

44 E. L. Good, "American Artists in Paris," *Catholic World* 66, no. 394 (January 1898), 456.

45 Aylward, "The American Girls' Art Club in Paris," 600; "An Art Students' Club for American Girls," 1.

46 Mariea Caudill Dennison, "The American Girls' Club in Paris: The Propriety and Imprudence of Art Students, 1890–1914," *Woman's Art Journal* 26, no. 1 (2005), 34.

47 "An Art Students' Club for American Girls," 1. In her article, Josephine Breekons adds an additional rule: "One thing the girls are obliged to do at the club, and that is to learn to speak French." While this was definitely the case for later iterations of the rue de Chevreuse buildings—like the AAUW, mentioned in Chapter 19—I have not been able to verify this for the Club. See Breekons, "Jolly and Busy Girls," 38.

48 "Dangers of Student Life in Paris," *San Francisco Call*, January 29, 1899, 23.

49 Rowland, "The Study of Art in Paris," 757.

50 Lorado Taft, "In French Studios: Lorado Taft's Estimate of Lady Art Students," *Baltimore Sun*, September 14, 1895, 7.

CHAPTER 8: EARLY REVIEWS

1   Harvey Levenstein, *Seductive Journey: American Tourists in France from Jefferson to the Jazz Age* (Chicago: University of Chicago Press, 1998), 207.

2   Geraldine Rowland, "The Study of Art in Paris," *Harper's Bazaar* 36, no. 9 (September 1902), 758.

3   Caro Lloyd, "The Club for American Girls Studying in Paris," *New Outlook* 50, no. 2 (July 14, 1894), 60. A later article notes that American girls were especially fond of purchasing hats from a Mme. Louie Le Gallienne, who made "wonderful headgear at prices ridiculously small." See "How the American Business Woman Has Invaded Paris," *Chicago Tribune*, September 27, 1908, F8.

4   "The World of Letters," *Wilkes-Barre Semi-Weekly Record*, November 20, 1894, 5. Minna Brown's birth and death dates have not been confirmed.

5   Alice Fessenden Peterson, "The American Art Student in Paris," *New England Magazine* 2 (August 1890), 670. This criticism of the Club continued even to the site's later years as the AAUW's Reid Hall. A 1928 article commented, "The criticism has been made that Americans coming to Paris tend to segregate, learning little of the language or of the people among whom they are living. [Reid Hall director Dorothy] Leet's aim, beyond that of making her girls comfortable, is to give them as broadening and as international an experience as possible." See "American Women's Club Names Its Paris Centre Reid Hall," *Paris Times*, December 15, 1928, 3.

6   Marianne Kinkel, *Races of Mankind: The Sculptures of Malvina Hoffman* (Champaign: University of Illinois Press, 2011), 37.

7   Ibid., 37.

8   Emily C. Burns, "Revising Bohemia: The American Artist Colony in Paris, 1890–1914," in *Foreign Artists and Communities in Modern Paris, 1870–1914: Strangers in Paradise*, eds. Karen L. Carter and Susan Waller (New York: Routledge, 2017), 105.

9   Ibid., 98. The American Art Association of Paris, like the Club, aimed to foster community and safety, similarly maintaining a residence and amenities to allow male students to "derive the greatest benefit from our French training and carry away with us the least of its evil influences."

10 Sterling Heilig, "Girls in Paris Find Freedom," *Baltimore Sun*, July 11, 1926, SF21.

11   Naturally, there are exceptions here: both Anne Goldthwaite and Alice Morgan Wright stayed on at the Club for several years each. For their final years in Paris, however, both vacated the premises for their own apartments.

12   "Girls' Club May Be Broken Up," *Chicago Daily Tribune,* March 4, 1894, 10.

13   Ibid., 10.

14   Ibid., 10.

15   "Newell," 1894, Décès, 06 (record V4E 8495), Archives de Paris. https://archives.paris.fr/.

16   Passenger Lists of Vessels Arriving at New York, New York, 1820–1897; National Archives, Washington, D.C., USA; Microfilm Serial M237, Ancestry.com.

17   "Girls' Club May Be Broken Up," 10.

18   William Stevens, "Homes and Clubs for Women in Paris," *Leisure Hour* (March 1896), 331.

19   "The Lafayette Home for American and English Lady Students," *American Register,* April 9, 1898, 1. Talk about another interesting life: according to author Jill Jonnes, Dr. Evans lived in "palatial splendor with his wife and a vast aviary, maintain[ed] a voluptuous mistress he shared with poet Stéphane Mallarmé, publish[ed] the weekly *American Register,* and supervise[d] the American Charitable Fund for impecunious 'unfortunates' marooned in the French capital." See Jill Jonnes, *Eiffel's Tower* (New York: Viking, 2009), 11.

20   Ibid., 1.

21   Heilig, "Girls in Paris Find Freedom," 21.

22   Kilbourne Cowles, "American Girl Students in Paris," *The Advance* 57, no. 2266 (April 1, 1909), 404.

23   Ibid., 404.

24   "A Club for Girl Art Students," *New York Times,* May 15, 1904, 7.

25   Ibid., 7.

CHAPTER 9: A DAY IN ANNA LESTER'S LIFE

1   Susan Gilbert Harvey, *Tea with Sister Anna: A Paris Journal* (Rome, GA: Golden Apple Press, 2005), 33.

2   Lorado Taft, "In French Studios: Lorado Taft's Estimate of Lady Art Students," *Baltimore Sun,* September 14, 1895, 7. Taft doubled down on

his insults of English women, calling them "girls richly endowed with front teeth and bangs."

3 Approximately 76 percent of known Club residents and exhibitors were painters, including miniaturists (the number of miniaturists is truly astonishing; miniatures were certainly enjoying a moment in the Belle Époque).

4 Harvey, *Tea with Sister Anna*, 33.

5 Ibid., 43.

6 Mariea Caudill Dennison, "The American Girls' Club in Paris: The Propriety and Imprudence of Art Students, 1890–1914," *Woman's Art Journal* 26, no. 1 (2005), 33. The other "favorite headquarters" of AGCP members was the Académie Colarossi, nearby on rue de la Grande Chaumière.

7 Catherine Fehrer, "Women at the Académie Julian in Paris," *Burlington Magazine* 136, no. 1100 (November 1994), 757.

8 Quoted in Charles Harrison, Paul Wood, and Jason Gaiger, eds. *Art in Theory 1815–1900: An Anthology of Changing Ideas* (Hoboken, NJ: Wiley-Blackwell, 1998), 765.

9 Gabriel P. Weisberg, and Jane R. Becker, eds. *Overcoming All Obstacles: The Women of the Académie Julian* (New York: Dahesh Museum, 1999), 16.

10 Harvey, *Tea with Sister Anna*, 45.

11 Ibid., 168.

12 Ibid., 44.

13 Quoted in Elaine C. Tillinger, "The Lure of the Line; Influences, Tradition and Innovation in the Education and Career of a Woman Artist: Cornelia Field Maury (1866–1942)" (doctoral dissertation, St. Louis University, 1995), 136.

14 Harvey, *Tea with Sister Anna*, 44.

15 Ibid., 99.

16 Ibid., 46-47.

17 Fehrer, "Women at the Académie Julian in Paris," 754.

18 Elizabeth Taylor, *The Far Islands and Other Cold Places: Travel Essays of a Victorian Lady*. Edited by James Taylor Dunn (Lakeville, MN: Pogo Press, 1997), 10–11.

19 Janet Scudder, *Modeling My Life* (New York: Harcourt Brace, 1925), 150.

20 Marie Adelaide Belloc, "Lady Artists in Paris," *Murray's Magazine* 8, no. 45 (1890), 375.

21 Harvey, *Tea with Sister Anna*, 199.

22 Ibid., 188.

23 Ibid., 58.

24 Enid Yandell, "Art in Paris," *Louisville Courier-Journal*, March 27, 1895, 26.

25 "They Had No Chaperon. Because They Entertain Men in Informal and Rather Gay Fashion American Girls Shock French," *Los Angeles Herald*, January 21, 1906, 2.

26 Ibid., 2.

CHAPTER 10: WHAT HOPES AND FEARS, AND TRIUMPHS

1 Margaret E. Handalman, "Artists in Summer. Making Preparations for the Next Salon. Girl Students Leaving Paris," *San Jose Mercury-News*, August 8, 1897, 15.

2 Alice Rumph, "Miss Alice Rumph Tells of Her Work and Travels While Two Years Abroad," *Birmingham* (AL) *News*, August 2, 1902, 3.

3 Vicki Leigh Ingham, *Art of the New South: Women Artists in Birmingham 1890–1950* (Birmingham, AL: Birmingham Historical Society, 2004), 124–25.

4 Rumph, "Miss Alice Rumph Tells of Her Work," 3.

5 Ibid., 3.

6 Annie Cohen-Solal, *Painting American: The Rise of American Artists, Paris 1867–New York 1948* (New York: Knopf, 2001), 36.

7 For a brief but thorough overview on the Salon(s), see the Art Institute of Chicago's webpage, "Paris Salons (1673–present)," https://www.artic.edu/library/discover-our-collections/research-guides/paris-salons-1673present.

8 Lois Marie Fink, *American Art at the Nineteenth-Century Paris Salons* (Cambridge: Cambridge University Press, 1990), 142.

9 Kathleen Adler, "'We'll Always Have Paris': Paris as Training Ground and Proving Ground," in *Americans in Paris, 1860–1900* (London: National Gallery, 2006), 40.

10 Charles Pearo, "Elizabeth Jane Gardner and the American Colony in Paris: 'Making Hay while the Sun Shines' in the Business of Art," *Winterthur Portfolio* 43, no. 4 (Winter 2009), 277.

11 Julia Dabbs, "Empowering American Women Artists: The Travel Writings of May Alcott Nieriker," *Nineteenth-Century Art Worldwide* 15, no. 3 (Autumn 2016), 21.

12 Adolphe Tabarant, *La Vie artistique au temps du Baudelaire* (Paris: Mercure de France, 1942), 12.

13 Adler, "'We'll Always Have Paris,'" 40.

14 Letter from Alice Morgan Wright to Edith Shepard, May 6, 1913, Alice Morgan Wright Papers, Sophia Smith Collection, Smith College, Northampton, MA.

15 *Catalogue illustré du Salon 1880* (Paris: Motteroz, 1880), 83.

16 Adler, "'We'll Always Have Paris,'" 40.

17 Susan Gilbert Harvey, *Tea with Sister Anna: A Paris Journal* (Rome, GA: Golden Apple Press, 2005), 139.

18 Fink, *American Art at the Nineteenth-Century Paris Salons*, 114.

19 Harvey, *Tea with Sister Anna*, 139.

20 Alice Fessenden Peterson, "The American Art Student in Paris," *New England Magazine* 2 (August 1890), 675.

21 Also spelled as "skied."

22 For an in-depth study of both the Salon des femmes and the Union des femmes peintres et sculpteurs, see Tamar Garb, *Sisters of the Brush: Women's Artistic Culture in Late Nineteenth-Century Paris* (New Haven, CT: Yale University Press, 1994).

23 Quoted in Kristen Swinth, *Painting Professionals: Women Artists and the Development of Modern American Art, 1870–1930* (Chapel Hill: University of North Carolina Press, 2001), 51.

24 Cohen-Solal, *Painting American*, 102. If the name Goupil et Cie rings a bell to some art aficionados, it might be because two brothers began their art careers as employees there: Vincent and Theo van Gogh.

25 "Marguerite Thompson Reaches San Francisco; Will Exhibit Paintings," *Fresno Morning Republican*, April 25, 1912, 1.

26 "Mrs. Newman Returns: Unsuccessful in Winning Salon Medal, But Not Daunted," *Nashville American*, June 27, 1902, 7.

27 Rumph, "Miss Alice Rumph Tells of Her Work," 3.

28 *Explication des ouvrages de peinture, sculpture, architecture, gravure et lithographie des artistes vivantes exposes au grand palais des beaux-arts* (Paris: Imprimerie Paul Dupont, 1901). In *Art of the New South*, author Vicki Leigh Ingham notes that Alice's submission was a fourteen by twenty-inch watercolor titled *Dutch Interior*, a work Rumph so enjoyed that she showed it again on at least three other occasions, including at the American Woman's Art Association in Paris. I have yet to find information to

bear this out and am thus using the Salon catalogue as a confirmation of title here.

29 "Social," *Birmingham* (AL) *News*, May 2, 1901, 5.

30 Rumph, "Miss Alice Rumph Tells of Her Work," 3.

CHAPTER II: AN EXHIBITION OF THEIR OWN

1 Enid Yandell, "Art in Paris," *Louisville Courier-Journal*, March 27, 1895, 26.

2 "Art Notes," *American Register*, March 1, 1901, 3.

3 Mariea Caudill Dennison, "The American Girls' Club in Paris: The Propriety and Imprudence of Art Students, 1890–1914," *Woman's Art Journal* 26, no. 1 (2005), 35.

4 Emily Meredyth Aylward, "The American Girls' Art Club in Paris," *Scribner's Magazine* 16, no. 5 (November 1894), 604–5.

5 A similar organization, the American Women's Art Club of Paris, may have been the AWAA's precursor, or could simply refer to an alternative name for the AGCP prior to its move to 4 rue de Chevreuse. We have the surviving records of the AWAA to thank for the most comprehensive listing of artists ever associated with the Club. Around 450 women—residents, exhibitors, tea-takers, journalists, and more—are known today as having participated in life at the Club, surely a vast underrepresentation of the true number of women who frequented it during its twenty-one years on the rue de Chevreuse. Of these 450 individuals, at least 80 percent showed their work at an AWAA exhibition at the Club or held positions on the AWAA's various committees.

6 Elaine C. Tillinger, "The Lure of the Line; Influences, Tradition and Innovation in the Education and Career of a Woman Artist: Cornelia Field Maury (1866–1942)" (doctoral dissertation, St. Louis University, 1995), 208; Dennison, "The American Girls' Club in Paris," 35. Nourse was also selected as a member of the exhibition jury at least once, in 1896.

7 "American Women Artists Show Pictures of Merit: Annual Exhibition of Oils at Students' Club Contains Much Excellent Work," *New York Herald* European edition, February 22, 1914, 2. See also "American Students' Display," *American Art News* 12, no. 12 (December 27, 1913), 5.

8 Katharine de Forest, "An Art Tea at the Paris Girls' Club," *Harper's Bazaar* 33, no. 2 (January 13, 1900), 33.

9   "American Girls' Club," *New York Herald* European edition, December 21, 1897, 4.

10   Dennison, "The American Girls' Club in Paris," 35.

11   Yandell, "Art in Paris," 26.

12   American Women Exhibit in Paris," *New York Times*, February 20, 1910, 2.

13   Dennison, "The American Girls' Club in Paris," 35.

14   "Exhibition at the American Girls' Club of Paris," *Quartier Latin* 4, no. 18 (January 1898), 651.

15   Lisa N. Peters, "Anne Goldthwaite: Modern Woman," in *Anne Goldthwaite: Modern Woman* (Greenville, SC: Greenville County Museum of Art, 2020), 27.

16   "American Women Artists Show Pictures of Merit," 2.

17   Laura McProud, *American Students' Census, Paris, 1903* (Paris: Laura McProud, 1903), 65.

18   "Les Femmes Peintres," *Le Matin*, December 20, 1897, 3.

19   "Paris Art News," *New York Times*, March 6, 1904, 4.

20   Storrs Lee, "The Sketch Exhibition of the American Girls' Club," *Quartier Latin* 2 (January 1897), 167. Storrs Lee here—dates unknown—should not be confused with W. Storrs Lee (1906–2004), an author and longtime professor at Middlebury College.

21   Ibid., 167.

22   "American Women Artists." *New York Herald*, December 10, 1899, 1.

23   Tillinger, "The Lure of the Line," 209.

24   De Forest, "An Art Tea at the Paris Girls' Club," 33. De Forest does not confirm which Salon—beaux-arts or artistes français—awarded Watkins this honor, but it is assumed to be the 1899 iteration of the Salon des artistes français, for which I cannot locate an online catalogue, but Watkins is not listed as an exhibitor in 1899's Salon des beaux-arts.

25   "American Women Artists Hold Annual Exhibition," *New York Herald* European edition, February 18, 1907, 6.

26   Letter from Alice Morgan Wright to Emma Morgan Wright, March 12, no year provided [1910 or 1911]. Alice Morgan Wright Papers, Sophia Smith Collection, Smith College, Northampton, MA.

27   Grace H. Turnbull, *Chips from My Chisel* (Rindge, NH: Richard R. Smith, 1953), 39.

28   "American Art Shown," *New-York Tribune*, December 15, 1912, 9.

29   Ibid., 9.

30   Ibid., 9.

CHAPTER 12: À NOTRE REGRETTÉ CAMARADE

1   Clive Holland, "Student Life in the Quartier Latin, Paris," *The Studio* 18, no. 69 (November 1902), 38.

2   Chas. W. Jarrett-Knott, *Paris artistic: indicateur des salons russes, anglais et américains en France, 1896* (Paris, 1896), https://gallica.bnf.fr/ark:/12148 /bpt6k64848575/texteBrut.

3   "In Society," *Boston Sunday Post*, December 05, 1897, 16.

4   "Miss Weil Buried," *Philadelphia Inquirer*, July 10, 1897, 3. Our Gertrude Weil here is not to be confused with the suffragist and philanthropist of the same name (1879–1971).

5   "Glimpses of the Academy of Fine Arts Exhibition," *Philadelphia Inquirer*, March 2, 1892, 4.

6   "Gossip of the Clubs," *Philadelphia Inquirer*, March 24, 1895, 15; "Art Notes," *Philadelphia Inquirer*, February 4, 1894, 16.

7   "The Latest Paris Mystery," *New York Herald* European edition, June 23, 1897, 3.

8   "Miss Weil Dead," *Philadelphia Inquirer*, June 23, 1897, 1.

9   Storrs Lee, "The Sketch Exhibition of the American Girls' Club," *Quartier Latin* 2 (January 1897), 167.

10   "Miss Weil Dead," 1.

11   Ibid., 1.

12   In "The Latest Paris Mystery," the author concludes that she had been sketching beneath it; in "Miss Weil Dead," such circumstances are questioned.

13   Most likely Joseph Michael Gleeson (1861–1917), a painter and illustrator who studied in Paris under William-Adolphe Bouguereau and Tony Robert-Fleury. "An American Girl Drowned" erroneously identifies him as W. M. Gleeson and is one of the articles that purports that the two were engaged to be married. The *Indianapolis News* article also names the deceased as "Gertrude Wiel," so accuracy seems not to be a strong suit here. See "An American Girl Drowned," *Indianapolis News*, June 23, 1897, 1.

14   "An American Girl Drowned," 1.

15   "The Latest Paris Mystery," 3.

16   Ibid., 3.

17   Raoul Duval, "Disowned Drowned: Parents' Answer Telling Gertrude Weil She Could Not Marry a Christian Drove Her to Die," *Buffalo Evening News*, August 8, 1897, 1.

18   "The Latest Paris Mystery," 3.

19   "Crowds Flock to Paris," *Chicago Tribune*, July 25, 1897, 27.

20   "In the Seine: Mysterious Death in Paris of Miss Weil of Philadelphia," *Los Angeles Herald*, July 18, 1897, 15.

21   Nancy L. Green, *The Other Americans in Paris: Businessmen, Countesses, Wayward Youth, 1880–1941* (Chicago: University of Chicago Press, 2015), 321. Green provides the additional example of the death of Lucinda Farrar, a music student who died by suicide after experiencing "discouragement in her studies, and weariness of life." Green, *The Other Americans in Paris*, 80.

22   "Paris Salons, 1898: The Day of the Vernissage," *San Francisco Call*, June 22, 1898, 6.

23   "A California Artist," *Janesville* (WI) *Daily Gazette*, February 10, 1898, 7.

24   "Les Femmes Peintres," *Le Matin*, December 20, 1897, 3.

25   Archambaud seems to have been a fairly well respected doctor who was later deemed an *Officier de la Légion d'honneur*. See http://mielcrestani.free .fr/genealogie/actes/paul_archambaud_legion_d-honneur_2.jpg.

26   "Death of a Young Artist," *San Francisco Chronicle*, May 7, 1899, 14.

27   "Pathetic Death of Artist: Miss Jessie Allen," *Chicago Daily Tribune*, May 7, 1899, 9. Acly is incorrectly identified as "Atlee" here and as the secretary of the Club, not its matron, though perhaps those terms were considered interchangeable.

28   Ibid., 9.

29   Ibid., 9.

30   Ibid., 9.

CHAPTER 13: WHY NOT TURN OUR ART INTO FOOD?

1   "The Parisian Café Decorated by a San Francisco Girl," *San Francisco Chronicle*, September 2, 1900, 26.

2   Some sources, like Edwards in *Jennie V. Cannon*, incorrectly note Lundborg's birth year as 1870. See Robert W. Edwards, *Jennie V. Cannon: The*

Untold History of the Carmel and Berkeley Art Colonies, Volume 1 (Oakland: East Bay Heritage Project, 2012), 489.

3   For an excellent summary of Lundborg's life and career, see Edwards, *Jennie V. Cannon*, 489.

4   "Here and There in Society," *San Francisco Examiner*, August 12, 1897, 12.

5   Katharine de Forest, "Art Student Life in Paris," *Harper's Bazaar* 33, no. 27 (July 7, 1900), 630.

6   Ibid., 630.

7   Floy Campbell, "Sunday on the South Side of Paris," *International Official Journal of the Brotherhood of Painters, Decorators, and Paper Hangers of America* XVIII, no. 1 (January 1904), 542.

8   De Forest, "Art Student Life in Paris," 630.

9   Campbell, "Sunday on the South Side of Paris," 542.

10   "Henrietta's Queen of Hearts Needs Restoring," *Baltimore Sun*, April 4, 1920, A14. In this article, produced twenty years later, the author claims it was Alice Mumford, not Lundborg, who had the idea. Since Mumford assisted Lundborg in her efforts, it is thus difficult to determine with any certainty which artist conceived of the project, but it is assumed that the concept originated from Lundborg.

11   R. E. Turpin, "A New American Colony," *Louisville Courier-Journal*, May 3, 1896, B2. Of the American delicacies available on "Robert Street," the most popular were "baked beans, cornbread, batter cakes, hot biscuits, any dish cooked American style." Other establishments in Paris included restaurants dedicated to producing pumpkin pie, buckwheat pancakes, and "New England–style fish balls," and by 1908, a "real American tea room" opened to the northwest of the Jardin du Luxembourg on the nearby rue de Bac. See Harvey Levenstein, *Seductive Journey: American Tourists in France from Jefferson to the Jazz Age* (Chicago: University of Chicago Press, 1998), 91–92, and "How the American Business Woman Has Invaded Paris," *Chicago Tribune*, September 27, 1908, F8.

12   Pablo Picasso, Diego Rivera, and Amedeo Modigliani were among those who frequented La Rotonde; Le Dôme was name-dropped in acclaimed works by Simone de Beauvoir, Ernest Hemingway, Henry Miller, and Anaïs Nin, among others; Paul Cézanne and Oscar Wilde enjoyed evenings at La Closerie des Lilas.

13   Frank Berkeley Smith, *The Real Latin Quarter* (New York: Funk & Wagnalls, 1901), 105.

14 Adelyn D. Breeskin, *Anne Goldthwaite: A Catalogue Raisonné of the Graphic Work* (Montgomery, AL: Montgomery Museum of Fine Arts, 1982), 25.

15 Frances Cranmer Greenman, *Higher Than the Sky* (New York: Harper & Brothers, 1954), 86.

16 Elizabeth Taylor, "The American Girls' Club in Paris," *The Churchman* 70 (October 20, 1894), 489.

17 Smith, *The Real Latin Quarter*, 31.

18 "The Parisian Café Decorated by a San Francisco Girl," 26. This, and "Henrietta's Queen of Hearts Needs Restoring," are the primary documents describing Lundborg's project.

19 "Henrietta's Queen of Hearts Needs Restoring," A14.

20 E. V. Lucas, ed., *The Works of Charles and Mary Lamb, Volume III* (London: Methuen, 1903), 336–37.

21 "The Parisian Café Decorated by a San Francisco Girl," 26.

22 Fellow Club resident Alice Rumph also completed an art project associated with the *Rubaiyat*: in 1914, she was among the artists who produced the scenery and backdrop for the Birmingham Art Club's "tableaux presentation" of Khayyam's lyrical poem. See Vicki Leigh Ingham, *Art of the New South: Women Artists in Birmingham 1890–1950* (Birmingham, AL: Birmingham Historical Society, 2004), 97.

23 "Miss Florence Lundborg's illustrations for the Rubaiyat . . . are unique and interesting, each one distinct by itself and not one in the least like any previous illustration for the famous poem. There is a faint influence of Aubrey Beardsley traceable in Miss Lundborg's present work. She is, however, strikingly original and bold in her decorative designs. Her lines are the most flowing and graceful." See "Studio Notes," *San Francisco Chronicle*, June 4, 1899, 22.

24 "The Parisian Café Decorated by a San Francisco Girl," 26.

25 Ibid., 26.

26 Ibid., 26.

27 Several other Club artists participated in the Panama–Pacific International Exposition, including Anne Goldthwaite, Janet Scudder, and Alice Morgan Wright. See Lisa N. Peters, "Anne Goldthwaite: Modern Woman," in *Anne Goldthwaite: Modern Woman* (Greenville, SC: Greenville County Museum of Art, 2020), 33.

28 Anna Pratt Simpson, *Problems Women Solved: Being the Story of the Woman's Board of the Panama–Pacific International Exposition: What Vision,*

Enthusiasm, Work and Co-operation Accomplished (San Francisco: Woman's Board, 1915), 41–42.

29 *After the Lights Went Out: Searching for What Remains from San Francisco's Spectacular 1915 Panama–Pacific International Exposition* (San Francisco: San Francisco Historical Society, 2015), 4.

30 "Henrietta's Queen of Hearts Needs Restoring," A14.

31 Helen Buckler, "Homesick Americans in Paris Comforted by Familiar Menus," *New York Herald*, May 16, 1926, D12.

32 "Henrietta's Queen of Hearts Needs Restoring," A14.

33 "News of Americans Day by Day," *New York Herald* European edition, December 19, 1920, 2.

CHAPTER 14: THE SCULPTOR OF HORRORS

1   H. Harrison Wayman, "Meta Vaux Warrick (Sculptress)," *Colored American Magazine* 6, no. 5 (March 1903), 330.

2   Judith N. Kerr, "God-Given Work: The Life and Times of Sculptor Meta Vaux Warrick Fuller, 1877–1968" (doctoral dissertation, University of Massachusetts at Amherst, 1986), 70.

3   William Francis O'Donnell, "Meta Vaux Warrick, Sculptor of Horrors: The Negro Girl Whose Productions Are Being Compared to Rodin's," *World To-Day* 13, no. 5 (November 1907), 1142.

4   Frances Cranmer Greenman, *Higher Than the Sky* (New York: Harper & Brothers, 1954), 82.

5   Meta Vaux Warrick, interview with Sylvia G. L. Dannett, quoted in Renée Ater, *Remaking Race and History: The Sculpture of Meta Warrick Fuller* (Berkeley: University of California Press, 2011), 15.

6   Meta Vaux Warrick's family claimed roots both in the Caribbean and in Europe and noted themselves in various censuses as "mulatto."

7   Meta Vaux Warrick, interview with Sylvia G. L. Dannett, quoted in Ater, *Remaking Race and History*, 15–16.

8   Kerr, "God-Given Work," 75.

9   Legend has it that Meta herself was named after one of her mother's white clients, a lady known as "Mrs. Vaux," though I have not been able to confirm this.

10 Henry O. Tanner, "The Story of an Artist's Life, Part I," *World's Work* 18, no. 2 (June 1909), 11664.

11 "Seeking Equality Abroad: Why Miss Edmonia Lewis, the Colored Sculptor, Returns to Rome—Her Early Life and Struggles," *New York Times*, December 29, 1878, 5.

12 Tyler Stovall, *Paris Noir: African Americans in the City of Light* (Boston: Houghton Mifflin, 1996), xiii–iv.

13 Some Black Americans did indeed find Paris to be the most liberating place. Notably, writer and diplomat James Weldon Johnson (1871–1938), who headed the NAACP in the 1920s, recalled, "From the day I set foot in France [in 1905], I became aware of the working of a Miracle within me . . . I recaptured for the first time since childhood the sense of being just a human being. I need not try to analyze this change for my colored readers; they will understand in a flash what took place." See Adam Gopnik, ed., *Americans in Paris: A Literary Anthology* (New York: Literary Classics of the United States, 2004), 199.

14 Stovall, *Paris Noir*, xiv.

15 Kerr, "God-Given Work," 76.

16 Eve Kahn, *Forever Seeing New Beauties: The Forgotten Impressionist Mary Rogers Williams, 1857–1907* (Middletown, CT: Wesleyan University Press, 2019), 197 (e-book edition).

17 C. F. M., "Another View of Negro Equality," *St. Louis Post-Dispatch*, October 30, 1901, 4. The South Carolina native discussed here has not been identified.

18 Ater, *Remaking Race and History*, 16.

19 Ibid., 16–17.

20 Ibid., 17.

21 John Sillevis, "Rodin's First One-Man Show," *Burlington Magazine* 137, no. 1113 (December 1995), 837.

22 Letter from Oscar Wilde to Robert Ross, July 7, 1900, in *The Letters of Oscar Wilde*, edited by Rupert Hart-Davies (New York: Harcourt, Brace & World, 1962), https://archive.org/stream/in.ernet.dli.2015.225943/2015.225943.The-Letters_djvu.txt.

23 Edward Steichen, "A Life in Photography," in Adam Gopnik, ed., *Americans in Paris: A Literary Anthology* (New York: Literary Classics of the United States, 2004),190-1.

24 Isadora Duncan, "My Life," in Gopnik, ed., *Americans in Paris*, 184.

25 Quoted in Ater, *Remaking Race and History*, 18.

26 Ibid., 19.

27 Quoted in Didi Hoffman, *Beautiful Bodies: The Adventures of Malvina Hoffman* (Meadville, PA: Fulton Books, 2018), 14.

28 Confusingly, Warrick sometimes called this work by two other names: *Man Eating His Heart* and *Secret Sorrow*.

29 Stephen Crane, "In the Desert," The Poetry Foundation, https://www .poetryfoundation.org/poems/46457/in-the-desert-56d2265793693:

> In the desert
> I saw a creature, naked, bestial,
> Who, squatting upon the ground,
> Held his heart in his hands,
> And ate of it.
> I said, "Is it good, friend?"
> "It is bitter—bitter," he answered;
>
> "But I like it
> "Because it is bitter,
> "And because it is my heart."

30 Kerr, "God-Given Work," 3.

31 Ibid., 117.

32 Quoted in Ater, *Remaking Race and History*, 19.

33 Kerr, "God-Given Work," 4.

34 Ibid., 137.

35 Velma J. Hoover, "Meta Vaux Warrick Fuller: Her Life and Her Art," *Negro History Bulletin* 40, no. 2 (March–April 1977), 679. Hoover notes that some Parisians may have linked Meta's horrific subject matter with her experiences of racism in America; while this may be absolutely correct, I have yet to find documentation to support it.

36 Though much of the (meager) twentieth-century literature about Warrick's career cites this fascinating and evocative title, I have yet to uncover its exact origin. The earliest English accounting of this nickname—a reference to her as a "sculptor of horrors"—is found in William Francis O'Donnell's article, "Meta Vaux Warrick, Sculptor of Horrors" (1907).

37 Ater, *Remaking Race and History*, 21.

38   Ibid., 21/23; Kerr, "God-Given Work," 140.

39   Kerr, "God-Given Work," 129. As the name suggests, Mary Fairchild MacMonnies had married the influential sculptor Frederick MacMonnies; the small worlds of both sculptors and American expatriates in Paris suggest that even prior to their mutual Salon acceptance, MacMonnies would have been familiar with Warrick's work, and he likely suggested her inclusion to his wife.

40   "Recent Art at 4 Rue de Chevreuse," *New York Herald* European edition, February 23, 1902, 9. Some modern-day readers may decry this as a bit of near-nepotism, considering that year's jury included none other than Henry Ossawa Tanner, Warrick's early Parisian guide and confidante, but the strength of her sculpture and the frequent praise she received prior to this point belittle such an argument.

CHAPTER 15: ANNE GOLDTHWAITE AND THE SHOCK OF THE NEW

1   Quoted in Karen Towers Klacsmann, "Bringing Modernism Home," in *Southern/Modern: Rediscovering Southern Art from the First Half of the Twentieth Century* (Chapel Hill: University of North Carolina Press, 2023), unpaginated.

2   Adelyn D. Breeskin, *Anne Goldthwaite 1869–1944* (Montgomery, AL: Montgomery Museum of Fine Arts, 1977), 11.

3   *Central to their Lives: Southern Women Artists in the Johnson Collection.* Edited by Lynne Blackman (Columbia: University of South Carolina Press, 2018), 84. See also Adelyn D. Breeskin, *Anne Goldthwaite: A Catalogue Raisonné of the Graphic Work* (Montgomery, AL: Montgomery Museum of Fine Arts, 1982), 19.

4   In her 1982 book, *American Women Artists*, Charlotte Rubenstein asserts that Goldthwaite opted for a career in the arts only after the death of her "beau" in a terrible duel. This information does not appear in credible sources, including Goldthwaite's incomplete memoir, so it is most likely a myth. Lisa N. Peters has recently suggested that Goldthwaite herself may have started this rumor as a handy excuse when questioned why she never married. See Charlotte Streifer Rubenstein, *American Women Sculptors: A History of Women Working in Three Dimensions* (Boston: G. K. Hall, 1990), and Lisa N. Peters, "Anne Goldthwaite: Modern Woman," in *Anne Goldthwaite: Modern Woman* (Greenville: Greenville County Museum of Art, 2020), 39.

5 Anne Goldthwaite, "How I Discovered Myself: Anne Goldthwaite, Artist, Tells How She Triumphed," *San Francisco Call*, November 24, 1915, 8.

6 Peters, "Anne Goldthwaite," 17.

7 Goldthwaite, "How I Discovered Myself," 8.

8 Anne Goldthwaite, *Memoir*, ca. 1910–39, Anne Goldthwaite Papers, Box 1, Folder 1, Archives of American Art, Smithsonian Institution Washington, D.C., unpaginated.

9 Ibid., unpaginated.

10 Ibid., unpaginated.

11 *Illustrations of Selected Works in the Various National Sections of the Department of Art, with Complete List of Awards by the International Jury, Universal Exposition, St. Louis, 1904* (St. Louis: Louisiana Purchase Exposition Company, 1904), 43.

12 Goldthwaite, *Memoir,* unpaginated.

13 Ibid., unpaginated.

14 Ibid., unpaginated.

15 Ibid., unpaginated.

16 Diana Souhami, *No Modernism Without Lesbians* (London: Head of Zeus, 2020), 317–18.

17 Arthur Lubow, "An Eye for Genius: The Collections of Gertrude and Leo Stein," *Smithsonian*, January 2012, https://www.smithsonianmag .com/arts-culture/an-eye-for-genius-the-collections-of-gertrude-and-leo -stein-6210565/.

18 Goldthwaite was by no means the only Club artist to visit the Stein salon, though her description of her visit (and its impact upon her career) is most vibrant. Other visitors included Malvina Hoffman, Janet Scudder, Grace Turnbull, Ethel Mars, Maud Hunt Squire (the prior two being immortalized in Stein's prose poem, "Miss Furr and Miss Skeene"), and Mildred Burrage, just to name a few.

19 Goldthwaite, *Memoir,* unpaginated.

20 Ibid., unpaginated.

21 Ibid., unpaginated.

22 Ibid., unpaginated.

23 Ibid., unpaginated.

24 The relationship between Goldthwaite and Rosen is unclear; recent research by Alabama author May Lamar confirms that when Goldthwaite returned to the United States in 1913, Rosen—a Russian

émigré—joined her. Together they shared a Greenwich Village pied-à-terre for a brief time, but whether as a romantic couple or platonic pals is unknown. A 1960 interview between art historian John D. Morse and curator Holger Cahill identifies Goldthwaite as Rosen's "assistant." Goldthwaite did help Rosen with the occasional conservation project, so this assessment is somewhat correct. See Breeskin, *Anne Goldthwaite: A Catalogue Raisonné of the Graphic Work*, 28; May Lamar, "The Anne Goldthwaite Nobody Knew," *Alabama Heritage,* no. 135 (Winter 2020), 34; and John Morse and Peter Pollack, Oral History Interview with Holger Cahill, 1960 April 12 and 15, Archives of American Art, Smithsonian Institution, Washington, D.C.

25 The Académie Moderne reformed under entirely different instructors, students, and styles in the 1920s to become the Académie Léger-Ozenfant. See Peters, "Anne Goldthwaite," 41. Confusingly, some sources still referred to this later iteration by the name of the Académie Moderne, though the two academies had little in common besides their street addresses.

26 Martin Birnbaum, "Anne Goldthwaite," *Catalogue of an Exhibition of Paintings, Watercolors and Etchings by Anne Goldthwaite, October 23–November 13, 1915* (New York: Berlin Photographic Company, 1915), 4-5.

27 See "A Modern Painter with a Strong Sense of Style," *New York Times*, October 24, 1915, 21, and Société du Salon d'automne, *Catalogue de peinture, dessin, sculpture, gravure, architecture et art décoratif* (Paris: Évreux, 1912), 124. A fellow Club resident, one Ethyl Canby of Wilmington, Delaware, is also listed.

28 Elisabeth Luther Cary, "Pictures and Quality: Anne Goldthwaite," *New York Times*, January 6, 1929, 124.

29 Goldthwaite is noted in the Salon des artistes français's 1907 catalogue as entry number 715; in the 1909 edition, she is catalogued as number 793.

30 "Chez Max Rodrigues," *Gil Blas*, January 19, 1913, 4.

31 "New Exchange Professor," *Harvard Crimson*, May 9, 1912, https://www.thecrimson.com/article/1912/5/9/new-exchange-professor-pthe-announcement-is/; "American Women Artists Hold Exhibition in Paris," *New York Herald* European edition, February 2, 1913, 3.

32 *Prince's Feathers* is now believed lost.

33 The Association of American Painters and Sculptors' Domestic Art Committee record book from the Armory Show indicates that Goldthwaite submitted five paintings for consideration: three, marked with

a letter "R," were rejected: *Nude*, *The Green Parasol*, and *The Red Hammock*.

34 In a 1982 catalogue, biographer Adelyn Breeskin insists that "Anne had returned in time to see the 1913 Armory Exhibition." But this cannot be true if Breeskin also asserts that Goldthwaite returned to the States in the *summer* of 1913. The Armory's New York iteration closed in mid-March, and the Chicago version—in which only one of Goldthwaite's works appeared—closed one month later. Due to a lack of space, the later Boston iteration of the show did not include any works by American artists. The official catalogue of the New York version bears out her absence, too: Goldthwaite's works are listed as in the care of a "Miss Gabay" on the Upper West Side, as Goldthwaite herself was, at that point, not yet living in the States.

35 "Art Notes," *New York Times*, February 17, 1913, 10.

36 Goldthwaite was not the sole representative of the AGCP at the Armory; several Club alumnae were showcased, including Enid Yandell, Marguerite Thompson Zorach, and Grace Mott Johnson. Mildred Burrage, though not an exhibitor, attended the show and documented her observations in an insightful article titled "The Post Impressionists at Home," which one scholar calls "an important statement . . . about the early twentieth-century art scene in America and France." See Earle G. Shettleworth Jr., "The Making of an Artist: Mildred G. Burrage's Early Years," in *From Portland to Paris: Mildred Burrage's Years in France* (Portland, ME: Portland Museum of Art, 2012), 22.

37 Susan Stamberg, "In 1913, a New York Armory Filled with Art Stunned the Nation," *Morning Edition*, National Public Radio, air date November 11, 2013, https://www.npr.org/2013/11/11/243732924/in-1913-a-new-york-armory -filled-with-art-stunned-the-nation.

38 Jennifer Pfeifer Shircliff, "Women of the 1913 Armory Show: Their Contributions to the Development of American Modern Art" (doctoral dissertation, University of Louisville, 2014), 162.

39 A. D. Defries, "Anne Goldthwaite as a Portrait Painter," *International Studio* LIX, no. 233 (July 1916), iv.

40 Quoted in Breeskin, *Anne Goldthwaite: A Catalogue Raisonné of the Graphic Work*, 30.

41 Ibid, 30.

42 "American Students in the Latin Quarter at Odds Over a $200 Award," *New York Times*, July 20, 1913, C2.

43 The unnamed author of "American Students in the Latin Quarter at Odds Over a $200 Award" wrote: "Mrs. Whitney Hoff then announced that her purpose was to 'bring a little religion across the river.' Women students who were the objects of this undisguised solicitude objected to having their private affairs thus interfered with, and few who lived in Paris at that time have ever become very active members of 'the hostel.'"

44 "American Students in the Latin Quarter at Odds Over a $200 Award," C2.

45 Ibid., C2.

46 Quoted in Mariea Caudill Dennison, "The American Girls' Club in Paris: The Propriety and Imprudence of Art Students, 1890–1914," *Woman's Art Journal* 26, no. 1 (2005), 34.

47 Société des artistes français, *Catalogue illustré du salon 1909* (Paris: Bibliothèque des annales, 1909), unpaginated.

48 Quoted in Breeskin, *Anne Goldthwaite: A Catalogue Raisonné of the Graphic Work*, 25.

49 Peters, "Anne Goldthwaite," 24–25.

CHAPTER 16: SCULPTURE OR SUFFRAGE, OR ALICE MORGAN WRIGHT
GOES TO JAIL

1 Alice Morgan Wright, "Sculpture and Suffrage," *New York State Business & Professional Women* XIV, no. 3 (December 1947), 7.

2 "Woman Sculptor Views Boxing as a Fair Sport," *Brooklyn Standard Union*, January 3, 1918, 8.

3 Wright, "Sculpture and Suffrage," 7.

4 Marla Frances Wagshal, "Alice Morgan Wright, 1881–1975" (undergraduate thesis, Mount Holyoke College, South Hadley, MA, 1978), 24. Alice Morgan Wright papers, Sophia Smith Collection, Smith College, Northampton, MA.

5 Wright, "Sculpture and Suffrage," 7.

6 Betsy Fahlman, *Sculpture and Suffrage: The Art and Life of Alice Morgan Wright (1881–1975): Catalogue of the Exhibition at the Albany Institute of History and Art, April 21–June 11, 1978* (Albany: Albany Institute of History and Art, 1978), 2; "Smith College Notes," *Boston Evening Transcript*, February 17, 1903, 7; "Smith College," *Boston Evening Transcript*,

April 28, 1903, 16; "Alice Wright Hard Worker," undated newspaper clipping from Alice Morgan Wright Papers, Sophia Smith Collection, Smith College, Northampton, MA.

7   In the archives of Wright's papers at Smith College, letters attest to a great interest in Wright's poetry. A representative from the publishing house Sherman, French & Company began negotiations with Wright to publish a volume of her writing, but nothing came of this attempt.

8   See Alice Morgan Wright Papers.

9   "Clever Art Students Who Won Awards," *Brooklyn Standard Union*, May 13, 1908, 2. O'Keeffe's surname is misspelled as "O'Keefe."

10   Tamar Garb, *Sisters of the Brush: Women's Artistic Culture in Late Nineteenth-Century Paris* (New Haven: Yale University Press, 1994), 129.

11   Wright, "Sculpture and Suffrage," 7.

12   Letter from Alice Morgan Wright to Emma Morgan Wright, February 5, 1912, Alice Morgan Wright Papers.

13   Undated letter from Alice Morgan Wright to unidentified recipient(s), Alice Morgan Wright Papers.

14   Letter from Alice Morgan Wright to Edith Shepard, September 2, 1910, Alice Morgan Wright Papers.

15   Quoted in Janet Robb, "Jack-Knife, Gift to '90s Albany Tomboy, Started Alice Morgan Wright's Career," *Albany Times Union*, undated (after 1937). Alice Morgan Wright Papers, unpaginated. *Cain* is now thought to be lost.

16   June Purvis, *Emmeline Pankhurst: A Biography* (London: Routledge, 2002), 67.

17   In a letter sent late in her life to Smith College archivist Margaret Grierson, Wright stated that she "crossed the ocean with Mrs. P . . . in Sept. 1909." This contradicts the timeline constructed by Pankhurst biographer June Purvis (see Purvis, *Emmeline Pankhurst*, 141), but if correct, it would mean that Wright met Pankhurst on the first transatlantic crossing of her France residency, when she moved to the country.

18   Shepard's dates have not been verified, but she should not be confused with Edith Shepard Fabbri (1872–1954), a great-granddaughter of Cornelius Vanderbilt.

19   Quoted in Wendy L. Rouse, *Public Faces, Secret Lives: A Queer History of the Women's Suffrage Movement* (New York: New York University Press, 2022), 102.

20 Wright, "Sculpture and Suffrage," 8.

21 Quoted in Fahlman, *Sculpture and Suffrage*, 5. It is likely that several Club associates attended this summit, and AGCP resident Mildred Burrage recalled having tea with Pankhurst during this period. See Earle G. Shettleworth Jr., "The Making of an Artist: Mildred G. Burrage's Early Years," in *From Portland to Paris: Mildred Burrage's Years in France* (Portland, ME: Portland Museum of Art, 2012), 28.

22 Rouse, *Public Faces, Secret Lives*, 101.

23 Ibid., 102–3.

24 Elizabeth Thompson Colleary, "Marguerite Thompson Zorach: Some Newly Discovered Works, 1910–1913," *Woman's Art Journal* 23, no. 1 (Spring–Summer 2002), 25.

25 Cameron Allen, *The History of the American Pro-Cathedral of the Holy Trinity, Paris (1815–1980)* (Bloomington, IN: iUniverse Press, 2013), 502.

26 Though we as researchers do not know how Squire and Mars identified, sexually speaking, their connection to the Gertrude Stein poem is enough to foster a strong assumption of their sexual preferences referenced in this section. It must be noted, however, that at least one scholar, Catherine Ryan, disagrees with this identification. See Catherine Ryan, *Très Complémentaires: The Art and Lives of Ethel Mars and Maud Hunt Squire* (New York: Mary Ryan Gallery and Susan Sheehan Gallery, 2000), 6.

27 Gertrude Stein, "Miss Furr and Miss Skeene," *Geography and Plays* (Boston: Four Seas Press, 1922), 17.

28 Gertrude Stein, "Sacred Emily," *Geography and Plays* (Boston: Four Seas Press, 1922), 187.

29 Stein, "Miss Furr and Miss Skeene," 20.

30 Martha Stone, "Who Were Miss Furr and Miss Skeene?" *Gay & Lesbian Review Worldwide* 9, no. 5 (September–October 2002), 29; Michael Abraham, "Out of the Closet and into the Home: Gertrude Stein, Alice B. Toklas, and the Affordances of the Domestic Interior," *Texas Studies in Literature and Language* 64, no. 4 (winter 2022), unpaginated.

31 Margaret Alice Friend, "Art: American Women in the French Salons," *Vogue* 40, no. 2 (July 15, 1912), 25. Club members Janet Scudder and Elizabeth "Betty" Edmond—Wright's studio mate—are also featured in this article.

32 Wagshal, "Alice Morgan Wright," 19.

33 National Archives (UK), "Extract of a Statement from Mary Richardson on Forcible Feeding, February 6, 1914," catalogue ref: HO 144 /1305/248506, accessible online: http://www.nationalarchives.gov.uk /education/resources/suffragettes-on-file/mary-richardson. Art historical fun fact: as part of a protest over a 1914 arrest of Emmeline Pankhurst, Richardson slashed a Diego Velázquez painting, *The Rokeby Venus* (c. 1647–51, National Gallery, London), with a meat cleaver, declaring, "I have tried to destroy the picture of the most beautiful woman in mythological history as a protest against the Government for destroying Mrs Pankhurst, who is the most beautiful character in modern history." The painting was successfully restored.

34 "Suffragette Out of Jail Relates Woes," Special Dispatch to the *Globe-Democrat*, April 27, 1912, Alice Morgan Wright Papers.

35 "London Police Hunt for Miss Pankhurst," *New York Times*, March 7, 1912, 1.

36 "Women Sculptors and Artists Will Give Half the Proceeds of an Exhibit of their Work to the Suffrage Cause," *Evening Sun*, September 22, 1915, unpaginated, Alice Morgan Wright Papers.

37 Fahlman, *Sculpture and Suffrage*, 6.

38 "Suffragette Out of Jail Relates Woes," Alice Morgan Wright Papers.

39 Ibid., unpaginated.

40 "Women Sculptors and Artists Will Give Half the Proceeds," Alice Morgan Wright Papers.

41 Wright, "Sculpture and Suffrage," 7.

42 Alice Morgan Wright Papers.

43 See Stone, "Who Were Miss Furr and Miss Skeene?" 29; Abraham, "Out of the Closet and into the Home," unpaginated.

44 "Women [*sic*] Proves Costly to the Cause; MISS PANKHURST SOUGHT," *Chicago Tribune*, March 7, 1912, 2.

45 "Suffragette Out of Jail Relates Woes," Alice Morgan Wright Papers.

46 Ibid., unpaginated.

47 "None Can See Miss Wright," March 6, 1912, newspaper clipping from Alice Morgan Wright Papers.

48 Undated and unpaginated news clipping photocopy, Alice Morgan Wright Papers.

49 "Women Sculptors and Artists Will Give Half the Proceeds," Alice Morgan Wright Papers.

50 Letter from Alice Morgan Wright to Emma Morgan Wright, June 7, 1912, Alice Morgan Wright Papers.

51 "To the Editor," undated draft of a letter, Alice Morgan Wright Papers.

52 Rouse, *Public Faces, Secret Lives*, 108.

53 Letter from Alice Morgan Wright to Edith Shepard, September 22, 1912, Alice Morgan Wright Papers.

54 "Militant Suffragette," undated newspaper clipping from Alice Morgan Wright Papers.

55 Undated and unpaginated news clipping photocopy, Alice Morgan Wright Papers.

56 "Women Sculptors and Artists Will Give Half the Proceeds," Alice Morgan Wright Papers.

57 Ibid., unpaginated.

58 "Smith College," *Boston Evening Transcript*, October 4, 1909, 12.

59 Fahlman, *Sculpture and Suffrage*, 5.

CHAPTER 17: EXTENDING THE CLUB'S SPHERE OF USEFULNESS

1 "American Art Students' Club House Annex, Almost Doubling Accommodation, Opened," *New York Herald* European edition, November 3, 1912, 6.

2 Ibid., 6.

3 Letter from Alice Morgan Wright to Edith Shepard, August 21, 1910, Alice Morgan Wright Papers, Sophia Smith Collection, Smith College, Northampton, MA.

4 Painting and (to a far lesser degree) sculpture were the predominant media for most artists studying in Paris at this juncture, and the demographics of the AWAA confirm this, too. For exhibitions of this kind, see as examples: "Women Miniature Painters Join in Showing Recent Work on Walls of the American Art Students' Club of Paris," *New York Herald* European edition, December 7, 1913, 2, and "American Women Open an Exhibition of Sculpture," *New York Herald* European edition, March 23, 1914, 3.

5 Bingham Duncan, *Whitelaw Reid: Journalist, Politician, Diplomat* (Athens: University of Georgia Press, 1975), 114.

6 Philip Davies, *Lost London 1870–1945* (Hertfordshire [UK]: Atlantic Publishing, 2009), 302. Sadly, Dorchester House is no longer extant; it was razed in 1929 and replaced by the luxurious Dorchester Hotel.

7   Charly Knight's artistic connections not only extend to his elder brother (Louis Aston Knight, a well-respected landscape painter), but also to Charly's own name: his middle name is a nod to his godfather, the Knights' Poissy neighbor, painter Ernest Meissonier (1815–91). For more on Meissonier and the Knight family, see "Daniel Ridgway Knight," https://mydailyartdisplay.uk/2018/01/26/daniel-ridgway-knight/.

8   "The Man of the Day," *Paris Times*, May 16, 1926, 4. Knight's work with the AGCP was only one of his American Colony projects: he also designed the Parisian outpost of jewelerTiffany and Co., and renovated writer Edith Wharton's Provence mansion. See Naby Avcioglu, "Notes on the Architectural History of the Institute Building (1910–2007)," *Columbia University Institute for Scholars Newsletter* 7 (2006–2007), 8–9, and "Who's Who Abroad," *Chicago Tribune* and *Daily News* (New York), February 4, 1926, 4.

9   "Property Improvements," https://reidhall.globalcenters.columbia.edu /content/property-improvements-1911-1912.

10   Emily Meredyth Aylward, "The American Girls' Art Club in Paris," *Scribner's Magazine* 16, no. 5 (November 1894), 604.

11   Ibid., 604.

12   "American Art Students' Club House Annex," 6.

13   Ibid., 6. Reid Hall's website asserts that there were seven private studios. As the building's updated plans no longer exist and given that the current structure has been altered several times, it is difficult to determine the true number of private studios, but a floor plan at the Library of Congress, illustrating the site's transformation into a World War One hospital, show six smaller spaces and one larger operating room, which might indicate that there were indeed six private studios. See "Floor plan of American Red Cross Hospital Number 3, Paris, France," Library of Congress, https://www.loc.gov/resource/anrc.18781.

14   Ibid., 6.

15   Grace H. Turnbull, *Chips from My Chisel* (Rindge, NH: Richard R. Smith, 1953), 40–41.

16   "American Art Students' Club House Annex," 6.

17   "Grande Salle Ginsberg-LeClerc: Inauguration June 8, 2023," Reid Hall and Columbia Global Centers, https://issuu.com/cgc.paris/docs /20230531_online_viewing_program_inaguration_spread.

18   "The History of Le Bon Marché," Le Bon Marché, https://www .lebonmarche.com/en/store/culture/heritage-lebonmarche.

19   "Grande Salle Ginsberg-LeClerc."

20   "American Art Students' Club House Annex," 6.

21   Ibid., 6.

22   "Whitelaw Reid Dies in London," *New York Times*, December 16, 1912, 1.

23   "American Art Students' Club House Annex," 6.

24   Reid Hall's official website notes two different years for Reid's purchase: 1911 and 1913. It is possible that Reid began the purchase process in 1911 but did not finalize it until two years later. See "Property Improvements."

CHAPTER 18: A BOLT FROM THE BLUE

1   Malvina Hoffman, *Yesterday Is Tomorrow: A Personal History* (New York: Crown Publishing Group, 1965), 125.

2   Quoted in Charlotte Streifer Rubenstein, *American Women Sculptors: A History of Women Working in Three Dimensions* (Boston: G. K. Hall, 1990), 120.

3   "Richest Race in the World Decided in Paris To-Day," *New York Herald* European edition, June 28, 1914, 1. The Grand Prix de Paris is not to be confused with the Grand Prix de France, which is its automobile equivalent; that race, less than a decade old at this time, would be held a week later, on July 4, 1914, in Lyon.

4   Ibid., 1.

5   "Many American Visitors See Race for Grand Prix," *New York Herald* European edition, June 29, 1914, 4.

6   Ibid., 4.

7   Frances Cranmer Greenman, *Higher Than the Sky* (New York: Harper & Brothers, 1954), 86.

8   The *Tribune*, coincidentally, was edited at this time by Ogden Mills Reid—the son of Elisabeth Mills Reid and Whitelaw Reid.

9   Charles Inman Barnard, *Paris War Days: Diary of An American* (Boston: Little, Brown, 1914), 14.

10   Ibid., 13.

11   Ibid., 20.

12   Elizabeth Nourse, "Extracts from the Diary of an American Artist in Paris, August and September 1914," *Art and Progress* 6, no. 2 (December 1914), 41.

13   Barnard, *Paris War Days*, 57.

14   "Children Dispel Gloom on Liner; Thirty American Girls Turned Out of Club," *New York Tribune*, August 31, 1914, 9.

15   "American Charity Made Ineffective: Students' Club, Organized for Girls in Paris, Closes its Doors to Refugees," *New York Times*, August 14, 1914, 4.

16   Ibid., 4.

17   Ethel Traphagen, an illustrator and designer, would later give her name to the Traphagen School of Fashion in New York, which ran from 1923 until 1991. See Durward Howes, ed., "Ethel Traphagen," in *American Women: The Official Who's Who Among the Women of the Nation* (Los Angeles: American Publications, 1937) 690.

18   "American Charity Made Ineffective," 4.

19   Ibid., 4.

20   "Whitelaw Reid Dies in London," *New York Times*, December 16, 1912, 1; "Squadron to Meet Reid Funeral Ship," *New York Times*, December 22, 1912, 3. A small memorial service was held in Paris at the "little tin chapel" of St. Luke's, on the grounds of the AGCP. A news article notes that members of the Girls' Club attended the service.

21   Barnard, *Paris War Days*, 31.

22   Quoted *From Portland to Paris: Mildred Burrage's Years in France* (Portland, ME: Portland Museum of Art, 2012), 22.

23   Eleanor S. Thackara and Enid Yandell, "A Correction," *New York Herald* European edition, September 6, 1914, 2. Roselle Shields produced a similar disclaimer in the same issue of the *New York Herald*, located directly above Yandell and Thackara's correction.

24   Hoffman, *Yesterday Is Tomorrow*, 124.

25   Ibid., 122–23.

26   Ibid., 126.

27   Ibid., 157.

28   "American Charity Made Ineffective," 4.

29   Barnard, *Paris War Days*, 89, 31.

30   Naby Avcioglu, "Notes on the Architectural History of the Institute Building (1910–2007)," *Columbia University Institute for Scholars Newsletter* 7 (2006–2007), 9.

31   Ibid., 9. The floor plans for these renovations are found today at the Library of Congress, as part of the American National Red Cross photograph collection. See American National Red Cross photograph

collection, Library of Congress Prints and Photographs Division, https://www.loc.gov/resource/anrc.18781/.

32 Ibid., 9.

33 "Ambulance Is Installed in American 'Girls' Club," *New York Herald* European edition, November 25, 1914, 2.

34 Elisabeth Mills Reid to Colonel Alfred Bradley, September 28, 1917. Hoover Institution Library & Archives, Washington, D.C. Hoover xx482 bx78 fl15, https://www.hoover.org/.

35 United States Congress, *Congressional Record* 56, part 11 (1918), 10704.

36 Laurie Lalla Wisdo, "'Je Suis Americaine'—Especially in France," *Columbia, The Magazine of Columbia University* 9, no. 2 (November 1983), 22.

37 "Mrs. Whitelaw Reid Receives Cross of Legion of Honor," *New York Times*, July 19, 1922, 11.

38 Grace H. Turnbull, *Chips from My Chisel* (Rindge, NH: Richard R. Smith, 1953), 69.

CHAPTER 19: REESTABLISHING USEFULNESS TO AMERICAN GIRLS

1 Virginia Gildersleeve to Elisabeth Mills Reid, July 6, 1921, Reid Family Papers, Library of Congress, Washington, D.C.

2 "Bienfaisance," *Excelsior*, August 10, 1919, 4.

3 Joyce Goodman, "Reassuring Mrs. Reid," Reid Hall, Columbia Global Centers, December 2020, https://reidhall.globalcenters.columbia.edu /content/reassuring-elisabeth-mills-reid.

4 Frederick Beekman to Elisabeth Mills Reid, February 17, 1925, Reid Family Papers.

5 Barbara Sicherman and Carol Hurd Green, *Notable American Women: The Modern Period: A Biographical Dictionary* (Cambridge, MA: Harvard University Press, 1980), 203.

6 Katherine S. Dreier to Elisabeth Mills Reid, March 1, 1920, Reid Family Papers.

7 "Making Bohemia Comfortable for Girl Art Students," *New-York Tribune*, February 15, 1920, 65.

8 Joyce Goodman, "A Potential Site in Paris," Reid Hall, Columbia University in the City of New York, December 2020, https://reidhall .globalcenters.columbia.edu/content/potential-site-paris.

9 Virginia Gildersleeve to Elisabeth Mills Reid, February 21, 1921, Reid Family Papers.

10   Undated draft of letter by Elisabeth Mills Reid (assumed 1920s), Reid Family Papers. The Klumpke girls—meaning Anna Klumpke and her sisters—are mentioned here, but as the Klumpke family lived in Paris, it can be assumed that the sisters did not reside at the Club. If they visited at all, it was most likely for tea or other social events, with Anna's participation, in particular, in AWAA shows (1901); she also attended the exhibitions at the rue de Chevreuse (see "American Women Artists," *New York Herald* European edition, February 23, 1895, 3). Lastly, the identity of "Miss Bowie" has not yet been established.

11   Virginia Gildersleeve to Elisabeth Mills Reid, February 21, 1921, Reid Family Papers.

12   "Reid Hall Incorporated," *New York Times*, March 24, 1929, 35.

13   Virginia Gildersleeve to Elisabeth Mills Reid, July 6, 1921, Reid Family Papers.

14   American Red Cross representative to Elisabeth Mills Reid, December 21, 1920, Reid Family Papers.

15   Janet Scudder, *Modeling My Life* (New York: Harcourt Brace, 1925), 111.

16   Quoted in Adelyn D. Breeskin, *Anne Goldthwaite: A Catalogue Raisonné of the Graphic Work* (Montgomery, AL: Montgomery Museum of Fine Arts, 1982), 25.

CHAPTER 20: THROUGH THE VISION AND GENEROSITY OF ELISABETH MILLS REID

1   "Women: Death of a Great Lady," *Time*, May 11, 1931, https://content.time.com/time/subscriber/article/0,33009,741612-2,00.html.

2   Quoted in "Reid Hall: Woman Student Headquarters," *New York Herald Tribune*, July 31, 1950, 10.

3   Ibid., 10.

4   Elisabeth Mills Reid to Virginia Gildersleeve, June 1, 1926, Reid Family Papers, Library of Congress, Washington, D.C.

5   Ibid.

6   Ibid.

7   "Exhibit 2: Report of the Secretary of Reid Hall," Reid Family Papers. The property was formally provided to the University Women's Realty Corporation, the AAUW's holding company.

8   Charlotte Streifer Rubenstein, *American Women Sculptors: A History of Women Working in Three Dimensions* (Boston: G. K. Hall, 1990), 251.

9   "Reid Estate Fitted for Siam's Royalty," *New York Times*, March 25, 1931, 29; "King of Siam to Live in Historic House Here," *New York Times*, November 9, 1930, 19.

10   Edward T. James, Janet Wilson James, and Paul S. Boyer, eds., *Notable American Women, 1607–1950: A Biographical Dictionary, Vol. 3* (Cambridge, MA: Belknap Press of Harvard University, 1971), 133.

11   "A Notable Career: The Scope of Mrs. Reid's Activities World-Wide," *New York Times*, April 30, 1931, 23.

12   "Women: Death of a Great Lady." See also "A Notable Career," 23.

13   Ibid.

14   "Hoover Lauds Mrs. Reid," *New York Times*, April 30, 1931, 23.

15   Ibid., 23.

16   "Memories of a Paris House," *New York Herald Tribune*, May 11, 1931, 14.

17   Virginia Gildersleeve, *Many a Good Crusade* (New York: Macmillan, 1954), 158–59.

18   "Wartime Refuge," https://reidhall.globalcenters.columbia.edu/content /wartime-refuge-1939-1947.

19   Ibid.

20   Laurie Lalla Wisdo, "'Je Suis Americaine'—Especially in France," *Columbia, The Magazine of Columbia University* 9, no. 2 (November 1983), 23.

21   "Cultural and Social Club," https://reidhall.globalcenters.columbia.edu /content/cultural-and-social-club.

22   Ibid.

23   Margaret Corwin to Helen Rogers Reid, February 25, 1963, Reid Hall Records, 1919–97, University Archives, Rare Book and Manuscript Library, Columbia University Library, New York.

24   Alice Kaplan, *Dreaming in French: The Paris Years of Jacqueline Bouvier Kennedy, Susan Sontag, and Angela Davis* (Chicago: University of Chicago Press, 2013), 17.

25   "Mrs. Ogden Reid Dies Here at 87," *New York Times*, July 28, 1970, 18.

26   Helen Rogers Reid to Kirk (?), January 13, 1964, Reid Hall Records.

27   "Helen Rogers Reid," https://reidhall.globalcenters.columbia.edu/content /helen-rogers-reid-1882-1970.

CHAPTER 21: THE HARD WORK OF REMEMBERING

1   Enid Yandell, "Art in Paris," *Louisville Courier-Journal*, March 27, 1895, 26.

2   Quoted in Kristen Swinth, *Painting Professionals: Women Artists and the Development of Modern American Art, 1870–1930* (Chapel Hill: University of North Carolina Press, 2001), 187.

3   Adelyn D. Breeskin, *Anne Goldthwaite: A Catalogue Raisonné of the Graphic Work* (Montgomery, AL: Montgomery Museum of Fine Arts, 1982), 30. At least one journalist has suggested that Goldthwaite's association with the suffrage movement may have produced this unwelcoming response at the stalwart art school, but little evidence backs this up; being that the artist's most ardent suffragist activities took place in the years following her return to New York, such a hypothesis might not hold water. See May Lamar, "The Anne Goldthwaite Nobody Knew," *Alabama Heritage,* no. 135 (Winter 2020), 35.

4   Ibid., 28. Goldthwaite also completed a print of Harry Wehle, now in the collection of the Montgomery Museum of Art, Montgomery, Alabama.

5   The Met purchased the iconic *Autumn Rhythm (Number 30)* in 1957, one year after Pollock's untimely death in a car accident.

6   Linda Nochlin, "Why Have There Been No Great Women Artists?" *ARTNews,* January 1971, https://www.artnews.com/art-news/retrospective/why-have-there-been-no-great-women-artists-4201/.

7   Quoted in Breeskin, *Anne Goldthwaite: A Catalogue Raisonné of the Graphic Work*, 14.

8   Quoted in Kevin Sharp, "How Mary Cassatt Became an American Artist," in *Mary Cassatt: Modern* Woman (Chicago: Art Institute of Chicago, 1998), 150.

9   See John Elderfield ed., *De Kooning: A Retrospective* (New York: Museum of Modern Art, 2011).

10 "Art: Heiress to a New Tradition," *Time*, March 28, 1969, https://time.com/archive/6634065/art-heiress-to-a-new-tradition/.

11 Whitney Chadwick, *Women, Art, and Society* (New York: Thames and Hudson, 1997), 279. Part of the development of Abstract Expressionism, et cetera, may be chalked up to the natural reaction of one generation to the choices of the previous one. To use the tried-and-true Jackson

Pollock as a prime example: his teacher, Benton, was a figurative painter whose exaggerated individuals still read as somewhat naturalistic; Pollock learned his gestural style from his instructor but applied it to abstract scenes rather than representational ones. These narratives are the ones that have been prioritized in typical art history tracts, too, with complete abstraction being viewed as the purest epitome of artistic development and with American artists being seen as the gods (note the male gender!) who reached this apotheosis.

12   For more on the reception of this work of art by Picasso's friends, see https://www.artcuriouspodcast.com/artcuriouspodcast/46.

13   Betsy Fahlman, *Sculpture and Suffrage: The Art and Life of Alice Morgan Wright (1881–1975): Catalogue of the Exhibition at the Albany Institute of History and Art, April 21–June 11, 1978* (Albany: Albany Institute of History and Art, 1978), 5.

14   Margaret E. Burgess, "Mildred Burrage's Painting Practices in Europe," in *From Portland to Paris: Mildred Burrage's Years in France* (Portland, ME: Portland Museum of Art, 2012), 36.

15   Similarly, some historians have posted the slow growth of American interest in avant-garde art as a by-product of Puritanism. See Emily C. Burns, "Puritan Parisians: American Art Students in Late Nineteenth Century Paris," in *A Seamless Web: Transatlantic Art in the Nineteenth Century*, eds. Cheryll May and Marian Wardle (Newcastle upon Tyne: Cambridge Scholars Publishing, 2014).

16   "Exhibition of Paintings by American Women," *Daily Boston Globe*, December 29, 1928, 7.

17   For more on this, see Laura R. Prieto, *At Home in the Studio: The Professionalization of Women Artists in America* (Cambridge, MA: Harvard University Press, 2001), 4.

18   Vicki Leigh Ingham, *Art of the New South: Women Artists in Birmingham 1890–1950* (Birmingham, AL: Birmingham Historical Society, 2004), 18.

19   While men were naturally not barred from creating works in any of these media, such works were nevertheless gendered as more typically "feminine."

20   Quoted in Charlotte Streifer Rubenstein, *American Women Sculptors: A History of Women Working in Three Dimensions* (Boston: G. K. Hall, 1990), 100.

21 Solomon Fuller is noted as the first person of African descent to practice psychology in U.S. history. See Benjamin Davidson and Pippa Biddle, "The Sculpture of Meta Vaux Warrick Fuller," *The Magazine Antiques*, September/October 2020, 35.

22 Renée Ater, *Remaking Race and History: The Sculpture of Meta Warrick Fuller* (Berkeley: University of California Press, 2011), 32.

23 This is not to assert that Meta Vaux Warrick Fuller's works, post-marriage, suffered indelibly. She still created several pieces that many consider to be among her best, like *Ethiopia* (also known as *Ethiopia Awakening*, ca. 1921) and *In Memory of Mary Turner: As a Silent Protest Against Mob Violence* (1919). The matter is complicated, however, by the fact that a 1910 warehouse fire destroyed most of her work created prior to that time, including most of the pieces that brought her so much acclaim in Paris.

24 In other words: the women highlighted in this book, whose stories are more easily known and accessible today.

25 Jennifer Pfeifer Shircliff, "Women of the 1913 Armory Show: Their Contributions to the Development of American Modern Art" (doctoral dissertation, University of Louisville, 2014), 15. As Shircliff later notes, most of the women at the Armory Show were also childless.

26 Catherine Hewitt, *Art Is a Tyrant: The Unconventional Life of Rosa Bonheur* (London: Icon Books, 2021), epigraph.

27 This manner of thinking was not limited to the visual arts but suffused many professional realms. Famously, Edith Wharton once declared that "On her wedding-day [the American woman] ceases, in any open, frank and recognized manner, to be an influence in the lives of the men of the community to which she belongs." See Shircliff, "Women of the 1913 Armory Show," 15.

28 Marion Porter, "This Girl Sculptor Was of Uncommon Clay," *Louisville Courier-Journal*, February 9, 1941, 67.

29 Kathy Zimmerer Kelvie, "A Century of Women Artists at Cragsmoor," *Women Artists News* 7, no. 1 (April–May 1981), 9.

30 "The Cragsmoor Inn," Cragsmoor Historical Society, https://www.cragsmoorhistoricalsociety.com/the-cragsmoor-inn.

31 Kelvie, "A Century of Women Artists at Cragsmoor," 9; Exposition des beaux-arts, *Salon de 1895 catalogue illustré peinture et sculpture* (Paris: Bibliothèque des annales, 1895), cat. no. 1760; Exposition des beaux-arts, *Salon*

de 1896 catalogue illustré peinture et sculpture (Paris: Bibliothèque des annales, 1896), cat. nos. 1872–73.

32 An artist identified only as H. Edwards exhibited a painting of a flower vendor at the 1905 exhibition of the American Woman's Art Association, per Reid Hall's website: https://reidhall.globalcenters.columbia.edu/artist_index.

33 Likewise, an 1896 article notes that a "Miss Gaspell" lived at the Club, but no other details about her have survived, per Reid Hall's website: https://reidhall.globalcenters.columbia.edu/artist_index.

34 According to Laurie Lalla Wisdo, some of these luminaries—particularly Scott Fitzgerald, Hemingway, and Gertrude Stein—enjoyed visits to Reid Hall in its interwar period as members of the Paris branch of the PEN Club, the global society for writers. See Laurie Lalla Wisdo, "'Je Suis Americaine'—Especially in France," *Columbia, The Magazine of Columbia University* 9, no. 2 (November 1983), 23.

35 During the writing of this book, the *New York Times* published an article documenting the reclamation of the terms "girl" and "girlies," suggesting that these words offer flexibility and inclusion. See Marie Solis, "Why 'Girls' Rule the Internet," *New York Times*, September 10, 2023, 13.

36 An internet search for "American Girls' Club" is more likely to return results for American Girl dolls, ultra-popular toys that stormed the US beginning in the mid-1980s that spawned books, movies, stores, cafes, and accessories. The company is now a subsidiary of toy behemoth Mattel.

37 A. D. Defries, "Anne Goldthwaite as a Portrait Painter," *International Studio* LIX, no. 233 (July 1916), iii.

38 Art Students League, *The Art Students League Winter Catalogue 1931–1932* (New York: Art Students League, 1931), unpaginated. Given that she was the only female instructor at the League, at least for a significant part of her stint there, one might be tempted to assume that children's education was foisted upon her. Women, after all, were—and still are—disproportionately saddled with child-teaching duties. But an introductory description in the Art Students League booklet belies this supposition. "The League is, in fact, a collection of private ateliers," it reads. "Each instructor has complete freedom in his ideas and method of teaching." Goldthwaite, then, must have specifically chosen to provide this service.

39 Vincent LoBrutto, *Stanley Kubrick: A Biography* (Cambridge, MA: Da Capo Press, 1999), 28.

EPILOGUE

1   "Grande Salle Ginsberg-LeClerc: Inauguration June 8, 2023," Reid Hall and Columbia Global Centers, https://issuu.com/cgc.paris/docs/20230531 _online_viewing_program_inaguration_spread.

2   The original work is located in a private collection and is number 6799 in the de László online catalogue raisonné. See https://www.delaszlo catalogueraisonne.com/catalogue/the-catalogue/reid-mrs-whitelaw -nee-elisabeth-mills-6799.

3   Quoted in Suzanne Kamata, "Blondelle Malone: The Sojourn of an American Garden Artist," *Sandlapper: The Magazine of South Carolina* (Summer 2008), 14.

4   As of this writing, Youki is still going strong and maintains a social presence on Instagram at @youkistanclub.

AFTERLIVES

1   See the Dixie Art Colony's website: http://dixieartcolony.org/artwork -artists/anne-wilson-goldthwaite-1869-1944/.

2   Quoted in Jennifer Pfeifer Shircliff, "Women of the 1913 Armory Show: Their Contributions to the Development of American Modern Art" (doctoral dissertation, University of Louisville, 2014), 160.

3   Susan Gilbert Harvey, *Tea with Sister Anna: A Paris Journal* (Rome, GA: Golden Apple Press, 2005), 212.

4   See Robert W. Edwards, *Jennie V. Cannon: The Untold History of the Carmel and Berkeley Art Colonies, Volume 1* (Oakland: East Bay Heritage Project, 2012), 489; Porter Garnett, "News of Art and Artists," *San Francisco Call*, August 25, 1912, 31; Porter Garnett, "News of Art and Artists," *San Francisco Call*, October 27, 1912, 36; and Anna Cora Winchell, "Artists and Their Work," *San Francisco Chronicle*, March 12, 1916, 19.

5   Kathryn Carse, "Tour: Worker Murals Paint Vivid Portrait of Staten Island History." *Staten Island Advance*, July 23, 2015, https://www.silive.com /entertainment/arts/2015/07/wpa_murals_in_st_george_provid.html.

6   Bill Conlin, "Expanding Halls of Fame," *Sacramento Bee*, April 16, 1979, C3.

7   "In the Bay Area: Art," *Santa Rosa Press Democrat*, July 12, 1991, 36.

8   Vicki Leigh Ingham, *Art of the New South: Women Artists in Birmingham 1890–1950* (Birmingham, AL: Birmingham Historical Society, 2004), 129.

9   "Pioneer Artist, Teacher, Alice E. Rumph, Dies," *Birmingham* (AL) *News*, August 30, 1957, 35.

10 Ingham, *Art of the New South*, 129.

11 Walter Vanast, ed., "Bird in the Bush: American Artist Elizabeth Taylor's Summer Journey to the Mackenzie and Western Arctic, 1892. Letters, Journals, Photos, and Sketches," draft 16, Historical Society Archives, McGill University, 2011, unpaginated.

12 Elizabeth Taylor, "Five Years in a Faroe Attic," *Atlantic Monthly* 128 (October 1921), 441.

13 Elle Andra-Warner, "Minnesota's Elizabeth Taylor: Victorian Adventurer on the Nipigon River," Northern Wilds, December 2, 2015, https://northernwilds.com/minnesotas-elizabeth-taylor-victorian-adventurer-o-the-nipigon-river/. This source erroneously notes Taylor's age at death as seventy-eight.

14 Grace H. Turnbull, *Chips from My Chisel* (Rindge, NH: Richard R. Smith, 1953), 167.

15 Elisabeth Stevens, "Grace Turnbull: Too Comfortable to be Great?" *Baltimore Sun*, September 21, 1980, D6.

16 John Dorsey, "Grace Turnbull: An Artful Life," *Baltimore Sun*, May 26, 1996, https://www.baltimoresun.com/1996/05/26/grace-turnbull-an-artful-life-art-baltimore-museum-of-art-will-exhibit-paintings-and-sculpture-by-baltimores-multitalented-artist/.

17 Renée Ater, *Remaking Race and History: The Sculpture of Meta Warrick Fuller* (Berkeley: University of California Press, 2011), 23–24.

18 Ibid., 25.

19 Charlotte Streifer Rubenstein, *American Women Artists* (New York: Avon Books, 1982), 208.

20 Ibid., 222.

21 Draft of advance obituary, prepared October 17, 1967, Alice Morgan Wright Papers, Sophia Smith Collection, Smith College, Northampton, MA.

22 Dorcas MacClintock, "Fifty Years Before Us: An Essay on Alice Morgan Wright '04," unpublished draft of Smith College article, Alice Morgan Wright Papers.

23 "Leaves Estate to Cats," *Simpson's Leader-Times* (Kittanning, PA), December 5, 1975, 3.

24 The National Humane Educational Society, https://www.nhes.org/.

A NOTE ON THE AUTHOR

Jennifer Dasal is the creator and host of the *ArtCurious* podcast, which has been featured in multiple local and national publications and websites, including *O, the Oprah Magazine*, *PC Magazine*, ArtDaily, NPR, Salon and more. She is also the author of *ArtCurious: Stories of the Unexpected, Slightly Odd, and Strangely Wonderful in Art History*. She holds an MA in art history from the University of Notre Dame and a BA in art history from the University of California, Davis. Dasal is the former curator of modern and contemporary art at the North Carolina Museum of Art, Raleigh, where she worked for thirteen years. She lectures frequently on art both locally and nationally. Dasal lives in North Carolina with her family.